Windows Server® 2008
Enterprise Administrato.

Study Guide

D0529018

...ned on or before

MCITP
Windows Server® 2008
Enterprise Administrator
Study Guide

Steven Johnson

WILEY

Wiley Publishing, Inc.

Acquisitions Editor: Jeff Kellum
Development Editor: Laurene Sorenson
Technical Editors: Randy Muller and Rob Shimonski
Production Editor: Rachel McConlogue
Copy Editor: Kim Wimpsett
Production Manager: Tim Tate
Vice President and Executive Group Publisher: Richard Swadley
Vice President and Publisher: Neil Edde
Project Manager: Laura Moss-Hollister
Associate Producer: Kit Malone
Quality Assurance: Josh Frank
Book Designers: Judy Fung and Bill Gibson
Compositor: Craig Johnson, Happenstance Type-O-Rama
Proofreader: Publication Services, Inc.
Indexer: Nancy Guenther
Project Coordinator, Cover: Lynsey Stanford
Cover Designer: Ryan Sneed

Library of Congress Cataloging-in-Publication Data

Johnson, Steven, 1981-
  MCITP Windows server 2008 enterprise administrator study guide (exam 70-647) / Steven Johnson.
    p. cm.
  ISBN 978-0-470-29316-4 (paper/cd-rom)
  1. Electronic data processing personnel—Certification. 2. Microsoft software—Examinations—Study guides. 3. Microsoft Windows server. I. Title.
  QA76.3.J6536 2008
  005.4'476—dc22

                    2008041523

10 9 8 7 6 5 4 3 2 1

Dear Reader,

Thank you for choosing *MCITP: Windows Server 2008 Enterprise Administrator Study Guide*. This book is part of a family of premium-quality Sybex books, all of which are written by outstanding authors who combine practical experience with a gift for teaching.

Sybex was founded in 1976. More than 30 years later, we're still committed to producing consistently exceptional books. With each of our titles, we're working hard to set a new standard for the industry. From the paper we print on to the authors we work with, our goal is to bring you the best books available.

I hope you see all that reflected in these pages. I'd be very interested to hear your comments and get your feedback on how we're doing. Feel free to let me know what you think about this or any other Sybex book by sending me an email at nedde@wiley.com, or if you think you've found a technical error in this book, please visit http://sybex.custhelp.com. Customer feedback is critical to our efforts at Sybex.

Best regards,

Neil Edde
Vice President and Publisher
Sybex, an Imprint of Wiley

This book is dedicated to anyone who remembers what it was like to optimize for conventional memory, and how much fun it used to be.

Acknowledgments

To say that it would have been difficult to write this book without the assistance of several people would be a lie. That's because it would have been totally impossible. First, it goes without saying that the team at Sybex is by far the best group of editors, crying shoulders, and understanding managers that has ever been corralled into a single location.

And also, were it not for Microsoft and its thousands of brilliant employees, this book would have never existed. From the lowest-ranking employee to the vaunted status of its legendary executives, we owe them for not just this and many other fantastic certifications but for revolutionizing the way we do business—and we should thank them.

I would also like to thank all the people at PrepLogic. Were it not for people like Jay, normal jobs would just be so blatantly normal. And last, but certainly not least, I have to thank my loving family. I love each and every one of you.

About the Author

Steven Johnson is the managing editor for PrepLogic, a leading IT training and preparation company, and he has been involved with IT since the days when "a computer" was a big deal. In addition to being MCITP certified, Steven has the A+, Network+, i-Net+, and Wireless# certifications. (If you were to ask him, he'd say there are a lot of other certifications he should probably just take the test for.) Steve got his start in IT as a salesperson for RadioShack with little knowledge or formal training in electronics or IT. From that point on, he studied more and more until he became a guru. When he's not studying IT or computers, Steve spends most of his time either writing or flying airplanes—the two best things in life. Steve is a graduate of Texas Tech University.

Contents at a Glance

Contents

**Chapter   7   Administering Security in an Enterprise-Level
Infrastructure   243**

Table of Exercises

Introduction

Microsoft's certification program now contains four primary levels of certification: Technology Series, Professional Series, Master Series, and Architect Series. The Technology Series of certifications are intended to allow candidates to target specific technologies and are the basis for obtaining the Professional Series, Master Series, and Architect Series of certifications. The certifications contained within the Technology Series consist of one to three exams and focus on a specific technology rather than job-role skills. When obtaining a Technology Series certification, you are recognized as a Microsoft Certified Technology Specialist (MCTS) on the specific technology or technologies you have been tested on.

By contrast, the Professional Series of certifications focus on a job role and are not necessarily focused on a single technology but rather a comprehensive set of skills for performing the job role being tested. The Professional Series certifications include Microsoft Certified IT Professional (MCITP) and Microsoft Certified Professional Developer (MCPD).

The Masters Series is a series of validations produced by Microsoft to indicate that not only has someone attained a professional-level series of certifications but that they have actively participated in that role for a certain number of years. (The exact number of years varies by topic.) The Masters Series concludes with a multiweek direct-focus training seminar that is designed to ensure that the professionals, by the end of this experience, are truly masters in their field.

The Architect Series of certifications offered by Microsoft are premier certifications that consist of passing a review by a board of previously certified architects. To apply for the Architect Series of certifications, you must have a minimum of 10 years of industry experience. Passing the review board for an Architect Series certification will allow you to become a Microsoft Certified Architect (MCA).

This book has been developed to give you the critical skills and knowledge you need to prepare for the Windows Server 2008 Enterprise Administrator exam (70-647) in the Professional Series of certifications.

The Microsoft Certified Professional Program

Since the inception of its certification program, Microsoft has certified more than 2 million people. As the computer network industry continues to increase in both size and complexity, this number is sure to grow—and the need for *proven* ability will also increase. Certifications can help companies verify the skills of prospective employees and contractors.

Microsoft has developed its Microsoft Certified Professional (MCP) program to give you credentials that verify your ability to work with Microsoft products effectively and professionally. Several levels of certification are available based on specific suites of exams. Microsoft has recently created a new generation of certification programs:

Microsoft Certified Technology Specialist (MCTS)   The MCTS can be considered the entry-level certification for the new generation of Microsoft certifications. The MCTS certification program targets specific technologies instead of specific job roles. Each MCTS exam is a stand-alone exam; you may need specific ones to earn an MCITP, but one MCTS exam equals one MCTS certification.

Microsoft Certified IT Professional (MCITP)   The MCITP certification is a Professional Series certification that tests network and systems administrators on job roles rather than only on a specific technology. The MCITP generally consists of passing one to three exams, in addition to obtaining an MCTS-level certification. The Windows Server 2008 Enterprise Administrator exam (70-647) that this book covers is one of the exams you must pass to gain MCITP certification.

Microsoft Certified Master   The Microsoft Certified Master certification is a step above the Professional Series certification and is currently offered for Windows Server 2008, SQL Server 2008, and Exchange Server 2007. By the time this book is in print, Office Communication Server and SharePoint Master certifications will be available as well. Qualified MCITPs attend advanced training specific to the certification track, must successfully complete in-class written and lab exams, and then complete a separate qualification lab exam.

Microsoft Certified Professional Developer (MCPD)   The MCPD certification is a Professional Series certification for application developers. Similar to the MCITP, the MCPD is focused on a job role rather than on a single technology. The MCPD generally consists of passing one to three exams, in addition to obtaining an MCTS-level certification.

Microsoft Certified Architect (MCA)   The MCA is Microsoft's premier certification series. Obtaining the MCA certification requires a minimum of 10 years of experience and requires the candidate to pass a review board consisting of peer architects.

How Do You Become Certified as a Windows Server 2008 Enterprise Administrator?

Attaining a Microsoft certification has always been a challenge. In the past, students have been able to acquire detailed exam information—even most of the exam questions—from online "brain dumps" and third-party "cram" books or software products. For the new generation of exams, this is simply not the case.

Microsoft has taken strong steps to protect the security and integrity of its new certification tracks. Now prospective candidates must complete a course of study that develops detailed knowledge about a wide range of topics. It supplies them with the true skills needed, derived from working with the technology being tested.

The new generations of Microsoft certification programs are heavily weighted toward hands-on skills and experience. It is recommended that candidates have troubleshooting skills acquired through hands-on experience and working knowledge.

Fortunately, if you are willing to dedicate the time and effort to learn Windows Server 2008 Active Directory, you can prepare yourself well for the exam by using the proper tools. By working through this book, you can successfully meet the exam requirements to pass the Windows Server 2008 Active Directory exam.

This book is part of a complete series of Microsoft certification study guides, published by Sybex Inc., that together cover the new MCTS and MCITP exams, as well as the core MCSA, MCSE, and MCDST operating system requirements. Please visit the Sybex website at www.sybex.com for complete program and product details.

MCITP Requirements

Candidates for the MCITP: Enterprise Administrator certification on Windows Server 2008 must pass a total of five Windows Server 2008 core exams. The core examinations are Windows Server 2008 Active Directory, Configuring (70-640); Windows Server 2008 Network Infrastructure, Configuring (70-642); and Windows Server 2008 Applications Infrastructure, Configuring (70-643). For the elective, you must take either the Configuring Windows Vista Client (70-620) exam or the Deploying and Maintaining Windows Vista Client and 2007 Microsoft Office System Desktops (70-624) exam. This culminates with the Windows Server 2008 Enterprise Administrator (70-647) exam.

For a more detailed description of the Microsoft certification programs, including a list of all the exams, visit the Microsoft Learning website at www.microsoft.com/learning/mcp. As mentioned, for the MCITP: Enterprise Administrator certification, the exams are 70-640, 70-642, 70-643, 70-647, and either 70-620 or 70-624.

The Windows Server 2008 Enterprise Administrator Exam

The Enterprise Administrator exam for Windows Server 2008 covers concepts and skills related to planning, configuring, troubleshooting, and managing Windows Server 2008 servers.

Microsoft provides exam objectives to give you a general overview of possible areas of coverage on the Microsoft exams. Keep in mind, however, that exam objectives are subject to change at any time without prior notice and at Microsoft's sole discretion. Please visit the Microsoft Learning website (www.microsoft.com/learning/mcp) for the most current listing of exam objectives.

Types of Exam Questions

In an effort to both refine the testing process and protect the quality of its certifications, Microsoft has focused its newer certification exams on real experience and hands-on proficiency. There is a greater emphasis on your past working environments and responsibilities and less emphasis on how well you can memorize. In fact, Microsoft says that certification candidates should have hands-on experience before attempting to pass any certification exams.

Microsoft tries to protect the exams' integrity by regularly adding and removing exam questions, limiting the number of questions that any individual sees in a beta exam, limiting the number of questions delivered to an individual by using adaptive testing, and adding new exam elements.

Exam questions may be in a variety of formats. Depending on which exam you take, you'll see multiple-choice questions, as well as select-and-place and prioritize-a-list questions. Simulations and case study–based formats are included as well. You may also find yourself taking what's called an *adaptive format exam*. In the following sections, I'll explain the types of exam questions and explain the adaptive testing technique so you'll be prepared for all the possibilities.

With the release of Windows 2000, Microsoft stopped providing a detailed score breakdown. This is mostly because of the various and complex question formats. Previously, each question focused on one objective. Recent exams, such as the Windows Server 2008 Active Directory exam, however, contain questions that may be tied to one or more objectives from one or more objective sets. Therefore, grading by objective is almost impossible. Also, Microsoft no longer offers a score. Now you will be told only whether you passed or failed.

Multiple-Choice Questions

Multiple-choice questions come in two main forms. One is a straightforward question followed by several possible answers, of which one or more is correct. The other type of multiple-choice question is more complex and based on a specific scenario. The scenario may focus on several areas or objectives.

Select-and-Place Questions

Select-and-place exam questions involve graphical elements that you must manipulate to successfully answer the question. For example, you might see a diagram of a computer network, as shown in the following graphic taken from the select-and-place demo downloaded from Microsoft's website:

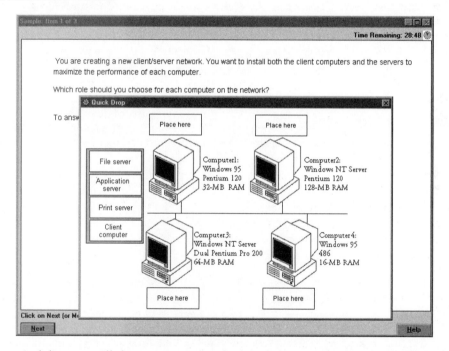

A typical diagram will show computers and other components next to boxes that contain the text *Place here*. The labels for the boxes represent various computer roles on a network, such as a print server and a file server. Based on information given for each computer, you are asked to select each label and place it in the correct box. You need to place *all* the labels correctly. No credit is given for the question if you correctly label only some of the boxes.

In another select-and-place problem, you might be asked to put a series of steps in order by dragging items from boxes on the left to boxes on the right and placing them in the correct order. Another type requires that you drag an item from the left and place it under an item in a column on the right.

For more information on the various exam question types, visit
www.microsoft.com/learning/mcpexams/policies/innovations.asp.

Simulations

Simulations are the kinds of questions that most closely represent actual situations and test
the skills you use while working with Microsoft software interfaces. These exam questions
include a mock interface on which you are asked to perform certain actions according to a
given scenario. The simulated interfaces look nearly identical to what you see in the actual
product, as shown in this example:

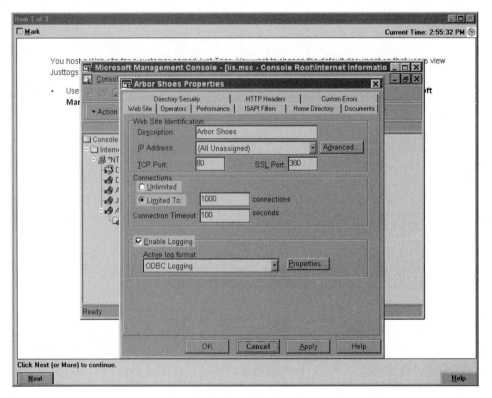

Because of the number of possible errors that can be made on simulations, be sure to
consider the following recommendations from Microsoft:

- Do not change any simulation settings that don't pertain to the solution directly.

- When related information has not been provided, assume that the default settings
  are used.

- Make sure your entries are spelled correctly.

- Close all the simulation application windows after completing the set of tasks in the simulation.

The best way to prepare for simulation questions is to spend time working with the graphical interface of the product on which you will be tested.

Case Study–Based Questions

Case study–based questions first appeared in the MCSD program. These questions present a scenario with a range of requirements. Based on the information provided, you answer a series of multiple-choice and select-and-place questions. The interface for case study–based questions has a number of tabs, each of which contains information about the scenario. Currently, this type of question appears only in most of the Design exams.

NOTE Microsoft will regularly add and remove questions from the exams. This is called *item seeding*. It is part of the effort to make it more difficult for individuals to merely memorize exam questions that were passed along by previous test-takers.

Tips for Taking the Windows Server 2008 Enterprise Administrator Exam

Here are some general tips for achieving success on your certification exam:

- Arrive early at the exam center so you can relax and review your study materials. During this final review, you can look over tables and lists of exam-related information.

- Read the questions carefully. Don't be tempted to jump to an early conclusion. Make sure you know *exactly* what the question is asking.

- Answer all questions. If you are unsure about a question, then mark the question for review and return to the question at a later time.

- On simulations, do not change settings that are not directly related to the question. Also, assume default settings if the question does not specify or imply which settings are used.

- For questions you're not sure about, use a process of elimination to get rid of the obviously incorrect answers first. This improves your odds of selecting the correct answer when you need to make an educated guess.

- Don't be surprised by seeing a technology you don't recognize. Part of the job of an Enterprise Administrator is to be familiar with just about everything, but that's a tough nut to crack. Just stick with your gut, and you should do well.

Exam Registration

You can take the Microsoft exams at any of more than 1,000 Authorized Prometric Testing Centers (APTCs) around the world. For the location of a testing center near you, call Prometric at 800-755-EXAM (755-3926). Outside the United States and Canada, contact your local Prometric registration center.

Find out the number of the exam you want to take and then register with the Prometric registration center nearest to you. At this point, you will be asked for advance payment for the exam. The exams are $125 each, and you must take them within one year of payment. You can schedule exams up to six weeks in advance or as late as one working day prior to the date of the exam. You can cancel or reschedule your exam if you contact the center at least two working days prior to the exam. Same-day registration is available in some locations, subject to space availability. Where same-day registration is available, you must register a minimum of two hours before test time.

You can also register for your exams online at www.prometric.com.

When you schedule the exam, you will be provided with instructions regarding appointment and cancellation procedures, ID requirements, and information about the testing center location. In addition, you will receive a registration and payment confirmation letter from Prometric.

Microsoft requires certification candidates to accept the terms of a nondisclosure agreement before taking certification exams.

Is This Book for You?

If you want to achieve the MCITP: Enterprise Administrator certification and your goal is to prepare for the exam by learning how to use and manage the operating system, this book is for you. You'll find clear explanations of the fundamental concepts you need to grasp and plenty of help to achieve the high level of professional competency you need to succeed in your chosen field.

However, if you just want to attempt to pass the exam without really understanding Windows Server 2008, this study guide is *not* for you. It is written for people who want to acquire hands-on skills and in-depth knowledge of Windows Server 2008.

What's in the Book?

What makes a Sybex study guide the book of choice for hundreds of thousands of MCPs? Sybex has taken into account not only what you need to know to pass the exam but also what you need to know to take what you've learned and apply it in the real world. Each book contains the following:

Objective-by-objective coverage of the topics you need to know   Each chapter lists the objectives covered in that chapter.

 The topics covered in this study guide map directly to Microsoft's official exam objectives. Each exam objective is covered completely.

Assessment test   Directly following this introduction is an assessment test that you should take. It is designed to help you determine how much you already know about Windows Server 2008 Active Directory and Windows Server 2008 enterprise environments. Each question is tied to a topic discussed in the book. Using the results of the assessment test, you can figure out the areas where you need to focus your study. Of course, I do recommend you read the entire book.

Exam essentials   To highlight what you learn, you'll find a list of exam essentials at the end of each chapter. The "Exam Essentials" section briefly highlights the topics that need your particular attention as you prepare for the exam.

Glossary   Throughout each chapter, you will be introduced to important terms and concepts that you will need to know for the exam. These terms appear in italic within the chapters, and at the end of the book, a detailed glossary gives definitions for these terms, as well as other general terms you should know.

Review questions, complete with detailed explanations   Each chapter is followed by a set of review questions that test what you learned in the chapter. The questions are written with the exam in mind, meaning that they are designed to have the same look and feel as what you'll see on the exam. Question types are just like the exam, including multiple-choice, and exhibits.

Hands-on exercises   In chapters, you'll find exercises designed to give you the important hands-on experience that is critical for your exam preparation. The exercises support the topics of the chapter, and they walk you through the steps necessary to perform a particular function.

Real-world scenarios   Because reading a book isn't enough for you to learn how to apply these topics in your everyday duties, I have provided real-world scenarios in special sidebars. These explain when and why a particular solution would make sense, in a working environment you'd actually encounter.

Interactive CD   Every Sybex study guide comes with a CD complete with additional questions, flashcards for use with an interactive device, and the book in electronic format. Details are in the following section.

What's on the CD?

This new member of Sybex's best-selling Study Guide series includes quite an array of training resources. The CD offers bonus exams and flashcards to help you study for the exam. It also includes the complete contents of the study guide in electronic form. The CD's resources are described here:

The Sybex e-book for *MCITP: Windows Server 2008 Enterprise Administrator Study Guide*   Many people like the convenience of being able to carry their whole study guide on a CD. They also like being able to search the text via computer to find specific information quickly and easily. For these reasons, the entire contents of this study guide are supplied on the CD in PDF. We've also included Adobe Acrobat Reader, which provides the interface for the PDF contents as well as the search capabilities.

The Sybex test engine   This is a collection of multiple-choice questions that will help you prepare for your exam. There are four sets of questions:

- Two bonus exams designed to simulate the actual live exam.
- All the questions from the study guide, presented in a test engine for your review. You can review questions by chapter, or you can take a random test.
- The assessment test.

Here is a sample screen from the Sybex test engine:

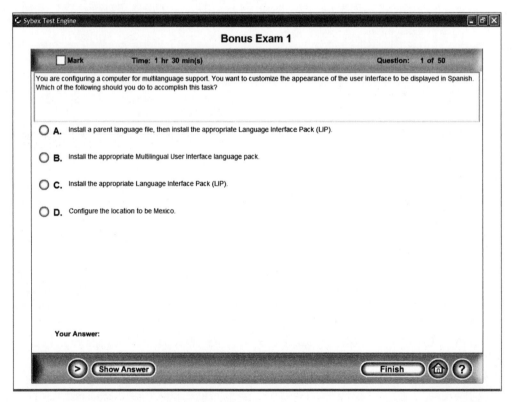

Sybex flashcards for PCs and handheld devices   The "flashcard" style of question offers an effective way to quickly and efficiently test your understanding of the fundamental concepts covered in the exam. The Sybex flashcards set consists of 100 questions presented in a special engine developed specifically for the Study Guide series. Here's what the Sybex flashcards interface looks like:

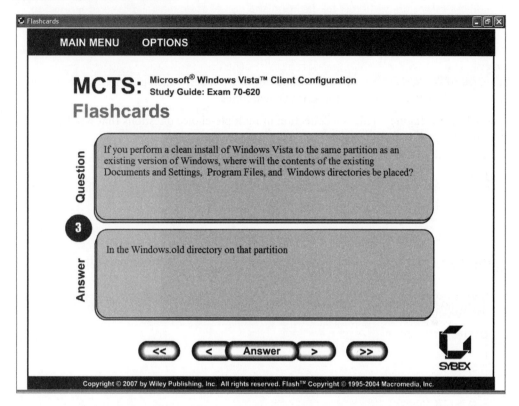

Because of the high demand for a product that will run on handheld devices, Sybex has also developed, in conjunction with Land-J Technologies, a version of the flashcard questions that you can take with you on your Palm OS handheld device.

Hardware and Software Requirements

You should verify that your computer meets the minimum requirements for installing Windows Server 2008. You can install Windows Server 2008 on a separate system or as a Virtual PC image on an existing operating system. Either way, you need to ensure that your computer or virtual PC environment meets or exceeds the recommended requirements for a more enjoyable experience.

 You can download a demo copy of Windows Server 2008 from www.microsoft.com/windowsserver2008/en/us/trial-software.aspx.

Contacts and Resources

To find out more about Microsoft education and certification materials and programs, to register with Prometric, or to obtain other useful certification information and additional study resources, check the following resources:

Microsoft Learning home page

www.microsoft.com/learning

This website provides information about the MCP program and exams. You can also order the latest Microsoft Roadmap to Education and Certification.

Microsoft TechNet technical information network

www.microsoft.com/technet

800-344-2121

Use this website or phone number to contact support professionals and system administrators. Outside the United States and Canada, contact your local Microsoft subsidiary for information.

Prometric

www.prometric.com

800-755-3936

Contact Prometric to register to take an exam at any of more than 800 Prometric Testing Centers around the world.

MCP Magazine online

www.mcpmag.com

Microsoft Certified Professional Magazine is a well-respected publication that focuses on Windows certification. This site hosts chats and discussion forums and tracks news related to the MCTS and MCITP program. Some of the services cost a fee, but they are well worth it.

WindowsITPro magazine

www.windowsITPro.com

You can subscribe to this magazine or read free articles at the website. The study resource provides general information on Windows Vista, Server, and .NET Server.

Assessment Test

1. If you work in an organization that has all your resources compiled into one location and that needs all personnel to access resources in that, and only that, location, what administrative design should you follow?

    A. Centralized

    B. Decentralized

    C. Hybrid

    D. Complex

2. Which technology supports single sign-on?

    A. AD RMS

    B. AD DS

    C. AD ALS

    D. AD FS

3. What is the minimum RAM requirement for Windows Server 2008, assuming no special services are required?

    A. 256MB

    B. 1024MB

    C. 512MB

    D. 2048MB

4. Which of the following is not a possible port exception for Active Directory Rights Management Services?

    A. Port 21

    B. Port 80

    C. Port 443

    D. Port 445

5. When creating a trust between a server deeply embedded in the network and another server in another branch of the network, which of the following trusts would be best implemented from a design perspective?

    A. External trust

    B. Resource trust

    C. Forest trust

    D. Shortcut trust

    E. Domain trust

6. Which of the following technologies encrypts hard drive information on a Windows Server machine in case it is physically compromised?

    A. Windows NTFS encryption

    B. FAT32 encryption

    C. Windows BitLocker

    D. Windows RODC

7. When Windows Server 2008 sends out replication over IP, what technology is it adding in addition to the IP protocol if you're in the same domain?

    A. RDP

    B. RPC

    C. SMTP

    D. FTP

8. When choosing your domain functional level, which level allows the use of the AES encryption for Kerberos?

    A. Windows NT

    B. Windows 2000 Server

    C. Windows Server 2003

    D. Windows Server 2008

9. To create forest trusts, what is the minimum functioning forest level that must be in use within your infrastructure?

    A. Windows NT

    B. Windows 2000 Server

    C. Windows Server 2003

    D. Windows Server 2008

10. Which of the following is *not* a design requirement to consider when planning your infrastructure?

    A. Legal requirements

    B. Organizational requirements

    C. Operational requirements

    D. Access requirements

11. If your enterprise is suffering periodic outages because of server overload and you would like to alleviate this overload by implementing a feature to split the process of Terminal Services across multiple terminal servers, what feature should you enable?

A. Terminal Services

B. Terminal Services Web Access

C. Terminal Services Gateway

D. Terminal Services Licensing

E. Terminal Services Session Broker

12. What Active Directory tool can be used to transfer accounts and Active Directory objects from one forest to another with Windows Server 2008?

A. ADMT 3.0

B. ADMT 3.1

C. Active Directory Users and Computers

D. The GPMC

13. Which of the following trust types is used for a Unix-based server in a Windows infrastructure?

A. Shortcut

B. Domain

C. External

D. Realm

E. Shortcut

14. By default, trusts within Windows Server 2008 that exist between a parent and child are what type? (Choose all that apply.)

A. One-way

B. Two-way

C. Transitive

D. Intransitive

15. Which of the following Active Directory technologies supports individual file security protection?

A. AD DS

B. AD CS

C. AD FS

D. AD RMS

16. Which of the following is not a Windows Server 2008 Terminal Services Licensing scope level?

    A. Workgroup

    B. Domain

    C. Forest

    D. Local

17. Terminal Services Gateway over Remote Desktop Protocol requires which port in order to connect successfully?

    A. 20

    B. 21

    C. 80

    D. 443

    E. 3389

18. What is the OU design concept that involves designing a specific part of an infrastructure to function on its own?

    A. Autonomy

    B. Automation

    C. Anonymity

    D. Administration

19. Which of the following group scope levels cannot be seen outside a local machine?

    A. Global

    B. Universal

    C. Local

    D. Domain local

20. Which of the following group conversions is not possible with Windows Server 2008?

    A. Global to universal

    B. Domain local to universal

    C. Universal to global

    D. Local to universal

21. Which of the following tools can be used for compliance auditing?

    A. SCW

    B. MBSA

    C. GPMC

    D. RSoP

22. Of the following four Group Policy application levels, which is applied first?

   A. Site

   B. Domain

   C. Local

   D. OU

23. When applying Group Policy, which of the following has the lowest precedence?

   A. GPO linked to an OU

   B. GPO linked to a domain

   C. GPO linked to a site

   D. Local GPO for a specific user

   E. Local GPO for administrators/nonadministrators

   F. Local GPO for local Group Policy

24. Using Windows Server 2008, Windows can identify computer components with what type of filter?

   A. GPO

   B. User

   C. Computer

   D. WMI

   E. Scope

25. Which type of CA exists outside the role of the primary CA and issues certificates to other CAs?

   A. Issuing CA

   B. Enterprise CA

   C. Stand-alone CA

   D. Policy CA

   E. Intermediate CA

26. Which editions of Windows support version 2 certificate templates? (Choose all that apply.)

   A. Windows Server 2003 Small Business edition

   B. Windows Server 2003 Standard edition

   C. Windows Server 2003 Enterprise edition

   D. Windows Server 2008 Standard edition

   E. Windows Server 2008 Enterprise edition

27. What is the maximum number of logical processors supported by Windows Server 2008 Hyper-V?

    A. 4

    B. 8

    C. 12

    D. 16

    E. 32

28. Windows Server 2008 security practices recommend a certificate authority tier model that contains no more than how many tiers?

    A. 1

    B. 2

    C. 3

    D. 4

29. When implementing IPv6, what method of transition allows you to access both IPv4 and IPv6 from the same IP stack?

    A. Dual stacking

    B. Dual layering

    C. Tunneling

    D. Teredo

30. Which type of tunneling methodology is applied by default to Windows Vista without Service Pack 1?

    A. ISATAP

    B. 6to4

    C. Teredo

    D. Host to host

Answers to Assessment Test

1. A. Centralized administrative designs involve the process of placing all your resources into one area. This can be further broken down into centralized/decentralized when you have resources in one area but personnel in another or into centralized/centralized when you have resources and personnel in one particular area. For more information, please see Chapter 1.

2. D. Active Directory Federation Services (AD FS) is a service that allows users to log on once and access resources across a complex network of servers by exchanging security resources. Essentially, a user can sign on once through single sign-on and be authenticated throughout the rest of the network without having to reenter a password. For more information, please see Chapter 1.

3. C. By default, the Microsoft minimum system requirements for Windows Server 2008 requires at least 512MB of RAM. If you're including other servers, or doing more complex tasks, this number will increase. Furthermore, the recommended setting is at least 2048MB of memory. For more information, please see Chapter 1.

4. A. Port 21 is the port required by File Transfer Protocol. Active Directory Rights Management Services requires ports 80, 443, 445, and 1433 to be enabled. For more information, please see Chapter 1.

5. D. A shortcut trust is a "quick pathway" between two forests that doesn't require authentication to be passed up and down the forest hierarchy. It alleviates the extra burden on already taxed domain controllers and creates a more stable environment. For more information, please see Chapter 3.

6. C. Windows BitLocker is a technology that encrypts hard drive information in case that drive is physically compromised. In such a case, the data cannot be accessed. NTFS does provide encryption, but not for the purpose of physical protection. FAT 32 does not provide encryption. For more information, please see Chapter 1.

7. B. When you are within the same domain, Windows Server 2008 uses Remote Procedure Call (RPC) over IP. However, if you are in separate domains, it is possible to use the Simple Mail Transfer Protocol for servers that may have unreliable WAN connections. For more information, please see Chapter 1.

8. D. Of all the domain functional levels, you must be operating at Windows Server 2008 level to use AES encryption for Kerberos. This allows tickets to be encrypted using this complex encryption for security purposes. For more information, please see Chapter 1.

9. C. To implement forest trusts, Windows Server 2003 is required. This was one of the major feature implementations of this version of Windows Server and was greatly needed within complex infrastructures with more than one forest. Windows Server 2008, because of the nature of the increase of functioning levels, also supports this technology. For more information, please see Chapter 3.

10. D. Legal, organizational, and operational requirements are all necessary in order to plan an appropriate design. Access requirements are embedded within operational requirements. If you require certain devices to be accessed at certain times, you can address this within your operational requirements. For more information, please see Chapter 5.

11. E. Terminal Services Session Broker (TS SB) is used to balance network traffic between terminal servers, similar to network load balancing. For more information, please see Chapter 4.

12. B. Windows Server 2008 requires the Active Directory Migration Tool (ADMT) version 3.1, as opposed to Windows Server 2003, which used version 3.0. For more information, please see Chapter 3.

13. D. External trusts are used for Unix-based operating systems that still need to communicate with a Windows environment. Unix systems exist in their own separate realm, defined by their own rules. For more information, please see Chapter 3.

14. B, C. Whenever child objects are created, a transitive, two-way trust is created between the child and parent object for the purpose of passing information between the two objects. For more information, please see Chapter 3.

15. D. Active Directory Rights Management Services is an enterprise level technology that is designed to support the deployment of individual protection for file security so that users can restrict permissions for their own individual files. For more information, please see Chapter 3.

16. D. Terminal Services Licensing is always applied at a "higher" level that includes overall design. This includes workgroups, forests, and domains. For more information, please see Chapter 4.

17. E. TS Gateway servers take advantage of the RDP protocol, which uses the standard port of 3389. For more information, please see Chapter 4.

18. A. Planning for autonomy is the process of setting up an individual part of the network, solely isolated for managerial reasons. For more information, please see Chapter 5.

19. C. Local groups are available only on the computers on which they are installed. By default, Windows Server 2008 contains several built-in local user types. For more information, please see Chapter 5.

20. D. Global to universal, domain local to universal, and universal to global group transitions are all possible in certain circumstances. However, a group cannot be translated from the local level to the universal level. For more information, please see Chapter 6.

21. A. Using the Security Configuration Wizard (SCW), a user can set up auditing and compliance for an entire network. For more information, please see Chapter 7.

22. C. Group Policy is always applied at the most granular level, so it can be overridden at the highest level. For more information, please see Chapter 6.

23. F. Group Policy is applied with the least precedence at the most granular level. This is because higher-tiered and linked GPOs should be more important. For more information, please see Chapter 6.

24. D. WMI filters are capable of surveying system components such as CPU, memory, and Windows version to test the application of GPOs in GPO filters. For more information, please see Chapter 6.

25. E. Intermediate CAs are used in higher-tiered models, such as three-tiered models, to provide intermediary CAs. For more information, please see Chapter 7.

26. C, E. Version 2 certificate templates always require Enterprise editions of Windows Server. For more information, please see Chapter 7.

27. D. Hyper-V can support up to 16 logical processors, but this does not necessarily mean there must be 16 physical processors. Hyper-V can split single processors into multiple logical processors. For more information, please see Chapter 10.

28. D. At a maximum, you should have a four-tiered CA model because of the complicated nature of having too many CA roles. At a certain level, a critical mass is reached. For more information, please see Chapter 7.

29. C. Dual layering is the process of layering both IPv4 and IPv6 on the same IP stack so that both versions of the IP protocol can access the network portion. For more information, please see Chapter 2.

30. A. By default, Windows Vista without Service Pack 1 includes ISATAP, which is a dual stacking technology used for public and private addressing. For more information, please see Chapter 2.

Chapter

1

Designing a Complex Windows Server 2008 Infrastructure

OBJECTIVES COVERED IN THIS CHAPTER:

✓ **Design of Active Directory forests and domains**

  ▪ May include but is not limited to: forest structure, forest and domain functional levels, intra-organizational authorization and authentication, schema modifications

✓ **Design of the Active Directory physical topology**

  ▪ May include but is not limited to: placement of servers, site and replication topology

Up until this point in your administration career, you've probably spent most of your time utilizing the technological aspects of Windows Server 2008. As you've probably read somewhere (either in another book in this series, on Microsoft's website, or in another one of your IT resources), succeeding at this exam is going to take a dramatic change from what you've gotten used to. That's because the certification exam concentrates on the idea of *design*. In other words, it's about how to create a network structure from the ground up. Thus, the beginning of this book is going to concentrate on one of the fundamental features of design: planning.

Planning is the process of realizing the needs of your network, the features that your organization will require, and the physical limitations placed on your environment, such as distance, office size, or even walls. Realistically, in the modern IT workplace, planning for an entire enterprise usually requires more than just one person. You can bet that most Fortune 500 companies make a lot of their decisions based on recommendations from a board or panel of administrators, each with their own individual experience, beliefs, and opinions. This makes a lot of sense, because when you're working with a lot of smart and experienced people on a collaborative project, you can usually create the best solution if you work together as a team, rather than doing everything by yourself.

This said, it's important for this exam (and for the real world) that you understand the overall concepts of design and most of the typical trends in the industry. To help with this, in the beginning of this chapter, I'll cover some of the basic concepts of design. I will then quickly move into what technologies are available with Windows Server 2008 and what tools you as an administrator have at your disposal. I'll end this chapter with a quick roundup of what I have covered, along with some good tips and suggestions for design.

Overview of Design Models

The first and most basic task in all designs is to determine a structure called an *administrative model*. Administrative models are conceptual logical topologies that mirror an organization's IT administration structure. In general, one of three administrative models is usually deployed:

- Centralized
- Decentralized
- Hybrid

Please note this chapter includes some content that will not be on your exam—specifically, the discussion of the administrative hierarchy. This content, which is from MCSE exam 70-297, is covered in much more detail in Sybex's *MCSE Windows Server 2003 Active Directory and Network Structure Infrastructure Design Study Guide*. However, I'll cover each of these models and their corresponding roles in an organization. Doing this will not only help you understand the concepts of design but will also lay the groundwork for later chapters that discuss much more complicated structures.

The Centralized Model

When you think of a centralized model, it's best to keep in mind the word root, *centra* (meaning center). In a pure *centralized model*, all your resources are in the same place, and all your administrators are in one spot. A good example of this would be a medium-sized business that has about 1,000 employees who each access applications, shared folders, and printers on your Microsoft network. In a centralized model, the business theoretically could exist in a large building with 20 floors, and the IT staff would all be stationed on the top floor where they could oversee all the dark deeds they must partake in on a daily basis. I'm kidding on that last part, but the concept of a pure centralized model is pretty simple. Everybody or anything who has to do with IT is in one spot!

In practice, a centralized administration model is a convenient way to run your IT function. If everything is in the same place, it's easy to get to what or whom you need to be in contact with very quickly. To top things off, you can usually get away with a lot fewer quality assurance practices because you don't have to connect across a slow WAN link to servers in your Japan office halfway around the world from your San Francisco location.

The only downside to this model is that sometimes when an organization grows, being centralized really isn't practical. Businesses open separate offices, they have remote employees, and they sometimes require IT resources in locations that don't make this realistic for a very large corporation with multiple offices. Thus, you'll fairly rarely see a pure centralized model in the wild. However, it's possible that you will see a variant of this practice called the *centralized-decentralized model*, where all of the IT *staff* is in one place but the servers are in various locations throughout the world. Figure 1.1 may help illustrate this.

FIGURE 1.1   Centralized model

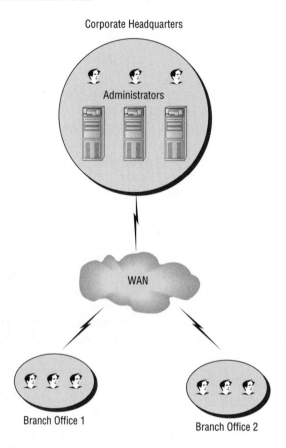

The Decentralized Model

If you understand the concept of a centralized model, I'm willing to bet that you will probably be able to guess what a decentralized model is. But, just in case you can't, a *decentralized model* is an administrative model where all your IT staff and resources are *not* in the same place.

Say, for example, you work for a company called MyCorp. If MyCorp has locations in Sydney, New York, and Paris, chances are that they probably have servers in those locations. And, if MyCorp happens to be a particularly big corporation, there's an even stronger chance that MyCorp will have *multiple* servers in each of those locations. Think about it for a minute. You have at least three locations, and at each of those locations you have multiple servers. Having multiple servers probably means multiple personnel. Thus, you have a lot of different people, managing a lot of different resources, in a lot of different places!

The main reason a company will choose to implement this method is because it's a requirement. Sometimes you end up with so many resources in a place outside your main location that you need to have individuals overseeing it. And, although it's sort of a pain to not have all your resources at your disposal in one location, this model does have its upside. For one, it's incredibly scalable. With a decentralized model, you can easily add another branch or expand one of your existing branches. This makes a lot of business professionals happy, because it means that in the long term they won't be stymied by the growth of their IT administration. Instead, as the business expands, the IT administration will be able to grow along with it.

The Hybrid Administration Model

Chances are that if you understood the previous descriptions of the centralized and decentralized administration models, you will pick up on this one. A *hybrid administration model* employs some of the concepts of a centralized approach and adds some of the elegance of the decentralized approach. Earlier, when I referenced the decentralized approach and alluded to how it involved multiple administrators, each responsible for various aspects of their particular network, I failed to ask one very important key question: who manages the overall enterprise?

The hybrid administration model seeks to remedy this by combining decentralized branch administrators with a centralized oversight staff. When you break it down to its basic parts, a hybrid model is almost the same as a decentralized model. The only real difference is that the hybrid model adds another layer of authority. Whereas in the decentralized model all branches are independent, in this model the branches are independent to the extent that they are responsible for governing themselves. However, they also are dependent because a centralized group of administrators at the home office has control over all IT resources in the entire administrative structure.

In effect, this person is what you are now studying to become! An *enterprise administrator* is someone who has authority over a great number of servers throughout the organization and normally has many administrators beneath them. Instead of concentrating on an individual server or a group of servers, you will instead concentrate on the big picture: your organization's IT health. You are the one who decides the corporate structure. You are the one who creates the Group Policy standards. And you are the one who sets the model for all other administrators to follow. It's quite an important position, and it's not one that you should take lightly. If all this authority scares you, stop now! Otherwise, keep on reading. It only gets better from here.

Designing a Forest Structure

The Active Directory *forest* is the topmost design structure that you as an administrator will normally deal with. A forest contains all the domains, trees, and objects for a particular organization. Ordinarily, most organizations use only one forest for the entire campus. However, in some large organizations, the design requirements may require multiple forests, or *forest collaboration*. Therefore, it's imperative that you as an enterprise administrator understand how a multiple-forest environment operates, as well as the domains within that environment. For our purposes, the Active Directory forest is simply a container that shares the same schema and global catalog. However, in order to design a forest for your Active Directory environment, you need to understand forest functional levels, trusts between forests, authentication within forests, and the forest schema.

Forest Functional Levels

As you've already learned from your study of Active Directory in Windows Server 2008, Windows Server 2008 currently has three functional levels at both the domain and forest levels:

- Windows 2000 Native
- Windows Server 2003
- Windows Server 2008

In previous exams, this feature wasn't quite as important as it is now. This is because each of these three functional levels has important and unique abilities, each of which is detailed in Table 1.1.

TABLE 1.1   Functional Levels

Functional Level	Available Features
Windows 2000 Native	Default Active Directory Domain Services (AD DS) features
Windows Server 2003	Forest trusts Domain renaming Linked-value replication Read-only domain controller deployment Creating dynamic objects Deactivation and redefinition of schema attributes
Windows Server 2008	No additional features, but all subsequent domain controllers will be at Windows Server 2008 level

The most important thing to know about these functional levels is that big changes will occur when you upgrade your infrastructure to the Windows Server 2003 level. Table 1.1 illustrates the drastic changes that were implemented with the release of Windows Server 2003. Beyond these major changes, the overall functional level of the forest is relatively simple.

In general, the best practice for an overall forest design is to use the most robust (and therefore highest) functional level possible. However, more often than not, because of the presence of certain older domain controllers or technological limitations, you will be forced to settle for less advanced deployments. Keep in mind, however, that if any domains within your forest are functioning at low levels, such as Windows 2000 Native, raising the overall functional level of the forest will raise any domains that are not already at that level to at least that level.

Forest Design Elements

When you first decide to design a forest in Active Directory, you have three important elements to consider:

- Organizational requirements
- Operational requirements
- Legal requirements

As much as you may like, you're not allowed to create a forest at whim. If you did that, almost every environment would be a single forest (unless you felt curious), and it's likely that none of these requirements would be met. To understand what you need to do to accommodate these elements, let's define them a little further:

Organizational requirements is a fancy term that means "doing what your organization says needs to be done." On a practical level, what it means to administrators like you and me is that some users in the environment may require their own individual playground (an area where they can make changes and not affect anyone else), or they may require access to more folders and shared documents (items that need to be accessed by them as well as users in the rest of the structure). When you choose your design, you have to keep in mind that situations may occur where you have to assume that there may be a lot of political reasons for separation or collaboration, and you should plan accordingly.

Operational requirements (or perhaps *restrictions* is a more apt term) usually stem from the fact that different groups within a company run different services at different times. For example, a branch of your organization may run Exchange Server 2007, while another may run a custom application that conflicts with Exchange Server's requirements by directly accessing the Active Directory structure and modifying it. Thus, these branches will have to be separated at the beginning of your design.

Legal requirements are laws and regulations that impact data access throughout the network infrastructure. Believe it or not, some businesses may be legally required to keep certain functions in a separate environment. From an IT person's standpoint, this may seem kind of odd, but it's true. Imagine what would happen, for instance, if you were working for an insurance company where the claims adjusters had direct access to the accounting applications. In practical terms, this could be a bad thing. The adjusters could make payments to claimants, get direct access to underwriting data, or figure out other ways to make a mess. But in addition to these practical business reasons, legal and regulatory rules mandate separation between the accounting, underwriting, and adjusting functions.

Autonomy vs. Isolation

When you first hear the words *autonomy* and *isolation*, they might strike you as nearly synonymous. In the non-IT world, *autonomous* describes something that is independent and functions of its own accord, and *isolation* describes something that has been set apart from the rest of any given group. However, when working with Windows Networking components and building an infrastructure, these terms have very distinct and important meanings.

Autonomy

In the world of Windows administrators, *autonomy* means that a particular resource is administered, but not completely controlled by, one group. It basically means putting things together in a spot that's independently operating. This means that if you have an autonomous group of administrators, they have the rights and authority to operate on their own group of servers, or even their own domain. However, you will most likely have another group of administrators that will have authority over this group and the ability to delegate their authority (or even supercede it). In general, administrators strive for two types of autonomy when they create an administrative design: *service autonomy* and *data autonomy*. Data autonomy is the result of creating an environment where particularly important pieces of data are placed in a location that can be overseen by administrators. Service autonomy, however, is the result of making sure part of service management is directly overseen by a particular group of administrators.

Just keep in mind that in both data autonomy and service autonomy, a single group of administrators will almost always *not* be the only ones in charge.

Isolation

There's something about the word *isolation* that seems to appeal to most administrators. That's a huge stereotype, but at least in terms of the enterprise, isolation can be a very good thing. The concept behind it is that sometimes pieces of data or services running within a forest require domains that are separated completely from others. This means that, no matter what, particular administrators are the only individuals who can administer a particular area in your environment. As with autonomy, you would likely consider isolation for two resources: services and data. With *service isolation*, you are preventing other administrators from controlling a particular resource. With *data isolation*, you are blocking other administrators from accessing important files and information.

Forest Models

When designing a forest, there are traditionally three models for breaking the forest up into understandable parts: organizational, resource based, and restricted access. Each of these structures is defined in the following sections, along with the pros and cons of the concept.

Organizational Forest Model

In the *organizational* forest model, administrators design the forest from the ground up to accommodate the needs of an organization according to its departments, locations, or other criteria that define the physical layout of the campus and the functional structure of the business model. These criteria take precedence over any customized scheme provided by the network designer. As an example, the domain model shown in Figure 1.2 was designed to represent the company in a single-forest organizational model. This model is designed logically to divide the company up: first by department, and then by location.

FIGURE 1.2   Single-forest organizational model

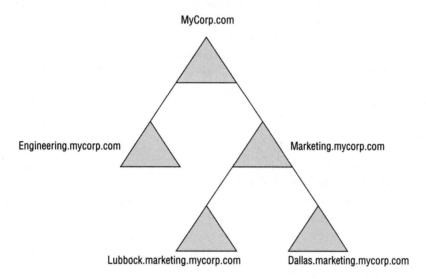

Figure 1.3 shows this same company but utilizes a trust with another forest. Each of these forests still maintains the concept of an organizational layout.

FIGURE 1.3   Organizational forest trust

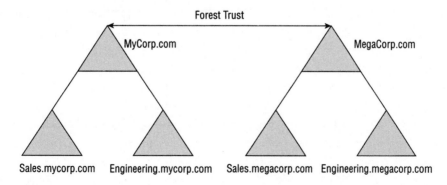

> Organizational forest models are useful for businesses with many different departments. Breaking up a campus by department is helpful because it alleviates the need to have a large amount of users in one location.

Resource-Based Forest Model

Fairly often companies will face situations where an environment contains valuable or highly demanding resources that have to be accessed by multiple personnel, and both users and business interests could be exposed to unnecessary liability if the resources are not separated from the rest of the organization at the forest level.

Sometimes, in an environment with a particularly useful or powerful application, shared folder, or other system resource, administrators will create a forest specifically designed for users who need to access that resource. Usually this type of forest—called a *resource-based forest*—is a new or additional forest in an organization, and trusts are established to access this forest.

Another advantage of a resource-based forest is that it is independent of any other forest; therefore, should there be a problem in a forest unrelated to the forest dedicated to the resource, the resource-based forest will be unaffected. This is particularly useful for backup strategies, which will be discussed later.

Restricted-Access Forest Model

A *restricted-access* forest, as shown in Figure 1.4, is a forest that is completely separated from another forest but (usually) is linked with a trust. This forest is administered wholly separately from the other forest and does not in any way share the administration needs with the other forest. Ordinarily, the administrators of this forest know nothing about other administration policies throughout the rest of the organization.

FIGURE 1.4   Restricted-access forest

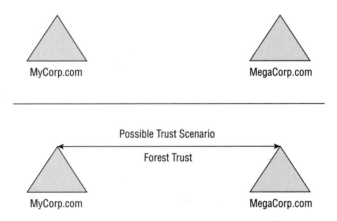

Forest Schema

Within all versions of Windows Server, the Active Directory schema acts as a guiding rule for what exists in Active Directory, what is allowed in Active Directory, and how everything within Active Directory is formally defined. At the server level, you might see the need to modify the schema in order to incorporate different versions of Windows or new objects in Active Directory. This process can be a little annoying at times, but it's all part of upgrading your environment, which will be discussed in Chapter 2, "Naming Conventions, Networking, and Access Principles." For now, I'll cover the Active Directory schema from a higher design level and show what you need to consider before you make changes to the schema or plan for future changes.

If you have the ability to make decisions in your network, it's a good idea to create a schema policy. This determines who can upgrade the schema and when they can do it. In an environment where such a policy has not been established, administrators can upgrade and modify the schema at whim, causing potential conflicts with applications and servers, as well as a myriad of other issues.

Single-Forest vs. Multiple-Forest Design

One of the biggest advantages of working with a schema is its all-encompassing quality. Most administrators dream of the day where they can operate in a campus that uses only one forest and where they can control all the domains within. Remember, all domains with parent/child relationships that are within a forest are linked by two-way transitive trusts by default, and they're all part of the same schema. This architecture is called a *single-forest* design.

On the other hand, most organizations have a good reason to keep multiple forests, with their own independent resources, in addition to their current forest. This architecture is (surprise!) called a *multiple-forest* design.

Autonomous model   An *autonomous model* is an administration concept that forces each independent forest or domain within your network to remain independent in its own administration and gives only a certain group of administrators the privilege to alter its contents. In terms of setup, this is by far the easiest model to implement. However, it can cause administrative headaches in the future because only a certain group has the authority to change permissions, and those permissions may need to be altered when the group is unavailable. Also, remember that this will affect the Active Directory application mode containers!

Collaborative Model   In a *collaborative model*, administrators assist each other across multiple forests. This eases the load of administration throughout the organization. Of the two forest administration models, this is by far the more difficult one because it requires the creation of forest trusts and the delegation of privileges.

Remember, the rule of thumb is one schema per forest. In terms of the schema, a multiple-forest design will have one schema per forest in the network. This means that unless you establish a form of trust between each of your forests, they will be completely different. Thus, the only way that forests in a multiple-forest architecture can communicate is by administrator intervention. From a design standpoint, this poses a couple of questions for you to consider: Who has the right to administer the separate forests? Should the administrators in one forest have access to the neighboring forest? These questions and many others have to be answered when you are considering your forest design. One issue is whether the forests will be autonomous or collaborative.

Schema Modification

Thankfully, with all the features that have been enabled in Active Directory through the years, the process of modifying your schema has become a less common process. However, sometimes this process still does occur. In particular, it is exceptionally common when an administrator decides to install a software package that creates its own individual object classes, which may require an update to be spread throughout the rest of your Active Directory environment.

As an example, Exchange Server 2007 creates numerous individual definitions before installation that must be replicated throughout the entire environment. This creates a problem because if new object classes are being created, the schema is being modified. If you're in a large organization with a lot of users, the process of replication can take quite a while because every machine needs to become aware of what's happening throughout the rest of the environment.

Therefore, it's best to adhere to the following steps before you alter your schema:

Plan   Determine what changes are required.

Plan again   Make sure you've considered all the changes that are necessary.

Test your plan   Simulate your changes in a test environment.

Roll out your plan   Begin the changes on a small scale when traffic is low.

By following this protocol, you can make sure the process goes as smoothly as possible.

These four steps apply to almost every aspect of server design. Plan, plan again, test your plan, and roll out your plan. At the enterprise level, you can't afford to make mistakes. A single downed server can costs thousands (if not millions!) of dollars in lost productivity, transactions, or application availability. Most large organizations have specific their procedures for major upgrades and make sure the administrators follow them.

Designing an Active Directory Domain Structure

Now that I've covered most of the decisions you need to make at the forestwide level, let's take a look at what most people consider to be the more "fun" container to play with—the Active Directory domain. Domains are more fun than forests because a lot of the real administrative work goes on at this level. It's where you place most of your users, groups, and resources. It's where you assign most group policies, and most of the time it's where the servers that run all your services are. Plus, there's something really neat about browsing through Active Directory and finding the machine that's running your web box, then finding the machine that contains your DNS, and knowing full well that you can make almost anything you want happen (well, anything within the security policy, that is). You don't want to start deleting or bringing down your servers. That wouldn't be pleasant at all.

Domain Functional Levels

For each domain—just as for each forest—you have to make a decision: at which functional level does the domain need to operate? Normally, this is based on the type of servers you have and the operations that are being conducted. But remember, a domain's functional level is limited by the forest's operating level. It's easy to go up, but not easy to go down.

Just like the Active Directory forest operating level, each domain functional level has its own advantages and limitations, as shown in Table 1.2.

TABLE 1.2   Functional Level Advantages and Limitations

Domain Functional Level	Available Features	Supported Domain Controllers
Windows 2000 Native	Universal groups Group nesting Group conversion SIDs—security identifiers	Windows 2000 Server Windows Server 2003 Windows Server 2008
Windows Server 2003	Netdom.exe Logon timestamp updates Set userPassword as the effective password on inetOrgPerson and user objects Ability to redirect User and Computer containers Authorization Manager can store authentication policies in AD DS Constrained delegation Selective authentication	Windows Server 2003 Windows Server 2008

TABLE 1.2   Functional Level Advantages and Limitations *(continued)*

Domain Functional Level	Available Features	Supported Domain Controllers
Windows Server 2008	Distributed File System (DFS) AES encryption supported for Kerberos Last interactive logon information Fine-grained password policies	Windows Server 2008

Source: Microsoft Corporation

Single and Multiple Domains

For the purposes of this book, which is geared at the large enterprise level, it is almost not worth discussing the concept of single-domain architecture, but I will for the sake of completeness. A *single-domain* architecture is a design where within a forest there is only one single domain, usually functioning as a domain controller. At this level, most domain administrators are also enterprise administrators. It's rare to see a situation in which a large organization has only one domain with no subdomains or other administrative breakdowns.

The advantage to having a single domain is simplicity. If you have everything in one spot, it's difficult to get lost in the maze of administrative breakdowns, the schema will not be complex, and Group Policy has less of a chance (but still a significant one) of running amok.

A much more realistic design structure (one much more often seen both in the real world and on the exam) is a *multiple-domain* architecture wherein an organization has multiple websites, locations, departments, or other signifying differentiations that require the administrative structure to be broken down into simpler parts. For the remaining portion of this book, you will almost always be looking at multiple domain architectures and the roles they play in the modern workplace. See Figure 1.5 and Figure 1.6, respectively, for illustrations of a simple-domain architecture and a multiple-domain architecture.

On the certification exam, it's much more likely you will come across a more specific domain model structure, such as a regional, x, or y model.

FIGURE 1.5   Single-domain architecture

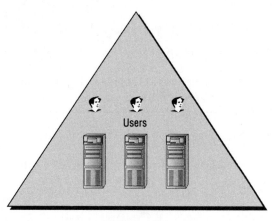

MyCorp.com

FIGURE 1.6   Multiple-domain architecture

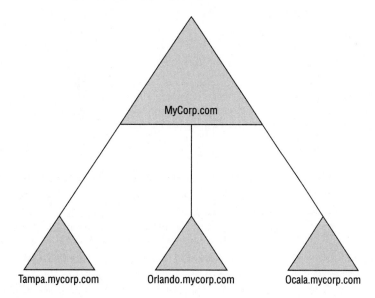

Regional Domain Model

In most international and large-scale companies, users are often divided into several geographic locations, such as Tokyo, Madrid, Hong Kong, and Los Angeles. Historically, the only way to connect these locations has been via a wide area network (WAN) connection over a relatively slow bandwidth link.

In a regional design, each of these regions is assigned their own specific domain where they can be further subdivided into more closely knit administrative groups. Figure 1.7 shows an example of this type of domain structure.

FIGURE 1.7   Regional domain model

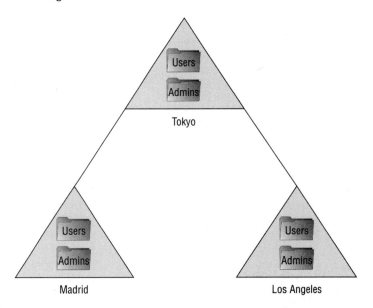

Sometimes when you need to isolate particular services using an autonomous model (not an isolation model!), it becomes necessary for you to create a multiple tree infrastructure wherein services or data are allocated among separate domain trees in a fashion that allows for a broader form of administration. You can see this model in action in Figure 1.8.

The main advantage of this model is that you manage to achieve a form of autonomous separation, but you also get to maintain the simplicity of a single schema. And if there's one aspect of Windows Server that's annoying to mess with, it's the schema.

Of course, this structure has drawbacks. Specifically, if you decide to use this form of administration, you remove the option to have complete isolation. Because the domain trees all are in the same forest, the root-level domain will have access to the rest of the trees and therefore will be able alter important information—something that you, as an enterprise administrator, may not want to have happen. Additionally, authentication paths usually take longer in this model because users have to cross separate servers to authenticate across links that are farther away.

FIGURE 1.8   Multiple-tree domain model

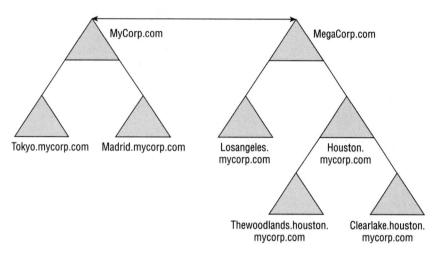

Creating Your Domain Structure

Now that you've seen the elements required to create an effective domain infrastructure, I'll discuss how to put them together effectively.

The process for this, once you understand the elements involved, is rather simple. Here are the steps for domain structure creation:

1.   Determine the administrative model.

- Centralized
- Decentralized
- Hybrid

2.   Choose a domain model.

3.   Choose the number of domains.

4.   Assign your domain functional levels.

5.   Assign a root domain.

Active Directory Authentication

One of the most important tasks when creating your overall design (if you ask your security administrator, *the* most important task) is to make sure the right people have access to the right information at the right time. In the administrative world, we call these processes *authentication* and *authorization*:

Authentication   In security administration, authentication is the process of verifying a user's identity. Is John Q. Smith really John Q. Smith? Or is he another user pretending to be John Q. Smith?

Authorization   Authorization is the process of determining what access a particular user has. For example, this is the process of determining whether John Q. Smith has access to the Shared folder on an office server located in the main building.

Overview of Forest and Domain Trust Models

No matter where you work, there will come a point in your administrative life where you simply have to break things down. As I alluded to earlier, it's rare that you will see a large enterprise using only one domain, or even one forest, to administer an entire facility. Unfortunately (or fortunately if you'd like to consider it in terms of job security), the real world is a lot more complex. Accordingly, designs and topologies become more complex as companies grow.

The main question that comes up as this process continues is this: how can you utilize resources that aren't part of your individual infrastructure? The answer, which originally came about in Windows Server 2000, is a *trust*. By now, you probably are familiar with trusts and the various types of trusts that can be implemented in Windows Server 2008. In the following sections, I will review the various types of trusts, cover their strengths and weaknesses, and discuss strategies for implementing trusts in your environment. The MCITP certification exam will ask a lot of questions on trusts from both your previous study and what you will learn here. It's a good idea to review what you've learned in the past before you take the exam. It could save your grade!

As mentioned earlier, trusts are connections—between either domains or forests—that allow various objects within Active Directory to access, modify, and utilize resources. In general, trusts exist on two levels: forest and domain.

Forest Trusts

With the release of Windows Server 2003, Microsoft made a previously unavailable function available to administrators. Forest trusts allow an administrator to connect two forests and establish a trust between them at the forest level. This is a big change from the previous iteration, which allowed this only on the domain level. Forest trusts can be either one-way, two-way, or transitive. In a two-way transitive forest, each forest trusts the other completely. Forest trusts offer several benefits, such as simplified resource access, improved authentication, improved security, and improved administrative overhead.

It's important to note that, unlike domain trusts (discussed next), forest trusts can be created only between two forests. They cannot be extended or joined to a third. This function is slightly limiting; however, this is utilized for security purposes and for administrative reasons. By accident, an administrator could easily end up making all components of a multitiered forest trust each other completely!

Domain Trusts

Just like at the forest level, administrators have the ability to create trusts between domains, albeit with a lot more flexibility and power than at the forest level.

In Windows Server 2008, three different trust types are available between domains in order to aid in the sharing of resources: realm trusts, external trusts, and shortcut trusts. Each of these types of trusts has various optional permissions and allowances. You will need to be familiar with them before you begin planning your infrastructure design.

External trusts   You can create an *external trust* to form a one-way or two-way, nontransitive trust with domains outside of your forest. External trusts are sometimes necessary when users need access to resources located in a Windows NT 4.0 domain that doesn't support Active Directory. Figure 1.9 illustrates this.

FIGURE 1.9   External trust

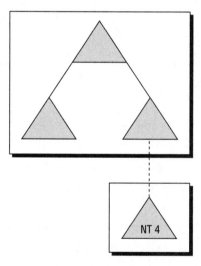

Shortcut trusts   Sometimes when you have a complex Active Directory forest, the "shortest path" between two servers is not as idyllic as you might desire. If, for instance, a particular domain is nested four tiers down in your tree and it wants to access resources in another domain that is four tiers down in another tree, it will have to go up four levels and then down four levels of authentication in order to access the resources it requires.

This is quite inefficient. There is another option. By using Kerberos, you can create a transitive trust between the two domains that allows one domain to directly access another, without having to traverse up and down their various trees. This is a *shortcut trust*. It's quite a useful trick, and it can save a lot of time. Keep in mind that once you create a shortcut trust, Windows Server 2008 will default to the shortest path it can to reach the desired server. This means there may come an occasion where a shortcut trust exists between a server and another server somewhere else in the network infrastructure. Undesired performance compromises can result if the server authenticates through its shortcut and then through another machine's trust. Because of this, it's best to use shortcut trusts in moderation. However, you can see a figurative example of a shortcut trust in Figure 1.10.

FIGURE 1.10   Shortcut trust

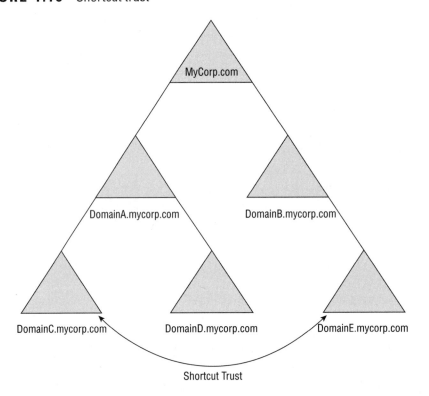

Shortcut Trust

Realm trusts   Since the whole world doesn't use Windows servers, it's a pretty good thing that Windows Server 2008 has a way to accommodate this. That way is a *realm trust*. Realm trusts are designed to give Unix users the ability to authenticate and have a relationship with a Windows server. This means the users on another operating system can have access to your files and resources. However, Unix realm trusts are one-way trusts and are not transitive, as illustrated in Figure 1.11.

FIGURE 1.11   Realm trust

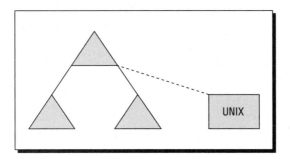

Overview of Physical Requirements and Physical Topology

With just about everything involving computers, there are two stages: planning and implementing. So far, I have discussed some of the more basic aspects of planning, a fair share of which you may already be familiar with. The following sections will address some of the concerns you'll face with topological implementation in the modern-day workplace—issues relating to where you put the servers and how you connect them to each other.

The Microsoft MCITP enterprise administrator exam will test two things: your knowledge of both design logic and your ability to make the right decision at the right time. With regard to physical topology decisions, it usually means choosing the right type of server to be connected at the right place, running the right services and features. Accordingly, I'll start with a brief discussion of the physical characteristics of the environment that you have to consider, then discuss WAN considerations, and finally discuss specific server roles that require attention by administrators, such as the global catalog.

Restrictions

When an administrator says that they have a "restriction," it doesn't mean they're bound by the rules of emissions or dumping waste (although that beast does wander into our backyards occasionally). Instead, it usually means that something about the campus design imposes a physical limitation that hinders the speed of the data. These limitations are usually the result of geography, obstructions, or inherited design.

Geography

If parts of your environment are separated by great distances, you will most likely have a slow WAN link that connects your offices. Today this is less of a problem. As of 2008, even home users can purchase 20-megabit up and down connections for their own personal use. That is an astonishing amount of data. However, even with the fastest WAN connections, the rule of thumb when it comes to distance still applies. If it's far away, it's probably going to be slow. Consider Figure 1.12. In this example, you have three offices; two are located in the same building in Seattle, and one is located in San Antonio. Obviously, the connection in San Antonio is going to be limited by its T1 connection.

FIGURE 1.12   Geographic concerns

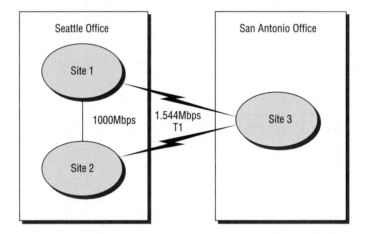

Obstructions

Have you ever been asked to install a server in one location and connect to another and then been blocked by a giant wall that is 8-feet thick? If you haven't, you're the single lucki-est administrator on the planet, or you simply haven't been in IT long enough to know the joys of dealing with the *other* kind of architecture. This is usually more of a building administration problem than an IT problem; however, it's good to note this, because it is a physical limitation.

Inherited Design

This is, by far, the most frustrating of all limitations. The dreaded *inherited design* occurs when you are trying to either upgrade an environment or reassign the topology of an environ-ment around a preexisting wiring system or topology design that has a serious bottleneck.

Here's a simple example of this: the last network engineer to work on the environment decided it would be a good idea to use only 100Mb switches instead of gigabit ones. After all, they're cheaper. But what happens when you have 100 users trying to access the same file? You're then extremely limited by how fast the server can communicate. Even though it might be capable of gigabit (or even 10Gb) performance, you're still stuck at 100Mb.

On the exam, this might sneak by you if you're not careful. Consider Figure 1.13, which shows a simple campus design. If you aren't paying close attention, it looks like a simple star topology design. However, the bottleneck of this entire environment is a relatively ancient switch. This small element can affect the entire network.

FIGURE 1.13   Inherited design concerns: the network is centered around a 10Mb switch that is slower than the rest of the network switches.

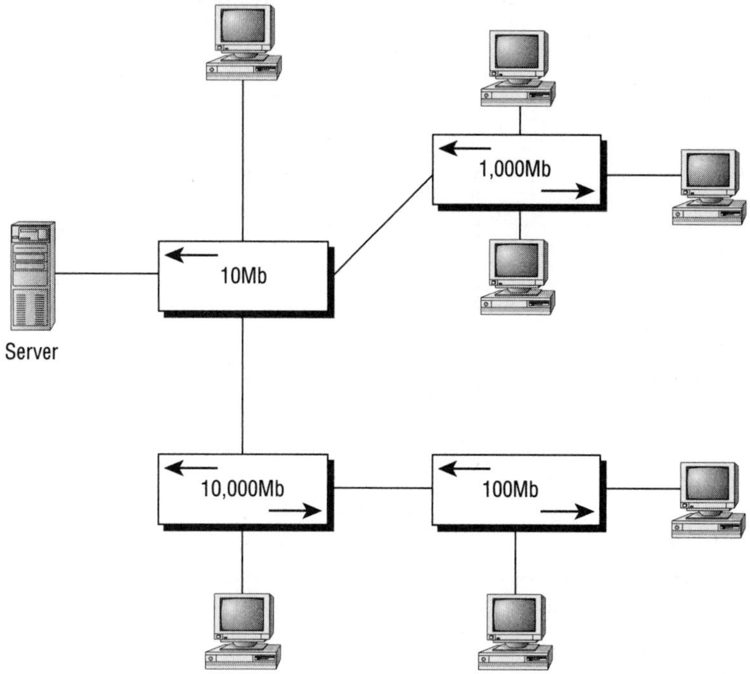

Placing Domain Controllers

The domain controller is the heart of your entire organization. It's the main location from which your users log in, and it also usually contains a copy of the global catalog, operations master, or other vital information that makes the domain controller not only the heart of your organization but several other very important organs as well.

In choosing the location for a domain controller, you should keep in mind several criteria:

Security   Security is your primary concern. Since a domain controller contains so much information, you have to make sure it is not just secure regarding software but also is physically secure. Generally, this means you want to make sure the domain controller is in a safe location, such as a data center, and that a hostile intruder couldn't easily compromise your server.

Accessibility   In terms of accessibility, you want to make sure this server can be accessed by your staff in terms of administration but also possesses adequate remote accessibility. Can it easily be accessed by all administrators? Are there any conflicts with the firewall or the router?

Reliability   Reliability by now is probably a given. Best practices for domain controllers indicate you should always have at least one backup domain controller in an environment, and the backup controller should be ready to take over at a moment's notice. Performance, likewise, is very important. Microsoft likes to test candidates on the specific hardware requirements of Windows Server 2008 in more ways than one. In addition to requiring you to know the basic requirements, they want you to know how much memory and disk space a domain controller will require based on the number of users. Table 1.3 breaks memory usage down into an easy-to-read format, and Table 1.4 shows how to calculate the recommended disk space, according to Microsoft.

TABLE 1.3   Domain Controller Memory Requirements

Users per Domain Controller	Memory Requirements
1–499	512MB
500–999	1GB
More than 1,000	2GB

TABLE 1.4   Domain Controller Space Requirements

Server Requirement	Space Requirement
Active Directory transaction logs	500MB
Sysvol share	500MB
Windows Server 2008 operating system	1.5 to 2GB; 2GB recommended
Intervals of 1,000 users	0.4GB per 1,000 users for the drive with NTDS.dit

You will have to plan for the number of domain controllers your environment will require according to the number of users, as shown in Table 1.5.

TABLE 1.5   Domain Controller Processor Requirements

Number of Users	Processor Requirements
1–499	One single processor
500–999	One dual processor
1,000–2,999	Two dual processors
3,000–10,000	Two quad processors

The Global Catalog

As you may remember from the 70-640 MCTS Windows Server 2008 Active Directory exam, a *global catalog server* is a server that contains a master list of all the objects in a domain or forest. The *global catalog* itself is the master list, and it is transmitted across servers for the purpose of informing individual machines throughout the environment of what objects actually exist and, more importantly, where they can be found. The Sybex 70-640 book *Windows Server 2008 Active Directory Configuration Study Guide* calls this list the "universal phone book" of Active Directory. Not only is that pretty clever, it's also very accurate.

The global catalog serves two more functions. First, it enables users to log on because it informs a domain controller of the universal group membership of the rest of the servers. Second, it resolves user principal names of which a particular domain controller may not be aware.

Global Catalog Server Locations

Deciding which server is going to contain your global catalog is one of the most important decisions you will make when you are beginning to design a network. Depending on its location, it can directly affect the speed of your site replication, the amount of time your servers spend updating themselves with the latest objects, and how quickly the rest of the environment becomes aware of changes.

By default, the first tree (domain) in a forest is always a global catalog server. This is because if a forest didn't have a copy of the global catalog, it really wouldn't achieve much, because no credentials would be cached and it wouldn't have a list of what user accounts existed. Beyond the initial global catalog servers, here are a couple of other reasons you might want to add a global catalog server: users of custom applications, unavailable WAN links, and roaming users.

Operations Master Location

Just like the global catalog server location, the operations master location is one of the most important design decisions you will have to make when creating your network infrastructure. However, unlike the global catalog server, the operations master server is broken down into five separate roles that have to be considered.

Schema Master

If you have a choice in the matter, the best decision for the schema master is to use it as little as possible. Modifying the schema isn't something you want to do very often, because it tends to be very heavy handed and can cause a lot of problems if you aren't careful. When placing the schema master, the main thing you have to keep in mind is the location of your schema administrators. They will be the sole benefactors of this location, and therefore you need to plan accordingly.

Domain Naming Master

In the old days of computing (the Windows 2000 era), the domain naming master was always placed on the global catalog server. With Windows Server 2008, this is no longer a requirement, but it's still considered a very good practice. The domain naming master is responsible for making sure that every domain is uniquely named and usually communicates when domains are added and then removed.

Relative Identifier Master (RID Master)

If you'll recall from your earlier study, the relative identifier (RID) and security identifier (SID) are used to distinguish uniqueness within Active Directory. Whenever an account or group of accounts is created, the RID will have to be contacted. Therefore, it's a good design practice to place the RID in an area that has access to domain controllers and can be easily communicated with whenever an administrator needs to make a new account.

Infrastructure Master

You can think of the infrastructure master in your environment as the person who makes sure everyone has everything named right. The best example of this is when someone gets married or has their name legally changed. Say a user changes her name from Maria Dammen to Maria Anderson. If she has her name changed in domain A, there is a chance that domain B may not be aware of this change and may need to be informed about it. Accordingly, something in the infrastructure has to search through everything (including network entities as well as users) and check the names and consistency.

The primary rule for placing an infrastructure master is to not place it on any machine that is a global catalog server. This is because when the global catalog server checks with other domains, it will not notice the inconsistencies between the two domains, because it's already aware of what they should be. Instead, you should try to place a domain controller in an area that is not a global catalog server but has access to a domain controller from another domain.

Primary Domain Controller

Maybe it's just a holdover from the days of old, but to this day when certain administrators hear the phrases *primary domain controller* and *backup domain controller* from their friend Windows NT 4, they shiver a little bit. This is because the world of Windows administration was nowhere near as friendly in the early days as it is now. You don't necessarily need a lecture on how things used to be, though. Instead, as a Windows Server 2008 administrator, you just need to know how to handle old equipment.

The only reason to use this role is if you have a machine running Windows NT 4 that doesn't understand Active Directory. In this situation, the primary domain controller can ensure that all older machines can change passwords as Windows Server 2008 emulates the older authentication process. Additionally, a primary domain controller makes sure that all machines with pre–Active Directory installations can keep their times synchronized.

Overview of Site and Replication Topology

In Active Directory, the concept of a site is very closely related to the concept of a subnet. A *subnet* is an isolated area in a network that is blocked by a router that stops broadcast traffic. From a design standpoint, this creates separation (and therefore isolation), and places physical firewalls between locations. The caveat to this design is that you will not have to route between IP based subnets by using a router.

Furthermore, in Active Directory the term *sites* means a collection of individual computers in a particular subnet that are logically collected into one container. This means that by default, each container will be autonomous and not communicate with any other container. To make the rest of your network communicate, you will need to establish a *site link* between the two sites within the various subnets so they can identify each other.

From a design standpoint, you are concerned with sites and subnets because of the concept of replication. As you'll recall from your study of Active Directory, *replication* is the process of notifying the rest of the network of when an object is created, deleted, moved, or changed. This is maintained by something called the *knowledge consistency checker* (KCC). The KCC generates and maintains the replication topology for replication within sites and between sites. It is a built-in process that runs on all DCs. When a system wide change takes place, the KCC (a dynamic-link library) will modify data in the local directory based on those changes and then by default, the KCC reviews and makes modifications to the Active Directory replication topology every 15 minutes to ensure propagation of such data, either directly or transitively, by creating and deleting connection objects as needed.

The KCC recognizes changes that occur in the environment and ensures that domain controllers are not orphaned in the replication topology. Due to this overhead, it is important that you take this into account when designing your site link topology and your overall infrastructure.

Site Links

Site links in Active Directory are reliable, usually WAN, connections between different subnets or collections of subnets. Remember, a site is a replication boundary. Thus, in order to communicate, you must establish a site link that connects these two different sites. Overall, each of these sites will send all their necessary replication over one individual connection, such as a T1 circuit.

Because not all site links are created equal, it behooves us as administrators to establish certain understood and quantifiable values within our site-link design:

- Site-link name
- Site-link cost
- Site-link schedule

The site-link name is pretty obvious—it's what you name your site link. The site-link cost is a little less obvious. A *site-link cost* is a value that is assigned by the administrator to identify the speed of the connection between the two different sites, with a lower number indicating a faster connection. Normally, Windows Server 2008 defaults all site links at cost 100, and it's up to administrators to manually establish costs for the rest of the topology. Table 1.6 shows a recommended cost-link table.

TABLE 1.6   Recommended Site-Link Cost Table

Available Bandwidth (Kbps)	Site-Link Cost
4096	283
2048	309
1024	340
512	378
256	425
128	486
64	567
56	586
35.4	644
19.2	798
9.6	1042

Keep in mind that site links are not limited to IP. In fact, they actually use Remote Procedure Call (RPC) over IP. But for your purposes here, IP will suffice. Site links can also use the Simple Mail Transfer Protocol (SMTP). However, SMTP is not available if you are within the same domain. Within the same domain, you are limited to RPC over IP.

The last value you need to be concerned with is the *site-link schedule*. If you read and did your exercises in Sybex's *MCTS Active Directory Configuration Study Guide*, you are probably familiar with how to set this up. Each site link requires a schedule for replication. This is because you don't necessarily want your servers replicating traffic all over the network while you have 1,000 users trying to access a particular file over a WAN. It creates a lot of traffic. For this exam, just keep in mind that schedules are a part of site links. The actual process of setting these up has already been covered.

Site-Link Bridges

The purpose of a site-link bridge is to function as a shortcut between two sites that are not actually linked together. In other words, if site A is linked to site B, and site B is linked to site C, site A can be linked through site C by using a site-link bridge.

If you have taken and passed exams 70-640 and 70-642, you are already quite familiar with this. Now you will be challenged to take what you have learned and apply it to a design environment. For instance, you may be given a scenario where you will be asked what the best solution is to connect site A to site C, as in Figure 1.14. Although it may seem like a site link would be the most logical answer, your knowledge of site-link bridges will indicate you can save some administrative overhead by using a bridge.

FIGURE 1.14   Site-link bridges

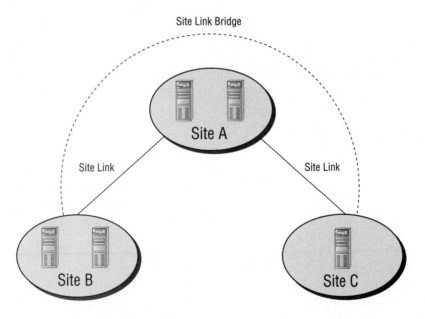

Site-link bridges can be a useful technique to implement if you already have preexisting site links in your environment. Later, in Chapter 3 of this book, I'll discuss a quick way to use this helpful feature.

Choosing Server Roles

Once you've taken the time to identify the overall structure and design scheme of your enterprise, the next logical step is to determine the role that Active Directory can play in your design. In the old days, this wasn't quite as complex a process. With systems such as Windows NT, you simply had to choose a primary domain controller (PDC), and possibly a backup domain controller (BDC), and then go through the much more arduous task of administering the environment after designing it.

Now, however, solution architects and IT administrators have the problem of not just choosing domain controllers but choosing among several types of domain controllers, DNS settings, server roles, server features, scripting, and hundreds of other options that can be implemented in your campus. Microsoft has adapted to this change in administrative design by introducing many new features and best practices that should be followed in your organization.

Part of the difficulty involved with designing an enterprise with Windows Server 2008 is that there is so much that can be done! In Windows Server 2008 alone, Microsoft released several major features that are particularly important to large environments. For the exam, you will need to be able to fire these features and their buzzwords off at whim, because you can bet a silver dollar that you're going to be seeing all them—either on the certification exam or when you enter the workforce.

Since you already have some familiarity with these new features, I'll briefly cover the most commonly tested features here and point out how you need to consider using these features in a Windows enterprise-level environment, as well as one or two old favorites that still raise their heads once in a while.

Security Design Features

Although Microsoft doesn't officially group Windows Server 2008's new features into categories such as security and delegation, it's useful for your purposes to consider the features this way, because it helps put you in the right frame of mind to think about how these features help your overall environment. The two features you'll concentrate on in the following sections are read-only domain controllers and Windows BitLocker encryption.

Read-Only Domain Controllers

As you probably already know, read-only domain controllers (RODCs) are a hot topic in the IT workplace right now. RODCs are new to Windows Server 2008 and can be run only on Windows Server 2008. However, Windows Server 2003 domain controllers can communicate with them.

An RODC is a domain controller that, as the name implies, contains a "read-only" copy of the Active Directory database that cannot be changed (written to). The primary use for this is in a situation where the *physical* security of an environment is compromised. In other words, an RODC makes sure that someone can't steal, tamper with, or alter your domain controller and acquire valuable intellectual property, such as usernames, passwords, or other such need-to-know information.

Something else you need to remember about RODCs is that they can use their own version of DNS, called *read-only DNS*. For design purposes, it's important to remember that read-only DNS functions by a referral system. Whenever a user makes a resolution request, the read-only DNS server makes a referral to another DNS server for name resolution. Effectively, this keeps the server from keeping a writable and updatable table of IP address mappings that can ultimately become compromised.

Figure 1.15 shows a typical example where a read-only domain controller could be used in a large enterprise environment. Keep in mind as you're studying RODCs that the RODC features fall under the purview of Active Directory Domain Services, along with the very snazzy new restartable Active Directory services feature, which I'll cover later in this book.

FIGURE 1.15 RODC placement

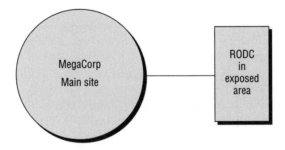

Windows BitLocker

Because of the release of Microsoft Vista, much of the true pizzazz of the incredible Bit-Locker feature has been downplayed. Why? Well, BitLocker is no longer new. However, the BitLocker feature is absolutely priceless in an enterprise environment. Single-handedly, this role ensures that your Windows server, along with its important data, is encrypted and cannot be read by a malicious intruder who nefariously acquires one of your domain controllers through deceit.

For design purposes, this feature actually opens an entire new level of consideration for the environment. Initially, you have to consider the physical placement of servers. Afterward, you have to think about whether the physical placement of those servers could possibly result in the servers being compromised. It's a rather disturbing thought, but in today's world you really just can't take the chance that your server might never be subject to malicious users.

In general, BitLocker encryption is almost never a bad thing. However, it isn't enabled by default. You, as the administrator, must turn it on. If it makes you feel safer, it isn't a bad practice to enable BitLocker encryption on almost any server that might ever have the chance of being visited by someone that isn't part of your organization. On the extreme end, you could also safely enable it on every Windows Vista and Windows Server 2008 machine in your environment. It's a bit taxing in terms of deployment but worth it in the end.

Administration and Delegation Features

It's no secret that administering several thousand users can be a big task that can take a lot of time. Not only is it a big job, but it can be rather complex. Without the ability to delegate some of the numerous tasks that have to be conducted every day, your job would be very difficult. It's because of this that nearly every day Microsoft is trying to incorporate solutions that make our lives as administrators a lot easier. Let's take a look now at some of the great new roles that you can incorporate in your design, such as Active Directory Rights Management Services (AD RMS).

Active Directory Rights Management Services

AD RMS is a true heavyweight in terms of the new features of Windows Server 2008. With AD RMS, an organization can give its users some administrative control of their individual documents and files, including office documents and emails. Additionally, with AD RMS, administrators and users can create privilege templates that can be defaulted for certain abilities in the environment. For instance, an administrator could create a "read-only" template that users could apply to a report that they'd like to make available on a shared drive somewhere in the organization.

The most important point you need to keep in mind for AD RMS in an environment is this: *Active Directory Rights Management Services requires a database server.*

If you are designing an environment and your organization doesn't plan to incorporate some sort of database server, you can't deploy this feature.

AD RMS has requirements that go beyond its hardware needs:

- Firewall exceptions (see Table 1.7)
- One AD RMS server per forest
- IIS with ASP.NET enabled

TABLE 1.7   AD RMS Port Exception Requirements

Port Exception	Description
80	HTTP port used for web traffic and communication
443	HTTPS port used for secure HTTP
1433	Microsoft SQL server port for database communication
445	SQL port for piper names

It's important to point out that AD RMS is not as simple to install as you might think. You need to keep in mind a lot of requirements, and although it might seem like a very convenient feature for your office environment, it does require some planning on your end. You can have an AD RMS server in an extranet, in a single-server environment, connected through a URL, or with several other setups.

For the certification exam, it's important to remember the basic features of AD RMS—the ones in the checklist at the beginning of this section.

If you're asked for a way to give users a right to secure their documents, remember that AD RMS is probably the solution. It's extraordinarily powerful, and if you implement it correctly, it can relieve a lot of headaches. However, if you don't consider the full ramifications of this setup, you can ultimately end up with a less secure network that is running more services than it needs, ultimately draining the usability and portability of your server.

Active Directory Federation Services

If there's one phrase you need to remember about Active Directory Federation Services (AD FS), it is this: *single sign-on* (SSO). The overall design purpose of AD FS is to create an environment where users don't have to repeatedly validate their credentials across an environment. From a design standpoint, you may have a situation that looks similar to Figure 1.16.

FIGURE 1.16 Active Directory Federation Services

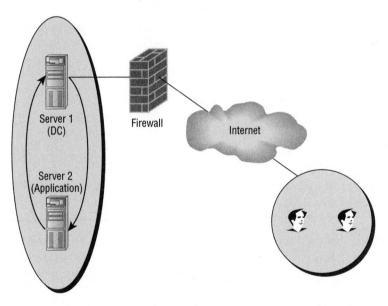

On the right side of the illustration, you have users who are trying to access an application on server 2. However, they authenticate through server 1. Once they've authenticated through that server, they then have to access yet another server in order to complete the tasks they need to do. As you can imagine, this can be quite annoying to users. It would be particularly irritating if they had to use the same username and password.

By using AD FS, administrators can create a trust policy between servers for the purposes of authentication. This means that in a situation such as Figure 1.16, you could create an environment where users could simply log on to their primary server and then be authenticated throughout the rest of the forest (or multiple forest) environment. It isn't just convenient for them; it's also less burdening on your servers. They get to automatically authenticate through a simple service vs. sending back and forth requests for user information that may require more demanding GUIs or other such programs they have to launch.

When you're first creating your design, Windows Active Directory Federation Services has several options on how it can be installed:

Federation Services   Federation Services is the underlying architecture that provides the ability for users to sign on once in an environment. It does this through a series of designed trusts and allocations that is decided upon far in advance of the actual implementation of the feature. In general, Federation Services can implement single sign-on through one of three general federation designs, also referred to as *federation scenarios*: Web SSO, Federated Web SSO, and Federated Web SSO with Forest Trust.

Web SSO design   In a simple Web SSO design, all users are external, and therefore no federation trusts exist because there are no partners. According to Microsoft, the primary reason an administrator would need a design such as this is if the organization had an application that needed to be accessed by users on the Internet.

Federated Web SSO design   Sometimes companies merge, form partnerships, or otherwise need to share infrastructures and applications. Before AD FS, the only real way this could be accomplished is by creating separate accounts for each account, as well as a new series of policies and information to remember in addition to the current passwords.

Now, when situations like this occur, administrators can incorporate a design policy that implements the concept of federation trusts. A *federation trust* is a type of agreement that's made between two organizations that gives them the ability to verify users from one organization to be granted access to another. Federation trusts represented with one-way arrows point to the account side of the trust, as illustrated in 1.17.

A quick but very important point to consider before continuing is that federation trusts require two servers to authenticate. You can't have a federation trust that authenticates to nothing.

Consider the example in Figure 1.18. In this figure, you can see a great example of where an organization could use Active Directory Federation Services. MyCorp, a service providing a resource, has a trust established with MegaCorp, an organization with several accounts. Within MegaCorp, several users will need to log in to MegaCorp and have access to the services provided from MyCorp. In this scenario, they can simply log in to MegaCorp and access their applications at whim.

FIGURE 1.17   Federation trust

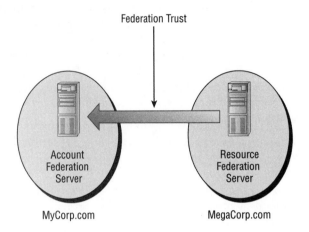

FIGURE 1.18   Federated Web SSO design

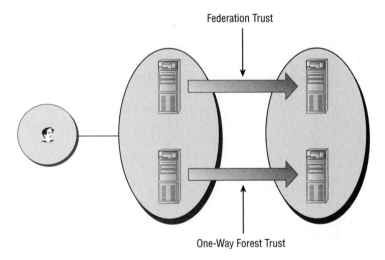

Federated Web SSO with Forest Trust design   In a Federated Web SSO with Forest Trust design, you are effectively combining Active Directory from multiple forests in different organizations so that users in the account portion can access applications in another organization with their standard username and password. The advantage of this design scheme is that user accounts in the MyCorp domain can also access the application, and therefore resource accounts or groups do not need to be created.

Federation Services proxy   A Federation Services proxy server is a role that serves two purposes for either the account or resource side. On the account side, a federation server acts as a proxy for the actual federation server and also distributes security tokens to web-based clients that need to access resources on the resource partner portion of the agreement. On the resource side, a proxy server just redirects clients to a federation server that can authenticate the clients. Overall, the benefit of a Federation Services proxy is to alleviate the workload of the actual federation server and add another layer of design complexity for best practices.

Claims-aware agent   If an organization happens to be running an application that is claims-aware and needs to have security tokens verified through Active Directory Domains Services, they can use a claims-aware agent. Loosely put, a claims-aware application is a Microsoft ASP.NET application that uses claims that are present in an Active Directory Federation Services security token to provide authorization and personalization to your environment. Normally, you won't be implementing this unless your organization has very specific needs.

Windows token-based agent   A Windows token-based agent is an agent that converts from Active Directory Federation Services to an impersonated Windows NT access token. The reason this might be used is if you have an application that requires Windows authentication and you have to connect via Federation Services. If this is the case, the web agent creates an impersonated authentication token that Windows can use. Some of the aspects of the Windows token-based agent are auditing, application logging, configuration details, and malformed requests.

If you're interested in learning more about Active Directory Federation Services and how it can be used in your environment, Microsoft provides a wonderful online resource on Windows Server 2008 TechNet that gives practical examples of how each of these designs could be implemented. However, for the purposes of the certification exam, the server-level implementation is beyond the scope of this book. What's important for you to remember is the purpose of the service and the different types of designs that can be utilized in your environment.

Summary

In this chapter, you examined the different roles of the administration process, the implementation and design of forests, and the design of the domain structure. Additionally, you examined some of the physical limitations and server roles within your infrastructure by examining WAN links, topologies, and new benefits released in Windows Server 2008.

For the exam, look over each of these individual processes, and remember the naming conventions for each theory, the features and strengths of each design structure, and what that structure will help to facilitate in your environment. In your own study, a good practice in preparing for the exam is to try to simulate a series of enterprise-level designs in your home laboratory. With just two machines, you can create a surprisingly complex amount of scenarios, such as a multiple-forest design.

Exam Essentials

Be ready to list design advantages and disadvantages.   A lot of the design-based questions for the exam revolve around limitations presented in a scenario. Within the question, Microsoft will give specific hints involving the limitations or design requirements of a specific domain or forest.

Know your server 2008 features.   This can't be stressed enough. Microsoft is very proud of the new features of Windows Server 2008, and truth be told, they're quite impressive. Know terms such as single sign-on, the purpose of a read-only domain controller, and where particular features can be used in your environment.

Understand the limitations of your functional levels.   What is the advantage of a Windows Server 2003 domain functional level? Windows 2000 Native? In your design, you need to accommodate the different application and architecture requirements that Microsoft will require.

Know where to place your servers.   If you are given a requirement for where to place your servers with a specific server role, you should be able to respond to a given diagram that shows server roles with the appropriate place in your topology to assign such a server.

Remember hardware requirements.   Part of administering an enterprise is to plan for growth and understand what hardware you will need in order to run Windows for a given period of time. When planning, make sure to accommodate the eventual number of users, not just your current capacity.

Understand autonomy vs. isolation.   These are not the same thing. Be able to differentiate between the two and, when asked, accommodate for the demands of each with a topology that responds well to each accordingly.

Be familiar with trust types.   Know what each trust type means. Is there an advantage to a shortcut trust over another type? What is an external trust? You'll need to know the answer to these questions instantly when you take the exam.

Review Questions

1. Which of the following administrative models would be the *most* efficient for a company that maintains several corporate offices in different locations, has a single master administrator in charge of the entire campus, and has three individual administrators within each branch who are in charge of their own resources?

    A. Centralized

    B. Decentralized

    C. Hybrid

    D. Outsourced

2. Which of the following functional levels within Windows Server 2008 support read-only domain controllers? (Choose all that apply.)

    A. Windows Server 2008

    B. Windows 2000 Native

    C. Windows Server 2003

    D. Windows NT

    E. Windows 2000 Mixed

3. If your design requires a single sign-on (SSO) feature to be enabled on your network, which of the following *must* be installed?

    A. Active Directory Rights Management Services (AD RMS)

    B. Active Directory Domain Services (AD DS)

    C. Active Directory Federation Services (AD FS)

    D. DNS

    E. Active Directory–integrated Domain Services

4. Which of the following server feature passes the authentication of users onto a federation server?

    A. Domain controller

    B. Domain naming master

    C. Federation proxy server

    D. Relative identifier master

    E. A federation trust

5. Which two of the following features need to be applied in order to make certain a domain controller in a compromised area is as secure as possible? (Choose two.)

   A. Read-only domain controller

   B. Active Directory Domain Services

   C. Federation Services

   D. Windows BitLocker

   E. Security identifiers

6. Which of the following is not a component of a site link?

   A. Site-link name

   B. Site-link cost

   C. Site-link schedule

   D. Site-link identifier

7. If you needed to support Windows NT in your domain, which of the following server roles would you require?

   A. Backup domain controller

   B. Federation server

   C. Primary domain controller

   D. Domain controller

   E. File server

8. Designing a domain to run completely independently of any other forest or domain structure other than itself in order to make certain it doesn't communicate with any other network is a design concept called what?

   A. Centralized administration

   B. Decentralized administration

   C. Centralized automation

   D. Autonomy

   E. Isolation

9. What is the maximum number of schemas that can exist in any given forest if the administrator installs a relative identifier master on the primary domain controller?

   A. 0

   B. 1

   C. 2

   D. 3

10. Which of the following is *not* a category of requirements you should consider in designing your forest structure?

   A. Organizational requirements

   B. Software requirements

   C. Operational requirements

   D. Legal requirements

11. You are the enterprise administrator for MyCorp, a medium-sized business with 200 employees. Your superior, John Mayer, has come to you with a new design concern. In the research and development branch of the company, the engineers have been designing a new program that is designed to stress test networks and examine computers that exist throughout the infrastructure. Because of this, John has asked you to create a solution in Active Directory that will accommodate the research and development group, as well as the group's new software. Which of the following summarizes the best action to take?

   A. Create a new group of users called "Research and Development." Assign a template to this group in Group Policy that restricts the usage of the network application to only those users, and then apply the policy.

   B. Create a new group of users called "Research and Development." In Group Policy, require that users of the network application log onto the centralized domain controller in order to authenticate the software.

   C. Create a new forest. Inside this forest, place a new group called "Research and Development" in the default domain, and adapt the isolation model.

   D. Create a new domain within your forest. Inside this domain, place a new group called "Research and Development," and adapt the isolation model.

12. At a local hospital, Exchange Server 2007 is almost constantly in use. Because most medical records are secure pieces of information, these records are highly sensitive, but occasionally doctors will have to communicate with other physicians via email regarding patients under an extremely restrictive security policy, governed by legal documents. Accordingly, you have been asked to deploy a domain controller solution at most hospital branches that will allow doctors to log on at will in potentially vulnerable environments. Security is a must, and physicians must be able to access email. Which of the following is the best solution?

   A. Deploy domain controllers at all branch locations with Windows BitLocker enabled. Enable single sign-on (SSO) with AD FS and require certificates to be used for each user.

   B. Deploy a read-only domain controller in the areas that may be exposed and ensure that certificates are used to protect sensitive data.

   C. Enable Active Directory Rights Management Services (AD RMS), and enable each physician to secure their own files. Additionally, enable Windows BitLocker.

   D. Deploy a read-only domain controller, and enable Windows BitLocker.

13. Phil, a new user in your engineering department, has been tasked with creating a new piece of hardware that drills microscopic holes in pieces of fiber. According to Phil, the budget for this project is in excess of $2 million. Additionally, Phil has asked that he be allowed to administer his own individual Windows NT server so that he can accommodate legacy user demands with the device. As the lead administrator for this 12,000-person company, what design choice would be your best decision?

    A. Create a new forest. Inside this forest assign the root domain to Phil, and give Phil administrative privileges.

    B. Implement a read-only domain controller. Add Phil as the administrator of this domain controller, and add the backup domain controller feature.

    C. Create a new forest. Inside the forest, create a new domain, and make Phil the administrator of this domain.

    D. Create a new domain in your existing forest, and enable the primary domain controller emulator. Then, implement the design model for autonomy.

14. In your large enterprise, your administrators have become constantly burdened by the need to keep up with the excessive amount of file permission reassignment that is required for certain important documents, including Excel spreadsheets and email. Accordingly, you are seeking to implement an elegant solution to this problem. What would you recommend?

    A. Enable Active Directory Rights Management Services (AD RMS), and allow users to assign their own file permissions.

    B. Create a template for each file situation, and enable delegation of this template to individual users in your environment.

    C. Elevate the authority of your standard user to server operators, allowing them to assign their own policies.

    D. Enable Active Directory Domain Services with DNS enabled.

15. Within your organization, you have three sites: Tokyo, Madrid, and New York City. From Tokyo to New York, you have a site link running over a T3 line at 45Mbps. From New York to Madrid, users are connected via a 1.544Mb T1 line. To connect Tokyo to Madrid, what should you recommend to your network administrator?

    A. Create a new site link between Tokyo and Madrid.

    B. Create a site-link bridge by maintaining a transitive link between the two existing site links.

    C. Enable remote logins for your Tokyo users, and extend a two-way transitive trust from your Tokyo to Madrid location.

    D. Enable remote logins for your Madrid users, and extend a two-way transitive trust from your Tokyo to Madrid location.

16. MyCorp is a larger enterprise supporting more than 10,000 users. Recently, the CEO of MyCorp has created another business within MyCorp called MyLittleCorp. As the enterprise administrator, your CEO has asked you to install a new domain controller for your organization that will support 400 users. Which of the following hardware requirements should you make sure to maintain?

A. At least two processors

B. More than 1GB of RAM

C. At least 512MB of RAM

D. RAID 5

17. If a forest is differentiated by the Engineering, Accounting, Human Resources, and Products groups, what administrative structure is it following?

A. Organizational

B. Resource

C. Restricted access

D. Single sign-on (SSO)

18. If a forest is differentiated into the Engineering, Accounting, Human Resources, and Products groups, what administrative structure is it following?

A. Organizational

B. Resource

C. Restricted access

D. Single sign-on (SSO)

19. Look at the illustration shown here. If domain D needed to communicate with domain G, which of the following trusts would you recommend?

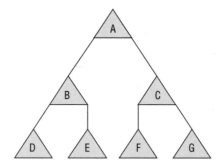

A. External trust

B. Shortcut trust

C. Realm trust

D. Friend trust

20. Consider the illustration shown here. If domain A needed to communicate with domain C, which of the following trusts would be best recommended?

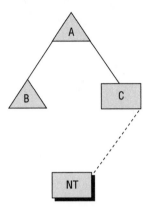

   A.   External trust
   B.   Shortcut trust
   C.   Realm trust
   D.   Friend trust

21. Consider the illustration shown here. If domain A needed to communicate with domain C, which of the following trusts would be best recommended?

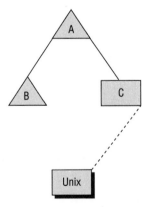

   A.   External trust
   B.   Shortcut trust
   C.   Realm trust
   D.   Friend trust

22. Which of the following technologies is responsible for verifying a user's identity across a network infrastructure, and what is the name of this process? (Choose all that apply.)

    A. Domain controller

    B. Domain name server

    C. Realm authenticator

    D. Operations master

    E. Authentication

    F. Authorization

Answers to Review Questions

1. C. Hybrid administrative models are used in environments where there needs to be a centralized corporate administrator (or administrators), as well as several decentralized locations where other administrators can maintain their own branches.

2. A, C. Windows Server 2008 supports three functional levels: Windows Server 2008, Windows Server 2003, and Windows 2000 Native. Windows NT and Windows 2000 Mixed do not exist. Of those three functional levels, only Windows Server 2008 and Windows Server 2003 support read-only domain controllers.

3. C. Active Directory Federation Services (AD FS) is a service that allows multiple users to authenticate once in a Windows environment and then access resources on the rest of the environment. Most often, it is used for Internet users.

4. C. Federation proxy servers authenticate users and pass on their credentials to Active Directory federation servers in order to reduce server load and increase security as the proxy services provide a security token for the authentication within the corporate network.

5. A, B. By using read-only domain controllers, the domain controller in the exposed area will not be able to be written to and will cache credentials. Additionally, if that server is physically compromised, Windows BitLocker will keep the server from having its hard disk exposed to data extraction.

6. D. The three main components of a site link are the site-link name, cost, and schedule. The name identifies the site link, the cost indicates the speed and priority of the connection, and the schedule indicates when the site can be used to replicate across the network. At the enterprise level, you have to make sure site links are assigned the appropriate speed so that they are as efficient as possible.

7. C. A primary domain controller emulator is used to communicate with pre–Active Directory systems in order to support the legacy software with Windows Server 2008 technology.

8. E. The process of isolation is ensuring that an individual piece of the network can be accessed by nothing else in the entire network. This is usually done to isolate pieces of software or volatile user accounts from the rest of the infrastructure.

9. B. Remember, the rule of thumb with schemas is that there is only one schema per forest. If there were multiple schemas per forest, it would be really bad because there would be constant conflicts over the overall design of the infrastructure.

10. B. Software requirements are definitely part of the design consideration process, but they are covered under operational requirements. When designing a forest, you have to consider an organization's organizational, operational, and legal requirements.

11. C. This scenario is a classic case of the need for the isolation model within a unique forest. If users are using a network application that could compromise the rest of your infrastructure, it's best to completely isolate these users. Thus, it's best to create a separate forest with a completely separate group inside an individual domain.

12. D. In a situation like this, the most important criteria are that the domain controllers be read-only, so that the information cannot be read if compromised, and that the hard drive's data be secured with BitLocker. This way, even if the hard drive is removed, the contents will not be useful to an intruder.

13. D. C is a very tempting option for this design but ultimately incorrect. The reason for this is that C would be designed using the isolation model, which isn't necessarily required for this design. Instead, you can use the autonomous model and still maintain control of your enterprise while implementing the required Windows legacy NT support and keeping overall control of the network.

14. A. Active Directory Rights Management Services is an administrative tool that allows administrators to enable users to assign specific rights to their files. To enable this feature, you must manually set it up and have access to a database server, such as Microsoft SQL Server 2008.

15. B. The best way to connect two sites that already have existing site links is to use a site-link bridge. By default, when you're creating sites, the Bridge All Site Links option is enabled. Thus, it's recommended you keep this enabled so you'll be able to communicate through preexisting sites.

16. C. If you have less than 500 users, Microsoft recommends at least 512MB of RAM and a single processor system. Above that, the minimum requirements are outlined in the tables in this chapter.

17. A. An organizational forest divides the administrative structure of its users by departments, products, or other definite separations of duties based upon the business model of the environment. In this case, the topology of the forest follows the structure of the organization.

18. A. An organizational forest divides the administrative structure of its users by departments, products, or other definite separations of duties based upon the business model of the environment. In this case, the topology of the forest follows the structure of the organization.

19. B. A shortcut trust would be best for this situation. This is because without it, the server would have to authenticate through five other domains in order to receive its credentials. With a shortcut trust, the need for this extra level of administration is removed.

20. A. Because domain C is a Windows NT domain, an external trust will be required. With pre–Active Directory domain controllers, this is the only way to properly authenticate.

21. C. To authenticate properly, a Unix server requires a realm trust to be created. This is so the standard Unix directory structure can communicate effectively with the Windows Active Directory.

22. A, E. The primary responsibility of a domain controller is the authentication and authorization of users. A domain controller logs in users by validating their credentials and then allowing them to access network resources.

Chapter

2

Planning Naming Conventions, Networking, and Access Principles

---

OBJECTIVES COVERED IN THIS CHAPTER:

✓ **Plan for name resolution and IP addressing.**

- May include but is not limited to: internal and external naming strategy, naming resolution support for legacy clients, naming resolution for directory services, IP addressing scheme, TCP/IP version coexistence

✓ **Design for network access.**

- May include but is not limited to: network access policies, remote access strategy, perimeter networks, server and domain isolation

In this chapter, I'll cover a few topics you've most likely spent a lot of time on already: naming conventions, network access principles, and IP addressing schemes. On the MCTS level, your experimentation with most of these technologies was very technical, as per the design of the certification exam. By now, you know how to subnet, you know your way around setting up a VPN connection, and you are generally pretty good at setting up DNS for zone forwarding and so forth.

On the MCITP level, enterprise administration digs into the idea of creating a very robust design that allocates room for growth, allows a certain amount of flexibility, and fits the overall infrastructural goals of the entire enterprise, rather than a small network. For our purposes in this chapter, this means I'll blend all of these concepts together for the first time into one very large and multipurpose design. The network I'll show you in this chapter will be hooked up and functioning and will incorporate all of the fun roles, features, and technical ideas that you've learned up until this point. By the end of this chapter, you should be reacquainted with the concepts you've already seen in your early study and understand how these concepts can be blended together into a complex mesh.

Network Addressing

When studying for the Microsoft 70-642 certification exam, you spent much of your time understanding how to administer and maintain a Windows network and the problems and challenges that can occur when doing so. Now, you'll take a broader look at the technologies available and develop an overall scheme that you can deploy in your Windows-based environment. You'll do this by using various addressing techniques, subnets, scopes, and variable-length subnet masking for host assignment.

Addressing Techniques

For the most part, you have used three different types of IP addressing techniques: automatic private IP addressing (APIPA), static, and dynamic (via DHCP).

APIPA

APIPA addressing is a Windows default mechanism for assigning IP addresses when a DHCP server is unreachable. This means that, no matter what the situation, machines running Windows will always have a logical address available to them within the 169.254.X.X range. For the most part, other than trivia, this addressing scheme is used at the MCITP level only as a reference to machines that are not communicating properly with DHCP.

Static

Static, or manual, addressing is the process of manually assigning an IP address to a machine based on a design created by an individual engineer or administrator. If network engineers could have their way, chances are that all IP addresses would be static. Unfortunately, in the modern day, that simply isn't possible because of the sheer number of addresses that have to be assigned.

Dynamic

Dynamic addressing is a technique that takes advantage of the Dynamic Host Control Protocol (DHCP) role that can be added to Windows Server. DHCP then automatically assigns addresses to requesting client machines through a predetermined pool within your DHCP server defined by the administrator. At the enterprise level, this is normally the most heavily used and implemented standard because of the ease, flexibility, and relatively equal efficiency of its addressing methods.

Address Ranges

When designing a network, the first step is to specifically establish the overarching breadth of what your design will need to encompass. This can vary wildly based on budget, number of users, addressing conventions (IPv4 or IPv6), and expectations of growth. At the top level, you first decide the addressing scheme you're going to use based on your needs within an address range.

IPv4 Address Ranges

Within a few years, the old method of IP address class ranges will become obsolete. With the advent of Internet Protocol version 6 (IPv6), the Internet now has simply so many different addressing assignments available on both the network and host levels that it's unlikely we'll run out any time in the near future, but stranger things have happened. Regardless, for the next few years, Internet Protocol version 4 (IPv4) will remain the most commonly used addressing assignment system in use.

IPv4 uses a set of four octets to create an individual, but not necessarily unique, logical address that can be used for the purposes of routing packets across networks. This is then further defined by a subnet mask, which partitions the address into different subnets for the purpose of sending and receiving broadcast traffic. At the top level, IP addresses are divided into five different classes that use a certain amounts of bits in the subnet mask for the network portion of your network and a certain amount of bits for your various hosts. It's rare that you'll discover a network administrator who uses all five classes of IPv4 addresses. For the most part, you are concerned with three different class levels of IP addresses: Class A, Class B, and Class C, which are described in Table 2.1. Each of these addressing classes has its own strengths and weaknesses, in that each can assign only a certain number of IP addresses based on the number of available host bits in the subnet mask.

TABLE 2.1 IPv4 Address Class Specifications

Address Class	Number of Network Bits	Number of Available Host Bits	Maximum Hosts
Class A	8	24	16,777,214
Class B	16	16	65,534
Class C	24	8	254

Furthermore, each of these classes of networks is assigned certain ranges that will be predefined for your network design. Given your address class, you will fall into one of the ranges of Table 2.2.

TABLE 2.2 IPv4 Address Class Network Range

Address Class	Network Range
Class A	1.0.0.0 to 126.255.255.255
Class B	128.0.0.0 to 191.255.255.255
Class C	192.0.0.0 to 223.255.255.255

When designing an addressing scheme, choosing (or *discovering*) your address class is your very first step. You need to determine both how many networks you require in your infrastructure and, perhaps more important, how many users are contained within these networks. Once you have determined this, you can then begin the process of subnetting your network.

IPv6 Address Ranges

Unlike its younger brother, IPv4, IPv6 no longer uses address classes. Instead, IPv6 uses prefixes that are subdivided by geographic locations around the world. Within those regions, the addresses are then subdivided more and more until its gets down to the individual level. In effect, this removes the need for the old fallback of the IPv4 addressing system, Network Address Translation (NAT). By design, IPv6 allows for every individual computer to theoretically have both a unique MAC address and a unique logical IP address, because so many addresses are available. Unlike IPv4, IPv6 uses eight quartets, making for a total of 128 bits worth of addressing space available.

> This book assumes you have a strong grasp of manual subnetting, including the ability to convert to and from binary, hex, and decimal. The examples from this point on require this and do not review that material. Thus, if you're struggling to remember all the mathematical techniques involved, it's a good idea to pick up the *MCTS: Windows Server 2008 Network Infrastructure Configuration Study Guide* (Sybex, 2008) and review the section on subnetting. The website www.learntosubnet.com is also a valuable resource.

Addressing and Subnetting IPv4

As you've experienced a lot by now in your 70-642 exam, the process of manually subnetting IPv4 addresses can be quite tedious and more than a little difficult. Just in case you've forgotten any of it in the process of attaining your other certifications to get to this point, such as 70-643, I'll now cover some of the most typical types of networking problems and solutions you'll be asked to handle on the MCITP Enterprise Administrator exam.

> The following sections assume you already know the basics of binary, hex, and decimal conversion. However, if you've forgotten, you can find a nice example of how to do so in *MCTS: Windows Server 2008 Network Infrastructure Configuration Study Guide* by William Panek (Sybex, 2008).

Working with the Number of Hosts and Subnetworks

In the past, Microsoft has asked lots of general subnetting questions of students just to make sure they understand the impact of choosing a particular subnet. The way that this is done is by examining both the host and network portions of the subnet mask and using a little mathematics to determine the number of available hosts and subnets that are possible.

For instance, you may be asked something akin to this: "If you're using a Class C address and you need to make sure your highly interactive network applications do not broadcast to more than five computers on the subnet, what would be the most appropriate mask to use?"

Or, building on the last example, you might be asked this: "Now that you have determined the amount of host bits required for your particular subnet, will you be able to accommodate 30 different subnetworks?"

In the following sections, you'll explore each of these questions and see whether you can find an easy way to calculate both of these answers. You'll start with determining the number of host bits.

Calculating Host Bits and Determining the Subnet Mask

In this scenario, you've been given a design requirement that no more than six computers exist on the same network (one application computer + five additional computers). Remember, the primary goal of a router is to stop broadcast traffic. And, in order to communicate from one subnet to another, you have to use a router. Thus, you have to determine the appropriate subnet mask to accommodate four hosts.

The following is the default subnet mask for a Class C address:

11111111.11111111.11111111.**00000000**

The part in bold is referred to as the *host* portion of the subnet mask. And the eight 0s refer to eight individual bits. The way you can determine the number of hosts is by taking 2, raising it to the number of available host bits, and then subtracting 2 again to give room for the broadcast address and the network address. In this case, the amount of available hosts would be $2^8 - 2 = 254$.

So, with that in mind, let's look at the example where you need four hosts per subnet. The easiest way to do this is by seeing which power of 2 gives you at least two more addresses than you need and then use that. You do this to accommodate for the broadcast and network addresses. Here are the powers of 2:

$2^1 = 2$

$2^2 = 4$

$2^3 = 8$

$2^4 = 16$

$2^5 = 32$

$2^6 = 64$

$2^7 = 128$

$2^8 = 256$

As you can see, in order to accommodate at least two more than 4 (in this case four more), you need to use 2^3 bits. In total, this gives you $2^3 - 2 = $ **6 hosts**.

So if you need three host bits to get six hosts, your network portion can take up all but 3 bits! That means the subnet mask for this problem is as follows:

11111111.11111111.11111111.11111000

The network portion is as follows:

11111111.11111111.11111111.11111000

And the host portion is as follows:

11111111.11111111.11111111.11111**000**

In shorthand, you would write this mask as /29, because it uses 29 bits. But the actual value for this mask is 255.255.255.X, where X is the last octet in decimal. And the number 11111 in decimal happens to be 248. Thus, the mask for this problem is as follows:

255.255.255.248

Determining the Number of Subnetworks

The next portion of the problem asks you to determine whether you can accommodate 30 different subnetworks. This can be easily answered by examining the *number* of subnet bits available to you. Since you're using a Class C address, you look at the network portion of the last octet only:

11111111.11111111.11111111.**11111**000

This is referred to as the *subnet bits* portion of the network portion of the subnet mask (that's a lot to say at once). But in reality, it's pretty easy to understand. This size grows and shrinks based on two factors. First, there is the address class. If you were using a Class A address, you'd look at all the networks bits in the second, third, and fourth octet combined. And if you were using a Class B address, you'd look at the third and fourth combined.

But since you're looking at a Class C address, you can just count those last five subnet bits. That is, you look at the 11111 portion of the 11111000 octet. And then, since you know it takes 5 bits, you can just raise 2 to the number of host bits (5) and derive the answer: $2^5 = 32$.

Thus, you have 32 subnetworks available, so, yes, you can accommodate the design requirements!

Addressing a Given Topology

The most common way you might be required to subnet on the MCITP exam is by being given a standard topology and then being asked to subnet the topology using only public addresses. The purpose of this exercise is to prove that you both understand how to subnet and can effectively design a complex infrastructure using Windows Server 2008. Normally, you will be given a diagram like Figure 2.1.

FIGURE 2.1   Publicly addressing a given topology

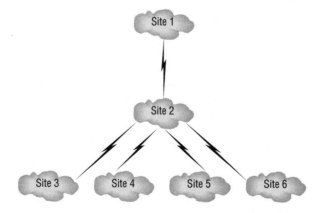

In the network diagram in Figure 2.1, your topology requires six different subnetworks because your overall design contains six different sites. Of course, from a Windows administrator point of view, this means you're going to have a lot of work on your hands: you have to subnet the network; connect the different subnets with site links; verify your replication strategy, schedule, and connections; and then do a little quality assurance to make sure everything is functioning properly. For now, you will stick to the initial process of sub-netting the network. Let's assume for the moment that you have been given the Class C IP address range of 209.81.3.0.

Remember, this address is Class C because the first octet is greater than 192. This also means there is only a single address, but you require six different subnetworks because of the earlier requirements. To support this many networks, you have to do a minor calculation with a portion of your subnet mask, the last octet. Normally, the default subnet mask for a Class C network is as follows:

111111111.11111111.11111111.00000000

Or, written in decimal format, it's simply 255.255.255.0. Now, because you're operating within the boundaries of a Class C address, you're concentrating only on the last octet: 00000000.

The first objective, as you might imagine, is to make sure you have enough space in your subnet mask to support the amount of networks you need to accomplish your objective. To do this, you simply take the number of networks you need (six in this case) and go up the binary digits of binary notation until you reach a number greater than your original number:

First digit 2^0 = 1 (not enough networks)

Second digit 2^1 = 2 (not enough networks)

Third digit 2^2 = 4 (not enough networks)

Fourth digit 2^3 = 8 (two more networks than required)

Whenever you're designing your network, keep in mind that you'll always want to have room to grow. In this case, you have room for two more networks. Thus, if you add more sites, you will be able to accommodate a few more networks without having to reorganize your entire structure.

So, you had to travel down four digits in binary in order to reach a number greater than six, your required amount of networks. Now, because you have this number, you can allocate the network portion of your subnet mask! Remember, the first bits of the subnet mask are the *network* portion, and the second bits are the *host* portion. So, instead of your default mask, shown in Figure 2.2, you move 4 bits in to subdivide your network, as shown in Figure 2.3.

FIGURE 2.2   Default mask

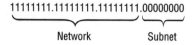

11111111.11111111.11111111.00000000

Network   Subnet

FIGURE 2.3   Subdivided mask

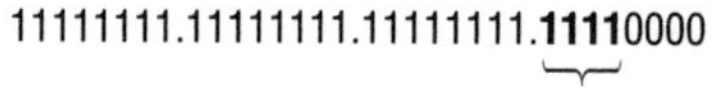

11111111.11111111.11111111.**1111**0000

And thus, you now have a subnet mask for the entire network! Pretty cool, huh? However, this isn't the end of the process.

Whenever you subdivide a network into different portions, you have to understand what the range of your IP addresses is. This is because, naturally, a subnetted network cannot communicate with an IP address that is out of the range of its own subnet without a router. Finding these address ranges is actually a pretty simple process. You just take the last number of your subnet mask and see what it corresponds to in decimal notation.

In this case, you take the value shown here:

11111111.11111111.11111111.11110000

This value of 1 in the fourth spot in the mask is actually 32 in decimal notation. What this number means to you is that by starting at zero in the *octet of concern* (the first octet for Class A, the second octet for Class B, and the third octet for Class C), you add by 32 until you reach the number 256, which is outside the scope of a single octet of numbers. This will give you the network addresses (or network IDs) for the available subnetworks.

This is a lot easier to understand if you see it. All it means is that you can take your starting address and find your network identifiers by starting at 0 and adding 32 like this:

209.81.3.0

209.81.3.**32** (0 +32)

209.81.3.**64** (32 + 32)

209.81.3.**96** (64 + 32)

209.81.3.**128** (96 + 32)

209.81.3.**160** (128 + 32)

209.81.3.**192** (160 + 32)

209.81.3.**224** (192 + 32)

Then, after you have your network identifier, you can find the broadcast address (the address that allows information to be sent to all devices within the subnet) by subtracting 1 from the last octet in all these numbers, with the exception of 0:

209.81.3.**31** (32 − 1)

209.81.3.**63** (64 − 1)

209.81.3.**95** (96 − 1)

209.81.3.**127** (128 − 1)

209.81.3.**159** (160 − 1)

209.81.3.**191** (192 − 1)

209.81.3.**223** (224 − 1)

209.81.3.**254** (256 − 1)

Then, you can find your usable addresses by looking at all the addresses between! You can see this illustrated in Table 2.3.

TABLE 2.3   Defining Network Address Ranges

Network Address	Broadcast Address	Usable Addresses
209.81.3.0	209.81.3.31	209.81.3.1–30
209.81.3.32	209.81.3.63	209.81.3.33–62
209.81.3.64	209.81.3.95	209.81.3.65–94
209.81.3.96	209.81.3.127	209.81.3.97–126
209.81.3.128	209.81.3.159	209.81.3.129–158
209.81.3.160	209.81.3.191	209.81.3.161–190
209.81.3.192	209.81.3.223	209.81.3.193–222
209.81.3.224	209.81.3.254	209.81.3.225–253

Most network administrators will steer you away from using the first and last subnet ranges, called the *subnet zero* and *all-ones* subnets. The reason behind this is that in the all-ones subnet, there can be confusion because you have a subnet with an identical broadcast address. Using the subnet-zero subnet was discouraged because you could have a subnet that was just 0. So, imagine seeing an IP address like 172.16.1.11 and having it be in the 172.16.0.0 subnet. Therefore, in practice, most administrators will say there are 2^{N-2} usable subnets.

However, the strategy I have just discussed is an exceptionally powerful tool, and truth be told, you will be able to use this technique on more than just your MCITP certification exam. Many, many certifications use this technique, and if you've already mastered it, you're well on your way to attaining even more impressive titles.

Now, take a look back at Figure 2.1 again. Now that you have your network IDs, broadcast IDs, and usable addresses, you can assign each of these sites to a subnetwork and then start assigning them accordingly. If you'd like to see this in action, check out the "Readdressing a Network" sidebar.

Real World Scenario

Readdressing a Network

You have just recently become employed with MegaCorp, a multibillion-dollar corporation that has placed you in charge of approximately 100 users within its organization. Currently, your portion of the organization is broken down into three separate networks connected by WAN connections. Today, the head office has decided it wants to readdress your network with the given address space of 209.113.60.0/27.

Specifically, MegaCorp wants to make sure the fewest number of possible subnetworks is used but that each of these sustains enough host bits to support the required number of users. Given the network topology shown here, what subnet mask would you need to apply for the entire network, and what three separate broadcast addresses would you need to assign, assuming that the corporate specifications for network design require the lowest incremental broadcast address to be applied to Site A, then the next highest to Site B, and so forth? Growth is not a consideration in this design.

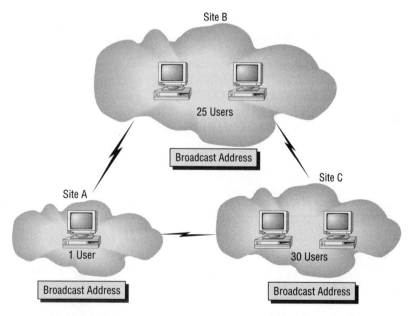

Answer: Since you have no network with more than 30 users, you know you will need to reserve only enough host bits to maintain 30 users. Additionally, you have been told that growth is not an issue.

The number 30 in binary is 00011110.

Thus, when you look at this number, you realize that you require 5 bits for your host portion and 3 bits for your network portion. Thus, your default mask assigned by the head office of /27 will be appropriate. This is because the default mask of /24 for Class C, plus the additional 3 bits for your specific requirements, creates a need for a /27 subnet mask. However, to complete the design, you must define your broadcast addresses. These are discovered by taking the incremental number of the network, which is found by taking the binary value of the last bit in the network portion, incrementing the IP address by that value, and then subtracting zero. In your case, your mask is as follows:

11111111.11111111.11100000

And the binary value of the 1 at the 27th spot is 32. Thus, your incremental value is 32, giving you this as your network addresses:

209.113.60.0

209.113.60.32

209.113.60.64

209.113.60.96

This allows you to subtract 1 from 32, 64, and 96 for your broadcast address:

Site A broadcast = 209.113.60.31

Site B broadcast = 209.113.60.63

Site C broadcast = 209.113.60.95

VLSM

Variable-length subnet mask (VLSM) is a technology concept that is used throughout networks that have great subnetting requirements but require the least amount of waste and most efficient use of broadcast traffic possible. Imagine for a moment that you work for MyCorp again and that you have a user situation in your office that breaks down as shown in Figure 2.4.

As you can see, the network is broken up into four individual subnets, and each of those subnets has a different user requirement. In the first subnet, you require 200 users, in the second you require 30, and so forth. Normally, you would break this network up by subnetting it into four individual groups, Subnet A, B, C, and D. But let's look at what happens if you do that; see Figure 2.5.

On the right side of the figure, you'll see the maximum number of hosts that can be contained on the subnet. To the right of this, you'll see your actual number of users, and then on the far right you can see the amount of wasted addresses within this space. Now, as you can imagine, especially with high-end networking, space matters.

FIGURE 2.4   Networks with various user requirements

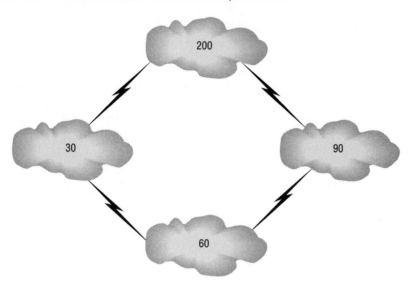

FIGURE 2.5   Standard subnetting applied

			Waste
Subnet A Max. Users = 510	Hosts = 200	310	
Subnet B Max. Users = 510	Hosts = 90	420	
Subnet C Max. Users = 510	Hosts = 60	450	
Subnet D Max. Users = 510	Hosts = 30	480	

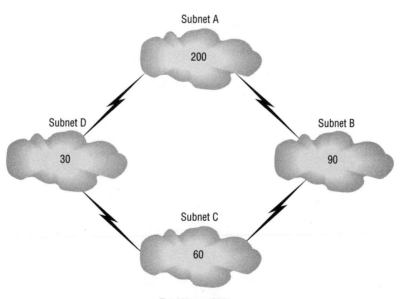

Total Users: 380
Current Mask: 23

Part of being an enterprise administrator is understanding that your ultimate goal for your enterprise is to make sure that everything is running as often as possible and as efficiently as possible. In your career up until this point, someone has undoubtedly told you that the best way to become successful in life is not to waste anything. This includes money, opportunities, and, of course, host addresses. Instead, consider what would happen if you could apply an individual subnet address for each of these subnetworks. For instance, using some basic calculations that you learned earlier, you could determine that the following masks could be used based on the host requirements:

Subnetwork A:	Requires 200 hosts	8 bits	255.255.255.0 subnet mask
Subnetwork B:	Requires 90 hosts	7 bits	255.255.255.128 subnet mask
Subnetwork C:	Requires 60 hosts	6 bits	255.255.255.192 subnet mask
Subnetwork D:	Requires 30 hosts	5 bits	255.255.255.224 subnet mask

This sure would be nice if you could do it, wouldn't it? The truth is, you can. VLSM allows administrators to apply a more specific subnet mask to a preexisting subnet mask to further define a subnet. This is extraordinarily useful for complex organizations and can really optimize your efficiency. Consider your first example, where the same mask was applied throughout, and consider your latest example, shown in Figure 2.6, which uses VLSM.

FIGURE 2.6 VLSM vs. standard subnetting

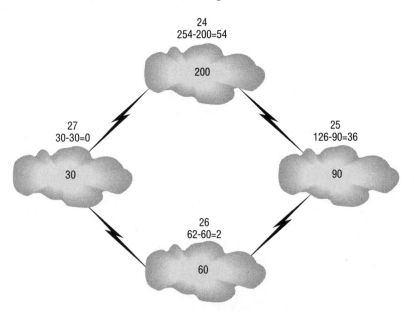

The numbers speak for themselves.

Now, if you wanted to apply these addresses to your network, you'd have to go one step further and calculate the address ranges where you would need to apply them. First you'd start by taking 2 and raising it to the required number of bits per individual subnet mask to find out an incremental number like you did earlier. Now, you've managed to subnet your network into several different areas and saved yourself tons of IP addresses!

Addressing IPv6

So, if you thought subnetting IPv4 was confusing, wait until you meet its younger brother, IPv6! That's actually only a joke. In truth, addressing IPv6 isn't as bad as you would think. But when most people even look at IPv6 addresses, they immediately assume they must be inherently evil because of their obvious unreadability. If you look at an IPv6 address like 4305:A93E:BADC:8956:3586:8D9C:7032:1423, it looks like garbage. You may know instinctively upon seeing it that it's been laid out in IPv6 format, but it just seems like a lot of random numbers and letters thrown together in one place. Thankfully, there's a lot of reason behind the seeming randomness.

IPv6 Shorthand Notation

One of the quickest ways you can identify and evaluate an IPv6 address is by using its shorthand notation. As you can tell, a full-length IPv6 address is very long. But thankfully, most of the time, you will see a lot of zeros in an IPv6 address. A very realistic example of one you may encounter is the reserved multicast address FF02:0000:0000:0000:0000:0000:0001:0002.

As you can see, this particular address has a seemingly excessive amount of zeros (25, in fact). Accordingly, you can shorten this by using the :: notation, which essentially means "use zeros until." When you see this symbol start, from that point on, you can insert zeros until you reach a number. Then, after this number, you can see how many sets of single : have been used to see what octet it represents. And just to make things even easier, if an octet is preceded by a few zeros, such as the octet 0002, you simply write this as 2 behind the : symbol. This sounds complicated, but it's actually pretty easy. The previous example in shorthand would be FF02::1:2.

In plain English, this means "FF02 is my first octet; then I keep going until I reach an octet that ends in 1, and then my last octet has a 2." Let's try it—it will probably make sense if you do it one part at a time by using a simple step-by-step procedure:

1. Count how many octets are at the end. In this case, there are two octets. One octet contains one, and the other octet contains two.

2. Place zeros until you reach the first of the octets at the end. Here, you start with FF02 and then place zeroes until the seventh octet, which ends in a 2:

   FF02:0000:0000:0000:0000:0000:0001:XXXX

3. Check the remaining octets for possible shorthand; then place zeros to fill them in.

You have one octet that has two written in shorthand. Therefore, the octet must be 0002. And thus, you have the complete address: FF02:0000:0000:0000:0000:0000:0 001:0002.

Anatomy of IPv6

IPv6 addresses are beautiful because of their absolute simplicity. Before, when you dealt with an IPv4 address, there was a lot of confusion. What part of the address belongs to the Internet service provider? Where is the subnet portion of the address? Better yet, where is the host? In IPv6, these are no longer concerns.

All IPv6 addresses can be broken down into two distinct portions, which can further be subdivided to a point that just about every portion of the address is accounted for. On the base level, IPv6 addresses are broken into two 64-bit portions, one of which is called the *prefix* portion and one of which is called the *host* portion, or the *interface ID*. Visually, the address looks like Figure 2.7.

FIGURE 2.7   IPv6 address portions

Network Portion	Host Portion

In one fell swoop, you can cover the second portion of the address. It's just the host portion of the network. In more technical terms, the 65th to the 128th bit of your address is completely dedicated to assigning the address to your hosts. That's a lot of hosts! It's more, in fact, than even some of the largest enterprises on the planet would ever use. However, when the IEEE designed IPv6, it didn't want to run into a situation where anyone would ever have to worry about having "enough" host addresses ever again. I think it's safe to say they've succeeded. 2^{64} is such a large number that if you were to take that many pennies and stack them up one after another, you'd be able to reach Mars more than 300,000 times. Or, if you'd like to think of it in more Microsoft terms, you'd be able to have 230,584,300 times the amount of money of Bill Gates (when he was worth 80 billion).

The first portion of an IPv6 address, called the *address prefix*, is a little bit more complicated, but not too much so. To begin, one of the real issues that IPv6 was meant to fix was to give service providers their own reserved section of the IP address that would identify whatever service provider was issuing the address. Accordingly, the IEEE assigned the first 48 bits of the prefix portion of the address to the service provider. Then, with the remaining 16 bits, it allocated a portion to be used for subnet addressing. You can see another visual interpretation of this in Figure 2.8.

FIGURE 2.8   IPv6 complete address portions

48-bit ISP Portion	16-bit Subnet Portion	64-bit Host Portion

The main reason that only 16 bits has been assigned to the subnet portion is actually pretty reasonable. After all, how often do you run across an organization that will need more than 65,536 subnets? The answer is not very often. And thus, only a small portion of the overall 128 bits is assigned. In just a moment, I'll go over how subnetting this portion of an address is slightly different than it was with IPv4. But for the moment, I'll take a step back and talk about those first 48 bits before the 16 bits of the subnet portion.

There are three organizations that take a bite out of the first 48 bits of addresses. These are the ICANN, RIR, and ISPs:

- Internet Corporation for Assigned Names and Numbers (ICANN)

- Regional Internet Registry (RIR)

- Your Internet service provider (ISP)

Thankfully, the exact scope of the importance of these organizations is outside the objectives of this exam. Suffice to say, the Internet address prefix goes through three filters going from ICANN to RIR to ISP that more and more uniquely define the coverage area of these addresses.

IPv6 Address Types

One of the biggest changes that came with IPv6 was the complete and total removal of the concept of a broadcast address. And if you ask most busy administrators, that's a good thing. The reason is that IPv6 has instead replaced the need for broadcast addresses with the concept of multicast addressing. The word *multicast* is getting a little ahead of myself, so I'll start by defining the three different types of addresses that are available to you in IPv6:

Unicast   A unicast address is an address that is assigned to a particular host so that host, and only that one particular host, can send and receive data. It's equivalent to saying "You and only you are identified as this."

Multicast   A multicast address is effectively a grouping of addresses that is addressed for the point of sending and receiving information to that group. So, if you wanted to send a broadcast of information, you could send it to a particular multicast group.

Anycast   The name is a bit confusing, but an anycast address is similar to a multicast address in that it's sent to a particular group of addresses, but only the address "nearest" to it. So, instead of sending it to every member of the group, it sends to a particularly near member of that group.

For the purposes of this book, I'll concentrate on unicast addresses, because they're what you as an administrator most care about. Concepts such as multicast addressing are more designed toward network administration and engineering, because they determine what particular routing protocols are used and where they can and cannot be broadcast throughout the network.

IPv6 Static and Dynamic Addressing

Just like IPv4, IPv6 addresses can be assigned both dynamically and statically. If an administrator for some reason wants to assign a particular address to some device within their network, they most certainly may. Furthermore, there are plenty of new methods to dynamically assign IPv6 addresses to devices through the use of Dynamic Host Control Protocol version 6 (DHCPv6).

However, there are a few differences to which you need to pay careful attention. In particular, you need to be interested in the conventions IPv6 uses to effectively assign addresses throughout the entire network. In total, there are four possible combinations—two of which are used for static addressing and two of which are used for dynamic. I'll talk about the static methods and dynamic methods. I'll go into this in more detail later in this chapter.

EUI-64

One of the great benefits of having such an incredibly long host field is not only the ability to have an absolutely gargantuan number of hosts but also the ability to specify a great deal of uniqueness toward an individual address. As you're familiar with from your study of basic networking, an individual interface normally contains two addresses, a logical Internet protocol address (IP) and a physical MAC address. In IPv4, the MAC address happened to be larger than the IP address. That is, IPv4 addresses were only 32 bits in length, but MAC addresses were 48 bits in length. The original purpose for this design (and still the purpose to this day) is twofold. First, a MAC address specifies a unique physical address for your computer. Second, it provides an address that a switch can use to forward a frame. Just in case you haven't seen one in a while, a typical MAC address looks like this:

00-1A-A0-05-2A-B7

Normally, a MAC address is divided into six different sets of two hex numbers for readability; let's do something different for a moment and split the example address into two sets of six hex numbers. The reason why will become clear in a moment.

001AA0 052AB7

Now that you've separated these two values, let's shift gears for a moment. Remember earlier when you read that IPv4 addresses were smaller than MAC addresses? Well, that simply isn't the case with IPv6. In fact, just the host portion alone is 16 bits larger than the entire MAC address.

Accordingly, a few networking geniuses decided it would be really fun (and really easy) to sort of semi-use the MAC address in the host field. It gives a unique address, and to boot, it allows static addressing without the need to manual enter every single number.

I say that the address is "semi-used" because in order to complete the 64-bit host fields, you're lacking 16 bits. Thus, you need to insert 16 bits somewhere in the host field to make up for this lack of bits. To do this, you use the hex field:

FFFE

Then, just to establish a little uniqueness (and for a few more technical reasons that are beyond the scope of this book), the seventh bit of the MAC address is flipped. So, for this example, the address is as follows:

001AA0052AB7

To achieve 7 bits, you need only the first two values (00). Thus, you take those first two hex numbers and convert them into binary:

00000000

And then, you "flip" the seventh bit:

00000010

In hex, this value comes out to 02. Thus, your new address is as follows:

021A:A0FF:FE05:2AB7

Visually, you can think of it like Figure 2.9.

FIGURE 2.9   EUI-64 visual breakdown

Flip 7th bit

Manual Assignment

The second way an address can be assigned statically in IPv6 is by doing it the old-fashioned way. And, although it may be a lot more tedious to implement, it's certainly more easily explained. Just like in IPv4, you can manually punch in an address piece by piece. The only real difference is that one takes decimal notation and the other takes hexadecimal notation and a subnet prefix. You can see the Windows Server 2008 manual assignment dialog box in Figure 2.10.

It may be old-fashioned, but it still works!

FIGURE 2.10   Windows Server 2008 manual IPv6

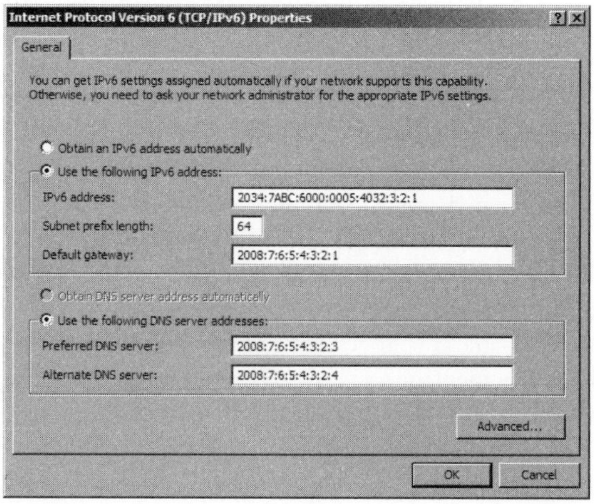

DHCPv6

In DHCPv6 there are two supported states of DHCP: *stateful* and *stateless*. Stateful DHCP is similar to what you've experienced in the past with DHCPv4; it just means that DHCP tracks the state of the interfaces it communicates with, such as information regarding the client and how long the lease on the dynamic address exists. The only real difference is that DHCPv4 uses broadcasts in order to find a DHCP. Clients, when first connected, essentially advertise themselves on their subnet by saying "Here I am!" And then the DHCP server responds accordingly. Although this works fine for DHCPv4, unfortunately DHCPv6 doesn't use broadcasts. So, it sets aside a default multicast address that I told you you'd probably see sometime in the future. That address is the following:

FF02:0000:0000:0000:0000:0000:0001:0002

I'll get into how to set this up in Windows Server 2008 a little later in this chapter, but for right now I'll talk about stateless DHCP.

In stateless DHCP, the "state information" (whether an interface is up or down, how long the lease exists, and so on) is ignored. Typically, stateless DHCP is used in conjunction with *stateless autoconfiguration*, which is a method used by IPv6 to automatically assign addresses to given interfaces based on their EUI-64 address. The main difference between stateless and stateful is that stateless doesn't remember IP addresses, but it can still supply information such as a DNS server.

IPv4 to IPv6 Transitional Techniques

Obviously, the entire networking world cannot shift from one networking scheme to another overnight. There are billions upon billions of networking address-bearing devices floating around to this day, and a good share of these devices are commonly used for legacy business operations and will most likely *never* be able to understand new networking technology. As of 2008, the year of the release of the MCITP Enterprise Administrator exam, IPv6 hasn't come into popular use. However, over the next several years it's possible that this will become more relevant. Thus, the next section will become valuable as administrators learn techniques to handle the dramatic shift from IPv4 to IPv6. For now, you are interested in three methods: dual stacking, tunneling, and translating.

Dual Stacking

The simplest of the transitional techniques designed to transition from IPv6 to IPv4 is the idea of a dual IP stack. In a dual IP stack, you operate both an IPv4 address and an IPv6 address. In Microsoft Windows Vista and Microsoft Windows Server 2008, this option is enabled by default. With dual stacking, using the ipconfig command will display both a hexadecimal address and an IPv4 address.

The reason that this is possible is that addresses are logical. So, there's no reason that a computer couldn't be logically identified two different ways. In practical implementation, this is done by one of two ways—by using a dual IP layer or by using a complete dual stack.

Dual IP layer   In dual layer addressing, both the IPv4 and IPv6 protocols access the same information in the same TCP/IP stack. This means that the network portion contains both the IPv4 and IPv6 implementations, and they both access the same transport layer. So, regardless of whether a packet is sent via IPv4 or IPv6, it passes through the same area. This technology is supported by Windows Vista and Windows Server 2008.

 Dual IP layer supports IPv4, IPv6, and IPv6 over IPv4.

Dual stack   Dual stack implementations differ from dual IP layer implementations in that dual stack creates a complete separate stack through which each protocol travels. What this means for network administrators is that routers will have to support both the IPv6 and IPv4 protocols. And, of course, each of these stacks has its own transport layer that interfaces with the application layer. By default, if you install IPv6 support for Windows XP and Windows Server 2003, both of these operating systems will use a separate stack, where the settings will be defined by `tcpip6.sys`.

Both dual stack and dual layer implementations get a little tricky when you start to throw in the confusing factor for any normal and well-functioning network: DNS. DNS, as I'll go into in the "Naming Conventions for Windows Server 2008" section of this chapter, relies upon the use of records and aliases to translate addresses into names. Unfortunately, the record types for IPv4 and IPv6 are completely different. Thus, you have to maintain records for both types of implementation.

Tunneling

If you've ever set up a VPN connection before, you've used a type of tunnel. *Tunneling* is the process of placing a protocol or piece of information within another protocol that serves as the primary method of connection. With VPNs, when you use Point-to-Point Protocol (PPP) to connect via the Internet to your internal network, you're using the VPN as a tunnel to transmit data via TCP/IP, where the server sees you as remotely connected across the network.

When working with IP transitional tunneling, you're doing something very similar. In effect, you're taking IPv6 information and passing it through IPv4 by adding on a header. Visually, an IPv6 over IPv4 packet looks like Figure 2.11.

This can be achieved by one of two ways, each with many different customer configurations. First, it can be achieved by manual configuration. And second, it can be achieved automatically. Configured and automatic tunnels can be configured in many different ways; in particular, the manually configured tunnels can be configured by using the `netsh interface ipv6 add v6v4tunnel` command. And automatic tunnels can be configured by using one of three different technologies: 6to4, Teredo, or ISATAP.

FIGURE 2.11 IPv6 over IPv4 packet

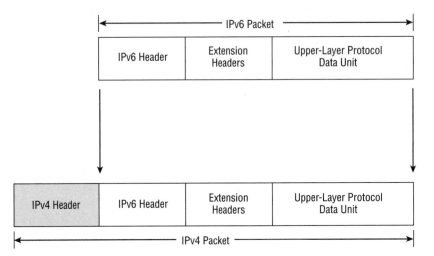

Tunneling Between Devices

As you know from basic networking, every device that sends a packet from one place to another exists in some manner on the network layer. Accordingly, every device that is connected on the network layer is logically connected in some fashion. Thus, every host and router (both of which are capable of understanding the network protocol) must have a way of communicating with one another. However, this varies with each device. In a tunnel, this breaks down to three types of communication between devices:

Router to router When tunneling between routers, two routers capable of both IPv6 and IPv4 communicate to one another by referencing a network behind each of the routers that operates on IPv6 and then send packets to one another across a tunnel that operates IPv4 with IPv6 packets embedded within. Figure 2.12 depicts this communications process. On the left side of Router A, there is an IPv6 network, and on the right side of Router B, there is also an IPv6-capable network. These two devices are connected via IPv4, and the messages sent between them contain IPv6 packets within IPv4 packets.

FIGURE 2.12 Router-to-router tunneling

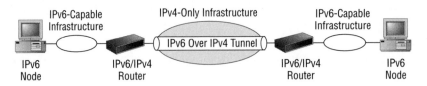

Host to host When two hosts running both IPv4 and IPv6 stacks in an IPv4 infrastructure communicate, IPv6 information can be sent between the two by creating a tunnel that sends IPv6 over IPv4. Since the two computers both understand the different stacks, the IPv4 information is interpreted and the internal information is recognized, forming a connection that allows them to communicate.

Router to host and host to router When operating between hosts that reside between firewalls or routers, a host running IPv4 can communicate between infrastructures operating different IP protocols by creating an IPv4 tunnel containing IPv6. The way this is accomplished is that the routers again understand both protocols, IPv4 and IPv6. And when an IPv4-capable computer sends a request to the router with an IPv6 packet embedded inside a tunnel that is usually a subnet route, the router receives the IPv4 packet, examines the internal IPv6 packet, and then forwards that packet onto the IPv6 host computer running in an IPv6 infrastructure. In Figure 2.13, on the left side of Router A is an infrastructure running IPv4, and on the right is a network operating IPv6. The left network can communicate to the right by using a tunnel to the router, which the router recognizes as a tunnel and then examines the internal contents.

FIGURE 2.13   Router-to-host and host-to-router tunneling

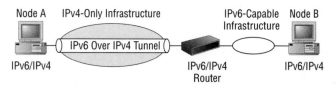

6to4 6to4, much as it sounds, is a direct method of transitioning from IPv6 to IPv4 over the IPv4 protocol. 6to4 accomplishes this by implementing both stacks of the IPv4 and IPv6 protocol and then translating the given IPv4 address into a standardized address for IPv6. This is done by inserting the given IPv4 address in this format—129.118.1.3—into the hexadecimal form:

2002:AABB:CCDD:Subnet:InterfaceID

AA is the first octet, BB is the second octet, CC is the third octet, and DD is the fourth octet. The subnet portion is the standard /48 to /64 subnet range, and the interface ID is the 64-bit portion of IPv6 dedicated to the host.

In this example, you could convert the portions of the decimal address into hexadecimal by using some simple math, which I won't dive into because you've most likely learned it by this point:

$$129 \quad = \quad 81$$
$$118 \quad = \quad 76$$
$$1 \quad = \quad 1$$
$$3 \quad = \quad 3$$

Thus, your full address would be as follows:

2002:8176:13:Subnet:InterfaceID

Within 6to4 tunneling, the entire subnet is treated as a single link. Hosts are automatically given their 2002:AABB:CCDD:Subnet address with a /64 mask, and then communication within the subnet is given directly to neighbors. If, for some reason, the given address is not found on the subnet, that information is passed onto a 6to4 router that exists on a /16 mask by default.

 A Windows Server 2008 or Windows Vista computer can act as a 6to4 router through Internet Connection Sharing (ICS).

ISATAP

ISATAP, which stands for Intra-Site Automatic Tunnel Addressing Protocol, is an automatic dual stacking tunneling technology that is installed by default in Windows Vista *without* Service Pack 1, Windows Server 2003, and Windows XP. However, in Windows Server 2003 and Windows XP, it is called Automatic Tunneling Pseudo-Interface. The ISATAP tunneling method can be used for either public or private addressing. With public unicast addressing, ISATAP uses this global address:

::5EFE:**A.B.C.D.**

A.B.C.D. in this case is a standard IPv4 address that is assigned within the IPv4 infrastructure. Additionally, ISATAP uses the private address of ::200:5EFE:**A.B.C.D.** where A.B.C.D. is again the assigned IPv4 address within the infrastructure.

By this method, ISATAP creates a link-local address that can be used to communicate between devices through tunneling. An important feature to note, however, is that ISATAP is *not* installed by default on either Windows Vista Service Pack 1 or Windows Server 2008 unless the name "ISATAP" can be resolved.

ISATAP allows computers operating IPv6 in IPv4 infrastructures to communicate with IPv4 clients in the same subnet. However, to communicate with additional subnets running either pure or mixed IP protocols, an ISATAP router is required. Normally, this router is resolved either through the mapping of the "ISATAP" hostname or by the use of the `netsh interface isatap set router` command, which allows the address of the router to be manually specified in either Windows Server 2008 or Windows Vista.

Teredo

As mentioned earlier, one of the primary goals with the implementation of IPv6 was to enable almost all organizations to use publicly assigned addresses throughout their entire organization without the use of Network Address Translation. Although this is good in theory (NAT was such a pain anyway), the problem is that NAT is still used…a *lot*. Therefore, to make the shift from IPv6 to IPv4, network administrators need to have an option at their disposal to shift from IPv4 to IPv6 and still make use of NAT or at least give the network the ability to interpret between these addresses. And that's where Teredo comes in.

Teredo is also known as Network Address Translator Traversal (NAT-T). What it does is provide a unicast address for each device located within the NAT pool. It does this by sending out IPv6 data over Uniform Data Protocol (UDP). In some ways, it's actually fairly similar to 6to4 tunneling. However, if you'll remember from the earlier discussion of 6to4, 6to4 requires a router to be used that comprehends 6to4 routing in order to get past its particular subnet. Instead of using a router to translate out the NAT pool, Teredo uses host-to-host communication and establishes a tunnel directly between two individual hosts.

For your exam, the most important point you need to remember about Teredo is the process it uses for the initial configuration and communication between clients. Beyond that, Teredo is quite complex and uses a series of XOR operations to determine a unique address; then it also creates a randomly generated series of numbers and a flag field for security purposes. So, it's unlikely you'll be asked to manually configure a Teredo address. However, the process breaks down into two portions: initial client configuration and initial client communication.

1. The client sends a router solicitation request (RS) to a Teredo server with the *cone flag* (a high-order bit that indicates a device is behind a NAT) set.

2. The Teredo server responds with a router advertisement (RA) from a router that is on an alternate IPv4 address so it can determine whether the address is behind a NAT.

3.   If the RA is not received, the client repeats the RS with the cone flag not set.

4. The server responds with an RA from the source address to the destination address. If the client receives the RA, it is behind a restricted NAT.

5. To make sure there isn't a symmetric NAT in place, the client sends another RS to an alternate server.

6. The alternate server responds. If the RAs are different, the map is mapping the same internal address and UDP port number, and Teredo will not be available.

Teredo has several different processes of initial communication based on what type of NAT the client is assigned under. The most commonly referenced one of these is a situation where a client resides on a restricted NAT. In which case, the process of two computers, A and B, communicating is as follows:

1. Client A sends a bubble packet to Client B.

2. Client A sends a bubble packet to Client B through Client B's Teredo server.

3. Client B's Teredo server forwards the packet to Client B.

4. Client B responds to the packet with its own bubble packet to Client A.

5. Client A determines NAT mappings for both NATs.

Legacy Networking and Windows Server 2008

Although it would be nice if we existed in a world where all technology was upgraded instantly at the same time and there were never any issues switching back and forth between technologies and we could just link with IPv6, that world simply doesn't exist. In fact, even before IPv4 and the current networking situation, the world of networks wasn't exactly laid out in perfect order.

To this day, there are many protocols that aren't used as often as others but that occasionally rise to make their presence known and require special attention from administrators who otherwise no longer encounter them. On the MCITP level, you actually encounter these sorts of scenarios frequently. This is because most complex networks will contain a lot of different technologies that mutually cohabit (or at least coexist) in the same environment. Because of this, Microsoft expects that all candidates applying for MCITP-level certification completely understand how to deal with even the most obscure networking protocols and understand their effect on their networking environment.

In the following section, I'll begin by explaining the most commonly encountered protocol: WINS.

WINS

In some ways, I've already addressed legacy technology at some level, but now you're going to dive into a concept that isn't used as commonly anymore and will probably go the way of the dodo after this incarnation of Windows Server, or possibly after the next incarnation. In case you hadn't guessed, I'm talking about Windows Internet Name Service (WINS).

Wins Components

When using WINS, generally four components are available to administrators using Windows Server 2008:

- Server
- WINS database
- Client
- Proxy

Each of these roles in self-explanatory by its name; the server serves WINS, the WINS database keeps a collection of records, the clients request WINS information, and the proxies provide resolution for WINS in TCP/IP configured networks.

Reasons for WINS

Normally organizations won't implement WINS without a valid reason. Among these reasons are the following:

- Legacy applications using NetBIOS
- Older version of Windows
- Dynamic registration of single-label names

Additionally, an organization may implement WINS if it is running logically older versions of Windows or applications requiring older versions of Windows, which include anything using Network Neighborhood or My Network Places.

WINS Name Resolution

The WINS name resolution process is pretty easy to understand. First, any given client sends up to three attempts to connect to a WINS server, but no response is given. If no response is given, it will attempt to find another. If it does, the WINS server responds with a given IP address.

Client Records

Within the WINS database, various pieces of information are stored that in total create the necessary components to resolve names to IP addresses, which is the given purpose of any general name resolution server. Within WINS, client records contain the following:

- Record names
- IP addresses
- Types
- State
- Static
- Owner
- Version

Each of these records within the database is occasionally changed, deleted, or somehow modified through a process called *scavenging*.

WINS Replication

Just like Active Directory, a WINS server knows very little about the world around it. In fact, it knows nothing about it. And, just like Active Directory, in order to understand the world around it, WINS uses replication to exchange information about its clients. However, in WINS, this process is called *push/pull*.

The push occurs after a certain server reaches a number of specified changes. For instance, a server may reach 10 changes in its database and decide that it needs to send its information to another WINS server. Thus, it informs the server that it has reached a certain amount of predetermined changes and needs to replicate, and the server that needs to understand the replication changes responds with a request to receive the changes. The original server then sends the changes across the subnets.

A pull replication is essentially the opposite of a push. Instead of requesting another machine to make a change after a certain number of events, a partner machine will ask another if changes have occurred after a period of time. This happens regardless of whether any changes actually *have* happened. And, as you might imagine, this can be combined with push to create a push/pull replication process.

WINS to DNS Using GlobalNames Zones

If an organization runs WINS, there's a strong chance that in addition to running WINS that it is also using DNS. The reason is because the modern standard for name resolution is DNS. Thus, Windows Server 2008 enables a simple transition from WINS to DNS by using a *GlobalNames Zone*. A GlobalNames Zone enables a WINS environment to resolve single-label, static, global names if the server is using DNS.

The GlobalNames Zone is a completely new Windows Server 2008 zone for DNS in addition to zones such as forward lookup, reverse lookup, and stub. It's responsible for resolving names without WINS and requires that the zone be available on all DNS servers. But, it's best if you place it within Active Directory. Another special fact about Global-Names Zones is that they use CNAME records for fully qualified domain names.

GlobalNames Zones work in a multistep process that's pretty easy to understand:

1. A user requests a URL.

2. The browser requests the address.

3. The client computer tries to request domain by domain from most granular to least (users.engineering.mydomain.com to users.engineering.com to users.com).

4. If the query fails, the DNS server checks the GlobalNames Zone.

 GlobalNames Zones support IPv6.

Naming Conventions for Windows Server 2008

When referencing naming conventions in Windows Server 2008, it's essentially the same thing as saying you're identifying the method of name to IP address conversion that is used throughout the enterprise. And of course, this brings to mind two different name resolution technologies that are used with Windows Server 2008: WINS and DNS.

Accordingly, this also means that the two technologies may either exist by themselves or coexist in the same environment. Furthermore, these technologies can be implemented either externally or internally. In the following sections, I'll discuss some of the most common usage scenarios for name resolution tactics and how they're implemented in an enterprise-level environment. I'll begin with a brief review of DNS and zone types. Then, since I've already covered WINS technology, I'll address the incorporation of WINS with DNS, and then I'll address how to include Active Directory within DNS. Afterward, I'll finish off this discussion on naming conventions by talking about some of the most commonly used migration, delegation, and transfer strategies used in a complex environment.

Internal and External Namespaces

When I reference the words *internal* and *external* in regard to namespaces, I'm actually referring to whether you're using the internal infrastructure of your enterprise, or how that enterprise is accessed from the Internet. On the internal level, you usually reference your enterprise by an extension such as .local, whereas the external namespace is referenced by a top-level domain such as .net, .com, or .org. And each of these types of naming conventions, internal and external, make way for several configuration options that are important in terms of administrative overhead and user accessibility.

In fact, the first design choice an administrator has to make when choosing an internal and external naming scheme is whether that naming scheme will actually be the very same scheme, that is, whether the internal and external naming address will be the same. It's certainly a tempting option, and it has lulled more than a fair share of (perhaps *lazy* is too strong a word) less involved administrators.

When designing an internal namespace and an external namespace that use the same name, an administrator is choosing to have the internal namespace be a subdomain of the external namespace. The problems with this are, first, security based (because resources are all in one place) and, second, that users in the internal organization won't be able to access external resources without a lot of overhead administrative work, which is basically taking away from one of the benefits of using them both at once.

When using different internal and external naming addresses, you're provided with the added benefit of security, and you create an additional forwarder in DNS. Plus, users who may be accessing your network externally will not have access to your internal resources, which is a huge benefit.

External Namespace Design

The first step in choosing an external namespace design is to determine the most appropriate registered domain according to your company. For instance, if your company name is MyCorp, it would be logical to attempt to register the MyCorp.com domain with a given domain registrar, such as domainsdoneright.com. Once this is complete, you can begin your design from the top down.

An important point to keep in mind about any good external strategy is that a good design practice is to keep any external resources assigned completely as external resources. This means that it's a good idea to not place your external users, or Active Directory objects, in a completely different place that cannot access your internal resources. The reason this is suggested is because if internal resources, such as a printer, can be accessed on the external namespace, it's possible that an external user can take control of this device or cause internal problems within your enterprise, which is never a good thing.

By the same token, certain specialty resources such as a web proxy server needn't be located in the external namespace. This is mostly because resources such as this don't rely upon being addressed externally and make use of preexisting conditions in the internal namespace in order to operate. But the most important reason for the separation of the external namespace is NAT. When using NAT, it's difficult for external addresses to be accessed by the internal network because of the inherent problems with referencing something else in another domain or possibly a different subnet.

Internal Namespace Design

The reasons for implementing an internal namespace design are many. One of the reasons for this portion of the naming convention design is that there needs to be an isolated area within your network that can be accessed only by authorized resources from within a certain area or that falls within the purview of a predefined set of security conditions for external access that is laid out originally by the enterprise administrator. But more important, the point of an internal namespace design is to create a robust design that creates an environment that provides a method for name resolution of all internal clients through the use of either hostnames or NetBIOS names.

 NetBIOS names have a maximum length of 15 characters, and each name must be unique within the entire organization.

Zone Types and Zone Transfers

Windows Server 2008 has four types of zones: primary, secondary, stub, and Global-Names. And each of these zones is designed for a specific purpose that can be incorporated with Active Directory. Throughout your study, you've already touched on a good share of these zone types, but for the sake of completeness you can review each of these shortly.

Primary Zones

A *primary zone* is the main standard zone type in Windows Server 2008. It can be either integrated or not integrated with Active Directory. The primary zone contains the main database associated with the DNS and is usually supported by secondary zones. If Active Directory is not associated with it, the primary zone hosts the only modifiable zone in the infrastructure, with all remaining zones being secondary to it. If it is integrated with Active Directory, the zone data is copied into Active Directory, and all other associated zones become peers of this zone. It is, by far, the most efficient way of managing DNS zones. On the enterprise level, it is highly recommended to integrate DNS with Active Directory; otherwise, the standard primary zone becomes a bottleneck for the rest of the enterprise that relies upon the primary zone to receive information from Dynamic DNS or other query resolution processes.

Secondary Zones

Secondary zones are zones set apart from the primary zone to aid in the replication and accessibility of DNS database records for the rest of the enterprise. Secondary zones are read-only, host a copy of known DNS information, and reduce traffic in an enterprise. Secondary zones are usually placed at logical places throughout the external and internal namespaces in order to aid users on either side in the acquisition of whatever DNS information they may require.

Stub Zones

Stub zones are not new to Windows Server 2008 but are still a relatively new concept to Windows Server in general. Originally released with Windows Server 2003, *stub zones* are zones that delegate information to another namespace. The main purpose of a stub zone is to act as a buffer between zones to eliminate traffic caused by excessive queries to a particular zone by delegating requests to another namespace. Stub zones receive their updates by an authoritative server and contain only the following:

- Start of authority (SOA)
- Name server (NS)
- Address (A)

Once it receives this information, the stub zone periodically updates itself whenever it requires additional information from its authoritative server based on administratively defined settings.

GlobalNames Zone

The completely new zone type in Windows Server 2008 is the GlobalNames Zone, which I briefly discussed earlier. It is a zone type that is designed to assist in phasing out the WINS technology by implementing a last-resort technique that resolves NetBIOS queries for DNS operating infrastructures. It supports IPv6, can integrate into a currently running WINS environment, and can affect an entire forest.

Zone Transfers

Within Windows Server 2008, zone transfers come in two types: authoritative transfers (AXFRs) and incremental zone transfers (IXFRs). An AXFR is a complete transfer of all components of the zone as it is authoritatively initiated, whereas an IXFR transfers only the differences since the last zone transfer. Normally, most organizations try to make as much use as possible of IXFR because of the inherently less bandwidth that is used.

Active Directory Replication with DNS

A friend of mine once told me that if Active Directory knew where, when, and how to replicate itself, I'd probably be out of a job. And, unfortunately, I have to agree. One of the major problems with any enterprise is the process of connecting various servers through the use of site links, bridges, and various routers across multiple subnets. It's time-consuming, difficult, and not necessarily reliable. Additionally, replication uses schedules that may not fit in perfectly well with your given organization.

However, the actual process of setting up replication was mostly covered in your exam on Active Directory. On this certification exam, you'll be concentrating on understanding the scope of your replication as it pertains to DNS. Remember, there are four scope levels, which are summarized in Table 2.4.

TABLE 2.4   DNS Scope Replication Levels

Scope Level	Effect
Forest	Every DNS server in the forest receives replication.
Domain	Only DNS servers for the domain will be replicated.
Domain controller in domain	Every domain controller holds a copy of the DNS server information.
Domain controllers in a DNS application	All domain controllers with a copy of the application partition will receive replication.

DNS Server Requirements and Placement

The exact DNS server requirements of your organization will be based on the number of users, the amount of queries, and the amount of traffic that you see both externally and internally within your organization. As a general rule of thumb, a resource record (RR) will take up approximately 100 bytes of RAM. Thus, based on the number of users and records associated with your organization, you can use this accordingly. If you are in an organization with 10,000 users, you will require 1,000,000 bytes of RAM just for resource records that can be accessed thousands of times per second based on the amount of traffic flowing back and forth between your network.

In general, the basic rule of DNS server requirements is that the DNS server must be highly available and accessible to all users in your organization. In an ideal world, this would mean you could place a DNS server in every subnet, and each server would have an incredibly light load. However, for an organization with, say, 500 subnets, this is not very realistic. This problem literally doubles when you consider that the first rule of thumb with network design is that you plan for the worst and then expect the worst. So, this means you will naturally need a backup DNS server for each server you are using. And, in your ideal "500 subnet" design, you'd be using a paltry 1,000 servers purely for DNS—probably not a good idea.

Normally, DNS servers are accessed across a WAN link or across routers that are connected in such a way that allow for easy throughput. When placing your DNS servers in design questions on the certification exam, consider the speed or your WAN links as well as the speed of the given switches in the topology, and place your DNS server in the most logical area of your network in terms of accessibility.

It's pretty unlikely that you will be asked about this on your exam, but a good tip to keep in mind for the real world is that Microsoft estimates that WINS servers can support approximately 4,500 queries per minute and register about 1,500 names per minute.

Planning for Network Access

In short, *network access* refers to any method an external or internal user will need to implement in order to securely or insecurely access a resource from a remote or internal location across a WAN or LAN. More simply put, *network access* refers to any user trying to access the network from any given location at any given time. Within Windows Server 2008, there are a myriad of ways for this to occur, such as VPNs, dial-up connections, RADIUS servers, or other such remote technologies.

Within the limits of network access, you also have to consider the concept of NAT pools, routing, and network policies (formally referred to as *remote access policies* in previous versions of Windows Server). On the enterprise level, you combine these technologies into a very broad scope. In fact, there's a strong possibility that some advanced enterprises may require almost every single, if not all, of the technologies available for network access to be in use at the same time. The days of an individual user working only from the office and then going home for the day are gone. Now, an employee can sit from home, log into the corporate network, and conduct business without ever having to leave their home. On the enterprise level, you are primarily concerned with the types of authentication used, the policies implemented, and the design of your perimeter network, all of which I will discuss now.

Password-Based Policy Authentication Protocols

When in the "authentication" portion of network policies, you are most likely using some form of password protocol on your WAN or LAN link as information is transmitted across your link. If this wasn't done, then passwords could be seen in plain-text format and could be easily compromised. Now, although this is an option (particularly with PAP), it's normally not recommended. Within Windows Server 2008 there are typically four password authentication protocols used:

MS-CHAP Microsoft Challenge Handshake Authentication Protocol (MS-CHAP) is an earlier, now mostly outdated, one-way authentication protocol that is used to support legacy clients such as Windows 98. If, on the certification exam, you encounter a question that asks you about this particular protocol, pay careful attention because it is usually necessary only if you need to support legacy equipment.

MS-CHAPv2   Microsoft Challenge Handshake Authentication Protocol version 2 (MS-CHAPv2) is a newer, more improved two-way authentication method that requires both the server and the client to authenticate. If certificates are not available, this is the recommended policy protection by Microsoft.

CHAP   Challenge Handshake Authentication Protocol (CHAP) is an authentication similar to MS-CHAP that is designed for clients who do not use Windows. If you are utilizing a realm trust or Unix-based machine, this may be an excellent suggestion for your infrastructure.

PAP   Password Authentication Protocol (PAP) is a plain-text, unencrypted password system that authenticates password strings and verifies them for accuracy. If the password doesn't match, authentication is denied. Both Microsoft and I strongly recommend against this method.

 Microsoft does not recommend password-based systems and instead suggests using certificate-based systems for all access systems that support their use.

Certificate-Based Authentication

The far more recommended and secure method of authenticating user identities for network policies is using certificates. Certificates, as you know, are individualized methods for ensuring user identity with a combination of public and private keys, normally utilizing 128-bit encryption. These certificates are assigned by a certificate authority, such as VeriSign, or any machine running Active Directory Certificate Services (AD CS).

In Windows Server 2008, remote network users authenticated by certificates using remote protocols such as VPN utilize powerful authentication protocols, such as Extensible Authentication Protocol-Transport Level Security (EAP-TLS), Protected Extensible Authentication Protocol (PEAP), or Internet Protocol Security (IPsec) to protect against unauthorized access:

EAP-TLS and PEAP   EAP-TLS and PEAP are two-way, certificate-based authentications that always authenticate on the server end and can be configured to require both client and server authentication. To implement one of these types of security certificates, they must have a purpose configured in the extended key usage (EKU) that matches the certificate use. Additionally, they must meet the requirements of X.509 for certificates and the requirements for Secure Sockets Layer (SSL).

IPsec   IPsec is a very secure, network layer authentication protocol that can support certificates. Its most common use is for VPN access, but it can be used for various network authentication purposes through the enterprise. However, IPsec is limited in that it is designed to work only over IP, so it is highly specified. But, it is available on Windows Server 2008, 2003, and Windows 2000 operating systems.

Additionally, IPsec has the ability to be configured within Group Policy at the domain, site, or OU level. This allows an administrator to create powerful authentication policies for individuals at a very granular level.

Network Access Policies and the Network Policy Server

With the release of Windows Server 2008, Microsoft has included a new server role called the network policy server (NPS). The network policy server is responsible for (as the name implies) the maintenance and enforcement of network access policies for services such as VPN, Routing and Remote Access (RRAS), and other features. NPS is a replacement for the Windows Internet Authentication Service (IAS) available on Windows 2000 and Windows Server 2003. In total, NPS is responsible for the following:

- Routing of LAN/WAN traffic
- Resource access via VPN and dial-up
- Network access policies
- VPN connection services
- Dial-up connection services
- RRAS
- 802.1X switch authentication

In effect, NPS is the Microsoft implementation of a RADIUS server and proxy. It's incredibly powerful in that it allows a lot more utilization than previous incarnations of Windows Server and doesn't require much setup or configuration. In addition, NPS is a prerequisite for NAP, which is responsible for maintaining the health of your network.

RADIUS   RADIUS stands for Remote Authentication Dial-In User Service and provides authentication for dial-up, VPN, and even wireless client authentication. Within Windows Server 2008, this is managed by the network policy server. The advantage of it is that you can configure RADIUS policies in each RADIUS server. Additionally, it supports auditing and logging in a centralized users database that is easily accessed by administrators. Specifically, RADIUS supports the following:

- Event logging
- Authentication and account logging
- RADIUS-based logging

VPN   A virtual private network (VPN) is a remote authentication technology that allows a computer that exists outside the LAN to act as part of that network via the WAN connection. VPNs are low-cost, low-upkeep solutions that utilize encryption in order to maintain security within the organization. From a broad perspective, you should be concerned with the type of encryption used on the links established from the Internet to the intranetwork. You need to pay attention to two of these encryptions:

PPTP   The Point-to-Point Tunneling Protocol (PPTP) is an extension of the Point-to-Point Protocol (PPP) that encapsulated PPP packets over the IP layer in TCP/IP networks. It is defined in RFC 1171, has been in existence for a very long time, and is someone antiquated. The advantage to PPTP in VPNs is that it is relatively secure and fairly easy to set up.

L2TP   The Layer 2 Tunneling Protocol (L2TP) is a standard established by the Internet Engineering Task Force. It combines Cisco's Layer 2 forwarding and Microsoft's PPTP. Technically, L2TP is an extension of PPP, it allows for vendor independence and multi-hops, and it is capable of being combined with IPsec to form a very secure connection. Recently, L2TP has gained popularity over the seemingly obsolete PPTP, and it has the added bonus of allowing tunneling of the already accepted PPP standard.

Network Access Policies

Network access policies are policies given to remote users that determine where, when, who, and how a network is remotely accessed. The way these particular policies are determined is by examining the number of users, type of environment, and overall feel of the organization in order to accommodate the exact needs of the users involved. Each of these policies is set in the network policy server under a certain set of *conditions*:

Groups   This can be Windows groups, machine groups, or user groups.

HCAP   Host Control Authorization Protocol Location Groups and User Groups (HCAP) is used to communicate between the network policy server and the network access server.

Day and time   This specifies when a policy can be active (specified by date and time).

Network access   This is a condition that occurs based on NAP policies.

Connection   This specifies conditions based on IP address type, authentication type, protocol type, and tunnel type (PPTP/L2TP).

RADIUS client   This specifies what type of role the client is playing in the RADIUS setup.

Gateway   This defines conditions based on the network access server role.

These conditions are further refined by certain *constraints*:

Authentication methods   This defines clients by authentication type.

Idle timeout   This defines the maximum idle time.

Session timeout   This defines how long a session can last.

Called station ID   This specifies the phone number of the network access server.

Day and time restrictions   These are date and time restrictions.

NAS port type   This defines the media type allowed to connect.

Lastly, these conditions and constraints are refined by *settings*, based on the type of connection being used:

- RADIUS attributes
- Network access protection
- RRAS

Perimeter Networks

A *perimeter network* is a network that exists internally but is completely exposed to the outside world and devoid of security. Outside the Windows Server world, a perimeter network is also called a *demilitarized zone* (DMZ). The purpose of a DMZ is to serve as a place set apart from the rest of the network that first exposes itself to any potential attack. More often than not, a DMZ will also be backed up by a *honey pot*, which is a machine designed to appear as if it has vital information to an organization that may be of interest to a malicious hacker but in reality is merely a trap to isolate the malicious user and identify them in order to prevent access or aid in prosecution. However, there are now certain legal issues in place that have made these less popular.

Almost always, a DMZ is separated from the internal network by a *firewall*, which is a hardware or software device that filters packets and determines where they will and will not be allowed to forward based on their origin, destination, protocol, and other such information. When designing a perimeter network, you have to take into account the available budget for your network, number of users, redundancy requirements, availability, and scalability. Each of these factors will determine what type of firewall you can use and how many of them you can use.

Possible Perimeter Intrusion Attacks

Although it may not be a complete list, Microsoft has listed in its recommendation for perimeter network design a list of possible attacks you will need to plan against in case of network instruction:

Packet sniffers   These are applications of hardware that monitor the network at the packet level for the purpose of exploitation.

IP spoofing   This is falsifying an IP address for the purpose of gaining false authorization.

Denial-of-service attacks   These are attacks that attempt to deny a service from running by compromising the service through constant software or with a hardware attack.

Application layer attacks   These are exploitations of software at the application level.

Network reconnaissance   This is using detailed information gained by extensive study to find weak points in the network.

Viruses   These are malicious programs designed to penetrate a network and cause adverse effects.

Firewall Classes

Firewalls can be either hardware or software and come in many different shapes, sizes, and capabilities. Microsoft has defined five classes of firewalls, as outlined in Table 2.5.

TABLE 2.5   Microsoft Firewall Classes

Class	Type	Design Purpose
1	Personal (software) firewall	Small, individual users requiring little to no extensive firewall protection
2	Router firewall	Small to medium businesses requiring packet-level routing and inspection NAT
3	Low-end hardware firewall	Dedicated firewalls that require little configuration and can incorporate switch and VPN capabilities
4	High-end hardware firewall	High-performance, dedicated firewalls that require setup and firewall specifications
5	High-end server firewall	Dedicated server-based firewall using both hardware and software procedures to ensure an incredibly fast and secure network

Active Directory Federation proxy servers should be placed within the perimeter network!

Firewall Options

Whenever you are setting up your firewall initially, you have a choice of three design options to use, each of which has advantages and disadvantages based on your overall network design. Usually, the firewall option will be of the following: bastion host, three-homed firewall, or back-to-back firewalls.

Bastion Host

A *bastion host* is a single firewall that is placed up front and is the only existing firewall on the network. The advantage of this design is that is cheap, easy, and usually pretty effective. However, it is also the single point of failure and, if bypassed, can cause serious concerns throughout the rest of the network.

Three-Homed Firewall

A *three-homed* firewall is connected to three different locations on the network. This sounds a bit more complicated than it actually is. In reality, a three-homed firewall is connected to the following three networks:

- The internal network, where all the internal user computers are located
- The perimeter network, where the honey pot or AD FS proxy may be located
- The Internet, from where the external requests and most of the filtering originate

Back-to-Back Firewalls

The inherent design of *back-to-back firewalls* is to have one firewall connected to another, which requires double authentication when crossing beyond the second firewall. Usually, this type of design is either implemented to reduce hardware/software load on a firewall or implemented in order to have a perimeter network.

Server Placement

The last topic I'll discuss in this chapter is server placement. Within Windows Server 2008 infrastructures you're going to have a lot of options in complex environments regarding where to place your network components. Accordingly, you should follow a few general guidelines when considering VPN, RADIUS, and DHCP server locations.

VPN Server Placement

VPN servers can be placed either in front of or behind a firewall. In truth, there are advantages to both. On one hand, VPN servers that are placed in front of a firewall ease the load on the overall infrastructure and can directly pass data received from Internet requests onto the rest of the network; on the other hand, VPN servers placed in front of the firewall are exposed to malicious users. When servers are placed behind the firewall, however, the VPN server is more protected, but it requires more load to be placed on the firewall and additional overhead from an administrator during setup to ensure traffic can be easily sent across the perimeter network.

NPS Placement

The easy rule of thumb when placing a network policy server is as follows: place it near or on a domain controller and near the user population that will be taking advantage of it. By placing the NPS near or on a domain controller, it enables the server to easily authenticate user accounts it will be using, and by placing it near the user accounts that may be using it for a feature such as RADIUS, you will ensure that they have the shortest link requirements possible.

DHCP Server Placement

When opting to use DHCP in your infrastructure, two options are available:

- Connecting directly to the subnet
- Using DHCP relay

Ideally, DHCP servers will be placed within the subnet. This is because by default DHCP servers can assign dynamic addresses only to the subnet to which they have been assigned without using a DHCP relay. Thus, if you require only one DHCP server in one particular subnet, the placing becomes simple: the DHCP server goes in the subnet.

However, if this isn't an option, the best place to place a DHCP server is in a secure location within your infrastructure that can be handed packets from all subnets. The exception to this is if you have multiple DHCP servers, in which case you would want each DHCP server to be placed in a location where it can easily access the subnets to which it needs access via router links. In either case, a DHCP server will need to be forwarded DHCP/BOOTP packets via a DHCP relay agent, which can be installed on any given Windows Server machine. All this requires is for you to assure that communication can be established with the appropriate server and that each relay agent points to the appropriate DHCP server for that subnet.

Summary

In this chapter, I discussed IP addressing strategies for IPv4 and IPv6, delved into namespaces and commonly used methodologies for resolving names using both modern and legacy design, and discussed remote network access strategies and server placement for robust Windows Server 2008 infrastructure design. Before moving on from this chapter, you should understand how to subnet IPv4 very well, have a familiarity of the overall IPv6 structure, and be familiar with the tunneling methods utilized to transition from IPv4 to IPv6.

I also covered namespaces and naming conventions, including the requirements of DNS, that it can be incorporated into Active Directory, and the relationship that DNS zones play with the infrastructure and with legacy naming mechanisms, such as WINS. Additionally, I covered the effect that DNS will have on your remote access strategy, which accounts for network policies, connection types, and overly infrastructure design goals, including perimeter networks. Lastly, on the server placement side, I covered where to place a DHCP server; general rules of thumb for RADIUS-based servers on NPS; and the purposes, classes, and types of firewalls you can use in any given environment.

Exam Essentials

Know your subnetting.   The MCITP certification exam will probably not have you manually subnet an IPv4 address, but you should still know how to do it. This is important, because it gives you a strong foundation in the basics of networking and will help you more easily understand the complex situations you may be presented with on the certification exam.

Remember network server-based roles.   These include DHCP, DNS, and other server roles that are strictly networking-related. Microsoft expects you to have learned these technologies for your 70-642 exam; now you will be expected to have them perfected.

Know how to handle IPv6.   This includes IPv4 to IPv6 tunneling, IPv6 addressing, and the allocated space available in the 128-bit address. IPv6 is a complicated subject and will slowly start appearing over the next few years.

Know access policies.   Access policies include VPN, dial-up connections, and other access strategies that Microsoft will expect you to be intimately familiar with. Don't be surprised!

Understand authentication and authorization.   You need to know and understand all the different types of authorization strategies and encryption strategies Microsoft has at its disposal, along with all their advantages and disadvantages. This can be a lot to take in, so make sure you memorize them.

Know DNS zone types.   You need to know the difference between primary, secondary, GlobalNames, and other different types of DNZ zones. They will pop up a lot, and more often than not, they will be the simple answer to a complicated question.

Don't forget the past.   Legacy technologies still exist. WINS is still actively used, as are tons of different networking technologies. Be prepared for questions about them.

Review Questions

1. How many host bits would be required if your IPv4 network required 36 different hosts per subnet?

 A. 3

 B. 4

 C. 5

 D. 6

2. How many subnetworks would a Class C IPv4 address with a /27 subnet mask support, including the subnet-zero and all-ones subnets?

 A. 2

 B. 4

 C. 8

 D. 16

3. Which of the following tunneling technologies transforms a standard IPv4 address into 2002:AABB:CCDD:Subnet:InterfaceID format?

 A. Teredo

 B. ISATAP

 C. VPN

 D. 6to4

4. Which of the following IPv4 to IPv6 tunneling conventions carries a different name in Windows XP and Windows Server 2003?

 A. 6to4

 B. ISATAP

 C. Teredo

 D. VPN

5. Which of the following is an accurate shorthand notation of the IPv6 address FF02:0000: 0000:0001:0000:0000:0001:0032?

 A. FF02::1:0:0:1:32

 B. FF02::1::1:32

 C. FF02::1::1::32

 D. FF02:0:0:1::32

6. Which of the following is the default broadcast address for IPv6?

   A. FF02::1

   B. FFEF::1

   C. 2002::1

   D. 2340::1

   E. FE00::1

   F. None of the above

7. You are a newly arriving administrator to a currently existing infrastructure that utilizes WINS technology, and you would like to upgrade your existing network to DNS. Accordingly, you have decided to install the DNS server role on your network. Currently, you utilize Windows Server 2003, combined with Windows 2000 Server. To maintain the most efficient implementation of DNS with Windows Server 2008, what should your first action be?

   A. Install a GlobalNames Zone for WINS support.

   B. Dedicate a reverse lookup zone.

   C. Implement AD FS within your infrastructure.

   D. Associate DNS with Active Directory, and implement Active Directory.

8. The address 129.118.1.9 is which class of IP address?

   A. A

   B. B

   C. C

   D. D

9. What is the broadcast address of 129.118.1.9/27?

   A. 129.118.1.31

   B. 129.118.1.32

   C. 129.118.1.1

   D. 129.118.1.63

10. A senior administrator comes to you early one afternoon and says he would like to make the current running network much more efficient. Specifically, he'd like to make your currently operating five-subnet bits not waste as many available addresses as you are currently using. If currently you are utilizing standard subnetting, what technology would help you reduce the number of wasted addresses?

    A. Teredo

    B. ISATAP

    C. IPv6

    D. 6to4

    E. VLSM

    F. CIDR

11. How many bits are available by default in the host portion of an IPv6 address?

   A. 16

   B. 32

   C. 64

   D. 128

12. If you have a given MAC address of 0045:4384:48A9 and you want to utilize EUI-64 conventional IPv6 addressing in your network, what would the host portion of this address be if you used the `ipconfig/all` command?

   A. 0045:43FF:FE84:48A9

   B. 0245:43FF:FE84:48A9

   C. 0045:43FF:FF84:48A9

   D. 2045:43FF:FE84:48A9

13. When using a WINS-supported network, what is the process of broadcasting changes made in the names database referred to as?

   A. Push

   B. Pull

   C. Push/pull

   D. Single-label push/pull

14. If your infrastructure's IPv4 to IPv6 transitional method requires that both IPv4 and IPv6 be implemented at the same time and that the IP address not be shared, which tunneling method are you using?

   A. Dual stack

   B. Dual layer

   C. Dual IP stacking

   D. Dual IP layer

   E. Dual stacking

15. Windows Vista and Windows Server 2008 can act as routers for 6to4 tunneling through what Windows feature?

   A. Teredo

   B. ISATAP

   C. DNS

   D. Active Directory

   E. AD FS

   F. AD RMS

   G. ICS

   H. IPv6

16. Of the following six aspects, which of the following is *not* part a WINS client record?

   A. Record names

   B. IP addresses

   C. Type

   D. Label

   E. State

   F. Version

17. What is the maximum number of characters that can exist in a NetBIOS name?

   A. 10

   B. 15

   C. 16

   D. 20

18. With Windows Server 2008, many new features and available roles are available. One of these particular features allows for a new transitional technique from WINS to DNS. Of the following listed, which is this transitional technology?

   A. Primary Zone

   B. Secondary Zone

   C. Forward Lookup Zone

   D. Reverse Lookup Zone

   E. GlobalNames Zones

   F. Stub Zone

19. Stub zones require what to receive updates?

   A. Zone transfers

   B. An authoritative server

   C. A primary zone

   D. A secondary zone

20. Which of the following protocols is a two-way protocol designed for use with certificates?

   A. MS-CHAP

   B. CHAP

   C. EAP-TLS

   D. PAP

Answers to Review Questions

1. D. To support 36 hosts per subnet, you would need to allocate 6 bits in your subnet mask. An easy way to do this is to start with the first bit, 0, and then hop to the second bit and multiply by intervals of 2 until you reach a number greater than your desired number (0, 2, 4, 8, 16, 32, 64). Since 64 is greater than 36 by a significant margin, you also allocate for the two addresses for broadcast and network addresses.

2. C. The number of subnetworks can be determined by taking the remaining number of bits in the subnet mask in addition to the default mask and raising to the power of that number. In this case, you have a default mask of 24 because it is Class C. Thus, three remain. If you raise 2 to the power of 3, it gives you the answer 8. Keep in mind, in practice, it's best to account for the all-ones and subnet-zero subnet, leaving you with six practical and usable subnets.

4. B. In Windows XP and Windows Server 2003, ISATAP tunneling is referred to as Automatic Tunneling Pseudo-Interface. This type of tunneling occurs by default in Windows XP, Windows Server 2003, and Windows Vista without Service Pack 1.

3. D. Only 6to4 tunneling works by transforming an IPv4 address in a portion of the IPv6 address, prefaced by 2002 and concluded by Subnet:InterfaceID. Keep this in mind, because it makes it easy to identify when this type of tunneling is in use.

5. A. When using shorthand notation, you can use the :: symbol to indicate 0s until the first bit that contains a nonzero. Afterward, you must use the standard : separator.

6. F. IPv6, unlike IPv4, does not use broadcast addresses. Instead, IPv6 relies on multicast addresses to send specific information to portions of the network decided by your infrastructure design.

7. D. Associating DNS with Active Directory is almost always a good choice. Active Directory can then easily replicate this information across the infrastructure and make it much easier for users to access DNS information via simple queries that can be handled by various servers throughout the network.

8. B. The Class B address range extends from 128.0.0.1 to 192.255.25.255. For your exam, you will need to be intimately familiar with these address ranges in order to save time and and quite numerous, so this sort of exercise is good to practice a day or two before taking the exam.

9. A. The broadcast address of a particular subnet is found by taking the incremental number found by the subnet mask last bit, raising to the place value of that bit, and then subtracting 1. In this case, the place value of /27 is 5, thus $2^5 = 32$, and subtracting 1 leaves you with 31. Therefore, the answer is 129.118.1.31.

10. E. VLSM, or variable-length subnet mask, is a technology that allows administrators to divide the number of subnetted networks and use different masks for each individual network to accommodate for a lesser amount of users.

11. C. IPv6 breaks the address into two specific portions, a network and a host portion. Each of these portions has 64 bits, for a total address length of 128 bits.

12. B. When using EUI-64, the MAC address is split in half with the arbitrary hexadecimal numbers FFFE placed in the middle. This is completing by "flipping" the seventh bit, which in hex is represented by 02. Thus, B is your address.

13. A. Periodic broadcasting of changes based on a threshold with WINS is referred to as push. When a certain number of changes occur in the database, these changes are reported throughout the network.

14. A. Dual stack refers to a transitional technique where both versions of the IPv4 stack and the IPv6 stack are implemented on one host device. When using this technique, you receive two logical addresses per device.

15. G. To implement a 6to4 router with Windows Vista and Windows Server 2008, you must utilize Internet Connection Sharing (ICS). Through this, you can set up your Windows device to function as a router for this type of tunneling.

16. D. WINS client records are associated with the WINS database and are used for queries and name resolution. The components of a WINS client record are record names, IP addresses, types, state, static, owner, and version.

17. B. NetBIOS names used for WINS can have a maximum length of 15 characters. Partially because of this, WINS is outdated and is being quickly replaced by DNS implementations.

18. E. GlobalNames Zone is a new zone type available to Windows Server 2008 that is designed as a last-resort method to evaluate WINS requests. It operates on the forest level and can provide an easy transitional method to integrate legacy devices.

19. B. Stub zones were released with Windows Server 2003 and are designed to reduce traffic in congested networks that receive multiple DNS requests. To update their information, they must receive updates from an authoritative server.

20. C. Extensible Authentication Protocol-Transport Level Security (EAP-TLS) is a two-way authentication protocol that can evaluate both the server and the client. It supports certificates using SSL and is highly secure.

Chapter

3

Planning for Forestwide and Domainwide Upgrades with Server 2008

OBJECTIVES COVERED IN THIS CHAPTER:

✓ **Plan for domain or forest migration, upgrade, and restructuring.**

 ▪ May include but is not limited to: cross-forest authentication, backward compatibility, object migration, migration planning, implementation planning, environment preparation

It's no secret that Windows Server 2008 isn't the first version of Windows Server ever made. In fact, it's far from it. And it's also no secret that along the way the saga of Windows Server has had some serious ups and downs, along with a lot of dramatic changes. What is commonplace now didn't even exist in the first few versions of Windows. If you speak to an administrator who started in the beginning and then quit before things started to get a little less hectic, there's a strong chance they may not even know what Active Directory is, much less how to administer it.

Like Windows, most enterprise-level businesses are not new creatures. Many of them (if not most) have been around since before the days of even the first version of Windows, much less Windows Server. What this means for administrators at the enterprise level is that although the versions of Windows might quickly change and the technology may very well adapt on a daily basis, businesses simply *do not*. In fact, the first rule of IT in a lot of businesses is as follows: "If it ain't broke, don't fix it."

Apart from being pretty funny, that is incredibly accurate. When new versions of Windows Server are added, it can create some incredibly complex problems. In this chapter, we're going to explore the process of mixing old technology with new. And along with covering the process of integrating that old technology, we're going to cover the process of *changing* from the old technology to the latest version of Windows Server, which is Windows Server 2008. By the end of this chapter, you should be able to transition your organization from whatever version of Windows is running to Windows Server 2008 or integrate Windows Server 2008 smoothly into your current architecture.

The Essence of Migration

One of the words that you're going to see used throughout your 70-647 exam and throughout your career in the IT world is *migration*. Migration is just a marketing term that means transferring from one place to another, transferring from one version to another, or both. In the older days of administration, migration was an ominous task that took a lot of planning, design, and best implementation practices. Mainly, this was because of the inherent difficulty of transferring from a non-Active-Directory-capable environment to an Active Directory–capable environment. Obviously, there were problems.

In the world of Windows Server 2008, those concerns are mostly gone. The days of Windows NT are numbered, and it is rare that you will find an organization that doesn't implement Active Directory in some form throughout the enterprise. This changing of the guard occurred in the age of Windows 2000 Server and Windows Server 2003.

Now, with Windows Server 2008, you'll face the lesser challenging of moving objects between Active Directory–capable versions of servers that aren't so up-to-date or moving objects between overall designs that perhaps aren't as evolved as they could be. To facilitate this transformation, you can take advantage of a very powerful administrative tool that must be installed by hand: the Active Directory Migration Tool (ADMT).

Using the Active Directory Migration Tool

The primary tool that we use to migrate objects from one domain to another is the Active Directory Migration Tool. As of the writing of this book, the Active Directory Migration Tool version most widely used at the enterprise level is ADMT 3.0. This is the version that is used with Windows Server 2003 and mostly facilitated transfers between Windows 2000, Windows NT, and Windows Server 2003.

With the release of Windows Server 2008, Microsoft introduced the ADMT version 3.1. This powerful, new version of the previous ADMT tool is designed from the ground up to support Windows Server 2008 and all previous versions of Windows Server. Because of the inherent power of this tool and how heavily it will to be used in the enterprise environment, it's important for us as enterprise administrators to understand the capabilities of this tool.

Accordingly, in this chapter we're going to spend some time in our test exercises going over the various methods used to migrate accounts between domains, forests, and servers. Additionally, we'll cover a few real-world scenarios where you will need to use the ADMT to facilitate an easy transition to Windows Server 2008.

Using Caution with Migration

There's a big difference between whether you *can* do something and whether you *should* do something. We all know that Windows Server 2008 is a powerful, new, and fancy operating system with numerous capabilities. From the perspective of an administrator, you'd like to incorporate as many features as possible into your design. But from the perspective of a business, migrating any machine from one platform to another means two things: money and liability.

We IT professionals might like to ignore such details, but migrating to Windows Server 2008 costs a lot of money. A business has to worry about the costs of Windows Server, which include the labor costs associated with installing the software and the cost of any additional hardware to support the upgrade with the appropriate amounts of RAM, CPU power, and other associated functionality. More often than not, this means purchasing new computers.

A business must also be concerned with liability issues. Gary Olsen, a software engineer with Hewlett-Packard, once commented in an article he wrote pertaining to migration with Windows Server 2008 that a customer was potentially losing up to $1 million per hour because of incompatibility between the version of SQL Server currently in use in the office and an upgrade to another application.

Just imagine that: $1 million per hour. A lot of regular, hardworking people barely make a million dollars in their entire lifetime. And this business was losing that much in a single hour. The moral of the story? Plan. And then plan again. Although we might want to jump into the situation headfirst and upgrade on a whim, we have to use caution. If you don't, you'll most likely regret it. Don't count on being lucky. Be certain.

Migrating Objects

Objects are, for the most part, the only reason you need to concern yourself with migration. This is because objects contain most of the information you need in order to conduct business. Remember from your earlier study of Active Directory that an Active Directory object is either one or a collection of important resources, user accounts, computers, printers, or other elements that exist as part of the Windows infrastructure. When we say that we are "migrating objects," we are simply taking objects from one source domain and transferring them to the target domain.

For example, say you have two different domains, MyCorp and MegaCorp. MyCorp is a small, independent seller of machine equipment for use in excavating archeological discoveries. MegaCorp, on the other hand, is a giant manufacturer of equipment used for thousands of purposes. MegaCorp is involved in coal mining, dumping, building construction, road construction, and many other endeavors. Recently, MegaCorp decided to purchase MyCorp for an undisclosed amount, acquiring all of its employees, resources, and assets. Accordingly, MegaCorp wants to migrate the resources of MyCorp to its infrastructure.

In a simple example like this one, you face the problem of migrating objects from a small domain to a larger one. Accordingly, you need to use the ADMT. You would start by migrating users from the MyCorp domain. You would do this by logging on to a server in the MegaCorp domain and executing an instance of the ADMT.

The reason you do this from the target domain and not the source domain is that the ADMT works in a similar fashion to a crane. If you're using the ADMT, it's like operating the crane. When you're operating, you can dig into a target area and move it to another one. More technically, when you're using the ADMT, you have to point the ADMT to a target and tell the ADMT what you would like to take.

Consolidating Objects

Beyond moving objects from domain to another, or from one Windows platform to another, a dramatically increasing usage trend is to use the ADMT to consolidate the number of servers within an existing Active Directory infrastructure. Consider that in the "older" days of computing, hardware was nowhere near as powerful and software was nowhere near as robust, stable, and capable.

Because of this, it is easy for administrators to use the ADMT to take objects from a previously overburdened server and place them into a higher-level server that has a much greater maximum capacity than the previous server. Consider Figure 3.1, where the forest root domain for the SuperCorp corporation is the supercorp.com server, and the extending child domains are children of the root.

FIGURE 3.1   SuperCorp topology with extra child domains

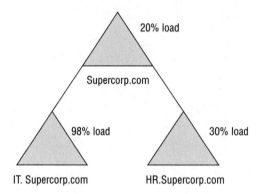

In this figure, you can see that the IT department domain (it.supercorp.com) is overburdened. Although it isn't illustrated in this figure, the reason for this is that the users in the IT department are running an outdated Windows 2000 Server machine with a whopping 400MHz processor and barely enough RAM to run Office 2007. But then again, that's sort of the way it goes in IT—just enough to get the job done.

To deal with this situation, you'd have to perform a common task—taking the existing user accounts from that Windows 2000 Server that existed in a child domain and integrating them into the domain a level up. In this case, you'd use the ADMT to consolidate the number of servers. You'd do this by first *instantiating* (which is just a fancy word for initializing) the ADMT on the server that you want to ultimately consolidate toward and take out the user accounts. After this, you could remove the child domain.

 Real World Scenario

Consolidating Domains

OmniCorp, a medium-sized search engine–based advertising company, has a central office in Washington, DC; four additional domains installed within the company for various projects; and departments throughout the enterprise. However, new government privacy regulations require OmniCorp to consolidate its existing domain structure into a centralized, focused environment with only one domain and one domain controller.

The reasons why this is necessary are complicated, but suffice to say that security is of great concern. Some of the data to which OmniCorp has access is very private and consequently very valuable. Currently, OmniCorp's corporate infrastructure appears as shown, with one root domain and four child domains.

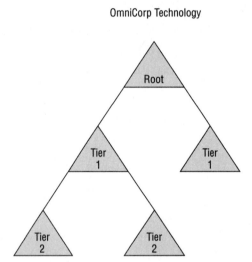

Within each child domain are multiple thousands of user accounts. Each of these domains may have its own policies and procedures regarding accounts. However, all the domains must now be consolidated into one domain. Currently, the entire OmniCorp enterprise is running Windows Server 2003 R2 with the domain and forest level at Windows Server 2003.

To solve this problem, you would need to use the Active Directory Migration Tool to migrate the objects from the child domains to the root domain. Once you have migrated the objects, you will have the opportunity to remove the child domains and reduce the overall amount of domains within the infrastructure. In this situation, it may be a good idea to upgrade the overall forest to Windows Server 2008, especially if the domain policies are so specific that they include multiple password policies. Remember, only Windows Server 2008 supports the new fine-grained user password policy feature.

Options with the Active Directory Migration Tool (ADMT)

After you've initially installed the ADMT, it appears in the Administrative Tools section of your Windows Server 2008 Start menu in a similar fashion to many other MMCs for

Windows Server 2008 Thus, you can access it by selecting Start ➢ Administrative Tools ➢ Active Directory Migration Tool. When you open this tool, you'll see a default screen, as shown in Figure 3.2, which will look relatively unimpressive until you begin the process of migrating objects back and forth and generating reports based on your actions.

FIGURE 3.2   Active Directory Migration Tool default screen

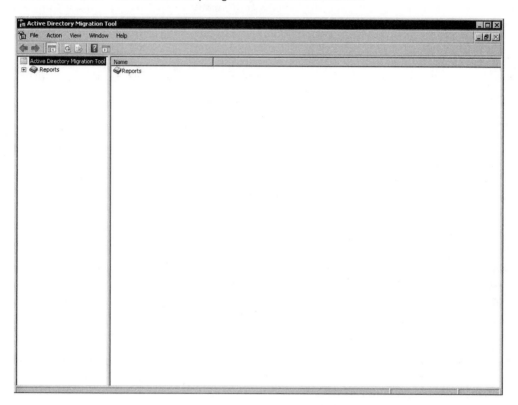

In the Action menu, you'll see several options that open wizards. In normal operation, you'll rarely use a wizard in a form other than the standard one. This is because Microsoft has gone through great pains to make sure that the ADMT doesn't just work but works very well. Thus, it behooves you to use the tools for the purpose they were designed— convenience. In total, there are nine wizards, only some of which you have to be concerned with for your exam. The nine wizards are as follows:

User Account Migration Wizard   The User Account Migration Wizard transfers user accounts between domains and keeps track of account information such as password settings and privilege levels. When complete, the users should see no difference between their previous accounts and their current accounts on the new server.

Group Account Migration Wizard   Using the Group Account Migration Wizard, administrators can move target groups from one domain to another. Within this wizard, there are options to select individual groups and user accounts, as well as the option to exclude certain groups and group members. But most important, in order to maintain group membership, groups need to be moved before user accounts to maintain membership during migration. Otherwise, the target server won't understand the groups, just the users within.

Computer Migration Wizard   The Computer Migration Wizard is designed to transfer computers from domain to domain anywhere within the infrastructure, including within organizational units. Just like the Group Account Migration Wizard, this wizard lets you select individual computers and configure the migration settings for each.

Security Translation Wizard   This wizard changes things up a bit in that it is designed to change security identifiers (SIDs) for access control lists (ACLs) and system access control lists (SACLs) on migrated objects. Without this translation, objects would have a lot of difficulty properly identifying themselves within the infrastructure.

Reporting Wizard   The Reporting Wizard is a web-compatible report tool that helps document the process of migration for your future use. You can choose to report domain changes, folder changes, security settings, and several other options. At the enterprise level, this is particularly recommended because of the good chance that this will probably occur again and again as technology continues to evolve. This way, you have a record of everything that has changed.

Service Account Migration Wizard   This wizard locates and identifies services on computers in the migration source domain (the domain that is being transferred) that do not use the Local System account. Once it does this, the ADMT identifies these accounts so that they are included in the migration at a later time.

Exchange 5.5 Mailbox Translation Wizard   If your enterprise is running Microsoft Exchange version 5.5, you can use this wizard to translate security and mailbox settings for Microsoft Exchange. However, this wizard is beyond the scope of this book.

Retry Task Wizard   You can use this wizard if you attempt to initiate a migration and the migration fails. If any settings are configured incorrectly, you can attempt to correct them with this tool.

Password Migration Wizard   It's no secret that sometimes domains can have a lot of passwords and different password settings. Using this wizard, you can both transfer all your password settings and then establish new protocols for your passwords in the infrastructure.

Migrating User Accounts

Migrating user accounts is probably the most common migration operation that you will ever have to perform in your administrative career. This is because of one main reason. That is, in certain enterprises, you may have hundreds of computers, dozens of printers, and even hundreds of group policies, but you will almost always have thousands and thousands of users. Without user migration, you'd have to go through the process of manually entering every one into the new version of Active Directory and, boy oh boy, would that be one serious pain.

To alleviate this pain and make the transition relatively simple, you access the User Account Migration Wizard, as you will see in Exercise 3.1.

EXERCISE 3.1

Migrating User Accounts

Prerequisites: To perform this exercise, you must have at least two domains and two domain controllers operating Windows Server 2008. These domains must be fully networked and accessible to each other. You will also need a 2003 server to host the ADMT.

1. Make sure you are logged in as either a domain or enterprise administrator.

2. Open the Active Directory Migration Tool by selecting Start ➢ Administrative Tools ➢ Active Directory Migration Tool.

3. Select the Action menu and then User Account Wizard. Click Next.

4. You will see the Domain Selection screen asking for the source and target domain and the domain controller. In the Source area, type the domain and the name of the domain controller from the source from which you want to migrate user accounts. In the Target area, place the destination for your user accounts with its domain and domain controller. In this example, we're using domain.com as our source domain and domain2.com as our new domain.

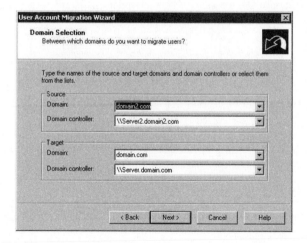

5. Click Next.

6. On the next screen, pictured here, you will be asked how you want to select users that you want to migrate. One option is to choose the users from a particular domain, and the other is to choose them from an include file. For this exercise, specify that you will choose them from a domain by selecting that radio button, and click Next.

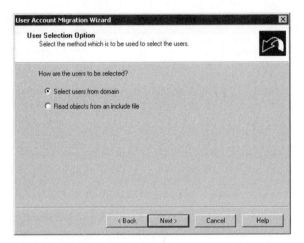

7. The next screen you will see is the User Account Migration screen. Here, you can choose accounts that you want to migrate from one domain to another. Most likely, this screen will appear blank. If so, click the Add button, type a known name into the Enter... box (you should be familiar with this box from other applications), and select the name. In this example, we have premade the mighty user "snuffleupagus," as shown here. Once the user is validated, you can close the box. Click Next.

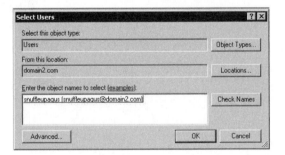

Note: Keep in mind that you can alternatively click the Advanced button after you have clicked Add and then click Find Now, where you can just select your user.

EXERCISE 3.1   *(continued)*

8. The next screen will ask you for the target organizational unit (OU) where the account will reside once it's migrated. Click the Browse button. Next, you can select where your target OU may reside. If you don't have any OUs set up, you can just select the Users folder. Afterward, the Lightweight Directory Access Protocol (LDAP) distinguished name will appear in your selection box. Click Next.

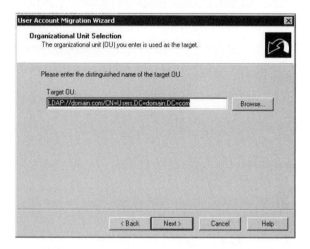

9. After you've clicked Next, you'll be presented with some password options for moving your accounts from one domain to another. For this exercise, select the Generate Complex Passwords radio button, and then click the Next button.

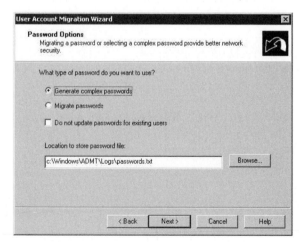

EXERCISE 3.1 *(continued)*

10. Leave the Target Same As Source radio button selected on the Account Transition Options screen. Click Next.

11. Leave the default options blank on the User Options screen, and then click Next.

12. On the Object Property Exclusion screen shown here, you can decide to exclude certain specified properties, such as account expiration. For our purposes in this chapter, leave this unselected. Click Next.

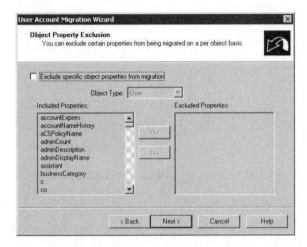

13. Keep the Do Not Migrate Source Object If a Conflict Is Detected in the Target Domain radio button selected, and then click Next.

14. Click Finish. You will then be presented with a Migration Progress button that should come out error free if the migration proceeded correctly. If not, you will be able to click the log and view a list of potential errors.

Snuffleupagus is now in the domain.com domain!

Migrating Computer Accounts

The second most common operation after migrating user accounts is migrating computers themselves. Migrating computers can save you a lot of headaches. Can you imagine how big of a pain it would be if you couldn't migrate computer accounts? You would have to manually reconnect each of your computers. Yuck! In Exercise 3.2, you'll go through the process of migrating computer accounts again with your preexisting domain.com and domain2.com domains.

EXERCISE 3.2

Migrating Computer Accounts

Prerequisites: To perform this exercise, you must have at least two domains and two domain controllers operating Windows Server 2008. These domains must be fully networked and accessible to each other. Additionally, you must have at least one computer account in the source domain. In this exercise, the domains are named domain.com and domain2.com, and the servers are named server and server2.

1. Make sure you are logged in as either a domain or enterprise administrator.

2. Open the Active Directory Migration Tool by selecting Start ➤ Administrative Tools ➤ Active Directory Migration Tool.

3. Select the Action menu, and then select Computer Account Migration Wizard. Click Next.

4. You will see a screen asking for the source and target domain and domain controller. In the Source area, you will type the domain and the name of the domain controller from the source you want to migrate computer accounts from. In the Target area, you place the destination for your computer accounts with its domain and domain controller. In this example, we're using domain.com as the source domain and domain2.com as the new domain. You can see this in Figure 3.3.

FIGURE 3.3   Computer migration source and target domain selection

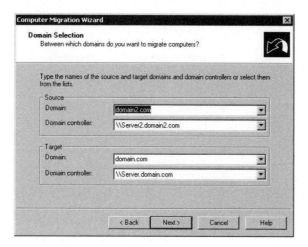

5. Click Next.

6. On the next screen, you will be asked how you would like to select computers that you want to migrate. (This is similar to Exercise 3.1.) One option is to choose the

computers from a particular domain, and the other is to choose them from an include file. For this exercise, you will choose them from a domain, so make sure that radio button is selected, and click Next.

7. The next screen you will see is the Computer Account Migration screen. Here, you can choose computers you want to migrate from one domain to another. Most likely, this will appear blank. If so, click the Add button, type a known name into the Enter... box, and check the name. In this exercise, we chose the computer Workstation1. Once it's validated, you can close that box. Click OK and then Next.

Note: Keep in mind that you can alternatively click the Advanced button after you have clicked Add, then click Find Now, and finally select your computer.

8. The next screen will ask you for the originating OU where the computers reside. Click the Browse button. Once there, you can select where your target OU will reside. If you don't have any OUs set up, you can just select the Computers folder. Afterward, the LDAP-distinguished name will appear in your selection box, as shown in Figure 3.4. Click Next.

FIGURE 3.4   OU selection

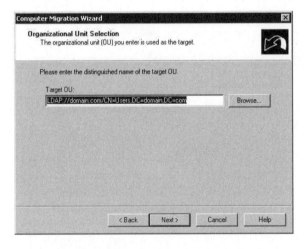

9. After you've clicked Next, you'll be presented with some options in moving your computers from one domain to another. For this exercise, you will again leave them blank. Click the Next button, and then click Next again to confirm the five-minute restart after the wizard completes (see Figure 3.5).

FIGURE 3.5   Computer account translation objects

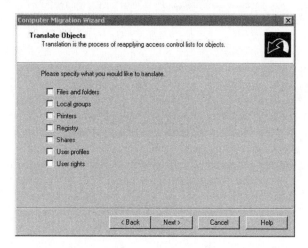

10. Leave the Object Property Exclusion page blank, and click Next.

11. Click Next on the conflict management screen, and then click Finish. Once you've click Finished, you will be presented with the migration log, as shown in Figure 3.6.

FIGURE 3.6   Computer account migration log

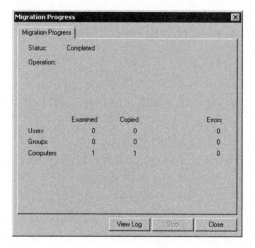

Cross-forest Authentication

Truly understanding cross-forest authentication doesn't just mean you understand authentication across multiple forests—it also means you understand the process of authentication and trusts within a single forest.

The term *cross-forest authentication* can take you aback a bit when you first hear it. But all this refers to is the authentication of credentials across multiple forests through the use of forest trusts. Since by now you've most likely seen forest trusts or been tested on forest trusts, this process should prove to be relatively easy for you. But for the sake of completeness and also because they are an absolutely vital aspect of the exam, we're going to cover forests in their entirety. More so than any other exam, the 70-647 exam asks you to understand every single aspect of forest trusts.

Recall that a large part of being an enterprise administrator is not just making administrative decisions but also making design decisions. There's certainly more than one way to organize an enterprise. What the enterprise administrator exam is going to test you on is not just whether you're capable of designing an enterprise but also whether you are capable of designing an enterprise in the best way possible. The best way to make sure you pass the exam is to familiarize yourself with the advantages and disadvantages of each type of trust and where they need to play a role in your environment.

Types of Trusts

In Chapter 1, we briefly covered the different types of trusts in Windows Server 2008 by name only. Let's review each of these trusts one more time in rapid fire, just so they're fresh in your mind:

Forest trusts   Trusts that exist between two entire forests. As an example, the MyCorp.com and MegaCorp.com forest could share a trust between them that exists on the entire forest level.

Domain trusts   Trusts that exist between two individual domains, somewhere within the forest. The majority of trusts placed in a multiforest environment are usually domain-based trusts, because they occur far more frequently than trusts between entire forests.

External trusts   Trusts designed for legacy Windows environments, such as NT 4, to exist within a modern-day trust.

Realm trust   Trusts designed to handle Unix-based servers in a Windows infrastructure.

Shortcut trust   Domain trusts that bypass the normal tiered hierarchy of domain trusts up and down the root domain and instead connect directly from one domain to another.

As you can see, or possibly have seen before, each of these types of trusts has a specific purpose and needs to be applied at a specific point. And furthermore, each of these types of trusts can be further refined by several categories of information.

To begin with, trusts can be either one-way or two-way.

One-Way Trusts

A *one-way trust* is the foundational trust that is used for all trust design. In a one-way trust, the trust flows in one direction, and the access direction flows in another. This is visually explained in Figure 3.7, with a one-way trust model. In this figure, you can see that the direction of the trust points in one direction. What this means is that the organization that issues the trust is saying "I trust this."

FIGURE 3.7   One-way trust

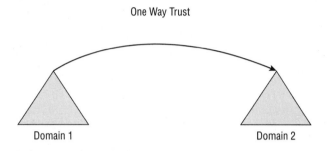

Because when the domain says that it trusts another, it points in one direction, and this means the other domain can take advantage of this trust. It's like when you give the key to your house to your house cleaner or to a friend. When your friend decides that she'd like to come over to use your coffee machine for a nice cup of joe, she's using your resources because you trust her. (We are assuming she doesn't make a mess and abuse your trust. That wouldn't be fun at all.)

One-way trusts can either be *incoming* or *outgoing*. If they are incoming, it means they will trust incoming connections. If they are outgoing, it means they will trust outgoing connections.

Two-Way Trusts

A *two-way trust* is a trust that is issued in two directions. However, unlike what you might think, a two-way trust is not simply a trust that exists in two directions. Instead, it is two individual one-way trusts that are applied to each domain. This is because trusts are, in practice, binary. Either you trust something or you don't. That trust goes just one way. Returning to the friend example, you may very well trust your friend, but your friend may not trust you.

You can see this type of trust in Figure 3.8. In this figure, the MyCorp and MegaCorp domains each trust each other and form two one-way trusts that allow the authentication of resources to each of the individual domains.

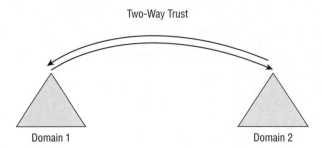

Accordingly, each domain in this figure will be able to access resources in the other domain.

Transitivity

Active Directory trusts come in two flavors: transitive and nontransitive. This happens regardless of whether the trust is two-way or one-way. In a *transitive* trust, the trust relationship extends upward, and the trust is established at the lowest level. So if you created a transitive trust to a domain that extends deeply within your forest structure, that transitive trust would accordingly trust all the domains up to the root domain.

In a *nontransitive* trust, the trust that is established is restricted to the two domains that have been joined. For example, if two lower-level domains are established by a nontransitive two-way trust, they will directly access one another's resources, but the trust will not be established in an upward direction throughout the forest. Those two domains, and those two domains only, will trust one another.

Forestwide Authentication and Selective Authentication

The easiest way to explain forestwide and selective authentication is to consider Figure 3.9, which shows two separate forests that each contain several domains. So, most likely, each of these forests represents an infrastructure that consists of several hundred or several thousand users. Each forest is a living, breathing system that has its own infrastructure and runs completely independently from the other.

But if for some reason these two independent structures had to merge or needed complete access to each other's resources, they could form a "forestwide" trust. This means one forest would trust each other in its entirety, and each forest would be able to use the other's authentication scheme.

In theory (and sometimes in practice), this is a good idea, because it really does ease the effort of having to administer two different structures. Effectively, they almost become one, because administrators can more easily define trusts and access. However, most of the time, administrators require a finer-grained level of control. Thus, forests can also trust each other through the process of selective authentication.

FIGURE 3.9 Authentication options

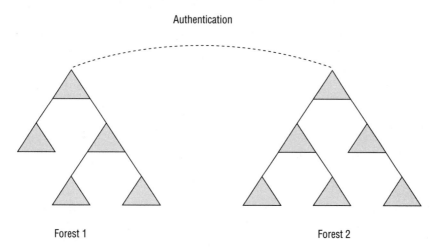

In *selective authentication*, users are not allowed to authenticate to a specific domain controller unless an administrator has specifically authorized this. The usefulness of this is that it keeps users from wandering into places that they aren't supposed to be and, well, messing things up. So, for instance, in our example, MyCorp could authenticate to Mega-Corp's resources through a selective trust that allows users only in an individual domain (say Tokyo) to access resources in the MegaCorp forest. Otherwise, the users would be denied. By doing this, we tighten up security and make sure there aren't any authentication leaks. It's a good security practice and usually required by most enterprises.

Trust Scopes

Trusts are said to either be *intraforest*, meaning that the trust exists solely in its own self-contained forest, or *interforest*, meaning the trust extends between two different forests. Within an intraforest trust, you will normally see the following types of trusts being utilized:

- Tree-root
- Parent-child
- Shortcut

This is because, by default, a two-way transitive relationship exists between the tree and root and accordingly between parent-child domains. Shortcut trusts are most usually seen on the intraforest level because they can remove a burden from machines higher up in the forest structure and can instead invalidate each other. It's like being in a classroom and giving two students permission to grade each other's homework. It's a shortcut, because they'll get it done more quickly than you will, plus it removes a burden from the teacher.

On the interforest trust level, you'll usually see only two types of trusts:

- Forest trusts
- External trusts

Using a little logic, you can see that this is because if two forests are to trust one another, they will need to have an external trust. Note that in an external trust, the legacy domain is not considered part of the live and active portion of Active Directory. Instead, it's considered an outside source.

 Real World Scenario

Establishing Forest Trusts Between Businesses

MyCorp, a small corporation based in the Midwest, is a manufacturer of combines and farm equipment that has been in business for more than 100 years. In the early days of MyCorp, its engineers designed steam-powered combines and tractors, and it has a great legacy of quality products and services. Accordingly, in the early 2000s, MyCorp purchased a small farm of Windows 2000 Server domain controllers to administer all of its 200 employees and dozens of printers and other pieces of hardware.

Now, for the first time, MyCorp has been entertaining the idea of a purchase offer made from MegaCorp. If the transaction were to go through, MegaCorp, as the owner, would let MyCorp operate as it has done for the past 100 years. However, MegaCorp needs an elegant way to allow the MyCorp users to access a specific domain within MegaCorp's pure Windows Server 2008 Active Directory forest, which is based in Los Angeles.

In the real world, Windows Server 2008 offers a few very elegant situations that would allow you to resolve this issue without a lot of excessive complexity. You could solve this either by migrating the users to the MegaCorp domain, where they could log in remotely and access the domain, or by using an Active Directory trust.

Because elegance is the goal and because MyCorp and MegaCorp have effectively merged, the most elegant solution you could implement is a forest trust. Specifically, you could establish a shortcut trust originating from the target domain to the MyCorp forest. The only decision beyond that point is whether you want the forest to be one-way or two-way. Obviously, both have advantages. But most likely, you'll want the trust to be one-way. This is because MyCorp is staying relatively independent in operation from MegaCorp but needs access to MegaCorp files. MegaCorp doesn't necessarily need access to MyCorp files; at the end of the day, MegaCorp just cares about the financial end of the business. Therefore, you need to implement a one-way forest trust between MegaCorp and MyCorp.

Trust Tools

When administering trusts, you have several tools available to you to make the process a lot simpler and more expedient. One of the best resources is a command-line tool called nltest, which lets you do the following five things that are documented on Microsoft TechNet:

- Get a list of domain controllers

- Force a remote shutdown

- Query the status of trust

- Test trust relationships and the state of domain controller replication in a Windows domain

- Force a user account database to synchronize on Windows NT 4.0 or earlier domain controllers

 Trusts make active use of SIDs, security tokens, and access lists to determine authentication and authorization decisions.

In Exercise 3.3, you'll create a forest trust between two different forests using the tools available to you through the Windows Server 2008 trust wizards. Using this, you can connect two different forests to share resources.

EXERCISE 3.3

Creating a Forest Trust

Prerequisites: To perform this exercise, you must first have two servers running Windows Server 2008 that have been elevated to domain controllers in their own respective forests. In this exercise, there are two forests with their root domains named domain.com and domain2.com. For this exercise, you will be executing the commands from the domain.com domain.

1. Make sure you are logged in as either a domain or enterprise administrator.

2. Access the DNS manager by selecting Start ➢ Administrative Tools ➢ DNS.

3. Expand your DNS server, and select Conditional Forwarders.

4. Right-click the whitespace to the right, and select New Conditional Forwarder. It will open the dialog box shown here.

EXERCISE 3.3   *(continued)*

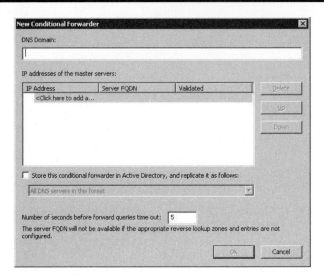

5. In the DNS Domain field, type **domain2.com**.

6. Select the Click Here To Add An IP Address Or DNS Name text, and enter the IP address of the domain2.com server.

7. Select Store This Conditional Forward In Active Directory.... Also ensure that All DNS Servers In This Forest is selected.

8. Click OK.

9. Repeat this process on the domain2.com, but point the DNS conditional forwarder to the domain.com domain.

10. Open the Active Directory Domains And Trusts tool by selecting Administrative Tools ➢ Active Directory Domains And Trusts.

11. Right-click domain.com, and select Properties.

EXERCISE 3.3 *(continued)*

12. Select the Trusts tab, as shown here.

13. Select New Trust, and then click Next. Enter **domain2.com** in the Name box.

14. Select the Forest Trust radio button, and then click Next.

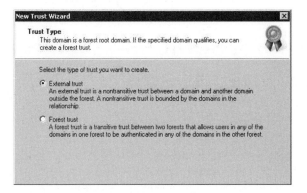

15. Select Two-Way, because this will be a two-way trust.

16. When the next screen appears, select the Both This Domain And The Specified Domain radio button. This will allow you to create the trust on both the domain.com domain and the domain2.com domain, which means you don't have to repeat the process. Afterward, click Next.

EXERCISE 3.3   *(continued)*

17. When prompted for credentials, enter the username and password of an account on the domain2.com server that is authorized to create a trust. A safe bet is an account in the enterprise administrator group.

18. Select the Forestwide Authentication button when asked about policies in the *target* forest, and then click Next. Alternatively, at this point you can select individual access to each domain and server that you want to make available with the Selective Authentication button.

19. Select the Forestwide Authentication button when asked about policies in the *local* forest, and then click Next. Alternatively, at this point you can select individual access to each domain and server that you want to make available with the Selective Authentication button.

20. Click Next on the summary screen.

21. Click Next on the confirmation screen.

22. On the next two screens, select the radio buttons to confirm the forest trust, and then click Finish.

23. You can test your forest trust by accessing the Active Directory Domains And Trusts tool once again, right-clicking the Active Directory Domains And Trusts section above the domain.com name, and selecting Change Forest. Then, enter the **domain2.com** domain name, and you will see the domains swap. It's a very rewarding feeling.

Planning for Upgrades in an Existing Forest

Most of the time, whenever you are trying to upgrade a server farm from one version of Windows to another, you're trying to upgrade within the same forest and more than likely within the same domain. Accordingly, you first have to remember the basic and essential commands to upgrade a domain controller, prep a domain, prep a forest, and prep an environment for a Windows Server 2008 read-only domain controller (RODC). In the following sections, you will examine these processes one at a time, beginning with the forest-level and domain-level prep commands.

Forest and Domain Preparation

> Both adprep /forestprep and adprep /domainprep require you to be logged in as an enterprise administrator.

adprep /forestprep   This command is used when first setting up an Active Directory forest for Windows Server 2008. This command prepares Active Directory to receive Windows Server 2008 from any version of Windows Server that supports Active Directory (Windows 2000 Server and newer). This command needs to be given only once for the entire forest. Afterward, you can go to the individual domains of your enterprise.

adprep /domainprep   By invoking this command, you are telling a domain within Active Directory that it needs to prepare itself for Windows Server 2008. According to Microsoft, this "prepares the domain for upgrade and adds inheritable access control entries (ACEs) to the Group Policy objects (GPOs) in the SYSVOL shared folder, which causes domainwide replication to occur." In other words, the individual domain is prepared for the impact and changes within Active Directory and Group Policy so that it isn't surprised by anything Windows Server 2008 may request.

In addition to the standard adprep /domainprep command, you may encounter an environment that is still running Windows 2000 Server. If that is the case, you will need to prepare the Windows 2000 Server environment for the accompanying Group Policy changes that occurred in Windows Server 2003 and Windows Server 2003. You do this by appending the **/gpprep** switch to the standard adprep /domainprep command, like this: adprep /domainprep /gpprep.

Preparing for a Read-Only Domain Controller

As we referenced earlier in this book, the first step in preparing for a read-only domain controller is to make certain that your domain and forest functional levels are operating at Windows Server 2003 or later. If this is not the case, the environment will not be prepared to receive a read-only domain controller, and it will be unrecognized upon connection. Furthermore, to use a Windows Server 2008 RODC, you must have a writable domain controller of Windows Server 2008 already running within the environment, that is, at the very least, connected by a site link. This is because in order to replicate information, the RODC will need to be fed from a preexistent domain controller with its native version of Windows.

> If your domain and forest don't match the appropriate level, you will need to run adprep /forestprep and adprep /domainprep before you install an RODC.

Once these prerequisites have been met, your environment will be prepared to accept a Windows Server 2008 RODC. However, to make any environment completely ready to take an RODC, you will need to execute the following command on the schema master: adprep /rodcprep. This will tell the schema master to look for an RODC and to expect that domain controller to not be writable. Afterward, on the installation level, you can install either an RODC as a normal RODC or an RODC running Windows Server Core. In Exercise 3.4, we show you the process of installing an RODC on a full installation of Microsoft Windows. The advantage of using Server Core is that the installation is light, efficient, and very stable. Administrators may choose to use a Server Core installation of an RODC if they're running in an insecure location that will not be accessed very often. That way, the server has an extremely light load and is running the bare essentials necessary to accomplish the task at hand.

EXERCISE 3.4

Installing an RODC

Prerequisites: To perform this exercise, you must have at least one Windows Server 2008 machine operating at the Windows Server 2003 domain and forest functional level. Additionally, you must have at least one writable domain controller operating Windows Server 2008 in your environment.

1. Make sure you are logged in as either a domain or enterprise administrator.

2. Open the command-line console on the Windows Server 2008 domain controller, and initiate the adprep /rodcprep command. (You must run this with enterprise administrator credentials.) Alternatively, you may log on to any given domain controller in the environment as long as you initiate the command from the source files on the Windows Server 2008 DVD.

3. Click Start, type **dcpromo** into the Search box, and then press Enter. This will begin the Active Directory Domain Services Installation Wizard.

4. Select Existing Forest and then Add A Domain Controller To An Existing Domain. Then click Next.

5. On the Network Credentials page, type the name of your domain and any usernames or passwords that are required for the Domain Admins group. Click Next.

6. Select the domain for the RODC, and then click Next.

7. Select the Active Directory site where you want to install your read-only domain controller, and then click Next.

8. On the next page, make sure you select the DNS Server checkbox as well as the Read-Only Domain Controller checkbox. Although it is not required, you should probably also make this machine a global catalog server. Click Next.

9. Reboot your new read-only domain controller.

Preparing for a Server Core Installation

If you are considering upgrading from an older version of Windows Server to Windows Server 2008 in any environment, you should consider whether it makes sense to implement a Server Core installation. Windows Server Core is a lightweight, minimalist installation of Windows Server 2008 that doesn't carry as many features and capabilities as a very robust, powerful generalized installation of Windows Server 2008. Basically, the idea behind the Windows Server Core installation is to create a server that is stable and lightweight and that serves a few dedicated purposes that don't tend to change very often.

Windows Server 2008 Server Core doesn't even have a graphical user interface. All the Server Core installations come by default with as few options enabled as possible. To use more features, you have to externally reference remotable MMCs, either through another Windows Server machine or through Microsoft Windows Vista. At the enterprise level, you can take great advantage of this installation capability. In earlier exams, such as the MCTS level, you may have learned about Server Core briefly. You may have installed it once, and you may be familiar with some of its most basic features. However, you most likely haven't considered the drastically impressive advantages that this server can provide. Consider a scenario in which you have a complex environment that has seven sites, six of which are branch offices that have employees who need to use Windows Server to log on to the network in order to access the Internet.

Without Windows Server Core, in this enterprise environment you as an administrator would need, at the very minimum, to be operating seven full-blown installations of Windows Server—one in each of these locations. If you think of it like a computer scientist, that's a lot of unnecessary extra data floating around. And remember, although some new features may become available and some new technologies may slowly begin to be adopted by the rest of the world, the number-one rule of the enterprise is to make it work and keep it simple. Windows Server Core installations do exactly that.

In this example, you could easily reduce the overall server load, hardware requirements, and complexity of your network by maintaining a full installation of Windows Server 2008 at the main office and then installing a Server Core installation in each one of the branch offices. It would keep the brass happy because the servers will still work and work well. And it keeps the administrators happy because there is less of a chance that something can go wrong.

In both my opinion and Microsoft's, Windows Server Core installation was *born* to be used in branch offices. It just fits! When you're considering an installation in the real world (or that you may see on an exam), remember that.

Windows Server Core does not support managed code, and the .NET Framework is not present. Even more important, PowerShell is not available in Windows Server Core. But in truth, although it may not be a "hot item" on the MCITP level exam, you should really know how to install a Windows Server 2008 Server Core installation and incorporate Active Directory domain services while joining a domain, which you'll do in Exercise 3.5.

EXERCISE 3.5

Installing Server Core and Joining It to a Domain

Prerequisites: Installing Server Core starts off as simply as an installation of any other version of Windows Server 2008. You can begin the process either by placing the Windows Server 2008 DVD into the drive and booting from the disk or by placing the disk into a machine with a previously running version of Windows and beginning the installation from that point. For the purposes of this exercise, it is assumed you have gone through the install GUI and are now staring at the default Server Core installation, which appears similar to the image here.

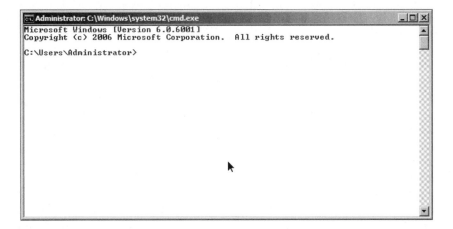

1. At the command prompt, type `Netsh interface ipv4 show interfaces`. This opens a listing of network adapters, each of which will have an identification number labeled in a column called Idx. Since our goal here is to assign an IPv4 address, you can ignore the default pseudo-IPv6 address and get the ID from the local interface, which is usually 2.

2. Next, type `Netsh interface ipv4 set address name=<idx number> source=static address= <A static IP address you would like to assign> mask=<Subnet Mask> gateway=<Default Gateway IP Address>`. This assigns an IP address so that this server has a static address that can be used for the purposes of Active Directory or domain services.

3. Once you've assigned an IP address to your Server Core server, you need to give it the DNS address of your main domain server. You can do this by again issuing the `netsh interface` command and appending the dnsserver field by typing `Netsh interface ipv4 add dnsserver name=<idx number> address=<dns server address> index=1`. This will add a DNS server to the Server Core installation.

4. And now, assuming that everything proceeded correctly and your computer is connected to the Internet, you should be able to ping an address such as Sybex.com from the command prompt using the ping command.

Note that, should you want, you can add DNS servers by increasing the index number incrementally for each additional address. For example, you could enter the command again with another IP address and increase the index value by 1 to 2.

5. To join the domain, type **netdom join** *<Name of computer you wish to join>* **/domain:**<*The Name of your Domain>* **/userd:**<*A Domain User that can add servers to the domain>* **/passwordd:***. (Note: The second d in passwordd is required.)

6. Restart the computer by executing the **shutdown /r /t 0** command.

Once this command is executed and the machine reboots, you can install various other roles and features to your specific needs.

Planning for Reduction

Surprisingly, and more often than not, one of the biggest processes in "upgrading" an enterprise to Windows Server 2008 is actually downgrading—well, at least downgrading the sheer number of servers. The reason behind this is that the overarching trend in the IT industry is consolidation—consolidation in terms of number of servers, consolidation in terms of roles of servers, and even consolidation in the virtualization of servers. Most of the time, this is because businesses just want their infrastructure to work and to work simply.

Consider that in the era of Windows 2000 Server, the average amount of available RAM was somewhere around 256MB. In Windows Server 2008, it's rare to find a server that doesn't have at least 2GB of RAM. And that's on the small side! We frequently see servers with 4GB, 8GB, and even 16GB of RAM just hungry and read for multitasking. And that's somewhere from 20 to 60 times the amount of memory that's available now per server.

Accordingly, when you're reviewing a campus for upgrades, keep in mind that it may very well suit the enterprise to not do any upgrading at all. Instead, it may make sense to downgrade to something more manageable.

Maintaining Connectivity

Whenever you think about the word *reduction*, the instant next thought in your mind should be this: "Will my reduction compromise my connectivity?" At the professional level, as we discussed in Chapter 1, it's pretty rare that you will find a single-domain or even single-forest architecture. Most companies have various branches, sister businesses, or completely separate aspects of their company that are divided across a purposefully created line.

Thus, whenever you encounter a fairly complex infrastructure, you need to look to see whether there are forests that are maintained by WAN links, or domains connected through sites by WAN links, and see whether your reduction or consolidation will interrupt or possibly compromise their connectivity issues. Consider Figure 3.10, where there are three forests that contain three child domains each. If you were to, say, decide to consolidate these into a single forest with a single domain, you would have a problem in that there are several servers still connected by WAN links. And, should a WAN link go down, it's possible that one of the servers may not communicate with another. Just imagine Joe or Jane User, on their first day at the job in the remote office, not being able to get any work done because the server in the branch office doesn't have connectivity to the root domain to receive new account updates from the global catalog.

FIGURE 3.10   Three forests connected by wide-area links

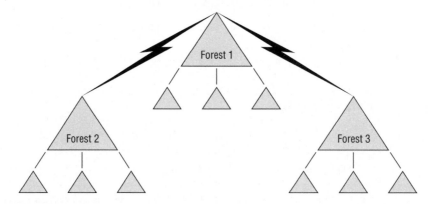

In the case of Figure 3.10, a much more elegant solution if you wanted to reduce the number of domains would be to reduce the number of child domains in each forest and instead maintain the three individual forests and allow each to keep its own Active Directory infrastructure. That way, if one of the WAN links fails, users can still log on to their computers and continue their work.

Adding Windows Server 2008 into a Live Environment

When you decide to place Windows Server 2008 into your existing environment, you're making one of two decisions concerning the overall infrastructure. You are deciding whether you want to directly upgrade a server to Windows Server 2008, and you are deciding whether you want to add a server in a pre–Windows 2008 environment; and, in some cases, you are deciding both.

In the first case—placing Windows Server 2008 within a preexisting Windows infrastructure—you really have only one option. You can directly upgrade to Windows Server 2008 only if the servers that you are upgrading are currently running Windows Server 2003. Windows 2000 Server does not support a direct upgrade path.

You can, of course, add a Windows Server 2008 to any Windows 2000 Server or Windows Server 2003 environment and use it as an additional domain controller. However, you will need to use the previously referenced `adprep` command to prepare the forest. To do so properly, you'd need to take the proper files from your Windows Server 2008 DVD and place them onto the Windows 2000 Server domain controller or the Windows Server 2003 domain controller so that it understand the most recent version of the command. Then, after you have run this command, you can easily place the new server into your environment.

But in some situations, neither of these solutions will suffice. Say, for instance, you are operating a Windows 2000 domain controller in a Windows 2000 native domain and forest mode. If you want to upgrade this forest to Windows Server 2008 with a Windows Server 2008 domain controller, the process is slightly more complicated. Because there is no direct upgrade path, you must instead do the following:

1. Run the `adprep` command from your domain controller armed with the latest Windows Server 2008 files to prepare the environment.

2. Install a new domain controller into the infrastructure.

3. Create a new DNS Active Directory–integrated server on the Windows Server 2008 machine.

4. Transfer the DNS from Windows 2000 Server to Windows Server 2008.

5. Transfer the appropriate masters from the Windows 2000 domain controller to the Windows Server 2008 domain controller.

6. Add the global catalog option to the Windows Server 2008 machine.

7. Demote the Windows 2000 Server, and then remove it completely.

8. Change the appropriate address and name of the Windows Server 2008 machine, and then reboot the domain controller.

9. Upgrade the functional level of the domain or forest if desired.

Summary

The process of upgrading and migrating is like most things involving the Windows world. It is complicated in explanation but relatively simple in practice. When you're thinking about migrating, remember that there are no direct upgrade paths between any version of Windows without Active Directory and Windows Server 2008. Furthermore, you need to remember the steps involved with upgrading a machine from Windows 2000 Server to Windows Server 2008.

But most important, you need to be familiar with using the Active Directory Migration Tool. The best way to do that is to follow the exercises in this book and to play with the ADMT on your own. Setting up a home lab is a very good idea. Or, if you don't have a home lab, running practical exercises at your office may be advisable. But don't make any changes that you can't undo, and never experiment on a production environment—that could be catastrophic.

Beyond migrating, one of the pillars of this exam is understanding trusts in all of their complexity. Unless you've built, used, and experimented with trusts heavily, the exam will probably confuse you. A full understanding of trusts is also required for your job when you actually become the person who this exam and technology was designed for: an enterprise administrator. As referenced earlier, it's rare that you'll run across a one-domain, or even one-forest, architecture. Currently, infrastructures are complex animals and require a great amount of due care and due diligence. Make sure that before you attempt these in the real world that you've mastered them in your own lab—your employers and fellow employees will thank you.

Exam Essentials

Know trusts like the back of your hand.   Trusts play a tremendous factor in the exam. You need to be able to spout off the advantages of different types of trusts and show where they belong in the infrastructure and how they should be implemented.

Understand the limits and advantages of migration.   Migration can't solve everything. You need to be familiar with what you can and cannot do with migration, as well as the procedure for doing it. Practice migrating several user accounts and groups between your domain controllers before you take the exam.

Know where, when, and how to use the Active Directory Migration Tool.   This is probably the most important point in this chapter to remember for the exam. Know how to use the ADMT and where you need to be to acquire your source and target domains. You can't just run the ADMT from anywhere.

Be aware of the limits of an RODC.   RODCs need to be installed where they have access to a writable domain controller running Windows Server 2008 that also has access to an infrastructure running at least Windows Server 2003 forest and domain functional levels.

Know where to place RODCs and Server Core installations.   Remember to place RODCs where you have access to a writable domain controller and in branch offices; they're built for it. On Server Core installations, you can place these where you have need for a low-intensity, long-life box that won't need access to advanced features such as PowerShell.

Review Questions

1. When upgrading and consolidating an environment consisting of servers using Windows 2000 Server and Windows Server 2003 to a Windows Server 2008 environment, the Active Directory Migration Tool will play a major role. Because you have many different versions of Windows available, which version of the ADMT will you need to use on Windows Server 2008 to consolidate?

   A. 3.0

   B. 3.1

   C. 3.2

   D. 2.0

2. If a trust needs to exist between two Active Directory forests, MegaCorp and MyCorp, and each of these forests requires access to one another's resources, along with all of their child domains, what type of trust needs to be established in order to ensure this type of connectivity?

   A. Two-way transitive forest trust

   B. Two one-way transitive forest trusts

   C. Shortcut trust between root domains

   D. Two-way nontransitive trust

3. OmniCorp, a major provider of consulting services to *Fortune 500* companies and small businesses alike, is a highly complex business that has many different deliverable requirements. Among these requirements are that consultants be familiar with the Windows architecture and with Unix administration. Accordingly, OmniCorp has set up several test domains within an expansive forest to provide remote consulting services. As a new Windows administrator, you have been asked to set up a new Unix server in your environment that can integrate smoothly into a preexisting Windows forest. Given what you know of Windows architecture, what would be an advisable forest trust type?

   A. Shortcut

   B. One-way

   C. Two-way

   D. Realm

   E. External

4. When migrating resources from the SuperCorp forest to the MegaCorp forest, you will need to make use of the Active Directory Migration Tool. From which location would you need to execute it?

   A. A server in the SuperCorp forest

   B. A server in the MegaCorp forest

   C. Any server in either forest

   D. A server in the SuperCorp forest and then a server in the MegaCorp forest

5. When designing your Active Directory environment, you see that it would be a good idea to implement a very secure structure because of the possibility of domain controllers being compromised. Accordingly, you have decided to implement read-only domain controllers. Given that your company has one main office and three branch offices, what would be the best location in which to implement your RODCs?

    A. The main office.

    B. The branch offices.

    C. The main office and the branch offices.

    D. RODCs are not recommended.

6. Within an intraforest relationship, trusts are automatically established between all but which of the following?

    A. Tree-root

    B. Parent-child

    C. Shortcut

    D. Internal-external

7. As a new administrator in your corporation, you have been put in charge of an individual domain deeply embedded within the overall infrastructure. Today you have been informed by your supervisor that your newly install domain will need to access resources within the resource.corporation.com domain, which is located in the logically opposite side of the forest. To bypass the need to traverse up and down the forest architecture, what type of trust could you establish between your new domain and the resource.corporation.com domain?

    A. External

    B. Realm

    C. Transitive

    D. Shortcut

8. Of the following versions of Windows, which do *not* support a direct upgrade path to Windows Server 2008 with Active Directory Domain Services? (Choose all that apply.)

    A. Windows NT 4

    B. Windows 2000 Server

    C. Windows Server 2003

    D. Windows Vista

9. With the Microsoft ADMT, a number of options are available by default within the wizard when you are initializing the process of migration from one platform to another. Which of the following choices is *not* one of those default options?

    A. User Account Migration

    B. Group Account Migration

    C. Computer Migration

    D. Reporting Migration

10. When migrating between versions of Windows Server, the process of eliminating child domains and placing their resources into top-level domains is known as what?

    A. Restructuring

    B. Processing

    C. Consolidating

    D. Alleviating

11. When migrating accounts between two different servers, what four pieces of information *must* be provided? (Choose four.)

    A. Source forest name

    B. Target forest name

    C. Source domain name

    D. Target domain name

    E. Source domain controller name

    F. Target domain controller name

    G. Source member server name

    H. Target member server name

12. The migration process that involves changing the composition of a forest is referred to as what?

    A. Domain consolidation

    B. Domain restructure

    C. Domain upgrade

    D. Domain refinement

13. Which of the following cannot be migrated as an object?

    A. User accounts

    B. Service accounts

    C. Groups

    D. Domains

    E. Computers

14. Which of the following are required to run ADMT version 3.1? (Choose all that apply.)

    A. Windows Server 2003

    B. Windows Server 2008

    C. AD DS

    D. AD FS

    E. SQL Server 2000/2005

    F. IIS

15. As a senior administrator for the MyCorp corporation, you are in charge of maintaining the reliability of all versions of the MyCorp infrastructure, which is extremely vast and has been existence since the early 1990s. Because of this, MyCorp has several preexisting domains that are operating early versions of Windows NT. These versions of Windows will need to associate within their respective forests, and therefore a trust will need to be established between the two. From what you know of trusts, which of the following types would be appropriate?

   A. Shortcut

   B. Forest

   C. Realm

   D. External

   E. One-way

16. When using a Windows 2008 Server Core installation, some of the options normally associated with Windows Server are not available. Of the following listed services, which is not available with Windows 2008 Server Core?

   A. AD DS

   B. AD FS

   C. IIS

   D. Windows SharePoint

   E. PowerShell

17. If you are trying to test the number of domain controllers and status of a trust in your forest, which command-line tool(s) could you take advantage of? Choose all that apply.

   A. nltest

   B. repadmin

   C. replmon

   D. ipconfig

   E. adprep

   F. gpresult

18. Migration from Windows Server 2003 to Windows Server 2008 is a fairly complex process. When transitioning between platforms, often administrators deal with password-related problems. Among the aspects of password aspects you can change when migrating between these two versions of Windows, which feature is not available unless specifically installed on the Windows Server 2008 destination platform?

   A. New password policies

   B. Simple migration

   C. "No update" password migration

   D. Fine-grained password policies

19. Which of the following options is not embedded within the SID of a user account object that you might need when migrating between Windows versions?

   A. Username

   B. Password

   C. Domain

   D. Group policies

20. When upgrading your environment to Windows Server 2008 from any version of Windows Server that supports Active Directory, what is the first command-line option that should be initiated?

   A. adprep /rodcprep

   B. adprep /forestprep

   C. adprep /domainprep

   D. adprep /forestprep /gpprep

Answers to Review Questions

1. B. When consolidating any given number of servers running Windows 2000 Server or Windows Server 2003, you will need to run the ADMT on Windows Server 2008, and thus you will be forced to use version 3.1 (or 31 depending on documentation). It is the only version of the ADMT that is compatible with Windows Server 2008.

2. A. Whenever you need to establish a trust that will both share resources and provide connectivity between two different forests, a forest trust will need to be established. By making this trust transitive, you will ensure that there are no communication problems between any of the other domains and will make everything function much more smoothly, given the requirements of the question.

3. D. Realm trusts are designed to ensure the easy connectivity of Unix servers to Windows infrastructures. By creating a realm trust, you are telling the Windows infrastructure to be looking for a different set of communication protocols. Furthermore, you are preparing the environment for a new server that other users will be able to access in the future.

4. B. Whenever you are moving resources from one domain to another or one forest to another, you must execute the ADMT from the destination area. This is because the ADMT works in a seizure-like method. First you must instantiate it, and then you must pick where the resources you want to acquire or migrate are located.

5. B. In a complex environment that spans several locations, the best location for an RODC is in branch locations that are either remote or isolated. By locating the RODC there, you ensure that your most compromised locations are secured. Furthermore, to implement an RODC, you must have at least one writable domain controller. Therefore, implementing it at all locations would not be feasible.

6. D. An external trust is considered an interforest trust, rather than an intraforest trust. This is because the relationship between NT domains that existed before Active Directory is considered to be a nearly completely foreign relationship, and therefore a trust is not established at the intraforest level.

7. D. A shortcut trust can directly connect two domains so that they can share each other's resources without having to traverse up and down the forest hierarchy.

8. A, B, D. Windows NT, Windows Vista, and Windows 2000 Server cannot be directly upgraded to Windows Server 2008 with Active Directory Domain Services. However, with some effort, Windows 2000 Server can be transitioned to Windows Server 2008.

9. D. Reporting is an option in the wizard, but it is just listed as the Reporting Wizard, not "Reporting Migration."

10. C. Consolidating involves the process of reducing the overall number of domains by moving their resources from one location to another and then removing either the extra servers or the child domains. Restructuring, however, involves the process of changing the overall forest or domain architecture to serve other purposes in the infrastructure.

11. C, D, E, F. When transferring information between two domains, you must have both the name of the target and source domain, as well as the names of the domain controllers associated with each. The forest name and member server names are not required.

12. B. According to Microsoft, domain restructuring is the process that involves changing the domain structure of a forest. Additionally, Microsoft says that a domain restructure can involve either consolidating or adding domains; thus, this can be sort of confusing when combined. To remember the difference, just keep in mind that the overall structure of the forest changing is the process of restructuring.

13. D. Although domains themselves can have aspects that may be migrated or accordingly placed into consolidation, they cannot be purely migrated as objects.

14. B, E. To run ADMT version 3.1, you must be running both a version of Windows Server 2008 (any edition) and any edition of SQL Server 2000 or 2005, including SQL Server Express Edition.

15. D. An external trust is associated with versions of Windows that predate Active Directory. To establish a connection between an outdated version of Windows and a version of Windows Server with Active Directory, an external trust needs to be formed.

16. E. In Windows Server 2008 Server Core installations, PowerShell is not available. Should an installation require PowerShell, you must install the full version of Windows Server 2008.

17. A. `Nltest` is a command designed to query trusts, find the number of domain controllers, and generally troubleshoot trusts and problems associated with authentication.

18. D. Fine-grained password policies is a feature available only with Windows Server 2008. Other than fine-grained password policies, administrators have the option to simply migrate passwords, create new policies, or choose to have freshly migrated accounts not update password information.

19. D. User account objects in ADMT have a page that displays the username, an option to change the password, and the associated domain the user account exists within. When migrating, administrators may need this information to make a proper migration decision.

20. B. Before you install Windows Server 2008, you must first prep the entire forest and then prep the domain to which you are installing the Windows Server 2008 computer.

Chapter

4

Planning for Terminal Services and Application Virtualization

OBJECTIVES COVERED IN THIS CHAPTER:

✓ **Plan for Terminal Services.**

- ▪ May include but is not limited to: Terminal Services licensing, Terminal Services infrastructure

✓ **Plan for application delivery.**

- ▪ May include but is not limited to: application virtualization, presentation virtualization, locally installed software, Web-based applications

In reference to an enterprise, "planning for Terminal Services" refers to the process of ensuring the accessibility and availability of virtualized applications on Windows Server 2008, all the way from simple Remote Desktop connections to highly available and highly scalable applications. Furthermore, on the enterprise level you are also concerned with the licensing of these applications. You do this through the distribution of licenses prepurchased from Microsoft for particular applications that are necessary throughout your infrastructure. In this chapter, I will briefly review the components, features, and aspects of Terminal Services and then discuss a strategy for implementing and designing a virtualization solution for your enterprise.

Reviewing Terminal Services' Roles

Although you've most likely seen all these components on your 70-643 exam, before you jump into planning, design, and licensing strategies for a Windows enterprise, it's a good idea to review these components in case you haven't used any of them in a while. Understanding how to deploy a complex Terminal Services (TS) infrastructure or licensing scheme requires that you intimately understand each of these components and their various purposes.

Throughout this chapter, I will use the terms TS and Terminal Services interchangeably.

These are the components:

Terminal Server   Enables a Windows Server 2008–based computer to host Windows-based applications through Terminal Services.

Terminal Services Web Access   Lets users use RemoteApp programs and Remote Desktop connections through the Internet

Terminal Services Gateway   Allows users to connect to internal servers running remote applications via an Internet device that can run Remote Desktop connections

Terminal Services Licensing   Maintains client access licenses for users of devices

Terminal Services Session Broker   Provides load balancing for Terminal Services in an enterprise

Terminal Services Server Load

One of the most convenient and useful features of Terminal Services is that it puts an extraordinarily light load on the server. As of this writing, Microsoft has not released a prescribed load for applying Terminal Services throughout a given enterprise. However, two tried and true methods for determining server load have existed since the release of

Terminal Services and (for that matter) have been in release since most computers were first functioning. Those two methods are experimentation and extrapolation. For particulars on using Roboserver and Roboclient, check `Microsoft.com`; the Enterprise Administrator exam will not test you on the particulars, so I will not discuss them here as to ease the burden of information.

When using *experimentation*, you take an existing server, give it a full test load of various applications, and place it under heavy use with various users requesting different applications at once. The information you derive from this experiment lets you determine where your Terminal Services server needs to be placed and what kind of hardware it will require. To aid in this process, when Microsoft released the Windows Server Deployment Kit, it included two useful tools: Roboserver (`Robosrv.exe`) and Roboclient (`Robocli.exe`). Using these tools, an administrator can place a heavy server load without having to go through the process of creating a custom load from scratch.

With *extrapolation*, you examine a previously existing instance of Terminal Services and plan accordingly based on the overall deployment needs of your organization. For example, if you have a currently running server with 10 users that is at maximum capacity (which, by the way, is pretty unlikely), you would extrapolate from that existing load that an organization that has 1000 users will require 100 servers to reach capacity.

In both methods, you are primarily concerned with the following:

- Network load
- Processor overhead
- Memory use
- Disk usage

If any one of these server requirements becomes a bottleneck, you will have to adjust your server deployment method and hardware accordingly.

Terminal Services Licensing

As mentioned earlier, one of the most important managerial processes in a complex network is making sure you have the right number of licenses—distributed in the right way, at the right time—in your Windows Server 2008 infrastructure. When using Terminal Services, users are required to have Terminal Services client access licenses (TS CALs). *Client access licenses* are licenses designated to a specific server that enable the authorization of applications through Terminal Services. By default, client access licenses are available free of charge for 120 days. This means that when first installing Terminal Services, you will not have to authorize every single account.

 Without Terminal Services, a maximum of two Remote Desktop users may log on to a Windows Server.

Licensing Types

One of the new features of Windows Server 2008 is a scheme of licensing that was unavailable in Windows Server 2003 or any previous iteration of Terminal Services on the Windows platform. Now, administrators can implement their licenses either per user or per device.

Per device   When using *per-device licensing*, a device is issued a temporary license the first time it connects. Afterward, when connecting for the second time, the device is issued a permanent CAL.

Per user   When using the new *per-user service*, Active Directory is queried to see whether an individual user has a CAL. If that user has such a license, the user is allowed to access any device or application requiring Terminal Services in the entire network. Note, however, that this is not enforced by Terminal Services Licensing. Therefore, it is fairly easy to accidentally violate Microsoft's terms of agreement when using this method, which can be bad for your business.

Licensing Scope

Within Windows Server 2008, administrators have the option of deciding how they want to implement their licensing authentication based on the overall design of their network. One of the options available to administrators pertains to the licensing scope. *Licensing scope* refers to which users are able to access which server based on their location within the network infrastructure. Within Windows Server 2008, there are three different scope levels:

- Workgroup
- Domain
- Forest

Scope levels allow computers on the same domain, workgroup, or forest to authenticate to their individual licensing server based on their location. Thus, at the workgroup level, computers in the same workgroup will be able to access the licensing server; at the domain level, computers within the same domain can access it, and so forth. In the internal documentation of Windows Server 2008, Microsoft recommends setting the default licensing server scope to Forest because licensing is a fairly lightweight service and because it is helpful to have a centralized place that all computers can access.

Another important point to note about Terminal Services Licensing is that any computer that has Terminal Services Licensing installed will be exempt from scope-level authentication because the computer can validate itself.

    Forest-level scope is always recommended, but it requires that a machine be a member of a forest. Similarly, workgroup-level scope is available only if a machine is part of a workgroup.

Licensing Process for Terminal Services

Just like Dynamic Host Control Protocol (DHCP), the licensing process for Terminal Services uses a unique and definite series of steps to configure itself based on its preferred priority of available information:

1. Computers in your network will check Group Policy and the Terminal Services configuration tool to see whether there is an available license server integrated within the network. If so, they will prefer that server over any other because of the nature of Group Policy.

2. A machine will check to see whether it itself is the licensing server and, if so, authenticate itself.

3. The server will check whether Active Directory has had a licensing server integrated with it. Using Active Directory's discovery methods, it will then choose that licensing server.

4. If no other server is available, the host will do the next logical thing and query the domain controller.

5. If no licensing service is found there, the domain controller will return a negative response, and the host will then stand by until otherwise notified.

Licensing Server Placement

Finally! We're now getting down to something a bit more interesting—server placement. The placement of a Terminal Services server takes a lot of thought. This is what most of your job as an administrator is going to be about. (It is also heavily tested on the exam.) Luckily for you, Microsoft has outlined a set of steps for placing a licensing server that you can follow to ensure the best possible results for your enterprise:

1. Determine the demand on the licensing server.

    This step involves taking a critical look at your server (or servers) and realizing how much of a load each of them is going to be enduring. Unfortunately, as of this writing, Microsoft has yet to release a predefined set of server requirements based on server load. However, the good news is that Terminal Services Licensing isn't a very demanding role, and thus it probably won't take too much of a load.

    However, if you are running an extremely busy network infrastructure, you can suffice by monitoring the performance of your various components and using capacity tools like `Robosrv.exe` and `Roboclient.exe` to find the best solution for your licensing server needs.

2. Determine the number of servers required.

    Once you've established how many users each server can support, you can divide the total number of users by the number of maximum-supported users and find the number of users you require.

3. Decide whether the server(s) that host TS Licensing can be shared. Essentially, a server can be shared either between farms or between services. This means if you have multiple farms, you can choose to use one or multiple licensing servers to lessen the burden of the role on other servers and keep them concentrated on the role they're already using. Additionally, you need to decide whether you want your licensing server to be dedicated or instead to host additional Terminal Services servers.

4. Determine where to place the TS Licensing role in the network. Ideally, the best place to put your licensing server is on a LAN where every computer can easily and quickly access it. However, if your organization is separated by a WAN, you will need to install multiple licensing services at each point of the WAN to alleviate the burden of communicating this information across distances.

5. Determine the fault tolerance requirements of TS Licensing. A good practice to use whenever you'd like to establish fault tolerance for TS Licensing is to acquire two servers, divide the licenses between each of those servers, and then publish each in Active Directory. This greatly reduces the chances of services being unavailable in case of a failure.

Terminal Services License Monitoring

When using TS Licensing per-user mode, administrators can monitor licenses that are being propagated through a network via a particular license server. This allows administrators to check for EULA compliance as well as proper usage of particular licenses throughout the enterprise. Windows Server 2008 can also produce a per-user license usage report via the TS Licensing Manager, which is useful if an administrator suspects that some licenses are being used improperly throughout their enterprise.

Terminal Services Licensing Services Events

A couple of issues tend to come up when using Terminal Services Licensing. You'll want to know the following two event IDs when administering a licensing server:

Event ID 28: "TS Licensing Service is unable to report status to the Service Control Manager"   This event sounds a lot more complicated than it really is. All event ID 28 means is that Terminal Services is unable to connect to the Service Control Manager. More often than not, the best solution for this is to reboot the server and make certain that the TS Licensing role has started.

Event ID 37: "TS Licensing Cannot Start. The following error occurred: %1!s!3"   Fun with cryptic errors! Normally, this event occurs when certain groups are given incorrect permissions. You can resolve this problem by making sure the correct permissions are established. If all else fails and the security is set correctly, rebooting will most likely fix the issue.

⊕ Real World Scenario

Determining a Licensing Scheme

MegaCorp, an international import/export corporation that specializes in foodstuffs, has recently signed a contract with the FoodInventory corporation to purchase a new inventory tracking program that monitors the thousands of containers of foodstuffs shipped by MegaCorp every year. The FoodInventory program is Terminal Services-capable so that field agents throughout the organization can add and subtract inventory amounts to the current fiscal year's spreadsheet.

MegaCorp is an organization with several hundred employees. However, the IT needs of the organization are very low, because most agents are field agents and need to log on to the server to update inventory only once every few days. However, there are still a great many employees to keep track of.

Your manager has asked you to deploy a Terminal Services Licensing scheme that will account for the many different users who will authenticate on a server in their corporate headquarters in Des Moines, Iowa. Given what you know about the organization, what licensing scheme would you recommend?

Because of the many different users in the many different locations throughout the world, the MegaCorp infrastructure is going to have a lot of remote users. These users may appear in various places throughout the Windows forest. From the description of the network, it sounds as if MegaCorp has a low-intensity infrastructure that is not used very often, so it would be best to set the licensing scope to Forest. This way, users can authenticate to the server from anywhere in the organization.

To complete the licensing scheme, you need to assign the per-device option for licensing. This is because this scenario mentions that there is only one server but several hundred employees. This eases administration and makes the organization more efficient.

Terminal Services Gateway

Terminal Services Gateway servers are a new and extremely neat feature available only in Windows Server 2008; they allow external clients to connect to internal Terminal Services servers via a gateway that redirects traffic to the appropriate areas of an infrastructure. Before the days of TS Gateway servers, users had to connect directly to Terminal Services within the infrastructure via a virtual private network.

This could get unwieldy, because you could authenticate only to the Terminal Services server after the VPN was engaged and authenticated. This was tiring and more than a little tedious. So, part of the goal of Windows Server 2008 was to create a secure system of communication that allows for single sign-ons in one location that authenticate throughout the enterprise. In the following sections, we'll briefly review some of the technology concepts used in Terminal Services Gateway servers and then discuss the role they play in the enterprise in terms of placement.

Terminal Services Gateway Protocols and Requirements

You can access Terminal Services Gateway servers in one of two ways. The first is via Remote Desktop Protocol (RDP), and the second is via RDP over HTTPS. Each of these has benefits and restrictions, which are outlined in Table 4.1.

TABLE 4.1   TS Gateway Protocols

Authentication Method	Advantages	Disadvantages
TS Gateway RDP	Easy to set up	Requires port 3389 to be open
TS Gateway RDP over HTTPS	Easy NAT, no open ports, more secure	More difficult to set up

Terminal Services Gateway requires you to do some initial setup once you decide to install it. Normally, these requirements will be added automatically, but if you decide to plan for Terminal Services early on, it's a good idea to keep the following in mind:

- RPC over HTTP proxy
- Internet Information Services (IIS) 7.0
- Network Policy and Access Services

Once these requirements are met and the gateway itself is installed, a lot of options are at your disposal. You can give specific users and groups access to the Terminal Services server through the use of Terminal Services connection authorization policies (TS CAPs). Additionally, you can use TS CAPs to set a number of conditions for security purposes (such as smart card authentication) for an individual device. On top of TS CAPs, you can install a Terminal Services resource authorization policy (TS RAP). This, as the name implies, allows you to allocate a specific resource to which users have access in your infrastructure.

TS RAP supports both fully qualified domain names (FQDN) and NetBIOS.

Normally, an administrator will create a TS RAP and associate a given group of users within Active Directory. These are the users to which the remote access policy applies. If users aren't in that group, they are denied access to that remote source.

When designing your Terminal Services infrastructure, you must include both a TS CAP and a TS RAP in your design. This way, you are ensuring that you use the most secure method in regard to access throughout your Terminal Services Gateway server.

Terminal Services Gateway Placement

The exact placement of a Terminal Services Gateway server is a process that depends on your particular business needs. Several customizable solutions are available; specific choices will be made based on your organization's security and availability requirements.

First, you have the choice of whether to place your server within the secure network or outside the secure network in the perimeter. Each has advantages.

If you place your server outside the secure network and within the DMZ (perimeter), your setup is relatively easy, and it will not take long to establish. However, it requires the internal port of 3389 to be opened behind the gateway.

If you place your Terminal Services Gateway server behind the perimeter and inside the secure network, you'll need to open port 443. This inherently creates a security risk, but it's not as bad as, say, port 21, which is under constant attack because of malicious users desiring access to data files placed on an FTP server.

Another issue to consider is whether to place the Terminal Services Gateway server in front of the firewall. Placing it in front of the firewall lowers the security for the server, but placing it inside the firewall lowers the overall security for the network.

Terminal Services Gateway Security

As we've touched on earlier, Terminal Services Gateway utilizes a lot of ports and encryptions when transferring users across the network. The reason for this is obvious: if a machine has access to the entire network, it will need to have serious authentication processes. Otherwise, a computer could access that machine and theoretically be able to hop around the entire network.

Accordingly, when first installing and designing your network, you will have to specify a security certificate for SSL encryption. This process is called *mapping*. When you first install Terminal Services, you will see an option like the one in Figure 4.1.

For the gateway, you can either choose to use an existing certificate or choose to create a new certificate for use specifically for the gateway. Both are acceptable practices. The more secure method is to create a custom certificate for the gateway, but this also entails a bit more work for you as the administrator. At least one of these methods is required to create a stable certificate-based gateway.

FIGURE 4.1   Terminal Services certificate selection

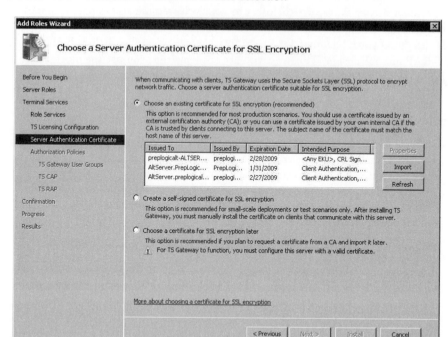

Terminal Services Gateway Events

Thankfully, there is only one really big event you want to pay attention to with TS Gateway servers: event ID 100. Normally, this error code is caused by either the TS Gateway service not being started or the NPS server or IIS server experiencing problems.

The solution to the first situation—TS Gateway not being started—is fairly simple. Just make sure the service is started in the Services section.

The second problem, however, is more complex. If the NPS server or IIS server is experiencing problems, you will need to start monitoring the events occurring using Event Log. Given the nature of these sorts of problems, it could be any number of issues. However, doing this gives you a very good place to start, because it tells you where the issue is originating.

Terminal Services Session Broker

Another one of the new and exciting features that I mentioned briefly earlier is the Terminal Services Session Broker. The Terminal Services Session Broker (TS Session Broker or TS SB) is a Windows Server 2008 feature that allows network load balancing across sessions within your entire infrastructure. Therefore, it's important that you understand the requirements and effect this can have at the enterprise level.

 Terminal Services Session Broker was formerly called Terminal Services Session Directory.

Terminal Services Session Broker Requirements

Most important, TS Session Broker requires that all Terminal Servers and all servers running TS Session Broker be operating at the Windows Server 2008 level. (Other Windows Server versions cannot use this functionality.) Additionally, clients using TS SB load balancing features need to be running Windows Remote Desktop version 5.2 or newer.

Terminal Services Session Broker Load-Balancing Process

One of the main advantages of TS SB is that it reduces the work being done on multiple servers. In a complex environment, chances are a great many users are trying to use the same resources at the same time. TS SB alleviates this by using a two-phase process. Let's examine that process piece by piece.

In the first phase, TS SB utilizes a load-balancing feature such as DNS Round Robin to query the initial authentication for the user's Terminal Services server.

The second phase is when the real work begins. In this phase, the Terminal Services server that authenticated the user will query the TS SB and ask, "Where should I send this user?"

TS SB will then examine the current load of each individual server running Terminal Services, find the server with the least load, and then assign that user to it. Additionally, TS SB will check to see whether the user who is reauthenticating has a previously existing session. If so, TS SB will try to reestablish that connection.

Terminal Services Session Broker Events

Two TS SB events in Windows Server 2008 are noteworthy. Event ID 1001 occurs when TS SB fails to start because of a problem with the RPC sequence. Event ID 1005 occurs when TS SB fails to start because of a problem with registering the TPC authentication information.

Event ID 1001   When this event occurs, it will be accompanied by the following message: "The remote procedure call (RPC) to join TS Session Broker to %1 failed."

The first thing to do if you receive this message is to confirm network connectivity between the two servers. Without it, there is no way the computers can communicate, so the error may keep reproducing. However, if they can communicate, the resolution for this problem is to first add the computer for the Terminal Services server to the Session Directory Computers local group on the TS SB server and then try to join once again. This will usually resolve the problem.

Event ID 1005   This event usually is signaled either with an affirmative message on the client side confirming that the client has established contact with the TS SB or with the following message: "The Terminal Services Session Broker service failed to start due to a problem registering RPC authentication information. The error code was %1."

This event causes a lot more concern than event ID 1001. However, it can more often than not be fixed by restarting the TS SB service. Once this is done, you can use Administrative Tools to confirm that the TS SB service is running and then manually start it or set it to automatic if, for some reason, it isn't.

Terminal Services Web Access

Another aspect of the new Terminal Services features for Windows Server 2008 is the Web Access role for Terminal Services. In effect, this role allows users to authenticate via Terminal Services and utilize applications over the Web. When properly set up, this role will allow a user anywhere in the world to be logged on remotely via the Internet and access a live application on their server without needing to install any software or special programs on their end. It is extraordinarily powerful and particularly useful for administrators. Now you can access a myriad of available applications using secure HTTP (HTTPS) over SSL.

Terminal Services Web Access Prerequisites

Just like other Terminal Services roles, TS Web Access has a few prerequisites that have to be established before it can be deployed. First, it must be installed on Windows Server 2008 running IIS 7.0 (which is available only on Windows Server 2008). Next, TS Web Access must be installed on top of IIS 7.0. However, the computer does *not* have to be a Terminal Services server. The only additional requirement on the Terminal Services end is that Remote Desktop Protocol 6.0 or above must be running on each of the hosts trying to access the various applications.

Terminal Services Web Access Setup

One of the features available with TS Web Access is functionality that enables administrators to deploy Remote Desktop files (.rdp). These can be customized by administrators so users can access remote applications on a server. Additionally, TS Web Access can be set up so users can access it via a web application. Figure 4.2 represents how access works via the Web and via manual .rdp setup.

FIGURE 4.2   Web site access and manual access

```
screen mode id:i:1
desktopwidth:i:800
desktopheight:i:600
session bpp:i:16
auto connect:i:1
full address:s:192.168.1.12
compression:i:1
keyboardhook:i:2
audiomode:i:2
redirectdrives:i:0
redirectprinters:i:0
redirectcomports:i:0
redirectsmartcards:i:0
displayconnectionbar:i:1
username:s:Administrator
domain:s:AKA
alternate shell:s:
shell working directory:s:
disable wallpaper:i:1
disable full window drag:i:1
disable menu anims:i:1
disable themes:i:1
bitmapcachepersistenable:i:1
```

Terminal Services Group Policy Options and Changes

Just like most aspects of Windows Server 2008, Group Policy plays a big role. Within Windows Server 2008, there is such a vast array of available information, including setup options and application/desktop customizations, that Group Policy infiltrates virtually the entire enterprise. On the Terminal Services and application levels, you can use Group Policy for deploying, publishing, and assigning applications access scripting and a cacophony of other easily (or not so easily) assignable policies. At the enterprise level, you need to pay close attention to three very important types of policy settings: Easy Print, TS Gateway configuration, and RemoteApp client settings.

Terminal Services Easy Print

Before Terminal Services Easy Print (or just Easy Print), printing could be a bit of a hassle with Terminal Services-based applications. The reason for this is that at the end of the day the application is actually on the server. So, what happens when the server is told to print? The server prints, of course! It finds whatever locally installed printer is available and goes to town. Obviously, this may not be what the user desires. In fact, it's sort of funny to imagine a high-powered executive flying first-class from London to New York while accessing a Terminal Services program and continuously hitting the Print button but not understanding why, for some reason, his portable printer isn't working. Meanwhile, back at the ranch, the print room keeps receiving dozens of requests for a 100-page spreadsheet. Good times.

To avoid these escapades, Microsoft really thought through Easy Print when it implemented the feature in Windows Server 2008. Easy Print works by using whatever locally installed drivers are available on the machine that is remotely connecting to the Terminal Services server. When it connects, it does so either through Group Policy or through a user interface tool that is customizable from the local machine. What makes this exceptionally grand is that Easy Print functions by proxy and supports almost all printer types, legacy or not. Thus, it really makes it a matter of pointing and clicking, without the hassle of installing drivers.

For the exam, you need to be familiar with the changes that were made in Group Policy (GP), because there's a strong chance you will be tested on them.

The first change Microsoft came up with is a way for you to forward only the default printer—instead of all printers—to the client machine. The policy is located at `Administrative Templates\Windows Components\Terminal Services\Terminal Server\Printer Redirection`.

This is quite convenient if you don't want all your printers forwarding to just one spot.

The second major change that Microsoft made (which was conveniently explained by the Microsoft Terminal Services team during beta 3—many thanks to them) is called *printer scope redirection.*

In Windows Server 2003, whenever printers were redirected with Terminal Services, an administrator could see every single redirection that happened, and it became a very big headache. Now, in Windows Server 2008, printer redirection is treated very much the same way as drive redirection, so printers now have a session ID based on their session in the list of Windows Server access control lists.

Along with printer scope redirection and default printer forwarding, Microsoft introduced per-session default printers. How this works in a nutshell is that it allows a different default printer to be established for each unique session that a user establishes.

The last major change in Windows Server 2008 is that the name of a redirected printer is much shorter. Now, instead of using the full printer name followed by the client name as in Windows Server 2003, the printer names in the Terminal Services session show up in this format: Printer Name (SessionID). For example, the ink-jet printer in the session ID number 1 would be Inkjet(1).

TS Gateway Policy

Just when you thought you were done with (and understood) Terminal Services Gateway servers, they raise their ugly heads again! Well, they are really not that ugly—in fact, they are quite convenient once you understand them. The important thing to remember about TS Gateway servers is that there are a lot of new Group Policy settings available and we need to understand them.

First and foremost, all policies implied on a gateway come in one of two forms: enabled and enforced. *Enabled* group policies are there for the users to implement if they desire.

Enforced policies, on the other hand, are demands that Windows Server 2008 places on users to require them to go along with certain policies.

Three Group Policy settings—which apply regardless of whether a particular policy is enabled or enforced—are important for you as an administrator of Windows Server 2008. They are as follows:

Set TS Gateway Authentication Method   This Group Policy setting allows you to set and specify the type of authentication method users will need to implement when they are connecting to your TS Gateway server from remote locations.

Set the TS Gateway Server Address   I bet you can guess what this one does! This Group Policy setting tells the user what connection method they should use whenever an internal resource is unavailable through a direct connection. It's a nice trick, because it makes users default to this location whenever they cannot connect, thus prioritizing it for the network.

Enable Connections Through The TS Gateway   This Group Policy setting actually *allows* users to connect to a TS Gateway server. Ordinarily, administrators will use the policy in conjunction with the Set The Gateway Server Address setting. This is because in order to connect, you have to specify a gateway. It's sort of like saying "OK, connect to a gateway" and then saying "Use the gateway specified at this location."

Controlling Client Behavior for RemoteApp Programs

This sounds a lot fancier than it really is. In reality, "controlling client behavior" just means that you as an administrator can specify certain Group Policy settings to ensure that resources are assessed in a certain way. For the exam, just remember that RemoteApp program client behavior can be adjusted by specifying a publisher as trusted or blocked from certain resources.

Terminal Services Maintenance and Error Recovery

If you remember the fundamental law of the universe known as Murphy's law, you will remember that if anything can go wrong, it will. That's not actually true, but it's certainly funny, and for computers in general it seems all too accurate. I'm happy to report that Windows Server 2008 gives us some procedures to use in case we see errors or problems with Terminal Services. In fact, in Windows Server 2008 Microsoft introduced a new mode to make logging maintenance issues even easier. I'll discuss it now.

Terminal Services' Terminal Server Drain Mode Feature

Back in the "old days" of Windows Server 2003, administrators would sometimes have to take servers hosting Terminal Services down for maintenance. Usually, this was a big hullabaloo and involved logging on to the server and using the command line to disable every single connection logging into the server and then bringing the server offline to do the maintenance. Now, with Windows Server 2008, there is a new and improved way of isolating problems using the Terminal Server Drain Mode feature.

The Terminal Server Drain Mode feature allows an administrator to shut down any new sessions being established with a server. This is useful because it doesn't cut off currently existing sessions. It just makes it impossible for new sessions to be established. You can put your server in the Terminal Server Drain Mode feature in one of two ways: either through the GUI or through the command line. Either way produces the same results. It's a matter of personal preference. Some administrators like to do everything via the command line, and some prefer to use the graphical user interface.

Using the GUI, you can go to Terminal Services configuration from the Terminal Services menu in Administrative Tools and then double-click Terminal Server Drain Mode, as shown in Figure 4.3, which brings you to a dialog box.

FIGURE 4.3   The Terminal Server Drain Mode feature

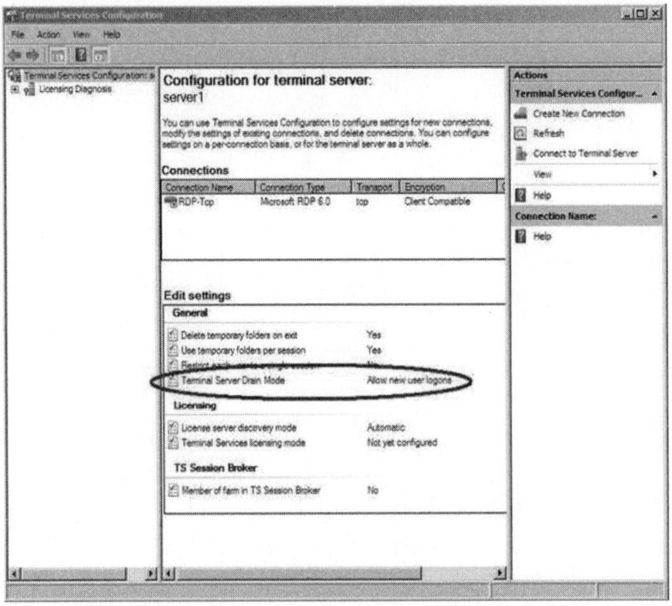

Alternatively, you can use the command line with the change logon command, chglogon.exe.

Common Event Codes

One of the best tricks you can do for yourself—both in order to pass the exam and to become a better administrator—is to memorize certain event codes. The reason for this is twofold. First, it helps you pass your exam. Second, if you immediately recognize an event code and don't have to look it up in Microsoft's documentation, you will save yourself a lot of research time.

Remote Desktop Event ID 1041

When this event occurs, the message "Autoreconnect failed to reconnect user to session because authentication failed. (%1)" usually appears. All this means is that on the initial attempt to authenticate, the process failed. The best way to resolve this error is to start a new session and try the process again. By default, Remote Desktop connections will try to reestablish themselves.

The most important thing to remember is that this error code is, surprisingly, not for troubleshooting—it's a security feature. If this code is occurring many times in your event log, there is a strong chance that someone is trying to access your server with evil intent.

Application Virtualization

One of the biggest high points of getting the MCITP enterprise-level certification is that it indicates you have the ability to support a multifaceted, multiplatform, multiuser environment. Before the release of Windows Server 2008, most of the IT implementations of on-demand applications and services usually involved deploying many different platforms. Certain programs would run only on Windows version X, other ones required version Y, and so forth. Most enterprises ended up with a collection of different computers and peripherals strewn around the facilities. Although this solution ultimately did the job (sort of), it didn't do it in a particularly elegant or cost-efficient way.

Windows Server 2008 makes the job of an enterprise administrator dual-pronged. On one hand, you have to administer all your users. On the other hand, you have to do it cheaply.

One of the tools at your disposal for this process is called Application Virtualization, which may be more familiar to you as Microsoft SoftGrid.

As of the release of this book, Microsoft SoftGrid is undergoing a name change to Microsoft Application Virtualization 4.5. Since this technology is still in beta, in this book I will be using the more tried and true name (Soft-Grid) and will refer to processes from that technological standpoint. For the purposes of the exam, this transition should not pose many problems because the technology is relatively the same. Additionally, where applicable, I have done my best to include information specific to the new features available in Microsoft Application Virtualization 4.5.

Application Virtualization Basics

The concept of application virtualization is simple in nature but more difficult in implementation. Effectively, all the words *application virtualization* mean are that an application can be installed on a server and be dynamically accessed by a user without needing to install a program or any other additional software. Instead, the application is run off the server in a dedicated server space. This allows for fewer user connections, more flexible deployments, and great cost reduction in terms of licensing, time, and technical difficulties.

The Application Virtualization Process

For an application to be "virtual," it has to exist somewhere other than on the primary operating system that resides on the user's computer. In the Windows enterprise environment, this means it can exist in several places:

Locally   A locally installed virtualized application is an application that is installed only on the host-based computer. Normally, this occurs through the use of other virtualization technologies, such as VMware or Microsoft Virtual PC.

Web-based   Web-based virtualization refers to any implementation of virtualization that allows clients to access an application remotely via a website URL. This includes technologies such as TS Web Access. When this is in use, the user installs no local software; instead, the application is run purely on the server side and is contained within an Internet browser.

Remotely   When an application can be accessed only remotely, it exists somewhere between the realms of locally installed and web-based. It isn't accessible via the web browser, and the client doesn't have the application installed on the host machine, but the client does have a configuration installed that allows it to access the remote program, which is accessed via IP packets across the network.

Anatomy of a Program

You can be pretty darn thankful for some serious improvements over the years in both the design and implementation or programs that make it unnecessary for you as an administrator to understand every single aspect of a program. In the "old days," when custom applications were made, teams of engineers would spend hours, days, months, or even years trying to create a system that would allow multiple users to access a program. They would create a program by hand from the ground up and then put it in a place that could be accessed by everyone in the organization at the same time, which wasn't easy. This is because a program might comprise one of two types of "libraries"—static libraries (.lib) and dynamic libraries (.dll).

Static libraries   A static library is a collection of classes, compiled objects, and executable code that has been created by a compiler for instantiation in a program in one area. In simpler terms, it's a collection of code that is used for one place at one time. At the enterprise level, you won't normally deal with this type of library. However, it's useful for understanding the next type of library, which is much more important—dynamic link libraries.

Dynamic link libraries (DLLs)   The main limitation of static libraries is that they are, for lack of a better term, static. They are created in one place and accessed by one program at a time. With DLLs, Microsoft invented a new way for libraries to be dynamically accessed by multiple processes at the same time. With a DLL, the same piece of information can be accessed by multiple portions of the program. So, if your program were accessing a particular piece of itself that needed to be accessed by another portion of the program, if that piece of information was in a static library, the other portion of the program would not be able to access this information. By contrast, a dynamic link library will happily let this happen.

At the enterprise level, you are most concerned about DLLs for two very important reasons. The first is that you are concerned about application deployment (where your applications exist on your server). The second reason you are concerned about DLLs is that they define the version of the program that your software is using.

The primary advantage of Application Virtualization is that it virtually (pun intended) eliminates the concept of "DLL hell," meaning the inability to find system libraries, or correct versions of system libraries, for certain programs. Because SoftGrid is designed in such a way that deployment throughout the enterprise can be universal, if an application is deployed, you can organize it in such a way that it is deployed the same throughout the entire enterprise.

MSI Files

The Microsoft .msi file extension stands for "Microsoft Installer." MSI files comprise executable code that contains installation wrappers for programs installed on Microsoft platforms that include the program base code, its required libraries, and other information required for the program to function. Typically, this type of file is manipulated and shared by the server as an application install file for clients or hosts.

Additionally, in traditional Group Policy deployment, MSI files are used to assign or publish applications throughout the network based on predefined policies set by the administrator. For virtualization, it's important to be familiar with MSI files because they are required for some forms of virtualization in different locations, such as client or server side, based on the type of install the administrator desires.

Line-of-Business Applications

Most of the programs that you'll deal with at the application virtualization level are what are called *line-of-business applications*. A line-of-business application is one that is absolutely essential to the production of a business and that is accessed by multiple employees. For a sales company, one example of a line-of-business application would be a custom utility that keeps track of large volume sales, allowing multiple users to log in to the same program, access the same data, make changes, and authorize certain actions, such as authorizing a discount, changing the quantity of items, or modifying customer information.

Line-of-business application is a catchphrase you'll see a lot, but if you are an administrator, you can just boil it down to two words: it's important.

Active Directory–Integrated Applications

An Active Directory–integrated program is a program that has been designed from the ground up to work alongside the data provided by Active Directory. Chances are you may have run across these either in the field or while studying for your application infrastructure exam for Windows Server 2008. A great example of something like this is an email client such as Exchange Server 2007. Because it needs a way to send email information from one Windows user to another, Exchange Server 2007 can query the Active Directory database for information regarding users and what they need to send information back and forth. The application falls right in line with Active Directory, and the user never really notices the difference.

Application Virtualization Components and Software

Application virtualization technology requires particular components. I'll begin the discussion of them by briefly touching on each of these concepts. Then I will discuss each one in more depth as you begin to learn more and more about application virtualization and the role it plays within a Windows Server 2008 enterprise.

Microsoft SoftGrid SoftGrid is the overall technology that makes it easy to deploy applications in a streamlined process, which in turn allows user to access various programs with very little overhead. When referencing enterprise-level deployment of applications, more often than not I'm referring to the use of Microsoft SoftGrid, which contains within it many of the features discussed later in this section.

Microsoft SoftGrid has two different types of deployment—Microsoft SoftGrid Application Virtualization for Universal Desktops and Microsoft SoftGrid Application Virtualization for Terminal Servers. Which to use is up to you and will be discussed in more detail later.

 SoftGrid is capable of creating individual per-user instances of the system registry, file system, COM/IPC, system libraries, process environment, and fonts, making it highly scalable and easy for users to integrate multiple applications in the same user environment.

Microsoft System Virtual Application Server Microsoft System Virtual Application Server (SVAS) is a component of Microsoft SoftGrid that is responsible for streaming application data to users who have requested that data throughout the enterprise. Normally, SVAS does this through security tokens and identifiers (SIDs). When SVAS is running, it runs a service called Microsoft System Center Virtual Application Server. This is located by default in the `Program Files\Softricity\SoftGrid Server\content` directory.

Microsoft SoftGrid Client: SystemGuard SystemGuard is what Microsoft describes as a "sandbox." It allows applications to run in a framework on an individual client computer using Microsoft SoftGrid. In Application Virtualization, the user never fully installs the program onto their own machine. Instead, only miniscule portions of the program are transferred to the user. The majority of the program is housed on the server. To protect the operating system and to communicate with the server, Microsoft SystemGuard creates a "safe zone" that users can operate from within without the risk of harming their machine. Additionally, SystemGuard can store information regarding an application for later use. Thus, if a user terminates a session, the session comes back in full force at a later point when the application is reinstantiated.

Microsoft SoftGrid Sequencer   SoftGrid Sequencer is the portion of Microsoft SoftGrid that determines which INI, DLL, and other files are required in the interaction between the operating system and the application. SoftGrid Sequencer then interfaces with Microsoft SystemGuard to determine what needs to be deployed to the end user and moves whatever is appropriate in the form of an executable file that can be used for virtualization. Ultimately, SoftGrid Sequencer "sequences" the application onto the virtual server for management purposes, such as the Management Web Services utility. To use SoftGrid Sequencer, administrators have to place data required for certain programs into "packages." These packages are then deployed based on administrative criteria.

Microsoft SoftGrid Management Web Services   This is a snap-in tool that integrates within the Microsoft Management Console. It is capable of interacting with Active Directory and database-driven applications for line-of-business or general virtualization purposes. It can integrate with both local and virtualized applications. Administrators can use Management Web Services through the Microsoft Management Console, just like other snap-in tools, to create individual groups, manage load balancing, or create fault tolerance. Additionally, Management Web Services can both create and manage the three licensing modes of applications:

- Time-based
- Concurrent
- Unlimited access

The primary use of Management Web Services is to directly assign applications to users, groups of users, or organizational units within Active Directory.

Microsoft System Center Configuration Manager   Microsoft System Center Configuration Manager (ConfigMgr) is a high-end utility designed to administer an extremely large-scale enterprise. To pass the 70-647 exam, you do not need to know how this operates, but you do need to know that it's designed for high-end administration purposes.

Microsoft Virtual PC 2004 and 2007   These are two versions of one piece of software designed to allow machines to install multiple different operating systems on one workstation. It is available as a free download, and in the enterprise it is rarely used, except on an individual user level.

Microsoft SoftGrid

As I said earlier in this chapter, Microsoft SoftGrid is a complex and highly scalable application virtualization platform that uses SQL Server and Active Directory for application availability. Within Active Directory, SoftGrid relies upon three different user groups:

SoftGrid browsers   This is a read-only account type that is designed to allow users to browse SoftGrid applications to see what is available.

SoftGrid administrators   SoftGrid administrators are granted access to the SoftGrid Management Console, as well as the SoftGrid Management Web Services tool. Administrators can also add, delete, and remove accounts within SoftGrid and manage application-based software.

SoftGrid users   SoftGrid user accounts are used to access available SoftGrid applications throughout the infrastructure.

Once the user accounts have been created in Active Directory and assigned their various roles, SoftGrid can deploy applications through SoftGrid Sequencer. The exact process is beyond the scope of this book, but it is *very* important for this exam that you be familiar with the technology and capabilities of the sequencer.

Scaling an Enterprise with Application Virtualization

The inherent difficulty with virtualization isn't necessarily the virtualization itself. In fact, that's almost easy. The difficult part of virtualization is working within an organization to derive a deployment method that will scale with an organization, no matter how much it may grow or reduce in size as the business ebbs and flows with its success or reduction.

The key to this is to remember that no single virtualization strategy will work throughout the entire enterprise. At the most granular level, individual workstations may have to be addressed for individual purposes. At the highest level, deployment methods such as Microsoft SoftGrid can be used to design the overall architecture of your organization.

To summarize, when you're designing an enterprise infrastructure, you have to keep the following questions in mind.

How Many Users Will Need to Be Supported?

This is a more complicated question than you may think. If you have several thousand users (rather than ten or a hundred or several hundred), you will have to make a lot of decisions regarding delegation and control of applications. Would Terminal Services work best? Or would SoftGrid? Generally, the best plan of attack is to take the current number of users and then multiply it by 2 times the number of years you are trying to scale for. Thus, if you currently have 1,000 employees and you are shooting for 5 years of scalability, here is the equation:

1000 (Users) × 2 (Growth) × 5 (Years) = 10,000

Obviously, on a large scale, this can lead to a drastic number of users. So, another general rule is to implement a "no more than 100,000" rule. This is because there are very few infrastructures that will need to support that many users.

What Operating System Do the Applications Require?

This answer alone can determine a lot of your deployment strategy. If you are deploying multiple different versions of applications that require different operating systems, you will need to select a virtualization method that accounts for this. On the client side, you can install Microsoft Virtual PC 2007 for implementing more than one operating system. If you want to use the program on the server side, you can include Microsoft SoftGrid. But ultimately, the best way to decide how to implement a program is to consider the limitations, capabilities, and features of the technology.

Your exam is going to throw a *lot* of technology questions at you. At the professional level, Microsoft exams expect you to be extremely familiar with the technology you are dealing with, both from experience and from the MCTS level exams you have already taken. The big secret of professional-level exams is that they throw all these technologies into one exam question and ask you to remember the features associated with the technology and what it can and cannot do. Thus, it's a really good idea to write down all of the technologies and their high points and then memorize that list. It will really help when the exam throws a dozen pieces of technology at you at once.

Are There Any Shared DLLs, INIs, or Other Resource-Required Files?

If so, you need to look into using a technology like Microsoft SoftGrid. This allows the Microsoft SoftGrid Sequencer and SystemGuard to interface between the applications and make sure there are no conflicts with the library files required to use the operating system.

SoftGrid Infrastructure Planning and Design

Microsoft recently released a series of new Windows Server 2008 guides called the *Microsoft Solution Accelerator Guides for Windows Server 2008*. An important one to know about is the *Infrastructure Planning and Design Guide for Microsoft SoftGrid*. This guide is available at www.microsoft.com/technet/SolutionAccelerators.

Although the scope of this guide is a bit beyond what you need for the MCITP level, reviewing this guide is an excellent way to prepare yourself for the real world and some of the challenges you will face. On top of that, if you have reviewed this guide, any questions you might face about SoftGrid planning and design on the MCITP exam will seem very trivial.

Real World Scenario

Implementing an Application Virtualization Strategy

You have recently been employed by a Fortune 500 company that has a large central office with more than 2,000 employees in the same building. The entire building is networked with a high-access, fault-tolerant mesh gigabit network. Users within the enterprise are using Windows XP Home, Windows XP Professional, and Windows Vista, and servers are running both Windows Server 2003 and Windows Server 2008. The Windows XP Home computers are personal computers brought into the campus by friends, guests, and families who still need access to the network.

Currently, your company is using an IPv4 networking scheme, but it plans to ultimately move to an IPv6-capable scheme to plan for future integration and scalability. Additionally, your company has several custom applications that it deploys throughout the enterprise. Each of these applications runs independently, and they are incompatible with one another. However, users are assigned only one workstation each. As the new lead administrator, you need to implement a technology that allows all the users on your network to be able to access all the applications from one workstation. Another criterion of the installation is that it must take as little space as possible on the host computers and preferably run on the server side instead of on the client. From what you know of application virtualization, what would be the best implementation?

This scenario gives you a few important pieces of information:

- The network is fast and redundant. This allows you to not be limited by any bandwidth issues that a virtualization solution might require.

- Nothing was mentioned regarding the need for Internet-based clients.

- The custom applications are incompatible with one another. Immediately, this tells you that virtualization is required in order to use two custom applications at the same time. This is because in order to use two incompatible pieces of software, you need two independent "sandboxes" (or platforms) that you can let your users play with.

The best solution would be to implement a Microsoft SoftGrid deployment. Using Microsoft SoftGrid, you can create two different application packages and make each available to users throughout the environment. When they need an application, they can access it on their desktop. Then, they can switch to the other application without causing instability because it is run on an independent server.

🌐 Real World Scenario

Using Old Applications on New (and Old) Operating Systems

You are currently administering a top-secret facility for the Department of Defense that requires the utmost security and discretion. Within this facility, there is important data sensitive to national security, which, if compromised, could have devastating results for millions of people. This facility consists of multiple different departments with various levels of security. However, none of these is lax.

Within the engineering department, fives users have been analyzing statistics for more than 30 years and do not adjust well to changes in technology. However, they were smart enough to design their own software. It is extremely stable and has never had a single problem. Recently, the Department of Defense decided to upgrade all computers in the department to Windows Vista. This means that the statisticians will also have to upgrade.

However, if the statisticians upgrade, their custom software will no longer function. It is incompatible with the Windows Vista operating system. The data contained by this application is vital to your organization, and if lost, it would require thousands of hours to recover. Thus, you must find a way to run this application that is efficient, low cost, and targeted toward the statisticians and *only* the statisticians. What would be the best implementation?

There are two pieces of key information here:

- First, there are only five users of this application.

- Second, the application is incompatible with Windows Vista—not necessarily with older versions of Windows. In fact, if the department is "upgrading," that implies the statisticians were already using a version of Windows.

In a situation like this, where there are few users and the fix would be relatively easy, it's best to implement an installation where you use Microsoft Virtual PC 2007. First, it meets the objective of being low cost—Microsoft Virtual PC is free. Second, it is efficient because it doesn't require the use of a server or any network bandwidth. Last, using Microsoft Virtual PC in this deployment method affects only the statisticians. Thus, other users won't be affected by their individual situation.

Summary

Terminal Services, Application Virtualization, and server consolidation play key roles throughout any large enterprise. As time moves on, more and more servers will be using these key elements to create a stable, fast, and effective platform for application deployment. To succeed on this portion of the exam, you should familiarize yourself with all the technologies available and what their restrictions are.

In this chapter, I covered the key elements to Terminal Services, including TS Gateway, TS Web Access, RemoteApp, Terminal Services Licensing, and Terminal Services Session Broker. I also explored the elements and software involved with application virtualization, including Microsoft SoftGrid and Microsoft Virtual PC 2007.

Before moving on from this section, you must know each of the technical elements discussed here intimately. The exam is going to ask you to identify each of these elements and how it can and cannot integrate with other components in an enterprise. If you are unable to remember these elements at a glance, your exam will be very challenging.

Keep in mind, also, that more information is available on these services, server roles, and applications via Microsoft TechNet, which is an extraordinarily valuable resource for all Microsoft professionals. If, after reviewing this section, you still have any trouble recalling the technology, refer to that web site for even more information.

Exam Essentials

Know your Terminal Server   You should make sure that before you take the exam, you've looked over every aspect of your terminal server. Chances are the exam will ask you something specific about it.

Understand the new Terminal Services Roles   There are a lot of Terminal Services roles available now! Session brokers, gateways, and so forth can get really confusing when a question throws a bunch of acronyms at you. Just know what technology does what and you'll be fine.

Know your Microsoft terminology   This is a pretty deep statement. You need to know all your Microsoft Terminology, including the various aspects of SoftGrid, Terminal Server, and all the different components that form application virtualization as a technology. Microsoft will try to fool you.

Understand the advantages of application virtualization   If you know *why* we virtualize applications, you'll be much further along than most. The key to using Terminal Services is to virtualize applications, but you need to know why we do it and how it can help an organization.

Review Questions

1. What three licensing scopes are available in Terminal Services Licensing? (Choose all that apply.)

   A. Forest

   B. Domain

   C. Computer

   D. Workgroup

   E. User

   F. Device

   G. Client

   H. Server

2. Which of the following are required for a TS Gateway server? (Choose all that apply.)

   A. A Domain controller

   B. A Perimeter network

   C. Port 3389 or 443 open

   D. A certificate

3. Which of the following file types can cause access errors that SoftGrid can alleviate? (Choose all that apply.)

   A. EXE

   B. DLL

   C. INI

   D. MSI

4. What is the service run by SVAS?

   A. Microsoft System Center Virtual Application Server

   B. Microsoft System Virtual Application Server

   C. Microsoft System Center Configuration Manager

   D. Microsoft Virtual Server Application System

   E. Hyper-V

5. What is the name of the Terminal Services feature that allows an administrator to shut down new logins?

   A. TS's Terminal Server Drain

   B. TS's Gateway

   C. TS's Session Broker

   D. TS's RemoteApp

6. How long is the default Terminal Services Licensing grace period?

   A. 30 days

   B. 60 days

   C. 90 days

   D. 120 days

7. Which of the following Terminal Services technologies supports network load balancing?

   A. TS Gateway

   B. TS RemoteApp

   C. TS Web Access

   D. TS Session Broker

8. Which of the following portions of SoftGrid is run on the client side?

   A. Sequencer

   B. SystemGuard

   C. SVAS

   D. System Center Configuration Manager

9. If an administrator wanted to configure a simple printing method that didn't require installing drivers for remote users, what would they most likely utilize?

   A. USB-based printing

   B. IEEE 1394 driver support

   C. Easy Print

   D. PostScript processing

   E. Generic drivers

10. If a program is said to be "required" in order for the business to function, it is deemed which of the following?

   A. Mission critical

   B. Primary

   C. Line of business

   D. Terminal Services

11. Which of the following Terminal Services *requires* IIS?

   A. TS Gateway clients

   B. Terminal Services RemoteApp

   C. Terminal Server

   D. Terminal Services Web Access

   E. Remote Desktop

12. Which of the following six commands can aid in placing a load upon a server for testing purposes? (Choose all that apply.)

A. Robosrv.exe

B. Robocli.exe

C. Ipconfig

D. RepAdmin

E. adprep /forestprep

F. adprep /domainprep

13. Which of the following account types is allowed only read access by default in Microsoft SoftGrid?

A. SoftGrid users

B. SoftGrid browsers

C. SoftGrid administrators

D. SoftGrid power users

E. Administrators

F. Enterprise administrators

14. Which of the following virtualization technologies should be used when there are a few users who need access to multiple Windows operating systems on the same workstation?

A. VMware

B. Terminal Server

C. Microsoft Virtual PC 2007

D. Hyper-V

E. TS Gateway

15. You have recently been promoted to be the administrator for your domain. Within your domain, you administer 400 users from various departments, spread out across several dozen OUs from throughout the enterprise. Within your domain, there are three Terminal Services servers, of which one is currently operating at maximum capacity and two are at less than 10 percent. You want to establish a more balanced load throughout your enterprise. What would be the best solution?

A. Implement a TS Gateway server to route TS traffic to the appropriate servers.

B. Implement TS SB to balance traffic across the three servers.

C. Implement IPv6 with a secure gateway for faster access.

D. Install TS Web Access on the other two servers for user access options.

16. Terminal Services Gateway policies can be implemented in one of two fashions. Which are they? (Choose two.)

- **A.** Assigned
- **B.** Published
- **C.** Enabled
- **D.** Enforced
- **E.** Installed
- **F.** Uninstalled

17. When a user sits down in front of a computer that is accessing a virtualized application via SoftGrid, a process occurs where portions of the application, including the registry, system libraries, and other important parts of the program are partially installed on the client machine. What portion of Microsoft SoftGrid is responsible for this?

- **A.** Microsoft System Center Configuration Manager
- **B.** Microsoft SoftGrid SystemGuard
- **C.** SoftGrid Browser
- **D.** Microsoft SoftGrid Sequencer

18. When a program has access to the database of available users, groups, organizational units, and other Windows server–based information, it is said to be what?

- **A.** Utilized
- **B.** Integrated
- **C.** Applied
- **D.** Informed

19. If a user has access to an icon on their desktop that launches a remote application on a server across the network, the user is most likely using a Remote Desktop file that gives access to the application via TS Web Access. If so, what type of file are they accessing?

- **A.** .rpc
- **B.** .rdp
- **C.** .rpd
- **D.** .rpx

20. Which of the following virtualization technologies lends itself the most toward a scalable, buildable, easily modifiable enterprise that can support multiple different versions of the same application for various operating systems and user requirements?

- **A.** Microsoft SoftGrid
- **B.** Microsoft Virtual PC 2007
- **C.** Microsoft Hyper-V
- **D.** Microsoft Virtual Server

Answers to Review Questions

1. A, B, D. Within Terminal Services, three licensing scopes are available: forest, domain, and workgroup. These licensing scopes determine the level from which the server can be accessed.

2. C, D. To function properly, a TS Gateway server must have Windows Server 2008 installed, have an SSL certificate, and keep port 443 or 3389 open. Additionally, IIS or Network Policy and Access Services can be optionally configured.

3. B, C. Microsoft SoftGrid is an application virtualization product that is designed to virtualize individual applications and allow multiple users to access application-critical files, such as DLL and INI.

4. A. When Microsoft System Virtual Application Server (SVAS) is run, it launches the Microsoft System Center Virtual Application Server service. This is located by default in the Program Files\Softricity\SoftGrid Server\content directory.

5. A. TS's Terminal Server Drain feature is a Windows Server 2008 feature that allows administrators to slowly siphon off new logins to a server in order to perform maintenance. It's normally used when a server needs to be brought down to minimum functioning condition to be worked on so that as few users as possible are interrupted.

6. D. By default, Terminal Services servers have a grace period of 120 days with which Terminal Services can be used without a license. After this grace period, a license must be installed. Keep in mind that using Terminal Services without a license during this 120-day grace period is most likely a violation of the end-user license agreement.

7. D. TS SB is a Terminal Services feature that allows network load balancing between Terminal Services servers and the management of session logins. By default, TS SB does not load balance, but load balancing can be set up manually through administration.

8. B. SystemGuard is a client-side interface that is responsible for creating a "sandbox" where client applications be installed and used without compromising the rest of the operating system. SystemGuard communicates with Microsoft SoftGrid Sequencer and receives the proper information required to run a particular application without completely installing on the client side.

9. C. Easy Print is a technology that allows users to utilize their own client-side printers without the process of having to install new drivers on either the client side or the server side. The user just clicks and watches as the server-side remote application interfaces with their client-side printer and prints the required information.

10. C. Line-of-business applications are applications that are essential to the functioning of the business. Examples of line-of-business applications are accounting apps, sales inventory programs, or other applications that must function in order for an organization to keep doing business.

11. D. Terminal Services Web Access is a method for users to access applications via a web browser. Because of this, Windows Server 2008 has to have IIS installed in order to receive the web-based requests and pass the application interface onto the users who request it. On the user side, Terminal Services Web Access is seamless. Users log on to a specific URL and request an application, and that application becomes available to them via the Web.

12. A, B. `Robosrv.exe` and `Robocli.exe` are two commands that were issued with the Windows Server 2003 Deployment Kit and are still available today. When determining server load, it's a good idea to use these tools to simulate a load on your server in order to ensure that you will receive steady performance when using an application.

13. B. SoftGrid browsers can, by default, only browse the contents of SoftGrid. To use applications, write to them, or manage them, the SoftGrid users must be elevated to SoftGrid administrators or SoftGrid users.

14. C. Microsoft Virtual PC 2007 is a free, downloadable program that allows workstations to utilize multiple different Windows operating systems within the same workstation. It is fast, effective, and very useful for small fixes in a large environment.

15. B. Terminal Services Session Broker (TS SB) is a service that is designed to balance Terminal Services loads between servers. Other Terminal Services roles, such as TS Gateway or Web Access, can assist in this but ultimately are not as sure and convenient a method as TS SB.

16. C, D. Terminal Services Gateway servers can interact directly with Group Policy to set policies as either enabled or enforced. When a policy is enabled, it is capable of being implemented throughout the environment. When a policy is enforced, it is required to be installed where the policy is in effect.

17. D. Microsoft SoftGrid Sequencer is the portion of SoftGrid that is responsible for proportioning the programs important resources and transporting them by "sequencing" these parts of the application across the network to a given client station.

18. B. An Active Directory–integrated application is one that has access to the Active Directory database. An example of an Active Directory–integrated application is Exchange, which can send mail to and from clients based on the Windows Active Directory user information.

19. B. `.rdp` files are files created by an administrator that simplify the authentication process for users to access virtualized applications. A user can double-click an `.rdp` file after the user has been set up by the administrator and be granted instant access to the application.

20. A. The greatest strength of Microsoft SoftGrid is its capability to be scaled almost endlessly. From the ground up, Microsoft designed SoftGrid to be capable of handling multiple requests for the same resource files and application d ata. Additionally, SoftGrid can support multiple installs of the same program throughout the enterprise based on user needs and administrator requirements.

Chapter

5

Designing an Effective Administration Model

OBJECTIVES COVERED IN THIS CHAPTER:

✓ **Design the Active Directory administrative model.**

- ▪ May include but is not limited to: delegation, group strategy, compliance auditing, group administration, organizational structure

In case you hadn't figured it out by this point, the whole root and core of Windows administration is the process of administering organizations full of objects through policies and procedures. And, yes, the word *policy* is a loaded term there. In fact, it's an extremely loaded term, because of our friend Group Policy, which can be summarized as the configuration settings of rules and regulations that control the behavior of the Windows infrastructure. In other words, Group Policy is what allows you to place limitations on objects by instituting policies at different points throughout your infrastructure that affect how you see and use various software and network resources.

Some of the classic examples of Group Policy deployments include removing access to the Control Panel, adding software to the default Start menu, and granting the ability to install said pieces of software without the direct need of an administrator. The full scope of Group Policy, however, is so broad that it probably couldn't be covered in a single book. If it could, it would probably be a fairly tremendous tome that you could use as a barricade to stop a charging elephant.

In fact, in the real world, a good share of your time in the enterprise is going to be spent administering and creating group policies to deploy to various users throughout your enterprise—actually, not just users, but computers, printers, pieces of software, and several different servers. This is because Group Policy is a huge undertaking, and if it isn't implemented properly, it can have drastic results on your enterprise. Just imagine how happy your boss would be if he suddenly received a call in the morning from your CEO claiming that, for some reason, she can no longer access her email and all of her office software no longer appears on the Start menu. It wouldn't be a happy phone call. Thus, for the certification exam, you're expected to have a very firm grip of Group Policy and the impact it can have throughout the enterprise at all deployment levels.

In this chapter, I'll cover Group Policy by explaining the important background you need to establish before you institute even your first Group Policy object: the administrative model. An effective administrative model is a network design that facilitates the organization of users, computers, and objects into compartmentalized and easily accessible organizational units (OUs) that will create a simple infrastructure that you can use for more complex enterprises at any level of granularity. By the end of this chapter, I'll have laid the framework for Chapter 6, "Planning and Designing Group Policy."

Object Essentials

According to Microsoft, an *object* is a distinct and named entity in the network infrastructure that has its own set of attributes and elements. There are many different types of objects:

- Users
- Computers
- Printers
- Contacts
- Groups
- Shared folders
- Domain controllers
- Organizational units
- inetOrgPersons
- MSMQ queue aliases

Within Active Directory, each of these objects can be assigned various permissions through the use of access control lists. Permissions are binary in nature; that is, something is either allowed or not allowed.

And beyond each permission, every object is assigned an object *owner*, who can control how each of these permissions are set, along with administrators with control levels higher than the object owner. Furthermore, Active Directory object control and permissions can be delegated to other users so that they can manage them themselves. At the enterprise level, this is common because it simply isn't practical for administrators to be responsible for every-day tasks, such as changing a password, for thousands of users. Accordingly, delegations can be assigned to various organizational units to administer other objects and free up load on the administrator.

Object Security Descriptors

Every object within Active Directory contains a certain amount of authorization data that secures the object. This information is included in the security descriptor, which, according to the Microsoft documentation on Active Directory delegation best practices, includes the following:

Owner This is the current owner of the object's SID.

Group This is the SID for the current owner's group.

Discretionary access control list (DACL) According to Microsoft, this is a list of zero or more ACEs that specify who has what access to the object.

System access control list (SACL) This is the list of access controls that are used for auditing.

Access Control Entities

Access control entities (ACEs) are Active Directory conventions that give specific permissions for object access; ACEs are compiled into access control lists and can take one of six values per ACE:

- Allow
- Deny
- System Audit
- Object Allow
- Object Deny
- Object System Audit

Additionally, ACEs contain permissions that are further refined by a series of standard permissions. This includes such values as Read Control, Standard Delete, and more permissions than I can include in this chapter. Suffice it to say, ACEs provide a fine-layered and very granular amount of control for individual objects.

Organizational Units

Organizational units form the basis for a lot of our work as administrators because they are the most easily mutable form of object collection available. As you know, OUs can comprise accounts, groups, computers, printers, or various other objects and can be very robust in their composition. They're generally implemented for one of two reasons: delegation or Group Policy.

More often than not, administrators use OUs for delegation because of how easy they are to assemble. In fact, they go further than just being easy to use, because OUs can contain other OUs in what is called OU *nesting*. And as OUs nest, they can create more and more complex infrastructures. Accordingly, on the 70-647 certification exam, a good deal of time is spent understanding OU design and understanding how to create the OU hierarchy.

Organizational Unit Hierarchy

If you've read Chapter 1, "Designing a Complex Windows Server 2008 Infrastructure," you're probably already familiar with the concept of breaking down organizations into more logical structures. Similarly, in this section, you'll explore how to break OUs down into more logical structures.

The reason I haven't covered this in detail up until this point is that in most small organizations, there really isn't as much of a need for this. Consider a business with, say, 50 employees. With 50 employees, there is almost no way that there could be more than 50 organizational units. There may be the rare case where someone could think up an OU structure that would make even the most seasoned administrator set down his glasses and say, "Well, that's a doozy." But more often than not, a small office will most likely look something like Figure 5.1.

The design is not very complex. But imagine you decided to apply this design to an organization with, say, 10,000 employees. Take a look at what happens in Figure 5.2, which shows the breakdown of just one OU, Sales.

Can you imagine applying a Group Policy to the sales group? The chance that all sales-people would need the same sorts of settings is infinitesimal at best, and moreover, in an enterprise that scales, you would essentially not have any delegation opportunities because there simply aren't enough OUs to delegate.

FIGURE 5.1   Typical small to medium business OU design

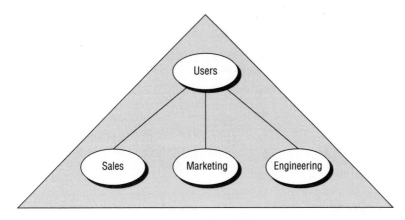

FIGURE 5.2   Large business with small business OU design

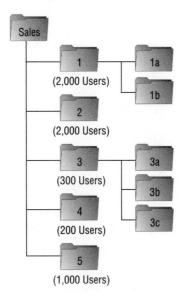

In most large-scale enterprises, OUs are implemented according to four administrative models approved by Microsoft:

- Location
- Business function

- Object type
- Hybrid/combination

These are, for the most part, self-explanatory by title. In a location-based OU model, objects are placed by their location, such as the United States or Canada. Beyond that, OUs are broken down into more specific locations, such as Los Angeles embedded within the United States or Montreal embedded within Canada, as shown in Figure 5.3.

FIGURE 5.3 Location-based OU hierarchy

Within a business function–based OU, users are divided up based upon their department or business duties and then divided down further, as shown in Figure 5.4.

FIGURE 5.4 Business function–based OU hierarchy

And within an object type–based hierarchy, objects are separated based upon object essentials, such as computers, which can then be divided into workstations and servers, or users, which can be divided down into users and groups of users, as shown in Figure 5.5.

FIGURE 5.5   Object type–based OU hierarchy

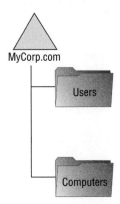

And, of course, a combination OU hierarchy involves the process of combining elements from either the location, business function, or object type OU and creating a customized model based on aspects of each of these OUs. For instance, an OU structure could be separated by location and then be further refined by object type, as shown in Figure 5.6.

FIGURE 5.6   Hybrid/combination OU hierarchy

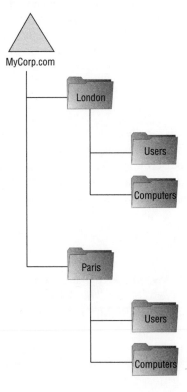

OU Design Requirements

When first deciding upon your OU design implementation, you need to consider a few factors beyond just the administrative model:

- Autonomy
- Group Policy
- Visibility

I will discuss these factors in the sections that follow.

Autonomy

Administrative autonomy is the process of ensuring that an individual location in the network has the freedom and capability to do whatever is necessary to conduct business and not interrupt the rest of the organization. Additionally, ensuring autonomy also means that outside users or devices cannot involve themselves in places that are specifically designed to be autonomous.

When you are designing OUs, this is an important design decision. Consider what would happen if you gave all midlevel administrators in a multithousand-employee company access to the All Users organizational unit. Granted, that's a bit of an overly exaggerated example, but if you did that, all midlevel administrators would be able to control objects at whim, which isn't a good situation to be in. Thus, if you're savvy, it behooves you to consider how autonomy will affect the rest of the environment as soon as you decide to implement an OU structure of any sort.

Group Policy

The discussion on Group Policy is mostly contained in Chapter 6, but suffice it to say that designing OUs for the ease of Group Policy is an extremely important step that has to be considered. Without this step, our group policies can have far-reaching and unintended results. It's rare you'll find the administrator who, when first starting to use Group Policy, didn't manage to do something like lock herself out of all applications permanently or take away the Control Panel.

Visibility

It almost goes without saying that when you're first designing a network infrastructure for an enterprise, there will be several objects you will not want users to access. Say, for instance, your company has a new $100,000 printer in the graphics department that can print full-scale color images with spectacular visibility. The only problem is, each time it prints, it costs the company around $100 worth of ink.

If you left the object in its default settings, any semisavvy user could add this printer to their computer and suddenly say, "It sure would be nice to print a full-banner size F-18 fighter jet picture that I could hang in my office cubicle." And nothing, except for a little thing called *ethics*, would stand in the user's way. However, with visibility, you can fix this problem.

Controlling visibility is the process of making objects not appear to users who don't need to have access to them. So, in the earlier example, when John Q. User decides he'd like to add a new printer and hits the Find Now button in Active Directory, he won't see the printer in the list of readily available devices for him to use. This relatively simple to explain concept can be accomplished by choosing to add an extra layer of extrapolation onto an existing OU structure.

For example, say you are working within the MyCorp corporation. Within MyCorp, two divisions of the company have access to sales resources, the sales and sales management departments. Accordingly, MyCorp has designed its administrative model according to business function and has broken its organization down as shown in Figure 5.7.

FIGURE 5.7   MyCorp administrative model without visibility considerations

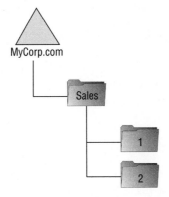

Recently, upper management at MyCorp has decided that the only users who should have access to the sales resources are sales managers—and only sales managers who have been directly approved by upper management. Thus, you could accomplish this new design requirement by moving the old Sales Resources OU inside your Sales Managers OU and setting up block inheritance. This way, you can manually assign the individual sales managers who will need to have access to these OUs and succeed in keeping out users who should not access this sensitive information.

Groups in Active Directory

Beyond OUs, the next important collective container you need to pay attention to is another you are readily familiar with, Active Directory groups. As you know, Active Directory groups are divided into two types: *security* and *distribution*. Distribution groups, for the purpose of this chapter, are mostly beyond the scope of discussion because they are mainly used as a convention to send email through applications, such as Microsoft Exchange. They can't take any permissions, and you can't assign them group policies.

Security groups, however, are *not* capable of directly receiving Group Policy, but they can control access to network resources and filter Group Policy settings, as well as set permissions. This can get a little confusing when you combine it with OUs, because in a way it seems almost like having double groups. But keep in mind that the purpose of OUs is to gather objects at a granular level for the purpose of administration. The primary purpose of security groups, however, is to set permissions and capabilities.

In fact, most seasoned administrators will create a security group that is designed to control permissions for a specific organizational unit. For instance, say you're in a company that has four telemarketing managers who need to control an OU of a dozen printers. Rather than giving each user permission to control the OU, you could assign the users to a group and then assign that group Full Control over that OU. Normally, the group that has full control over the OU is known as the *OU owner*.

An OU owner has complete authority over a specific OU and all children that reside within that OU (remember, OUs can be nested). In the enterprise, this is often done to aid in the process of delegation, which will be discussed in more detail later in this chapter. But suffice it to say for the moment, OU delegation occurs when an OU owner is responsible for administrating that OU, therefore becoming an *OU administrator*.

Group Scope

Whenever you create a group in Windows Server 2008, whether that group is a security group or a distribution group, the group is defined somewhere within the Active Directory forest. And that scope, once defined, shows the limitations of that group and where it can reach within the forest. When you create a group in Windows Server 2008 using the Active Directory Users and Computers tool, Windows Server presents you with three different choices of scope for your security groups if you are running in native mode: domain local, global, and universal. If you are not running native mode and are instead running in mixed mode, you will have access to two groups: domain local and global.

You can see a good example of group scope in Will Panek's *MCTS Windows Server 2008 Active Directory Configuration Study Guide,* published by Sybex.

Domain Local

Domain local groups are groups that are created from accounts that can come from any domain but that access only those resources on the local domain. All too often people try to make this a lot more complicated than it is, but that really is all there is to it.

As a simple example, if you have a domain local group on the server Domain 1, you can easily add *accounts* from Domain 2 into the domain local group, but it can access *resources* only on Domain 1!

 Keep this in mind for the exam. Domain local accounts are actually a very secure (arguably the most secure) form of account. Because of this, Microsoft likes to ask questions about them on the exam.

Global

The next group type is a global group. And the easiest way to think about a global group is that it is effectively the opposite of a domain local group. A global group can access *resources* on any domain, but it can contain *accounts* only from its unique domain. A great example of when you might use something like this is when you have three engineers in the engineering department who need access to a die cutter in another domain. Rather than set permissions for each engineer, you could simply create a global group for the engineers, place them in it, and give them access to the die cutter on the other domain with ease.

Universal

A universal group is the only group type that is available in Windows Server 2008 native mode. However, universal groups are certainly the most robust. A universal group can contain membership from any domain, and it can access resources in any domain. This type of group is useful to administrators, but it shouldn't be used excessively at the enterprise level. It's all too tempting to just add every group to universal status and remove the need for granular administration. However, there is a downside to universal groups in that any change that affects the group is placed in the global catalog and then replicated throughout the entire infrastructure, which can create some serious bottlenecks.

Built-in Local Groups

By default, Windows Server 2008 includes several built-in local user accounts within Active Directory for the purpose of administration. Each of these accounts serves a different purpose that can be used at various levels of administration. In total, these accounts are as follows:

- Account Operators
- Administrators

- Backup Operators
- Certificate Service DCOM Access
- Cryptographic Operators
- Distributed COM users
- Event Log Readers
- Guests
- IIS_IUSRS
- Incoming Forest Trust Builders
- Network Configuration Operators
- Performance Log Users
- Performance Monitor Users
- Pre-Windows 2000 Compatible Access
- Print Operators
- Server Operators
- Terminal Server License Servers
- Users
- Windows Authorization Access Group

Although local groups have been included in this book because they're often used for various purposes throughout the enterprise, you will rarely encounter questions on the certification exam specifically asking you about the purpose of a built-in local group.

Altering Group Scope

If you are a member of the Account Operators, Domain Admins, or Enterprise Admins in Active Directory, you have the option of changing the scope of a group if the current scope of your defined group is not to your liking. You can do this by using the Active Directory Users and Computers MMC; just right-click the individual group, and select Properties. On the General tab, in the Group Scope section, click the Group scope, as shown in Figure 5.8.

With Windows Server 2008, the following conversions are possible:

Global to universal This is possible if the group to be changed is not a member of another global scope group.

Domain local to universal This is possible if the group does not have another domain local group as a member.

Universal to global This is possible if the group does not have a universal group as a member.

FIGURE 5.8   Group scope's General tab

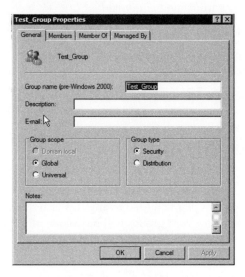

In Exercise 5.1, you'll create a universal group that contains membership from domains other than itself.

EXERCISE 5.1

Creating a Universal Group with Multiple Domain Membership

To perform this exercise, you must have at least two domains operating at the Windows Server 2003 or 2008 level that are either members of the same forest or connected via a forest trust.

1. Select Start ➢ Administrative Tools ➢ Active Directory Users and Computers.

2. Select the Users folder to display the complete list of users.

3. Right-click an area of whitespace within the Active Directory Users and Computers tool, and select New ➢ Group.

4. Select the Universal radio button and the Security radio button, and then name the group **AllUsers**.

5. Double-click the group, or right-click the group and select Properties.

6. Add a user of your choice. In this case, I'll use the previously created user snuffleupagus.

7. Click the Locations button, and select another domain in your forest.

8.   Add a user of your choice from another domain.

9.   Select OK and then OK again.

Your universal group will now contain members from multiple domains and can be assigned permissions in multiple domains.

Planning for Groups

To make sure your network properly supports the stringent requirements of the enterprise, before you begin to make groups you will need to administer in the future, it is extremely advisable to devise a plan for how your groups will be used at all levels—domain local, global, and universal.

Planning Domain Local and Global Accounts

The first thing to remember about both domain local and global accounts is that they are both listed in the global catalog; however, their members are not listed. One of the main reasons for this is security; another is bandwidth. If all members of groups were broadcast throughout the entire infrastructure, there would be a significant replication overhead. Therefore, you have to make sure to design your global and domain local groups from the ground up to optimize for efficiency and for association.

According to Microsoft and its administration best practices, the best way to design a domain local group is to follow this five-step procedure:

1.   Create global groups based upon various departments or similarly associated roles, such as Engineering or Accounting.

2.   Once these groups are created, add users who need to be associated with the groups.

3.   Create domain local groups that will contain various resources that need to be shared, and name these groups accordingly, such as the domain local group Printers.

4.   Once you've created your global and domain local groups, associate your global groups to the domain local groups by adding the global groups to the domain local groups. For example, you could take your Engineering or Accounting global groups and add them to the Printers group.

5.   Assign permissions to the domain local groups according to the required access. Thus, in the Printers domain local group you could assign permissions that would affect the global groups created earlier.

Keep in mind that although this is a good strategy, it has certain limitations. For one thing, domain local accounts are restricted to resources within the domain. Thus, the administration of multiple domains can become extremely complicated.

Planning Universal Groups

Universal groups are a little more powerful than domain local or even global groups because of their ability to associate users from multiple domains. Thus, as you might imagine, planning these groups is a little bit easier. However, keep in mind that universal groups can't be used unless you are running in native mode. Also, universal groups are an extremely large drain on your network infrastructure.

Thus, a strong recommendation by Microsoft is to add users first to global groups and then place these global groups into universal groups. By this design, the network doesn't have to broadcast every single member of the group throughout the infrastructure, which therefore increases your enterprise optimization.

 Real World Scenario

Designing for the Large-Scale Enterprise

The MegaCorp corporation is a large-scale business that contains 34 different departments with more than 1,000 users in each department. The MegaCorp corporation is operating at the Windows Server 2003 native level. Additionally, each of these departments has several layers of management, including department managers, floor supervisors, and others. In the initial design of the MegaCorp forest, the senior architect decided to create 13 domains to break down the forest into a more reasonable size.

To facilitate these users so that they can be accessed by anyone in the forest, the Mega-Corp corporation creates 34 different universal groups that can be accessed throughout the infrastructure. Then, after creating these groups, the MegaCorp corporation creates 34 different global groups and associates all members of the departments into those global groups. Afterward, the global groups are placed within the universal groups. Now, the changes made to the global catalog are minimal and can be replicated with ease.

For each domain, the local resources of the domains are placed into a domain local group that contains all the resources that need to be accessed by various users throughout the infrastructure. Then, using the universal groups that have been created, these universal groups are added to the domain local group. Once this is completed, users throughout the entire enterprise can access resources throughout the forest, and security policies can be placed on the domain local groups for the purpose of efficiency.

It's a good idea to make changes to universal groups as sparingly as possible. Remember, every time you change something in a universal group, it is replicated throughout the entire forest. This can bog your infrastructure down with unnecessary traffic.

Planning Delegation

As I've already referenced a couple times throughout this chapter, in a large organization delegation can become one of your best friends. But if you're not careful, just like with Group Policy, it can also quickly become one of your greatest and most terrible enemies. Keep in mind that whenever you delegate control to a user for some reason, you are, by the very nature of the word, delegating authority.

And whenever you delegate any type of authority, there's a strong chance you can make a mistake. So, just as a warning before you get started, tread carefully when it comes to delegation, and never delegate too much. The goal with delegation is to achieve a balance where you alleviate burden from yourself, but don't create a virtual Frankenstein in the process of doing so that may create huge problems for your overall infrastructure.

Delegation is done in two ways: through objects and through tasks.

Although the specific process of how to delegate a user does not appear on the Enterprise Administrator certification exam, understanding user delegation is extremely important in order to become a successful administrator. Before you take the exam and certainly before you delegate in the real world, be sure to try it in both a simulated environment and a live environment, especially before you try anything on a large scale.

Object-Based Delegation

When you delegate authority by assigning a user permission directly to an object, you're performing object-based delegation. For instance, if in your organization you have an OU called Computers that is accessed by several different users including managers and that periodically has machines added to it as new employees are hired and more hardware is acquired, you could delegate control of the objects contained within the Computers OU to the managers using the Delegation of Control Wizard in the Active Directory Users and Computers tool. Thus, from now on, the users or users you delegated control of the Computers OU will have access to any new computers that you may add at a later date. And within the Delegation of Control Wizard, there are numerous options that administrators can invoke to either assign or revoke privileges to further refine control of those objects.

Task-Based Delegation

A much more difficult to accomplish but still perfectly valid form of delegation is delegation based on task analysis. For example, earlier in the sales example there were users who needed access to a printer. Using task-based delegation, you could assign your managers the ability to, say, print to the printer but deny them the ability to modify any resources there, just for security purposes. As you can see, it's a bit fancier than just delegating objects, but if you're careful, it can get the job done—and possibly increase the overall security of your infrastructure.

Delegation Options

When you have decided to delegate a particular object to a given user or group, you start the Delegation of Control Wizard by navigating to Active Directory Users and Computers, right-clicking the given container you want to delegate, and selecting Delegate Control.

At this point, you can select what users you want to add as authoritative, as displayed in Figure 5.9.

FIGURE 5.9   Users selection for delegation

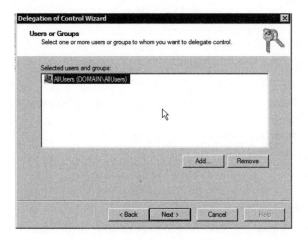

After hitting Next, you'll be presented with the section of the Delegation of Control Wizard that you are really concerned with at the enterprise level, which is the task delegation list, as shown in Figure 5.10.

FIGURE 5.10   Tasks to delegate

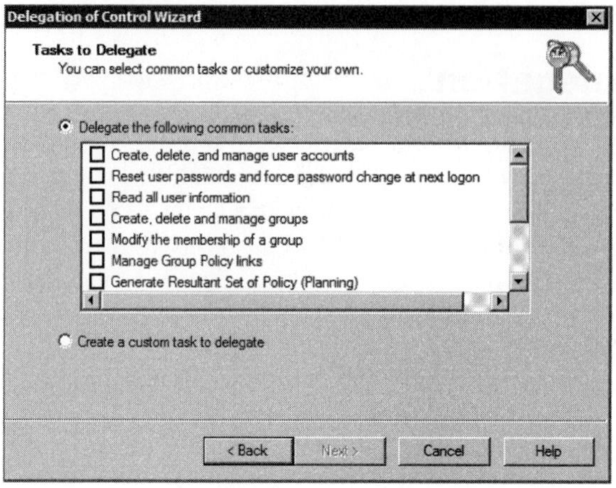

In total, this list contains eleven options that you need to be familiar with:

Create, Delete, and Manage User Accounts   This delegation is used when you need to give permission for a user or group to have control over the administration of accounts. With this permission, the user or group has the authority to create, delete, and modify accounts according to the design specifications they desire.

Reset User Passwords and Force Password Change at Next Logon   Probably the most often used delegation, this gives a user or group the ability to change passwords for the specific area that has been delegated for them.

Read All User Information   Mostly used for auditing and security purposes, this gives permission to read all user information in the entire account. This should be used sparingly.

Create, Delete and Manage Groups   This gives the delegate the authority to administer groups and is usually coupled with the ability to create user accounts. With this, the delegate has the authority to truly start managing the infrastructure.

Modify the Membership of a Group   A more finite and granular approach to delegation is to allow the delegate to modify the membership of a group, rather than the ability to manage the group with the permissions to delete and create groups. This is more secure and convenient for administrators.

Manage Group Policy Links   I'll cover GPOs more heavily in Chapter 6, but GPOs will sometimes need delegates to control them for ease of administration. With this option, the delegate can modify GPO links and alter their settings.

Generate Resultant Set of Policy (Planning)   This allows the delegate to use the RSoP snap-in in planning mode to view results.

Generate Resultant Set of Policy (Logging)   This allows the delegate to use the RSoP snap-in in logging mode to view results.

Create, Delete and Manage inetOrgPerson Accounts Sometimes delegates will deal with non-Microsoft LDAP and X.500 directory services that use inetOrgPerson mail accounts. With this delegation, delegates can create these accounts and modify them.

Reset inetOrgPerson Passwords and Force Password Changes at Next Logon Just like with normal accounts, this delegation lets the delegate modify passwords for their selected OU.

Read all inetOrgPerson Information This allows the delegate to read all inetOrgPerson information, generally for the purpose of security or auditing.

On the Microsoft Enterprise Administrator exam, several of the questions you may be asked will have to do with the process of delegation through groups, user accounts, OUs, and types of delegation. Thus, it behooves you to be very familiar with what you're capable of doing with delegation.

Furthermore, as you probably noticed in Figure 5.10, administrators are not confined to the default set of delegations. You can create a delegation from the ground up on a folder or object and specify exactly what you want to delegate. However, this will most likely not be covered on the exam and thus is not covered in this chapter.

Be aware that delegation is very granular by design, so you can't just delegate everything.

Inheritance

Just like in real life, inheritance in Windows architecture is the process of receiving from your parents. Of course, with inheritance in Windows, there is usually no death involved. Far from it, in fact. With Windows Server 2008, inheritance is designed to only increase the number of permissions and overall assets of the infrastructure and involves no taking away whatsoever.

By default, child OUs inherit all of their parent's attributes. This means that if the top-level OU dictates that they have full control over whatever objects that are in that OU, they will by default have control over all the objects that are in any succeeding OUs that are created there.

The complication comes, of course, when an administrator decides that for whatever reason the standardized process of inheriting all attributes from a parent object is not appropriate for the situation and thus the inheritance must be blocked. The block inheritance feature in an OU allows administrators to completely ignore the permissions once contained in the parent OU and allows them to instead define their own. Of course, when this is first initiated, the administrator who has decided to block the inheritance can initially copy the current permissions, block them, and then redefine permissions for the child object with relative ease.

In Figure 5.11, the Engineering OU will receive the settings of the top-level Departments OU. However, the Sales OU has blocked inheritance from Departments, and thus it doesn't have the same properties.

FIGURE 5.11   Inheritance and inheritance blocking

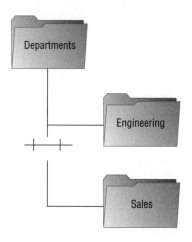

 Real World Scenario

New Accounts for New Hires

The MegaCorp corporation has recently gone through a massive hiring spree and has more than 1,000 new employees who are stationed on the eighth through tenth floors of the MegaCorp main office. Since the MegaCorp headquarters is an extremely large building, managers have also been placed at key locations in offices throughout the eight and tenth floors to both train and watch over the new employees while they transition through their orientation to MegaCorp.

When these new employees become ready to work as sales associates for MegaCorp, each of them will be given a unique user account in Active Directory that will be added to the MegaCorp forest. Accordingly, for every 50 employees who are in the company, there is at least one manager. To ease the process of administration, what MegaCorp might decide to do is create 50 different OUs that each contains the sales associates in a given location. That way, instead of having a large OU with every single sales associate, it's more easily refined based on location. Afterward, another step that could simplify the implementation of their new employees is by creating a security group called Sales Managers. Then, you could delegate control of the 20 different sales OUs to the Sales Managers group. That way, whenever the sales managers need to swap accounts between two different groups, they can do so. Additionally, they can reset passwords and take care of everyday tasks for their specific group.

By doing this, MegaCorp has utilized a location-based OU structure and delegated authority to a security group for more than 1,000 employees that higher-level administrators will, for the most part, not have to administer. The danger with an implementation like this, however, is that although this does ease the process of adding various users, resetting passwords, and the like, it also creates a fairly obvious security hole. Now, because of the implementation suggested, the Sales Managers security group has control of more than 1,000 users, which can lead to a potential disaster.

Alternatively, a more administratively taxing on the higher level but more secure method would be to create the OUs for the location-based users and then individually delegate authority to various sales manager user accounts. This way, they will have access only to their OU and do not run the risk of contaminating the rest of the environment.

Using the Security Configuration Wizard for Compliance Auditing

The process of *compliance auditing* is the everyday task of ensuring that users are adhering to the standards and purpose outlined by your organization's security design and policy. With Windows Server 2008, there are many ways of designing security audits and monitoring the access of various objects and resources to see whether they have been accessed according to their design. Of course, the inherent nature of any security design is that it can be compromised in some form or another. Therefore, another purpose of compliance auditing isn't just to make sure that the policy is being used well but that no one is abusing that policy.

With the release of Windows Server 2003, Microsoft included the Server Security Configuration Wizard. The Security Configuration Wizard (SCW) is an attack-surface reduction tool that assists administrators in creating security policies for the Windows administrators. With the SCW, you can create, edit, and apply security policies. Furthermore, Microsoft has thought ahead with the SCW in that the SCW uses XML files that can be swapped between servers.

At the enterprise level, you're most concerned with using the SCW to create an audit policy. The SCW has three default levels that can be set:

Do Not Audit No auditing is conducted, and no CPU hard disk cycles are consumed in the process of auditing.

Audit Successful Activities This type of auditing records when successful activities occur. This includes the auditing of logon events, object access, policy changes, process tracking, and system events.

Audit Successful and Unsuccessful Activities With this type of auditing, you can log all the audit activities of successful audits and also any failures that may have occurred. This process is mostly used if you are trying to track users who are attempting to gain access to unauthorized areas.

The SCW is not primarily designed for creating audit policies. In fact, the default loading screen for the SCW appears as shown in Figure 5.12.

FIGURE 5.12   Default Security Configuration Wizard loading screen

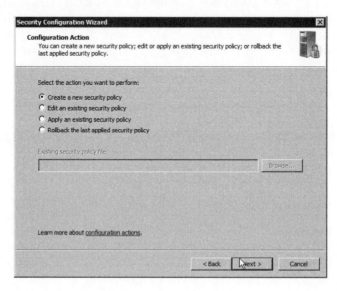

But when you create a new security policy, you will ultimately come to a screen where you can view the changes you made in the SCW.

For the certification exam, and for your real work in the enterprise, it isn't necessarily important that you understand how to use the Security Configuration Wizard inside and out, but you need to be familiar with the levels of audits that it can configure and what each of these audits corresponds to:

- Audit logon events
- Account management
- Directory services access
- Logon events
- Object access
- Policy change
- Privilege use
- Process tracking
- System events

Summary

Delegation is used in the Windows infrastructure to relieve the burden of administrative overhead, and groups are used in the enterprise to simplify the process of grouping users for various purposes. Within Windows Server, users are divided into two group types: security and distribution. Of concern to you for the enterprise certification exam and as a system administrator is the security group.

Security groups come in three types: universal, global, and domain local. Additionally, machines can contain local accounts for use on an individual machine. Along with these groups, individual user accounts can be delegated the authority to make changes in the enterprise, including adding user accounts and groups as well as changing user passwords and carrying out low-level administrative tasks.

When creating your OU design, it's best to keep in mind that there are three criteria that should be directly considered when beginning the first draft: Visibility, Group Policy, and Autonomy. Visibility controls the appears of objects, Group Policy design takes into account the effects of variously implemented group policies, and Autonomy regulates the independence of OUs apart from other containers.

Exam Essentials

Know the different delegation options. It's imperative for this certification exam that you be able to easily recite and understand the different options you have with delegation, such as resetting users' passwords.

Understand design criteria for OUs. Be able to readily identify weak points in OU structure, such as a lack of accountability for visibility or for autonomy.

Remember what can and cannot be an object. By now, this should be second nature. Remember also that most of the 70-647 exam is about implementing what you have already learned.

Keep in mind what you can do with auditing. Think like an auditor. Consider when it would be in your best interest to audit object access or directory access or perhaps whether it would be best to record a successful or unsuccessful attempt, or even both.

Know your groups inside and out. Different group scenarios will be tossed at you left and right. By knowing and understanding the different types of groups, you will prepare yourself for this eventuality.

Don't forget about inheritance. Keep inheritance in mind whenever you're studying a topology. If inheritance is going to affect you, you have to know what it does to your object access and your permissions and delegation decisions.

Understand the reasons for delegation. Your organization may be too big and need extra hands, or there may be a mundane task that is repeated far too often to be of concern to the senior administrator. But don't just implement delegation because it can be done.

Review Questions

1. Which of the following are not a design consideration for OU structure? (Choose all that apply.)

   A. Visibility

   B. Autonomy

   C. Access

   D. Control

   E. Group Policy

2. What are the types of delegation used in the process of delegating authority? (Choose all that apply.)

   A. Task-based

   B. Resource-based

   C. Object-based

   D. User-based

   E. Computer-based

   F. Control-based

3. Which of the following group types is viewable from the forest level and can contain members from any domain and access resources in any domain?

   A. Universal

   B. Global

   C. Domain local

   D. Local

4. A supervisor in your company has become concerned that night-shift employees who come into work after your supervisor has left the office are actually not showing up on time or not showing up at all. Accordingly, your supervisor has asked you to devise a method that will enable her to see when employees arrive to work. Which of the following solutions meets the objective of your supervisor?

   A. Create an audit policy to log object access between the night-shift's work hours, and report those log results to a file.

   B. Implement an audit policy that logs logon events for the enterprise and reports those events to a file that can be viewed by the supervisor.

   C. Create an audit policy that logs successful and unsuccessful logon events between the hours of the night shift, and save that to a file to be viewed by your supervisor.

   D. Create an audit policy that logs successful logon events only between the hours of the night shift, and only for the night-shift crew, have those results reported to a file and sent to your supervisor.

5. You are operating an enterprise running Windows Server 2008 at the Windows Server 2008 native level. Three different departments within your business need to access resources within a specific domain. In total, these departments represent a total of more than 3,000 users, or approximately 1,000 users in each department. You want to create a group structure for these users with the least amount of administrative overhead. What should you do?

   A. Create a global group for each department, and then assign each global group permissions to the resources in your domain.

   B. Create global groups for each of the departments, and add those global groups to a single universal group. Afterward, add those users to a domain local group on the domain with the resources, and assign permission to the domain local group.

   C. Create a universal group for each department, and assign permissions to the universal group. Afterward, create a domain local account on the domain with the resources, and add the universal groups to that domain.

   D. Add all users who need access to the resources to a universal group, and then apply permissions to the universal group.

6. When planning for best security practices, it's best to assign permissions to groups at what group scope level?

   A. Local

   B. Global

   C. Universal

   D. Domain local

7. As a newly appointed senior architect, the chief technology officer for your company has tasked you with creating a new OU strategy for your infrastructure. From what you know of OU strategy, which of the following is not appropriate criteria for design convention?

   A. Location

   B. Business function

   C. Title

   D. Object type

8.   Your organization consists of 10 Active Directory domains that are spread throughout 10 departments, with each department being placed in its own domain. The entire forest and all its domains are running at the Server 2008 functional level. In each of these domains, a department head needs to be able to control the users within the Users OU that is unique on each domain. Recently, the CEO has asked you to place the department heads into their own department called Upper Management. The Upper Management department should be able to control all users but not be able to make domain-wide changes or administer enterprise-level solutions. What should you do to facilitate this requirement?

A.   Create a universal group for the department heads called DepartmentHeads, and delegate the Users OU for each domain to the DepartmentHeads group.

B.   Create a global group for the department heads called DepartmentHeads, and delegate the Users OU for each domain to the DepartmentHeads group.

C.   Create a domain local group for the department heads called DepartmentHeads, and delegate the Users OU for each domain to the DepartmentHeads group.

D.   Create a DepartmentHeads OU, and delegate control of the Users OU for each domain to the DepartmentHeads OU.

E.   Implement a group policy that enables department heads to have control over all users.

9.   This morning you've received a memo that the MegaCorp corporation will be auditing your organization and that a senior administrator has accordingly created a universal security group called MCAuditors in Active Directory. Furthermore, in your email, the same administrator has asked you to set up this security group for the auditors. From what you know, the auditors will be auditing users in the AllUsers organizational unit. What is the first step you should take to facilitate this audit?

A.   Use the Security Configuration Wizard to set up an audit policy, and add the OU as a required field.

B.   Set up a GPO for the MCAuditors security group that allows them audit privileges.

C.   Delegate the MCAuditors security group the Read All User Information privilege.

D.   Assign the AllUsers OU the Read-Only permission for the MCAuditors security group.

10.   Your organization contains resources such as shared folders and printers throughout five different domains in your forest. Accordingly, 34 users in the Domain4 domain need to access all resources in the Domain1, Domain2, Domain3, and Domain6 domains. You need to give all these users access to the resources on the domain with as little administrative effort as possible, while still utilizing the best group design. What should you do?

A.   Create a domain local group on Domain4, add the 34 users, and then apply the appropriate permissions.

B.   Create a global group from the Domain4 group users, and apply permissions to the global group to access resources on the other domains.

C.   Create a universal group from the Domain4 group, add the appropriate users, and grant the universal group the appropriate permissions.

D.   Assign the users the appropriate permissions in Active Directory, and do not use groups to save network bandwidth.

11. You are an individual administrator for your domain in a large enterprise. In this domain, you have a total of 10 printers that need to be accessed by users throughout the rest of your domains. Because of this, your supervisor has asked you to create a group that will contain memberships from throughout the enterprise that will need to access these printers only on your domains. What should you do?

    A. Create a global group on your domain, and assign permissions to the global group.

    B. Create a domain local group on your domain, and assign permission to the domain local group.

    C. Create a universal group, and assign permissions to the universal group.

    D. Create a local group, and assign permissions locally without Active Directory.

12. Which of the following events is not a criterion for auditing events?

    A. Logon events

    B. Object access

    C. Policy change

    D. Privilege use

    E. Control use

    F. Process tracking

    G. System events

13. When delegating organizational units (OUs), all but which of the following can become delegates? (Choose all that apply.)

    A. Global groups

    B. Domain local groups

    C. Universal groups

    D. Servers

    E. Users

    F. Domain controllers

    G. Computers

14. The MyCorp infrastructure consists of a location-based OU design, as shown here. Today, the chief technology officer decided that all IT personnel should be able to create users and reset passwords for all OUs, regardless of their department. Based upon what you see in the figure, what would be the best solution to implement this design request?

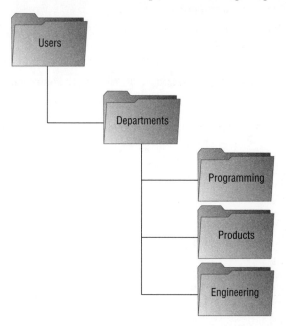

A. Create a security group called IT_Personnel, and add all members of the IT security team to that group. Then, delegate control of each OU to that group.

B. Create a security group called IT_Personnel, and add all members of the IT security team to that group. Assign permissions to change passwords for that group.

C. Create a security group called IT_Personnel, and add all members of the IT security team to that group. Delegate control of the parent OU, Departments, to the security group. Then choose the options Create, Delete, and Manage User Accounts and Reset User Passwords and Force Password Change at Next Logon.

D. Create a security group called IT_Personnel, and add all members of the IT security team to that group. Delegate control of the parent Departments OU to the security group, and choose the options Create, Delete, and Manage User Accounts and Modify the Membership of a Group.

15. Within your enterprise help desk, technicians have been delegated authority to add users to all OUs within the organization through the help-desk security group. This is designed to relieve the pressure from higher-level administrators whenever a new employee is added to the business. Today, a junior IT help-desk technician claims he is able to create a user account but unable to create a group within a particular OU. What is a possible reason for this?

   A. The help-desk technician is not a member of the Helpdesk security group.

   B. The Helpdesk security group has been assigned the incorrect delegation permissions.

   C. The OU being managed by the technician is set to block inheritance.

   D. The Helpdesk security group file permissions are incorrect.

16. If you are asked to adhere to the Microsoft-recommended standard practice for adding universal groups to your Active Directory infrastructure, what procedures must you follow? (Choose all that apply.)

   A. Create the universal group.

   B. Create a global group.

   C. Create a domain local group.

   D. Place the global group within the universal group.

   E. Place the global group containing the universal group within the domain local group.

17. Which of the following organizational structures cannot receive permissions?

   A. Global groups

   B. Universal groups

   C. Local groups

   D. Organizational units

   E. Domain local groups

18. The MegaCorp corporation is an enterprise that consists of three domains operating at the Windows Server 2008 functional level. You are the senior administrator for this company, and you are responsible for creating and implementing all administrative policies. Your organizational layout for the OU structure appears as shown here. Recently, you have decided to expand the IT_Technicians OU to three different departments; however, you do not want the delegation properties to be any different from the current layout. Which of the following methods will achieve this with the least amount of administrative effort?

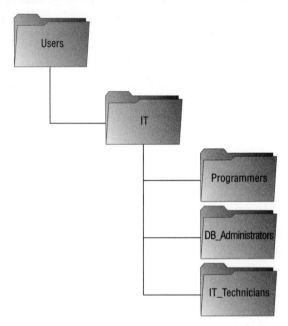

   A. Create three new OUs named IT_Tech1, IT_Tech2, and IT_Tech3. Nest the OUs within the parent OU, which is IT_Tech, and inherent the previous settings.

   B. Create three new OUs named IT_Tech1, IT_Tech2, and IT_Tech3. Replicate the settings via an ADMX file, and apply to each OU.

   C. Create three new OUs named IT_Tech1, IT_Tech2, and IT_Tech3. Assign permissions based upon the previously established template.

   D. Create three new OUs named IT_Tech1, IT_Tech2, and IT_Tech3. Nest the OUs within the parent OU, which is IT_Tech, and block inheritance so that each group can be administered separately.

19. Which of the following group scope conversions is not possible?

   A. Global to universal

   B. Domain local to universal

   C. Universal to global

   D. Universal to domain local

20. Which of the following group types can contain members from any domain but access resources only from within its own domain?

   A. Global

   B. Universal

   C. Domain local

   D. Local

Answers to Review Questions

1. **C, E.** OU structure is not a mandatory requirement, but it is a best practice laid out by Microsoft that ensures that your enterprise keeps operating smoothly. Three design considerations related to OU structure are visibility, autonomy, and Group Policy.

2. **A, C.** Delegation can be accomplished through either task-based or object-based delegation. With object-based delegation, delegation is accomplished through the delegation of specific objects in the enterprise. Task-based delegation is designed to facilitate the need to assign authority based upon a user's specific need to accomplish a task that may involve multiple objects and multiple security access requirements.

3. **A.** Only universal groups can access resources from any part of the forest and contain membership from any area of the forest. Remember, you must be running at a native level to use universal groups.

4. **D.** If the goal of the audit is to see what time users have been logging on, a successful logon event policy will record the times and user accounts that have logged into the domain controller. Thus, if an employee doesn't log in or logs in late, their name will show up in the log.

5. **B.** By placing each department into a global group, you are compartmentalizing your departments for best practices. Afterward, when you create a universal group, you are creating a group that can be read throughout the entire forest. Then, when you add this group to the domain local group on the domain with the resources, you are localizing the permissions associated with this domain.

6. **D.** Domain local groups are the best area to set permissions, because the scope is the least broad. By having a narrow scope, you can take extra security precautions as well as implement additional checks and balances to make sure your permissions are not applied to too many users or objects.

7. **C.** Organization by title can lead to a lot of confusion. Say your enterprise has 12 departments, and each of these departments has managers. If these managers were placed into one OU to have permissions assigned, it could get very confusing when you start to apply the sales managers permissions to use the die cutter in the engineering room because of lack of OU scope design.

8. **A.** By creating a universal group, you are creating a group that is visible to the entire forest. Then, by delegating the OU to the users, you are not giving the users enterprise- or domain-level authority, but they can still administer the users in their own departments.

9. **C.** The Read All User Information delegation allows the delegate to view all user information and is usually used in security audits. By doing this first, you ensure that the auditors will receive access to the information they need.

10. **B.** Both a universal group and global group will work in this situation, but you should use a global group because global groups can access resources in any location but can contain users from only one domain. Additionally, universal groups are much more intensive on network bandwidth, and global groups optimize efficiency for replication purposes.

11. B. Domain local groups can access resources on only one domain. However, they can contain members from other domains. Creating a domain local group ensures that users will be able to access the resources they need and not extend beyond the scope of the local domain.

12. E. Control use is not a criterion for auditing events. Using auditing, you can track a great deal of information, including successful and unsuccessful events. You can create auditing using the local security policy tool, the SCW, or other methods.

13. D, F, G. Only users or groups can become delegates. This is because the act of delegation is the process of giving authority to a person, not an object. Computers are not capable of making educated administration decisions—at least, not yet.

14. C. By creating a security group and delegating the control of the parent OU called Departments to the security group, the child OUs inherit the control from the parent OU through inheritance. Thus, the delegation occurs to multiple OUs without the need to apply to all OUs in the infrastructure.

15. B. If a technician is able to create users but unable to create groups, it's most likely that the Delegation of Control Wizard was used and the ability to create and manage groups was not applied. It is possible that the OU is using inheritance, but the question does not indicate that this OU is a child of another OU; thus, it must be disregarded.

16. A, B, D. The best practice of adding global groups to universal groups stems from the idea that global groups can reduce replication costs. This is done to enhance speed and lessen the effect of universal group membership changes on the infrastructure.

17. D. Organizational units are designed for delegation and for deploying group Policy. They cannot take permissions of any kind.

18. A. By nesting OUs within OUs, you ensure that the child inherits the parent settings of the top-level OU. This will ensure that the delegations do not have to be reassigned, so you can leave them at the default settings.

19. D. Although you can convert from domain local to universal, it is not possible to convert from universal to domain local. This is because universal groups may contain memberships that access resources outside of the local domain.

20. C. Domain local accounts can contain membership from any domain but can access resources only from within their own domain. This is because domain local accounts are designed to limit the scope of access to only the domain.

Chapter

6

Planning and Designing Group Policy

OBJECTIVES COVERED IN THIS CHAPTER:

✓ **Design the enterprise-level group policy strategy.**

    ▪ May include but is not limited to group policy hierarchy and scope filtering, control device installation, and authentication and authorization

An easy statement to make about Group Policy at the enterprise level is that if your network is the heart of your infrastructure, Group Policy is the circulatory system that directs it. The only difference is that with Group Policy you can't rely upon divine design to make it work. Instead, administrators have to do some of the hard work themselves.

When you took the MCTS-level certification exams on Windows Server 2008, you briefly looked at the topics of creating Active Directory objects and linking them to appropriate users, containers, and so forth. And even at that level, where you had to concern yourself with only one or at most two Group Policy objects, you had to consider the impact that even one change could make. If you didn't implement your policy right, you could lock yourself, the head administrator, out of important software to which you need access or important files that have to be shared.

At the enterprise level, your primary concern regarding Group Policy is making sure that it spreads to the right place at the right time. On average, a large infrastructure will have several dozen or possibly several hundred policies in place. If these policies aren't carefully designed, they won't be implemented effectively.

In this chapter, you'll examine the scope and impact of Group Policy, as well as how Group Policy can authorize and authenticate users. I'll also talk about controlling the installation of device drivers and then touch a little bit on software installation, which will be discussed later in this book. Lastly, I'll discuss two notable features of Server 2008: searching Group Policy objects and using the Group Policy modeling tool.

Understanding Group Policy Scope

Whenever you create a Group Policy object using the Group Policy MMC, the first step is to define the policy and establish all its settings. Afterward, a little bit of Active Directory magic happens, and a *Group Policy object* (GPO) is created. However, in and of itself, that GPO doesn't do a whole lot. In fact, it does absolutely nothing until that policy is linked to one of three different administrative structures:

- Sites
- Domains
- Organizational units (OUs)

Once that link is established, the location where that link is referenced is called the *scope of management* (SOM). The Scope of Management basically tells the areas defined what they should pay attention to and how it affects them. Of course, multiple structures can contain multiple GPOs, and each can be linked to multiple GPOs, which can create multiple scopes of management. But by default, all users contained within the SOM will have the GPO applied to them and their children through inheritance.

Applying Group Policy

A lot of administrators say that the most fun, or at least the most worrying, job in an enterprise is applying Group Policy. To do so safely, an administrator has to understand the impact of each decision. To begin with, you have to understand the order in which Group Policy is implied, which is summarized in Figure 6.1.

The order in which Group Policy is applied is as follows:

1. Local
2. Site
3. Domain
4. OU

FIGURE 6.1   Group Policy application order

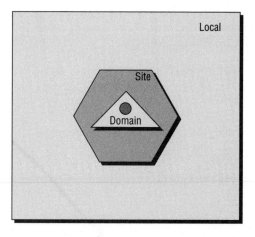

First, Group Policy is applied locally. Every computer running Windows Server 2008 that uses Group Policy has a Group Policy object that will apply its own individual settings, which come into play before any other. Afterward, any policies that are linked to the site are applied to the individual machine. Only after both the local and site policies have been applied are the domain policies applied. Ironically enough, it's only at the end of this process that OUs are applied.

This is for good and logical reason. The main reason OUs are applied last is that the policy is designed to go from the most localized to the least localized. Considering that OUs can spread across a wide area and contain a lot of different object types, it's best to apply them last and only after all other policies have been applied. What makes it ironic is that most administrators spend most of their time applying GPOs to OUs!

Keep in mind that although this is how Group Policy is applied, there is a default *precedence* regarding how important Windows Server 2008 considers the policy. The order is as follows, from strongest precedence to weakest precedence:

1. GPO linked to an OU

2. GPO linked to a domain

3. GPO linked to a site

4. Local GPO for a specific user

5. Local GPO for administrators/nonadministrators

6. Local GPO for a local group policy

And, in the case where two policies are overlapping, the policy with the strongest precedence is declared the winner and is applied.

Inheritance

By default, all group policies are passed from parent to child when the policy is contained within a single domain. However, for child domains, the group policies are *not* inherited from one domain to another. This means that, as in Figure 6.2, users in the Users OU in Domain 1 will receive the Group Policy from the domain, but users in the More Users OU in Domain 2 will not inherit the Group Policy.

FIGURE 6.2   Inheritance not received by domain

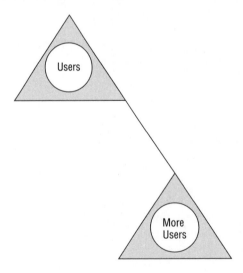

You need to know a couple of other facts about Group Policy inheritance rules. First, the rule of thumb within a domain is that if the policy is configured for the parent and not configured for the child, the child will automatically inherit it. However, if the policy is *not* configured for the parent, the child will not inherit any policies either. The last exception is, of course, if an administrator decides to manually block inheritance from a child, then the child does not inherit any group policies.

No Override Inheritance and Block Policy Inheritance

Group Policy objects, by default, have two ways they can be applied through inheritance. The first of these options is called No Override. With No Override, policies are continuously applied and ignore any settings beneath them from child OUs or containers that may contain different settings. So, for example, a higher-level OU may have a policy that conflicts with a policy at a lower level. If the No Override policy setting is selected, the higher-level policy will take precedence and ignore the lower-level policy.

Alternatively, a policy can be set to Block Policy Inheritance. If this is done, the lower-level child policy blocks the inheritance of the higher-level policy. Of course, it bears noting that the Block Policy Inheritance setting is not as high priority as the No Override option. This means that the No Override option will always take priority over the Block Policy Inheritance setting. So the Block Policy Inheritance setting will come into effect only if No Override is not selected.

Within a multitiered infrastructure, such as pictured in Figure 6.3, the Block Policy Inheritance setting is used often. This is because, using this utility, administrators don't have to go through the bother of creating new OUs or specifically applying OUs at multiple levels. In Figure 6.3, you can apply a policy at a higher OU level and add an exception for the Employees OU, instead of having to apply this OU four different times for each sublevel OU.

FIGURE 6.3   Multitiered OU infrastructure

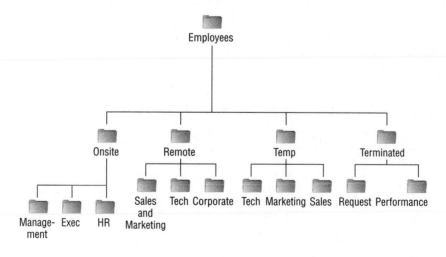

With this configuration, the Computers, Servers, and External Employees OUs receive GPO1, but the Employees OU doesn't receive the option because the Block Policy Inheritance setting is on. However, if the No Override options were set on GPO1 on the All Users OU, the Employees OU would still receive the policy, regardless of the Block Policy Inheritance setting.

> The No Override and Block Policy Inheritance settings are applied at the GPO level, not at the individual policy level.

Understanding Loopback Processing

When Group Policy is implemented, it's applied based on the design of Active Directory and how Group Policy has been applied within that Active Directory. Using Group Policy loopback processing, administrators are granted a more finite level of control based on the settings of the machine in question, regardless of its place in Active Directory.

More often than not, loopback processing is used on Terminal Services machines to make sure that users, regardless of their location, are applying specific policies according to that individual Terminal Services machine. In a way, it's a convenient method for administrators to say, "OK, I don't really care what the rules say; in this location I want the following settings to be applied."

Within loopback processing, two modes are available:

Replace mode   With Replace mode, all policies that were once granted to a user are now instead defined by the machine on which the user is logged on.

Merge mode   Using Merge mode, a user's policies and a machine's policies are combined. However, in the case where a user's policy may in some way conflict with a machine's policy, the machine's policy takes priority instead of the user's policy, again implying the administrative decision to let the machine make the appropriate decisions for the infrastructure.

The decision of which of these modes to use is, of course, up to you.

Understanding Group Policy Security Filtering

As I've mentioned a few times already in this book, one of the tasks that administrators face on a daily basis is the challenge of creating a policy that applies only to a specific area within Active Directory. Accordingly, one of the tools available to administrators in this process is the ability to use Group Policy security filtering.

With Group Policy security filtering, administrators can actively select users or groups of users that will receive direct policy application. The whole basis for this is that all GPOs are created and associated with access control lists (ACLs). These ACLs contain a series of access control entities (ACEs) that define the security principals within. In Figure 6.4, I'm using the Group Policy Management Console (GPMC) you are already familiar with to look at the security principals defined for the default domain controllers policy.

FIGURE 6.4   Default domain controllers policy setting

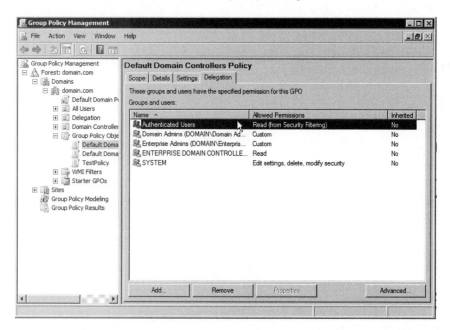

You can access this screen by opening the GPMC, expanding the Group Policy Object folder, selecting a GPO, and choosing its Delegation tab. From here, you can add users or groups, as well as choose to look at an advanced view that will allow you to set individual security privileges. It's important to note, though, that if you want a GPO to be processed by a security principal in a container linked to the GPO, you must have at least the following permissions applied:

- Allow Read
- Allow Apply Group Policy

Most of the time when administrators decide to implement security filtering, it's done when a particular OU that contains all the users to which the administrator wants to distribute the policy but also contains several users that do not need to have that policy applied to them. For example, examine the Managers OU in Figure 6.5.

Within that OU, ten different managers will be affected by a policy by default whenever a blanket policy is applied on that OU. If, for instance, you needed to give access to three of the managers to a particular printer or piece of software in the enterprise, you could apply a Group Policy to their OU, and the policy would take effect not just for those users but for all managers in the OU. It would achieve one goal in that managers would get access to the resource, but ultimately it would leave a security hole in that more users would have access to the resource than necessary.

FIGURE 6.5   Managers OU security filtering

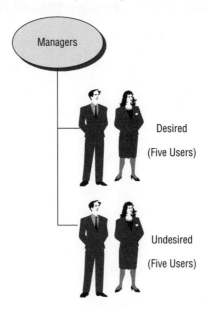

Using Group Policy security filtering, an administrator could create a singular group that contains just these users and then apply a security filter to the GPO linked to that OU, which applies the policy only to the group that the administrator created. Therefore, the rest of the users do not receive the implications of that Group Policy implementation.

As you can see in Figure 6.6, I have added my friend Snuffleupagus to the Security Filtering section of the GPO. Of course, to have this security filter truly apply properly, you would have to remove the Authenticated Users group. This is because the Authenticated Users group includes every user who is authenticated by the Windows Server environment (or in other words, any users who have logged on to a domain controller and authenticated themselves through the domain controller). In most environments, this will include just about every given user in the infrastructure. But of course, there are exceptions.

FIGURE 6.6   Security filtering on the GPO

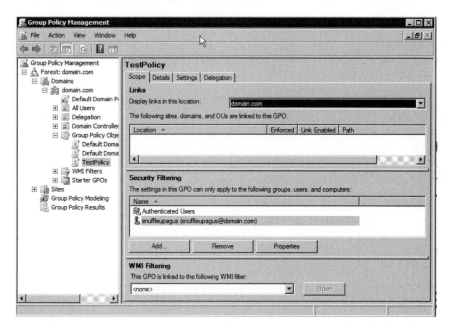

Windows Management Instrumentation Filters

In addition to filtering by users and by groups, another option available to administrators is to filter GPOs by the attributes of the individual computer that is the target of the Group Policy object. When a Windows Management Instrumentation (WMI) filter is applied, the target computer is tested and evaluated. Based on this evaluation, the WMI filter is issued either as true or as false and then applied or not applied accordingly.

One benefit of using WMI filters is that WMI makes data regarding a specific computer readily available for administrators. This includes features such as CPU, memory, disk space, and other important information that can be used when evaluating aspects for Group Policy application.

In the enterprise, WMI is used primarily for scripting purposes. Queries that are issued to WMIs are written using the WMI Query Language, which is similar to SQL database coding. Each of these queries is checked against a certain namespace that is defined when the query is created.

WMI filters can be applied on the Scope tab of a GPO. It's important to note, however, that a GPO can have only one WMI filter attached to it. Additionally, WMI filters are stored on a per-domain basis and must be used within the domain they are linked. Lastly, WMI filters work only on Windows XP and newer operating systems. Windows 2000–based products will not recognize WMI filters.

Planning Group Policy

Since the early days of Windows Group Policy, Microsoft has been very supportive of administrators in defining a set series of procedures that administrators should use when planning and designing Group Policy. Some of the reasons for this include the complicated nature of Group Policy, as well as the necessity to aid administrators in understanding the impact and scope of Group Policy when it is deployed correctly. In the following sections, I will cover the planning and design process recommended by Microsoft for deploying Windows Server Group Policy.

Step 1: Create a Reasonable OU Structure

This material, which I covered in Chapter 5, is the first step in planning for Group Policy. OU design is the fundamental base upon which the rest of Group Policy will be implemented. Therefore, to facilitate an easy implementation, it is best to start with a strong foundation.

Step 2: Define Restrictions and Objectives

After you've decided on the OU structure, the next step is to determine the entirety of the restrictions placed upon your organization and the objectives it wants to achieve. Microsoft breaks these objectives down into several facets:

- Complying with service-level agreements
- Defining Group Policy objectives
- Establishing Group Policy operational guidelines
- Recognizing interoperability issues
- Recognizing software installation issues

In the real world, these sorts of decisions are usually made by a team of administrators who sit down in a room and plan the long-term implications of the decisions made by Group Policy. However, for the enterprise certification exam, Microsoft will likely ask you direct questions that may involve issues from any of these planning and defining steps. And unfortunately, the guidelines for these steps require a lot of intuition on your behalf.

The best advice when dealing with these sorts of issues is to take them one at a time, whether you are dealing with a question on an exam or with a question in the real world. For example, when defining your Group Policy objectives, one of the requirements for your deployment might be to make sure a certain policy is not linked to a particular OU that is embedded within your OU design. Thus, the best step would be to make sure the No Override option is not set and to allow blocked inheritance. Remember, a large portion of what you will be tested on with the enterprise certification exam and what you will be working on in the real world involves taking the technology you learned from your earlier studies and applying it by using sound judgment and common sense.

Step 3: Design Group Policy for Your Infrastructure

When you eventually come to the third step, you should already have a good grasp of what your organization needs in order to function. You already have a strong organizational structure and know the limitations, goals, and perhaps even a few deliverables. During the design phase, you need to do the following:

- Define the scope of your group policies.
- Determine the number of GPOs.
- Determine whether GPOs will be enforced.
- Set Group Policy for all users.
- Determine Group Policy delegation.

The overall goal here in your design is to make sure your policies go from the most general to the most specific. A good design practice is to determine the highest-level policies that will be enforced at all levels and then ensure that those policies are followed by designating those links as Enforced. However, you should strive to use this as little as possible, because if you use this feature consistently, it can become difficult to troubleshoot in any issues that may arise with Group Policy.

When you go down to further levels of granularity, you can pick and choose where to apply GPOs that will have the least impact. Accordingly, at this level you can also decide how to place your GPOs in such a fashion that you can use filtering as little as possible.

Last, when you deploy your design, make sure you implement a staging area of some sort. Many environments have been collapsed or improperly implemented because of improper testing. By having a dedicated lab, you can spare yourself from this.

Working with the Default Domain Policy and Domain Controllers Policy

The first rule of thumb when working with the default domain and domain controllers policies is as follows: don't do it unless absolutely necessary.

In any enterprise that is going to require ongoing updates to Group Policy, you want to strive to not change this crucial portion of your network. Alternatively, you can create a domain policy that overrides the default domain policy and implement changes on this. This means that any additions you make to this new policy won't affect your settings.

Keep in mind that the default domain policy is the policy that is created as soon as an administrator logs on for the first time. It contains account policy settings, password policies, Kerberos policies, and other vital information. It's absolutely essential in order for your Windows network to operate properly.

However, if the situation arises that for some reason the default domain policy has been altered, the best solution for resolving it is to use the `dcgpofix.exe` tool. This tool can restore the default domain policy. However, it's not designed as a disaster recovery tool. It restores only the default domain policy and nothing else.

What's important to remember about the default domain and domain controllers policies is that they will affect settings for just about everything. On the exam, you may be asked questions regarding this particular topic. If so, remember that in the real world this isn't a very good practice; however, on the exam, it's more important that you understand the impact of modifying the policy. If it's changed, then it affects everyone in the domain.

Delegating Group Policy Administration

Similarly to how delegation is used in other parts of their network infrastructure, administrators can use delegation with Group Policy to relieve the burden of a large number of everyday tasks involving deploying and implementing Group Policy. With Windows Server 2008, administrators can delegate many Group Policy tasks as defined in the Microsoft Group Policy deployment guidelines, including the following:

- Managing GPOs
- Managing GPO links
- Performing tasks on GPOs
- Creating GPOs
- Creating and editing WMI filters

As with all delegation, you need to exercise extreme caution. Putting too much authority into the hands of one user or a group of users can have serious ramifications if the proper due diligence isn't done regarding the amount of control they have over the enterprise.

For each individual GPO, five settings are created by the direct Microsoft data, as summarized in Table 6.1.

TABLE 6.1   GPO Permissions Table

GPO Permission Option	Low-Level Permissions
Read	This allows read access on the GPO.
Read (from Security Filtering)	This is the same as Read, but it's set only if Read and Apply Group Policy have been established.
Edit Settings	This allows Read, Write, Create Child Objects, and Delete Child Objects.
Edit Settings, Delete, and Modify Security	This allows Read, Write, Create Child Objects, Delete Child Objects, Delete, Modify Permissions, and Modify Owner. It gives nearly full control, except Apply Group Policy is not granted.
Custom	This is based on administrator settings.

You can adjust these settings on the Delegation tab of the GPMC; they are up to the administrator's discretion. Keep in mind that Group Policy security, by default, is divided into six separate categories:

- Creating GPOs
- Linking GPOs
- Editing, deleting, and modifying the security of GPOs
- Editing GPOs
- Modeling GPOs
- Performing RSoP of GPOs

When making delegation decisions, you have to keep each of these abilities in mind. Sometimes the default set of groups or users can be useful in determining GPO delegation. You can add an individual user to a default group without having to go through the process of customizing an individual group for that user.

 Real World Scenario

Deploying Group Policy in a Single Large Domain

Within the OmniCorp campus there is a single domain with two different sites that have been set up for the New York and Los Angeles locations of the OmniCorp offices. Within each of these sites, more than 4,000 users have been divided into approximately 100 OUs.

Just last week, OmniCorp decided that because of the large size of the organization and its need for scalability and structure, it would be necessary to upgrade to Windows Server 2008. Accordingly, OmniCorp has upgraded all of its servers and is now functioning at a Windows Server 2008 domain and forest functional level.

Today, the OmniCorp CEO has decided that all employees within the OmniCorp corporation should have access to the OmniCorp company software, OmniSoft. Furthermore, the CEO has also decided to deploy removable storage devices to the sales department contained within the Sales OU and to restrict the use of Internet Explorer and browsing from the Los Angeles location because of consistent abuse of the privilege of web surfing.

As the head administrator, your responsibility is to deploy these requirements using Group Policy and to design Group Policy in such a way that the GPOs you create do not prevent one another from operating properly. The way you would accomplish this is by starting at the top level and moving down from most to least broad deployment. In this case, the broadest decision is to deploy OmniSoft to all employees. And, because of the single-domain nature of the organization, you can deploy OmniSoft with a new GPO at the domain level that installs OmniSoft on all computers.

Next, you can examine the site level. Since the changes to Internet Explorer involve users in only one site location, you can deploy another GPO to the site that restricts the use of Internet Explorer completely. And, since it is at a lower level, this implementation will not affect the rest of your users.

At the most granular level, you can apply a final GPO to the OU containing the sales department. With this GPO, you can grant them access to these removable devices if this has been blocked by an earlier exception. With this action, you will need to look up your levels of Group Policy and examine where the privilege has been taken away and react accordingly. However, if this privilege has not been removed, you will not need to apply a GPO in this area because the users should be able to install these devices through Plug and Play by default.

Exploring New Windows Server 2008 Group Policy Features

With every new iteration of Windows, Microsoft makes improvements and adds features to assist in the use and administration of their powerful operating system. With Windows Server 2008, one of the biggest advancements Microsoft made was in the use of Group Policy. With its release, Windows Server 2008 revealed a series of impressive new features for Group Policy. With Windows Server 2008, Group Policy is more secure, is categorized in different manners, has the ability to manage power settings, and implements many additional features that you need to become familiar with in order to properly take advantage of it.

Most of these changes stem from multiple requests by administrators, as well as internal requests from Microsoft engineers for more features and functionality with Windows Server 2008 as opposed to Server 2003. For starters, you need to be familiar with the following five new features:

- Administrative template files
- Starter GPOs
- Comments for GPOs and policy settings
- Network location awareness
- Preferences

Administrative Template Files

As you're probably already aware of from your previous study of both Windows Vista and Windows Server 2008, a major change in Group Policy for Windows Server 2008 is the implementation of a central store for Active Directory ADMX GPO templates. The reason for this creation was twofold. First, Microsoft wanted to create a more secure version of Windows Server with Group Policy implemented. ADMX achieves this by creating a centralized store that runs on the XML format for ease of readability both by the machine and by the necessary administrator.

The second reason for this change is the XML format itself. Previously, ADM files (the convention used in Windows Server 2003) used their own markup language. With ADMX, XML allows a much more readable and standardized method for viewing ADMX files.

To achieve a centralized store, Windows Server 2003 previously stored ADMX files in the `%systemroot%\inf` folder. Now, ADMX files are stored in the `%systemroot%\policyDefinitions` folder, and language-specific files are stored in a subfolder that reflects the localization of the individual policy.

The major change that this brought along is that ADMX files will no longer follow the convention of ADM files and become copied to each object. Instead, they are contained in a central repository. The main advantage of this is that all domain controllers in a single domain will use the same store, thereby increasing efficiency.

Group Policy in general, however, can still read and use legacy ADM files. These files are Unicode-based and store what is recorded in the system registry. It should be noted, however, that ADM files do not affect actual policy processing through administrative template client-side extensions. For the certification exam, it's likely you won't be asked about ADM files, because Microsoft is trying to get administrators adapted to the idea of using central store–based ADMX files. Just remember that they are still supported.

Starter GPOs

One of the most common situations administrators used to encounter before Windows Server 2008 was having to repeatedly create extraordinarily similar Group Policy objects and then apply those objects to various OUs throughout the infrastructure. Ultimately, this could become a bit tedious. So, with Windows Server 2008, Microsoft created what are called *starter GPOs*.

Starter GPOs are GPOs that can be created based on administrative template settings that can be defined in the GPMC and then applied to a newly created GPO with that starter as a base. As an example, a common task administrators may use Group Policy for is to make users unable to change the desktop background of their machines. Now, administrators can make a starter GPO that contains the desktop restriction setting by default. Then, when an administrator desires, they can create a new GPO with the default settings of the starter GPO, plus any additional Group Policy settings they care to make.

In effect, a starter GPO forms a base for Group Policy objects to be created that by default have all the settings of the originating starter GPO. It's quick, it's convenient, and it can save a lot of time if you have to create a lot of similar GPOs in your environment.

EXERCISE 6.1

Creating and Applying a Starter GPO

1. Open the Group Policy Management Console by selecting Administrative Tools ➢ Group Policy Management.

2. Select Starter GPOs in the GPMC. You may see an option that says Create Starter GPOs Folder. If you do, click it.

3. In the right pane, right-click Starter GPO, and select New. The New Starter GPO dialog box opens.

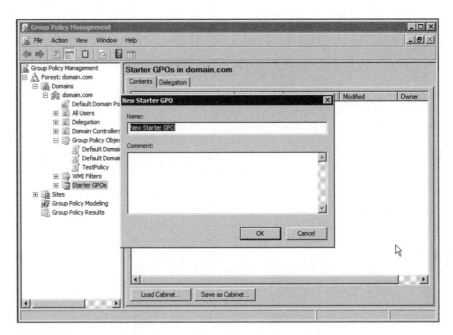

4. Name the GPO **Base GPO**.

5. Click OK.

6. Right-click Base GPO, and select Edit

7. Expand the Administrative Template: Policy Definition (ADMX Files) retrieved from the local machine under User Configuration.

8. Select Control Panel ➢ Add or Remove Programs

9. Double-click Hide Add New Programs Page, which opens the dialog box shown here.

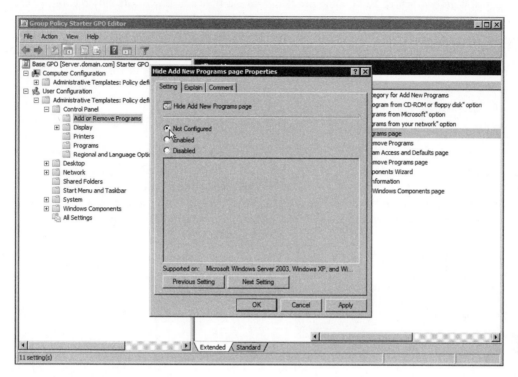

10. Choose Enabled.

11. Exit the dialog box.

12. In the GPMC, right-click Base GPO, and select New GPO from Starter GPO.

13. Name it **PolicyFromBase**. You will notice that by default the source starter GPO is based on the Base GPO starter GPO.

14. Click OK.

15. PolicyFromBase will appear in your Group Policy Objects folder. Select PolicyFromBase, and then select the Settings tab.

16. You will notice that if you expand the PolicyFromBase Show button under Policies and then select Control Panel ➢ Add or Remove Programs, the Hide Add New Programs setting has been enabled.

Now any additional edits that are made to this Group Policy object will take place on top of your preexisting settings that you've gathered from the starter GPO you created!

Comments for GPOs

Before Windows Server 2008, a big problem that multiple administrators would come across is that one person would create a GPO but nobody else would know what it did at first glance. You had to open the GPMC, look at the settings of the Group Policy object, and then figure out for yourself exactly what those settings meant based on the configuration. But other questions remained unanswered. For instance:

- Who made the GPO?
- Who edited this GPO at a later date?
- What's the general purpose of this GPO?

With Windows Server 2008, Microsoft introduced a nifty new feature called *commenting*. Commenting allows Microsoft administrators to place notes on Group Policy objects on the Comment tab within the Group Policy Management Editor. As you can see in Figure 6.7, the comments show the purpose of this GPO, as well as the author and date it was created. This way, within a few seconds whoever is using this GPO can know all about the creator of the GPO and any other information you want to leave.

FIGURE 6.7 GPO Comment tab

Once this information is placed on the Comment tab, you can view the comments from the Details tab using the GPMC. Furthermore, you can refine comments by not applying them just to the GPO, but to all the comments within the GPO if the policy is an administrative template policy.

Another reason comments are particularly useful is that with a little administrative work, you can filter your GPOs by comments and find individual policies. If you'd like to try this on your own, you can open the Group Policy Management Editor and then select a filter option. Within the filter options, you will see check boxes for commenting and other filter options. And, if you're in a large enterprise with a lot of GPOs, this can make finding an individual GPO a lot easier.

Network Location Awareness

Any good administrator knows that a good share of the time you spend troubleshooting your network is spent using the following two commands: `PING` and `IPCONFIG`. The reason for this is that all too often administrators are in the position where they're wondering two questions:

- "Where am I?"
- "Where is that?"

Before network location awareness, Windows Server Group Policy was no exception. More often than not, a firewall between locations could suddenly cause a tremendous problem. This is because previous versions of Group Policy relied on `PING` to resolve the network location. Now, using network location awareness, servers are alerted to changing network conditions, and Group Policy reacts accordingly. Additionally, network location awareness even lets Group Policy know about any changes in events, such as a computer suddenly dropping into hibernation or standby.

Moreover, what really matters even more about network location awareness is that it is readily aware of changes in virtual private networks (VPNs) and firewalls. VPN changes are very important, because at the enterprise level associates will frequently need to log in from remote locations and access resources. Having Group Policy become aware of any changes in VPNs saves a lot of administrative overhead.

This is because network location awareness is now capable of understanding any conditions that may prompt the return of a domain controller. Previously, establishing VPNs, standby, hibernation, docking laptops, or several other useful Windows features could cause a machine to suddenly stop communicating with the domain controller for an extended length of time. Now, the momentary loss is minimal at best, and the recovery period is extremely fast.

Last, although it's only a minor benefit, a handy new addition that network location awareness provides on the server end is a serious reduction in reboot time. Because of its knowledge of the network situation, the server can use network location awareness to jump "back to life" a lot faster than previous versions of Windows Server.

Preferences

The best way to sum up Group Policy preferences is by comparing Group Policy preferences to Group Policy itself. For starters, what is a policy? A *policy* is something that is strictly enforced throughout the network infrastructure. For instance, an administrator may completely take away the Control Panel from a user, and that is just the way it is going to be. A *preference*, however, is something that is not necessarily enforced for the user but is instead just something that recommends a practice that a user can override with their own settings.

To function properly, Group Policy preferences require a small amount of client-side operation. Namely, users of Windows XP Service Pack 2, Windows Server 2003 Service Pack 1, and Windows Vista must download a piece of software called the Client-Side Extension (CSE) from Microsoft. However, if Microsoft Windows Vista has the Remote Server Administration Tools toolkit installed, it will already come preinstalled with the CSE.

 Group Policy preferences are not supported on Windows 2000 or earlier operating systems

Upon examining Group Policy preferences in the Group Policy Management Editor, as shown in Figure 6.8, you will notice that there are seven preferences that you can now set with Group Policy preferences under Computer Configuration/Windows Settings.

FIGURE 6.8   Computer Configuration/Windows Settings preferences

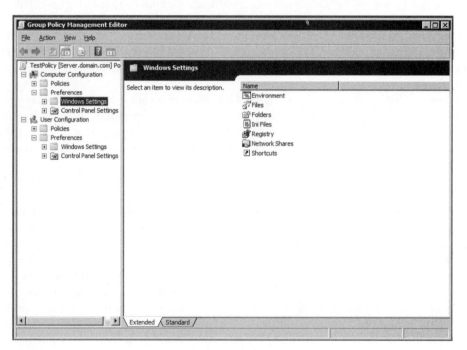

Environment   This allows administrators to set environmental variables for the user or system.

Files   This allows the administrator to set attributes (such as write or read-only) and allows you to create, update, or delete files on client machines.

Folders   This is similar to the Files option, except it can be used at the folder level.

INI Files   This enables the creation or deletion of INI files, as well as the ability to specify property values.

Registry   This allows you to browse the registry on a client machine you want to modify and set certain registry values.

Network Shares   You can use this to create or delete network shares for clients.

Shortcuts   You can use this to create or delete shortcuts for clients.

Furthermore, as shown in Figure 6.9, also within Computer Configuration you can set the following nine Control Panel settings.

FIGURE 6.9   Computer Configuration/Control Panel Settings preferences

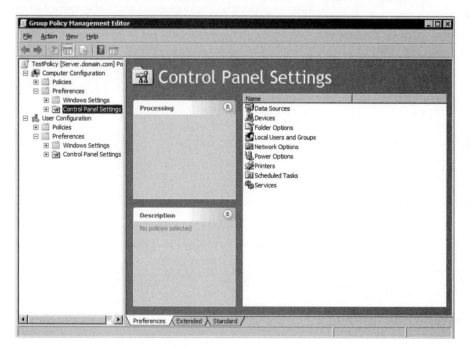

Data Sources   This creates or deletes users and system data sources.

Devices   This enables or disables devices based on GUIDs.

Folder Options   This controls file types and associated classes.

Local Users and Groups   This creates, replaces, and updates groups.

Network Options   This configures, deletes, or modifies VPNs and other network connections for individual users.

Power Options   This adjusts default power schemes for users.

Printers   This updates and modifies local printers for individual users.

Scheduled Tasks   This creates and modifies tasks.

Services   This adjusts the properties of various services.

Within the User Configuration option, as shown in Figure 6.10, you will see eight preferences that can be set in the Windows Setting preferences.

FIGURE 6.10   User Configuration/Windows Settings preferences

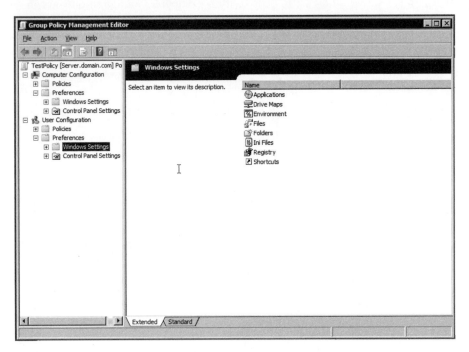

Applications   This modifies the access and deployment of various applications through Group Policy.

Drive Maps   This creates, modifies, and deletes mapped drives for individual users.

Environment   This sets environmental variables for the user or system, as well as modifies previously set variables.

Files   This creates, modifies, and deletes files.

Folders   This is similar to permissions set with Files, but this sets permissions at the folder level for more control.

INI Files   This creates, modifies, replaces, or deletes system INI files.

Registry   This modifies the registry.

Shortcuts   This creates, modifies, or replaces shortcuts.

Lastly, within User Configuration, you can adjust the following eleven Control Panel settings, as shown in Figure 6.11.

FIGURE 6.11   User Configuration/Control Panel Settings preferences

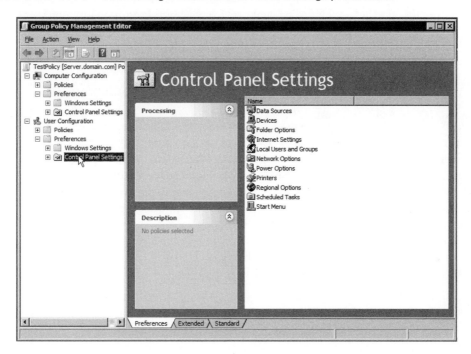

Data Sources   This creates, modifies, and deletes database connectivity.

Devices   This controls hardware device enabling and disabling.

Folder Options   This creates, modifies, and deletes folders and control file associations.

Internet Settings   This controls user access to Internet Explorer and Internet Explorer settings.

Local Users and Groups   This creates, modifies, and deletes groups on the local machine.

Network Options   This is similar to user network options, but it's for the Control Panel.

Power Options   This is similar to user power options, but it's for the Control Panel.

Printers   This is similar to user printer options, but it's for the Control Panel.

Regional Options   This modifies the regional options for individual users so they do not have to personally set them.

Scheduled Tasks   This creates, modifies, and deletes tasks for future or immediate use.

Start Menu   This controls the additions and deletions to the Start menu, as well as appearance options.

Overall, the important information to take away from user preferences is that they are useful for configuration options that don't need to be set in stone. Furthermore, they are easy to use for common tasks and allow for a great deal of complexity and granular control. Some of the other added features that preferences create are improvements in IT productivity because policies are able to be deployed from a central source. This, along with limiting possible errors in configuration, can add to a very satisfying user experience that was previously unavailable in other versions of Microsoft Windows Server.

 Real World Scenario

Creating a Central Location

If SuperCorp, an international conglomerate of three previously acquired businesses, recently decide to deploy a branch office in New York City, one issue it would have to consider is how to create a central location where users and computers can access files. SuperCorp could create a centralized shared folder that deploys throughout the entire enterprise and potentially risk security concerns. Or, SuperCorp could create a Group Policy that deploys a dedicated folder to various users based on group membership, computer use, location, or other situations. However, there may arise a situation in the future where users don't necessarily need access to the shared folder. Or, if they do, they may want to access it in a different manner.

A third option that exists for SuperCorp is deploying Group Policy using preferences. This way, SuperCorp could make the shared folder available by default through a mapped drive. And, if the users decide they no longer want access to the mapped drive, they can instantly remove it, without the need for a script or any other complex deployment process.

Configuring Automatic Updates with Group Policy

Whenever you're supporting an operating system that has as many components as Windows or any of its supported applications, there are ultimately going to be times that the software will need to be updated in order to function either properly or in a more improved manner. Later in the chapter, when I talk about configuring automatic updates for an entire enterprise, I'll dive much deeper into this subject. But for now, I'll briefly touch the subject of using Group Policy for automatic updates.

With Group Policy, you can directly link a GPO to an Active Directory container that can be used to deploy updates through Windows Software Updates Services (WSUS). According to the rules of Group Policy objects, you can of course link this to any container you desire. Thus, in a simpler environment, administrators commonly make a practice of deploying a WSUS GPO to an entire domain. However, at the enterprise level, this is neither practical nor recommended, because of the increased complexity of an enterprise environment. There could be situations where employees are receiving updates that could compromise previously established objectives or disrupt workflow.

Thus, according to Microsoft, at the enterprise level GPOs with WSUS specifications should be avoided at the default domain and domain controllers levels. But instead, you can place them on an individual domain or OU level.

 It will normally take 90 minutes for a freshly created GPO with WSUS settings to update throughout your infrastructure. However, you can choose to manually force it to update by using the gpudate /force command. Of course, one of the most common uses of Group Policy with WSUS at the enterprise level is to point computers in an organization toward an actual WSUS server. This way, by default, all members of the organization that need to access the WSUS server will have these settings defined by default and not have to manually look for any updates. Then, the WSUS server can determine the appropriate update requirements needed for the individual computer.

Restricting Group Membership with Group Policy

One of the best tricks in the book for a seasoned administrator who has had more than a couple issues with group membership not working properly with Group Policy is to use the power of *restricted groups*. Restricted groups are permissions lists that can be established within GPOs to determine who a GPO does and does not apply to.

The name itself can be a little confusing. At first, when you hear *restricted group*, you may think it's used as a filter that restricts users from doing something. And in truth, it does. But the easier way to think about restricted groups is that they are designed to choose who a policy *does* apply to, not who it does not. For instance, say you have a GPO you're creating to deploy a piece of software to 300 users who are members of the IuseSoftware group. If you wanted to make sure the GPO you're using applies only to those users, you could create a GPO and then use a restricted group that made sure only the IuseSoftware group could use it, regardless of where that policy is applied. This adds a lot of flexibility, because you can now deploy a GPO where you need and ensure that this GPO is accessible only by certain groups.

Of course, if you are given the option, it's best not to use restricted groups unless your situation demands it. The best practice is to create both your Active Directory structure and your OU design in such a way that you can easily deploy GPOs to areas that will not affect one another. However, sometimes there is a "needs-must" situation where you must use them. Don't feel bad if you have to; sometimes life has its demands.

In Exercise 6.2, you'll use Group Policy to create a restricted group that you can use for policy appliance.

EXERCISE 6.2

Creating a Restricted Group

To complete this exercise, you must have at least one user group and an available Group Policy object to restrict.

1. Open the Group Policy Management Console by selecting Start ➢ Administrative Tools ➢ Group Policy Management.

2. Expand your domain and the Group Policy Object container, and select a test policy. For this example, I will use the GPO TestPolicy, as shown here.

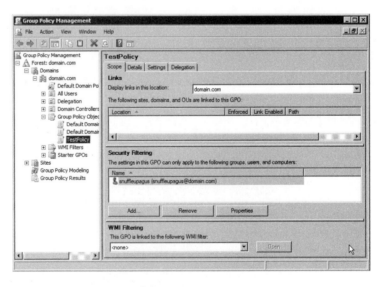

3. Right-click the policy, and select Edit.

4. Expand Computer Configuration/Policies/Windows Settings/Security Settings, and then select Restricted Groups, as shown here.

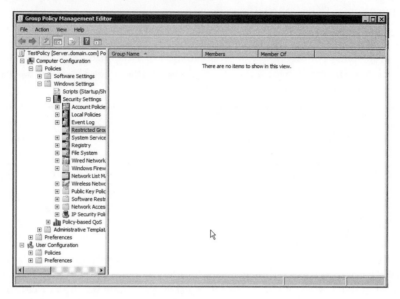

5. Right-click the right pane, and select Add Group.

6. Click Browse.

7. Click Advanced.

8. Select a given group, such as All Users. Note, however, that this should be a test policy and should be blank. You don't want to cause any problems in a live environment.

9. Select OK, and then hit OK again.

10. On the screen shown here, click the Add button. Do not worry if your screen looks slightly different or has group members already in the Members of This Group area.

11. Type the name of a user you want to include, such as **snuffleupagus**. Alternatively, you can browse for a user and select the one you like. Just make sure the domain path is listed after you select a user, and click OK. For instance, my user, snuffleupagus, shows up as DOMAIN\snuffleupagus.

12. Click Apply and then OK.

With this completed, your test policy now is restricted to a user group that contains only the users you are interested in including. In this case, snuffleupagus now has his own unique Group Policy object that applies only to him.

Controlling User Installation of Devices

If there was ever a true statement, it is that in the modern day it is far too easy for a user to gain access to a large amount of extremely important, extremely sensitive data and potentially do massive damage to a legitimate company. Consider that less than five years ago the average jump drive was about 128MB. Today, users are commonly seen with multiple-gigabyte jump drives and MP3 players that can range to nearly a terabyte in space. When you think about it, that's a *lot* of data. And what's scary is that although computers and devices can contain more data, the fact is that what you can actually manage to do with a small amount of data has never changed. A corporate report, mail list, account file, or other sensitive piece of data might be only a few kilobytes or perhaps even less than that. Thus, a major concern you have to worry about with an enterprise is driver signing in order to ensure the authentication of authorized devices. As enterprise administrators, you don't want users to be able to use any device except the ones you want them to use.

Using Group Policy, you can achieve this. Furthermore, using Group Policy with Windows Server 2008 you can specifically control the type of device a user can install, the time periods they can use it, and hundreds of other options without the costly need for an administrator to be present for even the most minor administrative changes (such as allowing someone to install a jump drive).

One of the ways you can accomplish this with Server 2008 is by implementing a *driver store*. A driver store is an area either on the local computer or on the network that is completely dedicated to the installation of a device that is recognized and trusted by the enterprise or system administrator and that will not affect the rest of the computer. Therefore, any regular user can have access to this area with the permission of a higher-level authority, such as yourself. You can also use your corporate structure's certificate layout and use digitally signed certificates to make the device available to computers outside your network. But I'm getting a little ahead of myself.

For now, you can concentrate on the fact that drivers in a secure Windows Server environment use digital certificates to sign the driver as an authoritative driver that won't compromise the integrity of the environment. What this means is that the driver is authentic and intact. Otherwise—if the driver isn't from a trusted source or is incomplete—this process will fail. In general, you can think of the process of driver signing in Windows Server as a linear process that loops back to the beginning toward the end, as shown in Figure 6.12.

FIGURE 6.12   Driver signing

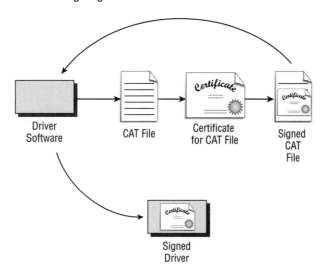

In the beginning, the driver package is sent by the user as an unsigned package. Then the drive has a CAT file and digital signature attached to it and becomes a signed driver.

Through design, Windows Server 2008 and Windows Vista allow this process to occur manually. However, in an enterprise infrastructure, it's advisable for the lead administrator to design the deployment in such a way that Group Policy maintains an extremely important role. Namely, Group Policy should be used to deploy the drivers in an authenticated manner.

Searching GPOs

With Windows Server 2008, it's easy for the average administrator to search through a Group Policy object that resides anywhere in your forest. Beyond that, you don't have to search just for a particular GPO, but you can search for a GPO setting as well. It is very, very cool. This is accomplished using the Windows Server 2008 GPMC search tool.

You can access the GPMC search tool by following these steps:

1. Open the GPMC, and select Group Policy Management. Then, right-click your forest, and select Search. This will open the tool you see in Figure 6.13.

FIGURE 6.13   The GPMC search tool

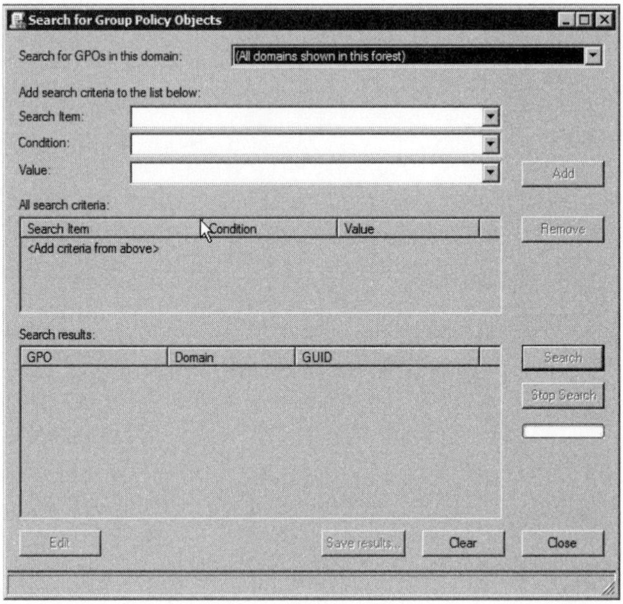

2. Once the tool opens, you can use the Search Item drop-down list to select from the following choices:

   - GPO Name
   - GPO-Links
   - Security Group
   - User Configuration
   - Computer Configuration
   - GUID

3. Once you've selected one of these choices, choose from a series of conditions based upon each particular choice. For instance, if you chose GPO Name, you'd be presented with conditions such as the following:

   - Contains
   - Does Not Contain
   - Is Exactly

4. Now specify a value. For example, I could set my search item as GPO Name, then set the condition Contains, and then type **Test** as my search criteria. This would spit out the output you see in Figure 6.14, complete with the domain name that the policy lies in and the GUID of the GPO.

FIGURE 6.14   Search output

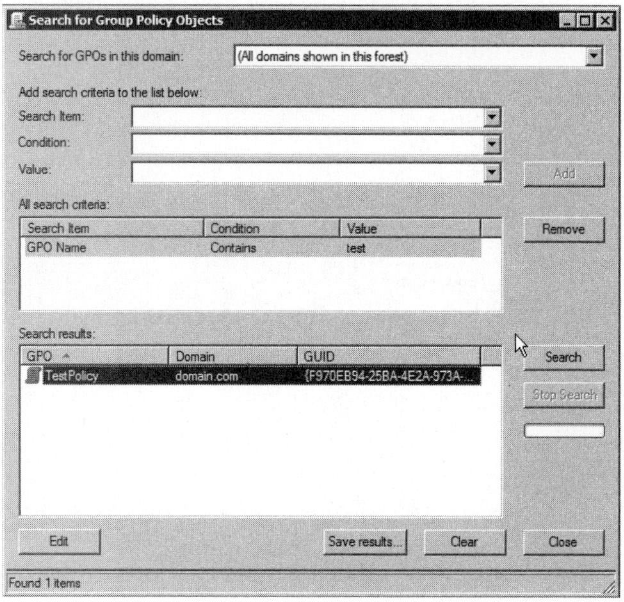

Both for the certification exam and for all practical purposes, it's not necessary to be familiar with every condition and value that can be set in the search tool. Thus, I haven't included a complete list of every option available to you. However, it is a good practice to play with this tool a bit. It's very powerful and can be a lot of fun.

Using the Group Policy Modeling Tool

One of the best methods you have at your disposal for evaluating the impact of Group Policy with Windows Server 2008 is the Group Policy modeling tool. Using Group Policy modeling, administrators can determine the impact of Group Policy on a specific user or computer in a specific location within Active Directory. This tool is located within the GPMC and is labeled Group Policy Modeling.

When properly used, the modeling tool will provide you with an excellent and easily understandable report that will show you the complete impact of your policy decisions throughout the entire infrastructure. In Exercise 6.3, you'll put this tool to use in a practical but simple demonstration.

EXERCISE 6.3

Using the Group Policy Modeling Tool

To perform this exercise, you must have a domain controller running Active Directory and at least one active Group Policy.

1. Start the GPMC by selecting Start ➤ Administrative Tools ➤ Group Policy Management.

2   **Select the Group Policy Modeling folder.**

3. Right-click the Group Policy Modeling container, and select Group Policy Modeling Wizard, as shown here.

4. Click Next.

5. On the Domain Controller Selection screen, choose the domain you want to simulate the performance on, and choose the Any Available Domain Controller Running Windows Server 2003 or Later option.

6. Click Next.

7. On the User and Computer Selection screen, click the Browse button for both the User and Computer Information screens, and select the same domain for each for the sake of ease in this exercise.

8. Click Next.

EXERCISE 6.3 *(continued)*

9. On the Advanced Simulation Options Mode screen, you can select Slow Network Connection if you are communicating between domains that have a very slow link, or you can select Loopback Processing if you are utilizing it. Furthermore, you can refine your search to a specific site. For our purposes, leave this blank. Click Next.

10. Leave both the Security Groups and Computer Security Groups screens defaulted to Authenticated Users. Normally, on these screens you can select specific groups to determine the Group Policy on these individual users. The WMI filters Users and Computers page will be left blank in this exercise, but by default it searches for all linked filters.

11. Refine your search by selecting the Only These Filters option and then clicking the List Filters option.

12. Individually select the filters you want to use. Click Next two times.

13. On the Summary screen, review the settings you have made, and go back if you want to change anything. Click Next.

14. The process will complete, and then you can click Finish.

At this point, a very easy-to-understand and usable report appears. By clicking the Show and Hide buttons, you can view individual reports, as well as check policy settings and review the exact query that was iterated. This way, you have a long-term record of the report you created and under what conditions the report was created.

Additionally, you can select advanced views of your report by right-clicking the report under the Group Policy Modeling container and selecting Advanced View. You can even rerun the query if you want!

Summary

Group Policy is the fabric of high-level administration and arguably the most difficult but fundamentally required skill in order to become an effective administrator. On the enterprise level, Group Policy can become maddening and involve the addition of policies that can single-handedly destroy the functionality of an entire business infrastructure. On the enterprise administrator certification exam, students are expected to be familiar with Group Policy to a point that they can administer even the toughest installations.

Remember that with the addition of Windows Server 2008, Microsoft introduced the following new features:

- Administrative template files
- Starter GPOs
- Comments for GPOs and policy settings
- Network location awareness
- Preferences

But you also need to take away from this chapter an understanding of how Group Policy is managed and implemented, from the most local taking the highest precedence to the most broad taking the least precedence. With Windows Group Policy and a firm understanding of Windows administration, an administrator can accomplish some really amazing things. Give it a try!

Exam Essentials

Know the new features of Windows Server 2008.   The new features include the ability to use ADMX templates, starter GPOs, and several other features. You need to know the changes these make to the power of Windows Server.

Know how Group Policy applies.   Know this at all levels. It's important to understand which policy takes priority over another.

Understand network location awareness.   You need to know how to implement this to save yourself a lot of network administration overhead. In today's growing business and on the certification exam, this is a must.

Know how to set up preferences.   Know the requirements for preferences and how to set them up. These are going to become a lot more common in the future.

Review Questions

1. In your organization you have three member servers, two domain controllers, and thirteen organizational units that exist within a three-domain architecture using the naming conventions Domain1, Domain2, and Domain3. Today, you have been asked to deploy a universal Group Policy that will encompass the entire policy. Domain2 and Domain3 are child domains to Domain1, and all domains exist within a single site. Knowing this, at what level should you apply your Group Policy?

    A. Apply the policy at the Domain1, and inherit the policy through the child domains, thereby applying the policy to the entire organization.

    B. Apply the policy at the site level to ensure maximum coverage.

    C. Apply the Group Policy individually to each OU in the organization to ensure that the policy is applied to every user.

    D. Apply the policy only to the member servers, because this way it will apply to all servers.

2. If you are planning a Group Policy deployment strategy and you're most concerned about deploying a policy before any other policy but not necessarily concerned about whether later policies may override this policy, at what level should you deploy this policy?

    A. The site level

    B. The local level

    C. The domain level

    D. The OU level

3. Which of the following GPO deployments has the highest precedence?

    A. GPO linked to a domain

    B. GPO linked to a site

    C. Local GPO for local group policy

    D. GPO linked to an OU

4. Your organization has a multitiered OU structure that envelops all employees into an easily manageable structure. Within this OU, there are multiple sales-level OUs that go from the lowest-level managers to the highest-level managers. At each of these OUs, a policy has been applied that adds new privileges, folder shares, and other abilities to other managers. Recently, you've decided to add a new OU at the most embedded level that will contain a new set of permissions completely apart from the rest of the organization. What should you do?

    A. Create a new OU using loopback filtering that contains its own permissions set.

    B. Create the new OU, set the OU to block inheritance, and then apply your new permissions set.

    C. Use WMI filters on the new OU, and set its filter to ignore previous settings.

    D. Create a new OU from a starter GPO, inherit the settings from the previous container, and then add the permissions you need.

5. Last week OmniCorp decided to deploy a Terminal Services machine running Windows Server 2008. The machine has been running well, but you have been experiencing Group Policy issues through conflicts that have been resulting in inappropriate permission issues. What should you do to resolve this conflict?

   A. Implement loopback processing, and use Merge mode so that all your policies are enacted.

   B. Implement loopback processing, and use Replace mode so that all previous policy settings are removed and new policy settings are applied.

   C. Implement a Group Policy filtering for the server, and set the policy to block inheritance.

   D. Set all group policies on the server to use No Override. Apply policies as usual.

6. Which of the following command-line tools can be used to restore default domain controller policies?

   A. `repadmin`

   B. `gpupdate /force`

   C. `dcgpofix`

   D. `replmon`

   E. `dcrestore`

7. One of the major changes from previous iterations of Windows Server to Windows Server 2008 is the transition from `.adm` to `.admx` files that are created in a central store. With Windows Server 2008, where is this central store located?

   A. `%systemroot%\inf`

   B. `%systemroot%\policyDefinitions`

   C. `%systemroot%\policy`

   D. `%systemroot%\groupPolicy`

   E. `%systemroot%\GPolicy`

8. You currently administer a Windows Server farm operating Windows Server 2003. And naturally the organization is running at the Windows Server 2003 domain and forest level. Your organization has recently begun to have problems with machines logging in and out of VPNs as well as machines hibernating and entering standby mode and then having to reauthenticate to their local domain controller. What can you do to alleviate this situation?

   A. Centralize the location of all servers, and place them into a single site formation.

   B. Create a GPO that allocates when machines can enter hibernation and join VPNs.

   C. Implement network-level authentication.

   D. Upgrade to Windows Server 2008 using network location awareness.

9. Part of the requirements that have been set forth by the executive branch of your company include that users in the Employees OU be allowed to have access to a network share called Share. However, you understand that most users will not need to have access to the Share network share, and therefore they should be able to remove it if they desire. How should you proceed?

   A. Implement a GPO that allows the deployment of a network share, and link the GPO to all users.

   B. Implement a GPO preference that deploys the network share to the Employees OU.

   C. Implement a GPO link for the Employees folder that deploys the network share to the Employees folder.

   D. Implement a GPO preference that links the network share to all users.

10. Which of the following options are not listed in Group Policy preferences? (Choose all that apply.)

    A. User Configuration/Control Panel

    B. User Configuration/Windows Settings

    C. User Configuration/Policy Settings

    D. Computer Configuration/Control Panel

    E. Computer Configuration/Windows Settings

    F. Computer Configuration/Policy Settings

11. The Group Policy Management Console in Windows Server 2008 added several powerful new features to its already impressive tool set. Among them is the Group Policy Management search tool. Of the following options, which cannot be searched in Windows Server 2008? (Choose all that apply.)

    A. GPO Name

    B. GPO-Links

    C. Security Group

    D. GUID

    E. SID

    F. User Configuration

    G. Computer Configuration

    H. ACE

    I. ACL

12. MyCorp, a small business based in Texas, is a distributor of manufacturing equipment for a major facility, OmniCorp. Accordingly, a forest trust exists between MyCorp and Omni-Corp, which allows MyCorp to access OmniCorp's resources. However, OmniCorp has requested as part of the partnership that it have full administrative control over MyCorp, and therefore it services all help desk and administrative tickets that are passed up from MyCorp. Today, OmniCorp has asked MyCorp to see whether it could reduce the amount of requests it receives regarding simple driver installation. What should you do?

    A. Implement a Group Policy object that gives local users administrative control over their various machines for local driver installation.

    B. Promote users to administrators on their local machines.

    C. Upgrade the facility to Windows Server 2008 and Windows Vista.

    D. Implement a Group Policy object that prompts for administrative credentials at driver installation and then evaluates each on a per-case basis.

13. What permissions are required in order to process a security principal in a container linked to the GPO? (Choose all that apply.)

    A. Allow Read

    B. Allow Read and Write

    C. Allow Apply Group Policy

    D. Allow Edit Group Policy

    E. Allow Create Group Policy Objects

14. What set of individual GPO settings are required in order to allow a user to read, write, create, and delete child objects?

    A. Read

    B. Read (from Security Filtering)

    C. Edit Settings

    D. Edit Settings, Delete, and Modify Security

    E. Custom

15. According to the best practices outlined by Microsoft, a WSUS update policy shouldn't be deployed at all but which of the following?

    A. Default domain

    B. Default domain controller

    C. Top-level domain

    D. Lower-level domain

16. You are working in an organization with more than 20 users that currently has more than 40 different applications deployed through GPOs. The organization has three sites, Site1, Site2, and Site3. Within each site, users need to access a different set of mapped network shares. How can you make sure your users have access to the proper shared folders without disrupting the current environment?

A. Place users into organizational units, and then create a GPO to apply the printers. Link the GPO to the appropriate OUs.

B. Create three different GPOs to share the folders, and link them to the appropriate sites.

C. Create a single GPO, apply that GPO to the domain, and filter it appropriately.

D. Place users in organizational units, create nested OUs, and set the OUs up to use block inheritance as necessary.

17. SuperCorp is a corporation with 20 different locations and 13 different domains. Additionally, SuperCorp has a Group Policy scheme that is very complex and can be at times overwhelming. SuperCorp is using Windows Server 2008, operating at the Server 2008 forest and domain functional level. SuperCorp has begun to experience problems keeping track of and searching for policies that were created by various administrators. What should you recommend as a solution?

A. Utilize the Group Policy Management Console search tool to search for various policies.

B. Create a requirement that all policies must be implemented in such a way that they follow a direct OU path that can be easily traced.

C. Use Group Policy commenting.

D. Set Block Policy Inheritance.

18. Your company has developed a very solid OU structure that has worked well for the past five years. Because of this, management is reticent to change the working structure. However, one issue that has recently emerged is that they want to deploy a group policy that deploys an application to one particular group that is contained within an OU that has more than 13 different groups within it. What could you do to maintain the current OU structure and apply this policy?

A. Upgrade to Windows Server 2008.

B. Raise the domain and forest functional level to at least Windows Server 2003.

C. Create a GPO with the required settings, and link it to the OU. Set the rest of the groups to block inheritance.

D. Create a GPO with the required settings, and link it to the OU. Filter the GPO so it applies only to the required group.

19. Which of the following is not a Group Policy security category?

   A. Create GPOs

   B. Link GPOs

   C. Edit, Delete, and Modify Security of GPOs

   D. Edit GPOs

   E. Edit and Modify GPOs

   F. Model GPOs

   G. Perform RSoP of GPOs

20. Windows Management Instrumentation (WMI) is a feature available to administrators that makes them able to create certain limitations and flagged conditions based on machine components and status. Using this technology, administrators can create specific queries to examine. Which of the following technologies is used to create these queries?

   A. SQL

   B. WMI Query Language

   C. XML

   D. TXT files

   E. UML

Answers to Review Questions

1. **B.** By applying a Group Policy at the site level, you apply that policy to the entire site, and thus you ensure that it will apply to everything within that site.

2. **B.** Before any other group policies are deployed, local policies will be applied first. However, local group policies should be used sparingly. This is because many locally applied policies will be incredibly difficult to administer over time.

3. **D.** GPOs linked to an OU have greater precedence than any other GPO deployment. This means that in terms of how Group Policy will interpret the policy, OU-level policies will take the highest priority.

4. **B.** Using Block Policy Inheritance, you can define the settings you want the new OU to contain without having any of its parents settings. WMI filters are mostly used for machine states, and starter GPOs are used to create policies, not to determine deployment.

5. **B.** Using loopback processing and Replace mode, you can ensure that your Terminal Services machine has its own policy deployment. This is useful because it removes any external policies that may conflict with the Terminal Services machine.

6. **C.** `dcgpofix` is a command-line tool used to restore the default domain controllers policy if it becomes altered. Remember, you should refrain from monitoring the default domain controller unless it is necessary or truly fits the situation.

7. **B.** `%systemroot%\policyDefinitions` is now the default location for the central store. With this central store, administrators can now deploy easily accessible and centralized stores for ease of access throughout the enterprise.

8. **D.** Windows Server 2008 is capable of using network location awareness to understand when machines enter and leave hibernation states. Additionally, network location awareness can understand where VPNs can be placed.

9. **B.** GPO preferences allow Group Policy to be deployed and not necessarily be enforced. This way, users can remove policies that they don't necessarily need to keep in place.

10. **C, F.** Group Policy preferences can be applied to both the user and the computer. The two places within each of these Users and Computers areas are Control Panel and Windows Settings.

11. **E, H, I.** The Group Policy search tool is a powerful and modular tool that allows you to search through Group Policy with relative ease. Using this tool, you can search through GPO names and links, various groups, and configurations. You cannot, however, search through access permissions lists or security identifiers.

12. **C.** Windows Server 2008 and Windows Vista take advantage of a driver store, which is a secure area that allows users to install simple devices, such as a flash drive, without needing to get administrative authority.

13. A, C. To process a security principle in a container linked to the GPO, you must have both the Allow Read and Allow Apply Group Policy permissions. This allows you to read the policy and apply it to give it effect.

14. C. The Edit settings option allows all of these. Additionally, many other default GPO settings are available to use without the need to create custom permissions.

15. D. The important point to note in this question is that WSUS policies should be avoided at the default level and at a level that encompasses a top-level domain. This is so that you can make sure the enterprise is easily adaptable.

16. B. GPOs can be linked on top of GPOs as long as there will be no conflict. In this case, shared applications will not interfere with a policy to deploy network shares.

17. C. Group Policy commenting allows administrators to make comments that show who created a policy and on what date, as well as any custom information they would like to include. This makes the process of searching for creators of various GPOs very easy, because you can search through comments for any desired field.

18. D. Using filters, you can apply Group Policy to an OU to make sure it is applied only to certain groups within it. Upgrading to Windows Server 2008 is not required.

19. E. All but the Edit and Modify GPOs category are part of the default Group Policy security categories. These categories are available as options that you can deploy to users to delegate their authority on GPOs.

20. B. WMI uses its own native language that is similar in nature to SQL. Using WMI, you can make a refined query specific to your enterprise requirements.

Chapter 7

Administering Security in an Enterprise-Level Infrastructure

OBJECTIVES COVERED IN THIS CHAPTER:

✓ **Design the branch office deployment**

- May include but is not limited to: authentication strategy, server security

✓ **Design and implement public key infrastructure**

- May include but is not limited to: certificate services, PKI operations and maintenance, certificate life cycle management

✓ **Plan for interoperability**

- May include but is not limited to: inter-organizational authorization and authentication, application authentication interoperability, cross-platform interoperability

One of the main objectives of the Enterprise Administrator certification is to be able to create and manage a stable infrastructure that is both reliable and secure. Using Windows Server 2008, this is achieved via a number of different methods, including security certificates, various forms of encryption, and a vast number of technologies that are accessible throughout the suite of tools and features available in Windows Server 2008.

Security is not a small subject. In fact, security has to be considered at all levels of the infrastructure, from the most basic LANs to how a web server will allow external users to access a web page through a Secure Sockets Layer connection. In this chapter, you will focus on the impact of security decisions as they affect the enterprise. This includes decisions about certificates, email, firewalls, network traffic, virtual networks, security policies, security audits, authentication, and authorization.

Enterprise Security Concerns

When you're dealing at the enterprise level, two of the primary concerns are implementing a secure public key infrastructure (PKI) and ensuring this infrastructure has secure policies to back it up. Microsoft recommends that before your enterprise implements an infrastructure of any sort, it should have the following three documents easily available to users:

- Security policy
- Certification policy
- Certification practice statement

Security Policy

A general *security policy* is a document that outlines the company's security practices and best policies. This typically covers all the computers and other technological assets that the company holds, and it identifies which assets it considers particularly valuable. It also usually contains information on what is considered acceptable use and what is considered a violation of security or a serious security threat.

Without a security policy, the old saying "I didn't know" can become a valid excuse. For example, what if security concerns mandate that a certain folder on the infrastructure server can never have its name changed? If a user doesn't know this, they can always use the "I didn't know" excuse after the folder's integrity has already been compromised.

Certification Policy

Although not used by all organization, a good practice when implementing a complicated certificate structure is to implement a *certification policy* that outlines the processes and measures taken to ensure both the validity of a user and the validity of the certificate they are using. This may be something as simple as an email to a higher certificate authority requesting permission for a certificate or as complex as an intensive background check. Either way, outlining this policy can ease some of the burden of informing users how to attain and manage certificates.

Certification Practice Statement

The last document recommended by the Microsoft best practices for a public key infrastructure is a *certificate practice statement* (CPS). According to Microsoft, a CPS essentially outlines how a certificate authority manages its security and certificates.

Using Windows Server 2008 PKI Additions in a Legacy Environment

Although you are most likely familiar with all of these technologies from your previous study of Windows certificate services for your 70-640, 70-642, and 70-643 exams, it's important to note that in order to support Windows Server 2008, you must update the schema master to support the new Windows Server 2008 features of the public key infrastructure, including the following:

- Version 3 certificate template support
- Online responders
- Network device enrollment
- Qualified certificates

For more information on how to update your organization's schema operations master, see *Windows Server 2008 Active Directory Configuration* by William Panek (Sybex, 2008).

Designing a Certificate Authority Hierarchy

The underlying fabric of any public key infrastructure is the design of the underlying certificate authorities. This includes the number of certificate authorities (CAs), as well as what type of certificates they will use and how the certificate authorities will be used, implemented, and so forth.

Choosing a Tier Model

The first step in creating a CA hierarchy is to choose an effective tier-design model. Therefore, the best way to start a certificate services design is to decide how many servers are going to be operating as certificate authorities and how the process of accessing certificates from these CAs will proceed.

According to Microsoft best practices, certificate authorities can exist in single-, two-, three-, or even four-tiered models, each of which has its own advantages and reason for implementation. In the following sections, I will briefly touch on each of these models and highlight the strengths and weaknesses of each.

Single-Tier CA Structure

For our purposes, the discussion of this level of structure is relatively moot. This is because a single-tiered CA hierarchy is usually used only in small organizations, typically with fewer than 300 user accounts. The focus of the enterprise-level exam is organizations that have more than 5,000 employees.

Regardless, in a single-tier CA infrastructure, the CA is a member server of the domain that exists as the only enterprise root-level certificate authority. Obviously, the advantages of this design are that it is both easy to design and easy to implement. However, it is limited. For example, there is absolutely no available backup. If the main root authority fails, then the entire structure fails. Furthermore, without additional tiers to rely upon, a single member server issuing certificates can (and most likely will) become overburdened in a large organization.

Two-Tier CA Structure

In a two-tiered CA structure, multiple levels of certificate servers perform different roles. Best practices dictate that at the top of the tree the root-level enterprise authority is standalone. That is, it exists apart from the network for the sake of security. Then, below that root-level authority, other member servers exist to issue certificates, as shown in Figure 7.1.

In this figure, the root certificate authority exists independently from the rest of the network, and the extending second-tier computers can either issue certificates or exist as policy issuance certificate authorities. Policy issuance CAs are similar to certificate authorities, except they define the way certificates can be issued but often do not issue certificates themselves.

The advantage of this design is that it allocates a single level of infrastructure for each of the roles being played in the process of dispersing certificates. Furthermore, it adds more physical security because it creates barriers of separation between the root CA, the policy CA(s), and the issuing CAs.

FIGURE 7.1   Two-tier CA hierarchy

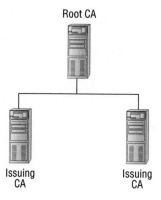

FIGURE 7.2   Three-tier CA hierarchy

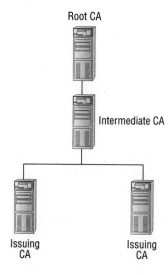

Four-Tiered Structure

A four-tiered CA structure is often used in organizations that have to issue many certificates and require an infrastructure that can support that need. Using a fourth tier, the issuing CAs that existed in the previous three-tier structure expand into a new layer of certificate authorities that build on the previous third tier and create a new tree structure that sort of resembles a "multitiered" third tier. This is pictured in Figure 7.3.

FIGURE 7.3   Four-tiered structure

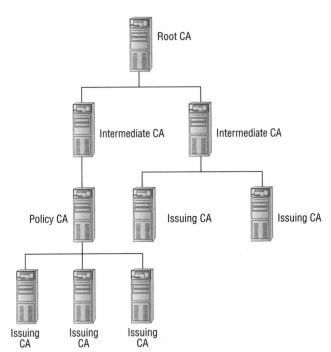

Modeling Your Structure

When choosing how to design your CA hierarchy, one of the first decisions to make—before you make any other crucial decision—is to pick the model that your entire PKI follows. What this means is that you need to answer the following question: Will the CA architecture follow the administrative structure, or will it follow its own independent structure?

Following the Administrative Structure

One of the most commonly practiced methods of working with a PKI is to model it to mirror your organization. In Chapter 1, "Designing a Complex Windows Server 2008 Infrastructure," I discussed various ways to model your organization based on resources, departments, locations, and various other quantities that make for an easily understandable architecture. Using these practices, you can model the CA structure the same way. If the organization has multiple branch offices, you can model them with certificate authorities that represent each branch office. If there are multiple departments, you can implement multiple servers that follow the model of each department.

The advantage of this method is that it is simple and creates uniformity in your infrastructure. Both Active Directory and certificate services will follow the same architecture, making it easy for administrators at all levels to understand

Following an Independent Structure

A case can be made that it is best to have a CA follow a structure that is independent of the standardized methods established by your Active Directory structure. For one thing, there may be organizational or legal standards that require your CA to be placed in a manner set apart from the Active Directory structure. This plays an especially important role in compliance with government standards and industry regulations. Some organizations, such as the FBI or CIA, might require that sensitive security data be laid out in a fashion that may seem strange at first but is ultimately the most secure method.

Design Factors

As I discussed earlier in this book, these are some of the major factors that play into your design decision:

- Organizational requirements
- Software requirements
- User requirements
- Business requirements

Only you, the administrator, can make these decisions (or perhaps you and several other people tasked with the duty). But the point is that all of these factors have to go into making the decision, and it can't be taken lightly. Usually, the decision of how to implement a CA structure is labored over for several weeks. Think about it. In the modern day, even jump drives can be issued certificates. Just think about how many keys there can be floating around if there are 10,000 of those devices in your enterprise!

X.509

An X.509 digital certificate is the most common form of certificate used in modern infrastructures. It contains information regarding the owner of the certificate, the public key of that certificate, and certain other fields:

- Version number
- Serial number
- Algorithm identifier

- Issuer name
- Validity
- Subject name
- Subject public key information
- Issuer unique identifier
- Subject unique identifier
- Key identifier

X.509 certificates can be used in almost every area of security, including just about any form of communication or application. The main function of a certificate, as you know from your study at the MCTS level, is to link a user with certain identifiers that label them as an individual (or entity) that your infrastructure can recognize and authenticate in a process called *verification*.

There are three versions of X.509:

- X.509 version 1
- X.509 version 2
- X.509 version 3

You do not need to understand the intricate differences among these three versions to become a capable administrator.

Using Certificate-Monitoring Tools

For the certification exam, you need to be familiar with two important and useful certificate-monitoring tools that come with Windows Server 2008:

`pkiview.msc`   **The `pkiview.msc`** command launches the PKI Health tool, which allows you to monitor the activity and health of your currently existing public key infrastructure. Additionally, it monitors Authority Information Access (AIA) and CRL distribution (CDP) extensions to ensure that the line of communication for the distribution of authority for certificates is properly monitored.

`certutil.exe`   **The certification utility (`certutil.exe`)** command allows you to determine the validity of issued certificates through the use of two switches:

- `-verify -urlfetch`
- `-viewstore`

Using the –verify –urlfetch *FileName* switch allows you to see the output of the URL for each certificate. If it succeeds, it will display a "verified" output. If it fails, it will display an "error" output.

The –viewstore output allows you to see the contents of a specific Active Directory Domain Services store or object, which lets you choose to view all certificates in that store.

Reasons for a PKI

Whenever an organization uses technologies such as smart cards, IPsec, SSL, digital signatures, EFS, or other technologies that rely upon levels of encryption, the organization needs to create a public system of encryption and identification. But the most common reason for using a system of certificates is Secure Sockets Layer (SSL), which verifies a user's identity and securely transmits data. Without a system of certificates, this would be almost impossible.

Therefore, in most companies, because of the need for the Web, there have been numerous examples of simple PKIs just to support a website on IIS. Without a PKI and certificates, you can't even use HTTPS!

Components of the Public Key Infrastructure

The PKI (the technology that your infrastructure uses to validate the identity of user or entities) is composed of many different components, but at the MCITP level you are primarily concerned with the following:

- Certificates
- Certificate authorities (CAs)
- Certificate revocation lists (CRLs)
- Certificate templates
- The Online Certificate Status Protocol

Some of the material you may read here will seem like review—and some of it may be. But remember, on the Enterprise Administrator certification exam the strongest concentration of material is not necessarily on any one new technology but on a mix of all technologies available to you within a modern infrastructure and your ability to apply those technologies in complex situations.

Certificate Authority

A *certificate authority* is part of the PKI that is responsible for validating certificates, issuing certificates, and revoking certificates. At a minimum, an enterprise using Active Directory Certificate Services (AD CS) must have at least one CA that issues and revokes certificates. Normally, as you'll see in this chapter, there's more than one CA deployed in an organization. Additionally, CAs can be either internal or external and can exist at several different levels, acting as a root CA or an issuance-only CA, for example.

Certificate Revocation Lists

When certificates are revoked before their period of expiration, they are added into a list called a *certificate revocation list*. Within Windows Server 2008, there are two types of CRLs: base CRLs and delta CRLs.

    Base CRLs are complete lists of certificates revoked by a CA; this list also contains the reason for their revocation. A *delta CRL*, on the other hand, contains only the serial numbers and revocation reasons for a revoked certificate that has been revoked since the original incarnation of the base CRL. It's sort of like a differential backup, because it lists only what has changed since the original list was added.

Certificate Templates

Certificate templates are categories of certificates that allow AD CS to store certificates within Active Directory and categorize them according to how they are used and what they contain. They are still relatively new and can be used with either Windows Server 2003 or Windows Server 2008. In effect, what a certificate template does is issue a set of rules that can be applied to certificates, such as where certificates can come from and how they can be created.

Certificate Authority Roles

Within the enterprise, the PKI is usually comprised of multiple certificate authorities, each of which contains one of several roles. These range from the most fundamental of all roles—the root CA role—to a simple CA issuing certificates, all of which fit somewhere within the CA hierarchy.

Root CA Role

The *root* CA in an organization is the first installed and most important CA in the entire infrastructure. Ultimately, the root CA contains the authority to sign certificates as well as authorize other subordinate CAs throughout the organization. And authorizing subordinate CAs is the activity that most root CAs spend the majority of their time undertaking.

Logically, what happens with a root CA is that whenever a client or subordinate receives a certificate, the client will validate that the certificate is trusted by the root CA. Thus, because of this vital role, most root CAs are kept offline, protected from the outside world and stored in a secure location for fear of being compromised.

Intermediate CA Role

An *intermediate* CA is any certificate authority that exists outside the role of the root CA and issues certificates to other CAs somewhere in the CA hierarchy. Normally, this intermediate CA exists in a state between the root CA (which is offline) and the issuing CAs, which are online. This way, issuing CAs have a method of contacting the root CA while ultimately exposing the root CA's private key the minimum number of times.

Policy CA Role

The *policy* CA is technically a subcategory of intermediate CA, but it has a special category in and of itself because of the vital part it plays within a Windows Server 2008 infrastructure. Within that infrastructure, a policy CA contains the policies and procedures an organization uses to secure and validate both the CA and the certificate holder identity. Normally, policy CAs communicate only with other CAs.

Issuing CAs

By far, the most common and lowest-level certificate authority is the CA that is responsible for actually distributing certificates to users and devices within the infrastructure—the *issuing* CA. Typically, the issuing CA receives policies from a higher-level policy CA and responds to requests for certificates and other information. However, an issuing CA is capable of holding its own policies and making its own policy decisions in a smaller architecture, such as a one- or two-tiered hierarchy (discussed later in this chapter).

Enterprise and Stand-Alone CAs

It's most likely that you have encountered an explanation of enterprise and stand-alone CAs in your previous study, but in case you have forgotten, an *enterprise* CA is a CA that takes advantage of Active Directory to control the enrollment process. Thus, because it involves the use of Active Directory, it can logically be further controlled and refined through the use of Group Policy.

Stand-alone CAs do not take advantage of Active Directory and cannot be managed by Group Policy. Furthermore, stand-alone CAs are limited to either web-based or command-line deployment.

Using the Online Certificate Status Protocol

One of the drawbacks of using certificates is that as the number of certificates grows, expires, or ultimately become revoked, the number of revoked certificates in the CRL becomes very large and cumbersome to send back and forth. Using the Online Certificate Status Protocol (OCSP), administrators are able to implement a system that, instead of sending the complete list of revoked certificates, is able to respond to a request about a single certificate within the organization. This greatly reduces the amount of data traffic and optimizes the infrastructure for other tasks.

Online Responders

Any computer that is currently running the Online Responder service can function in the online responder role. The responsibility of the Online Responder service is to communicate responses upon requests for OCSP responses, along with the use of CRLs. Normally, in the enterprise architecture the online responder is an individual machine that is responsible only for the online responder role.

According to Microsoft, online responders can respond to requests much more quickly stances involving the following:

- External clients connected via low-speed WAN connections

- Overloaded networks

- An organization with numerous certificates

- An organization that does not want all expired certificate data to be exposed

In Windows Server 2008, Microsoft encourages the use of the OCSP with its responder system over the use of traditional CRLs to increase the network efficiency of your infrastructure capabilities.

 Responses from online responders are digitally signed and indicate the status of only the certificate to which they have been requested to respond.

The online responder server should be set up and running the Online Responder service before any client certificates are issued. This server must be running Windows Server 2008, but the data can come from a published CRL, which can exist on either Windows Server 2008, Windows Server 2003, or even a non-Microsoft CA.

However, in order to install the Online Responder service, the following prerequisites must be met:

- IIS installed and operating
- OCSP response signing certificate template must be configured on the CA with autoenrollment
- URL placed in the AIA extension of certificates by the CA

OCSP Components

OCSP is divided into several different components, including the OCSP client, responder, and revocation providers.

OCSP Client

The *OCSP client* is integrated within Windows Vista and Windows Server 2008. This allows these two operating systems to interact with an OCSP implementation by default without any further implementation. However, earlier operating systems by Microsoft do not include support for OCSP; thus, you must look for a third-party software provider program.

Online Responder

The *online responder* consists of the service that holds the web proxy cache for the online responder, the revocation configuration to determine how the responder responds to requests, the ability to issue digitally signed keys, and audits.

Revocation Providers

The separate *revocation provider* components function along with the online responder by caching revocation information for the online responder. Then, whenever the online responder receives a request, it may request a revocation provider to cross-check the requested certificate serial number.

In Exercise 7.1, you will learn to install the Microsoft Online Responder service, an essential role for Windows Server 2008 enterprises. Using this service you can expedite the requests that servers will receive.

EXERCISE 7.1

Installing the Microsoft Online Responder Service

To complete this exercise, you must be logged in as at least a member of the local Administrators group. Furthermore, it is assumed you do not have AD CS installed at the time of this exercise.

1. Open Server Manager by clicking the button next to your Start menu.

2. Select Roles.

3. Click Add Roles.

4. Select Active Directory Certificates Services, as shown here, and click Next twice.

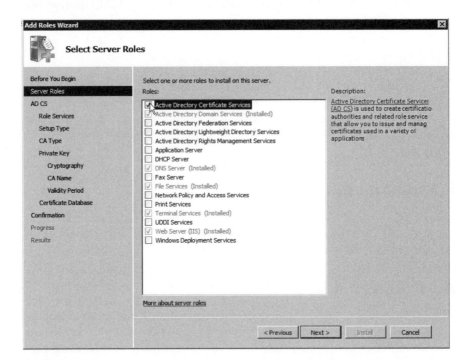

5. Select Online Responder, as shown here, and deselect Certification Authority if it is autoselected.

EXERCISE 7.1   *(continued)*

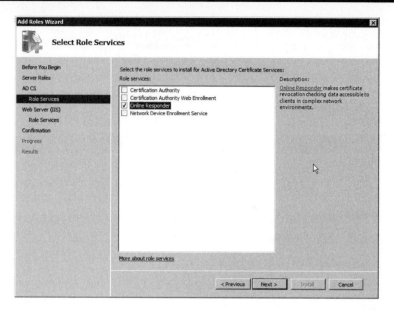

6. Click Next twice.

7. On the Select Role Services screen, leave the default settings, and click Next twice.

8. Click Install.

9. You should see the install screen, as shown here.

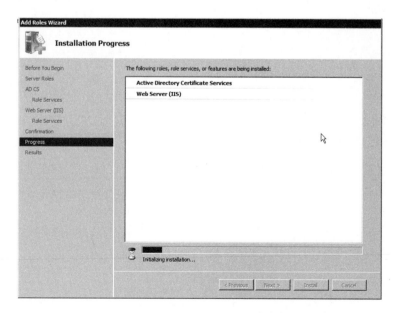

10. Click Close.

Once this is complete, you will have installed the Online Responder service onto your computer. However, there will be no currently installed certificate authorities.

In Exercise 7.2, you will configure the online certification authorities for the OCSP.

EXERCISE 7.2

Configuring a Root CA

To complete this exercise, it's advisable to be logged in as the enterprise administrator, and you should have completed Exercise 7.1.

1. Under Server Manager, select Roles, and navigate to Active Directory.

2. Select Add Role Services.

3. Select Certification Authority, as shown here.

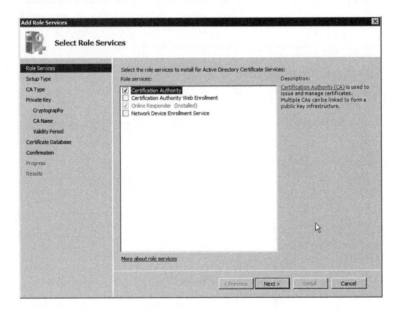

4. Click Next.

5. Select the Enterprise radio button, as shown here.

EXERCISE 7.2 *(continued)*

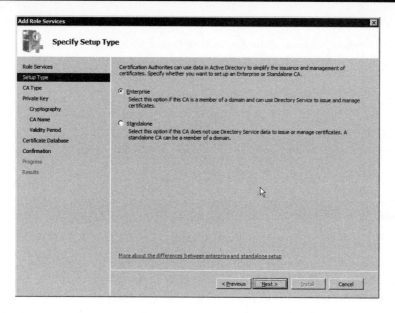

6. Click Next.

7. Select the Root CA radio button. Click Next.

8. Select the Create a New Private Key radio button, and click Next.

9. Leave the default options, as shown here, and click Next.

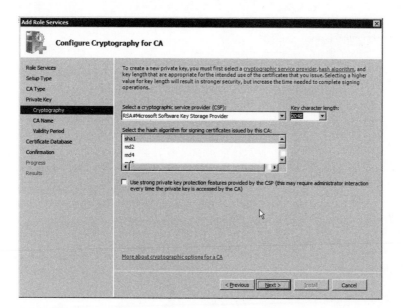

10. Click Next on the Configure CA Name screen.

11. Leave the default options on the Set Validity Period screen, and click Next.

12. Click Next again, and then click Install.

13. During the install, you may see a warning. Ignore it.

14. Click Close.

In Exercise 7.3, you will learn about managing a CA to communicate with an online responder.

Managing a CA to Communicate with an Online Responder

To proceed with this exercise, you must have completed Exercises 7.1 and 7.2. Please note that after you follow all the steps described, this exercise will not be totally complete unless you have an easily accessible online responder.

1. Open the Certification Authority tool by selecting Administrative Tools ➢ Certification Authority.

2. Right-click the CA name, and select Properties, as shown here.

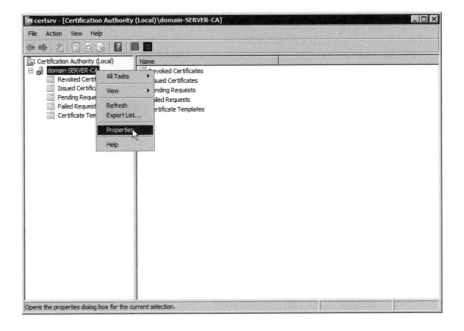

3.   Select the Extensions tab.

4.   Click Add.

5.   Under Location, you could place the URL of your OCSP. For our purposes, leave it blank.

6.   Click Cancel.

Note that if you were able to complete this exercise, you could click OK and then choose from any additional options on the Extensions tab, such as Include in the CDP Extension of Issued Certificates.

Working with Certificate Templates

Not all applications and not all certificates are created equal. In fact, they're created unequally by design. Many different types of certificates exist to meet various purposes in the enterprise, and you need to learn how to use them. This is why Windows Server 2008 comes with several types of ready-made certificates. However, you can also create custom certificates for various devices and users within your organization. Ultimately, the use of certificates achieves one very important goal: it relieves the burden of issuing certificates without complicated certificate requests.

Another interesting fact is that although not all certificates are created equal, various versions of certificate templates are also created even less equal. Windows Server 2008 takes advantage of Windows Certificate Template Version 3. This new type of certificate is supported by Active Directory Certificate Services and includes a new feature, called Cryptography Next Generation, which allows the use of Suite B algorithms in certificates.

You are probably inferring that there must have been a version 1 and version 2 of the certificate template. You're right: version 1 templates were not customizable and had very few of the handy features now available to administrators. Windows Server 2003 Enterprise edition supported version 2 of these certificate templates, which revolutionized the original version 1 certificates by enabling features such as key archival, recovery, and certificate autoenrollment.

For the certification exam, remember that Version 2 certificate templates are supported in Windows Server 2003 and Windows Server 2008 Enterprise edition certificate authorities.

Using Cryptography Next Generation

Using Windows Server 2008, administrators now have the option of utilizing a new suite of encryption algorithms that allow the creation of custom security for digital signatures, key exchange, hashing, and other features for all encryption-requiring applications in the enterprise. This new set of features is called Windows Server 2008 Cryptography Next Generation (CNG).

Cryptography Next Generation with Windows Server 2008 takes advantage of the U.S. government's Suite B cryptographic algorithms. Using these, CNG can provide a new level of complicated encryption for technologies such as AD CS, SSL, and IPsec. Furthermore, CNG is robust in that CNG requires a certain level of government certification by Federal Information Processing Standards (FIPS) to evaluate common criteria.

Unfortunately, CNG is not supported on legacy Windows Servers, such as Windows 2000 Server or Windows Server 2003. To use these, both your certification authority and your applications should support an elliptic curve cryptography (ECC) algorithm. Thus, the use of CNG is rather limited, but it is extremely powerful and useful for organizations that require an extra level of encryption and certification of the methods of that encryption.

Managing External Clients

Occasionally at the corporate level businesses can find themselves in positions where they will have to work with another business externally. This might occur in situations such as a merger or when outsourcing services to a consulting firm. To accommodate this possible design change, it's important to remember when you create your PKI that you may need to account for external users who might have their own PKI or not have a PKI at all. Normally, when the need to deal with an external organization presents itself, an administrator will create *cross-certification* trust-to-trust certificates that are originated from other infrastructures.

Enrollment Strategies

The next big hurdle—after you've designed your organization, you've picked the technologies you'd like to use, and you've determined when and where you are going to roll out your PKI—is deciding precisely how to do so. That is, you have to determine how you are going to issue certificates!

This process is referred to as an *enrollment strategy*. Using an enrollment strategy, you decide how users will receive certificates depending on the type of CAs you have deployed, the operating systems you're utilizing, and other various requirements. Most important, your enrollment strategy depends on the following:

The client operating system   This determines whether you can utilize autoenrollment. Modern Windows-based machines, such as XP or Vista, will be able to take advantage of this, while non-Windows or legacy machines will not.

The type of CA you're utilizing   Unless you're utilizing an enterprise CA, you cannot support autoenrollment.

Active Directory integration   Are you going to utilize Active Directory?

Types of Enrollment

Using certificates, you can determine various types of enrollment, including web, the Certificates MMC, the command line, and autoenrollment.

Web Enrollment

The primary way to interface with a server and obtain a certificate manually is through the use of a web-based browser. Using this method, you can either use a stand-alone or enterprise CA to obtain almost any type of certificate. However, web enrollment does not support certificates templates, so all the information regarding the certificate must be provided by the user.

Web-based enrollment can be used for smart card authentication.

Command-Line Enrollment

Using the command `certreq.exe`, you can manually create, manage, and retrieve certificates. Additionally, `certreq.exe` will allow you to map the CA policy to a set of policy restraints.

Certificates MMC

Using the new Certificate Request Wizard, you can use the certificates MMC to enroll a device with a certificate. Primarily, this method is used to set up computers and local devices for certificates, such as a computer, user, or server.

Autoenrollment

The preferred method for modern infrastructures needing certificates is to use Microsoft Windows autoenrollment, available in Windows XP, Vista, Server 2003, and Server 2008. With autoenrollment, you can enroll smart cards, EFS, SSL, and you can even manage S/MIME certificates for email and other applications. Additionally, you can use Group Policy to manage autoenrollment for specific network devices and users.

Enrollment Agents and Restricted Enrollment Agents

Whenever a user is configured with the ability to issue smart card certificates on behalf of users, that user is referred to as an *enrollment agent*. Through the use of an enrollment agent certificate, the user is able to distribute certificates. These users are usually part of the security infrastructure and help relieve some of the burden upon senior IT staff in the distribution of certificates.

Within Windows Server 2008, Microsoft has provided a new feature for enterprise-based CAs called *restricted enrollment agents*. With restricted enrollment agents, administrators are able to pick users or security groups and give these groups the ability to enroll other security groups or users. This is particularly useful, because previously Windows Server wasn't able to specify a user or group of users.

For the 70-647 exam, you need to know what a restricted enrollment agent is and that you should have as few as possible to optimize performance on your CA. Furthermore, your organization must be using version 3 certificates. You should also note that restricted enrollment agents cannot be used with Active Directory containers such as OUs, but only with users and groups.

The Network Device Enrollment Service

As you learned in your previous study of Active Directory Certificate Services, with Windows Server 2008 Microsoft released its own version of the Simple Certificate Enrollment Protocol for network devices and called it the Network Device Enrollment Service. Using this service, administrators can create a simple method for network devices, such as routers and switches, to attain certificates and become part of the PKI.

For the 70-647 certification exam, you need to remember that the purpose of NDES is to enhance security in your environment. However, it is by no means required. The main reason an organization would want to use it is to secure multiple Windows Server 2008 CAs by using IPsec on routers and switches.

Virtual Private Networks and Security

From your study in Chapter 2, "Naming Conventions, Networking, and Access Principles," you should already be familiar with the fact that virtual private networks use the following five authentication protocols through a VPN server:

- Password Authentication Protocol (PAP)
- Challenge Handshake Authentication Protocol (CHAP)
- Microsoft Challenge Handshake Authentication Protocol (MS-CHAP)
- Microsoft Challenge Handshake Authentication Protocol Version 2 (MS-CHAPv2)
- Extensible Authentication Protocol (EAP)

Furthermore, you should understand that VPNs are refined through the use of either the Layer 2 Tunneling Protocol (L2TP) or the Point-to-Point Tunneling Protocol.

These authentication methods and protocols have existed for a long time, and each of them in their own right has become the industry standard. However, with the release of Windows Server 2008, Microsoft has created a new standard protocol for VPNs that is available only for Windows Vista with Service Pack 1 and Windows Server 2008. The name of this protocol is the Secure Sockets Tunneling Protocol (SSTP). And as you might imagine from its name, SSTP takes advantage of the SSL channel of the Hypertext Transfer Protocol Secure (HTTPS) protocol.

The reason for this technology is that very frequently in the enterprise individual users face the problem of having to authenticate to servers, or navigate to servers, that are behind physical barriers that could cause connectivity problems, such as a firewall or any form of Network Address Translation (NAT). The way this is conquered is by combing a series of technologies. Although it isn't necessary to completely understand the anatomy of SSTP, you should understand that SSTP attaches an IPv4 or IPv6 header to a Point-to-Point protocol frame, and then it encrypts this frame using SSL.

Here are a couple of key points about using SSTP:

No TCP ports need to be opened on a firewall.   Using SSTP, no TCP ports need to be opened on a firewall because of the design of the technology.

You must use HTTPS.   Part of the design of SSTP is a requirement to use HTTPS.

Ultimately, the point to keep in mind with VPNs is that there almost always is a way to solve the problem of creating a secure and viable connection to even the most complicated networks. It really just depends on the type of security you want to implement and how tight you'd like that security to be.

Summary

Designing a public key infrastructure is one of the final and most important steps in completing an enterprise implementation. Part of this process includes creating a CA model that can be multiple tiers in its implementation; using various CAs in different roles, including the root role, policy role, and issuing role; and choosing whether to implement CAs as stand-alone or enterprise implementations.

The goal of any well-designed PKI is to provide an easy form of enrollment that allows for as little user involvement as possible while maintaining the highest level of security. This can be accomplished through automatic enrollment or manual enrollment through forms such as the Web, the Certificates MMC, or the command line. With Windows Server 2008, implementations can include the features of the Microsoft Online Certificate Status Provider that can aid in the alleviation of network traffic caused by requests for certificate status that are located in a standard certificate revocation lists (CRLs), which contain the information regarding certificates that have been revoked for various reasons in the enterprise.

It's important to remember as you review this chapter and begin to implement PKIs on your own that there is no such thing as a completely secure infrastructure. No matter how much work you do, there will always be holes. However, best practices prove that creating a strict security policy, maintaining vigilance, and accounting for all circumstances can produce incredible results and ultimately stable networks.

Exam Essentials

Know the roles that CAs can perform.   For the certification exam, you need to intimately understand the roles of all CAs and what they are and are not capable of doing in the enterprise.

Know the different between stand-alone and enterprise CAs.   This is tested frequently, along with what types of implementations can be made with each CA type. This ultimately leads back to enrollment and what can and cannot participate in certain forms of enrollment.

Know the technology.   Understand what can be used in your environment. Are smart cards capable of handling certificates? What about individual computers? Will this add any additional requirements? You need to know the answer to these questions.

Know how to secure servers in the PKI.   Know which servers should be stored online and which servers should be stored offline in your infrastructure. This leads back to understanding deployment models and the roles CAs can perform.

Review Questions

1. Which of the following certificate template types is compatible only with Windows Server 2008 and not Windows Server 2003?

   A. V1

   B. V2

   C. V3

   D. V4

2. Which of the following is *not* a CA role in the Windows Server 2008 infrastructure?

   A. Issuing CA

   B. Policy CA

   C. Root CA

   D. Enterprise CA

3. With Windows Server 2008 there are various types of certification revocation lists (CRLs). Which type of CRL contains only the serial numbers and revocation reasons for a revoked certificate?

   A. Base CRL

   B. Delta CRL

   C. Enterprise CRL

   D. Root CRL

4. Of the following, which is an available certificate enrollment option with Windows Server 2008? (Choose all that apply.)

   A. Web enrollment

   B. Command line

   C. Autoenrollment

   D. Certificate enrollment

5. Part of the decision of how to implement your CA modeling structure is by creating a tiered architecture for your CAs. According to Microsoft, this helps alleviate servers and secure the network. But also according to Microsoft best practices, you should not exceed how many tiers of CAs?

   A. 1

   B. 2

   C. 3

   D. 4

   E. 5

6. If you are required to monitor the AIA state of a certificate, which of the following monitoring tools would best suit your purpose?

   A. `pkiview.msc`

   B. `certutil.exe`

   C. `certutil.exe – fileview`

   D. `pkiview.msc – fileview`

7. Within the enterprise there are several reasons to incorporate the use of certificates. Of the following applications, which would most likely *not* require a PKI architecture?

   A. Win32 Apps

   B. Smart cards

   C. EFS

   D. Email

   E. SSL

8. What is the minimum version of Windows server required in order to support autoenrollment?

   A. Windows Server 2008

   B. Windows Server 2003

   C. Windows 2000 Server

   D. Windows NT

9. Which of the following enrollment methods is not available if you are using a stand-alone certificate authority?

   A. Web enrollment

   B. Autoenrollment

   C. Manual enrollment

   D. Certificates MMC

10. When you are installing a CA from a given three-tier design, which of the following CA roles should be installed first?

    A. Root

    B. Issuing

    C. Policy

    D. Any intermediate

11. Within OmniCorp, a vast enterprise with more than 2,000 external employees located offsite and performing job functions such as sales and marketing, there is a complicated four-tiered CA model. Currently, external users are logging in over WAN links to access an internal secure web page. However, they have been experiencing problems with the quantity of revoked certificates. If OmniCorp upgraded to Windows Server 2008, what technology could alleviate this problem?

    A. OCSP

    B. Version 3 templates

    C. X.509 version 3

    D. AD CS

    E. Delta CRLs

12. MegaCorp, a large corporation based in the Midwest, is planning on launching a new secure website that will be accessed by users from locations throughout the world on the public Internet. The website needs to utilize SSL and the HTTPS protocol for security purposes. Given this information, what design implementation would be best suited to the organization?

    A. Create a stand-alone CA, and install it along with IIS 7 on the server.

    B. Create an enterprise CA by accessing a public C, and then install it along with IIS 7 on your server.

    C. Use a self-signed certificate with IIS 7.

    D. Install a stand-alone certificate on the root authority.

13. At minimum, how many tiers must be present in your infrastructure in order to support an offline root certificate authority?

    A. 1

    B. 2

    C. 3

    D. 4

14. To install an enterprise authority CA, you must be logged in with at least what level of privileges?

    A. Local administrator

    B. Server administrator

    C. Enterprise administrator

    D. Administrator

15. SuperCorp, an oil company based out of Tokyo, is interested in deploying smart cards to its users. Additionally, SuperCorp wants the benefit of making sure certain groups within their organization are capable of enrolling others users with certificates. Based on these requirements, what would you suggest?

    A. Implement an autoenrollment strategy that assigns privileges to groups.

    B. Utilize certificate restriction strategies.

    C. Implement OCSP.

    D. Implement restricted enrollment agents.

    E. Utilize the `certreq.exe` tool.

16. What is the command that will allow you to create, submit, accept, and retrieve certificates?

   A. `certreq.exe`

   B. `pkiview.exe`

   C. `certutil.exe`

   D. `certconfig.exe`

17. In an enterprise, the Microsoft-recommended practice for creating a secure and informed environment is to create several different documents outlining various security practices and the acceptable and understood use of various resources within the infrastructure. Of the following documents that are used in this design, which of the following documents outlines how a certificate subject is verified before it is issued?

   A. Security policy

   B. Certificate policy

   C. Certification practice statement

   D. User Security Guide

18. What is the term used when two separate organizations utilize trusts in order to validate each other's credentials?

   A. Cross-certification trust

   B. Forest trust

   C. Domain trust

   D. Trust

   E. Certification trust

19. In an enterprise, the Microsoft-recommended practice for creating a secure and informed environment is to create several different documents outlining various security practices and the acceptable and understood use of various resources within the infrastructure. Of the following documents that are used in this design, which outlines the rules and accepted practices associated with acceptable use of security assets?

   A. Security policy

   B. Certificate policy

   C. Certification practice statement

   D. Policy statement

20. When operating within an organization with fewer than 300 user accounts, what is the recommended certificate authority infrastructure?

   A. Single-tier

   B. Two-tier

   C. Three-tier

   D. Four-tier

Answers to Review Questions

1. C. Version 3 certificate templates are new to Windows Server 2008 and available only for Windows Server 2008. Windows Server 2008 also supports version 1 and 2 certificates. There's no such thing, at this point, as version 4 certificate templates.

2. D. Enterprise is a type of certificate authority, not a role it plays within the infrastructure. When implementing your CA, you have to choose between stand-alone and enterprise CAs.

3. B. A delta CRL contains only the serial numbers and revocation reasons for a revoked certificate that has been revoked since the base CRL has been invoked.

4. A, B, C. Using Windows Server 2008, you can set up your PKI to enroll automatically, through the Web, via the command line, and through the Certificates MMC, which is the tool most commonly used by administrators to handle certificates.

5. D. According to Microsoft, it is not advisable to exceed four tiers of CAs. In fact, your organization will probably benefit from a three-tier or even two-tier infrastructure. Both of these still allow for an offline root CA and for it to be exposed as little as possible.

6. A. The PKI Health tool (`pkiview.msc`) allows you to monitor the activity and health of your currently existing public key infrastructure. Additionally, it monitors Authority Information Access (AIA) and CRL distribution (CDP) extensions to ensure that the line of communication for the distribution of authority for certificates is properly monitored.

7. A. Most normal Win32 applications do not require the use of certificates. However, chances are that your smart cards, EFS, email, SSL, and many other additional components may require them.

8. B. At minimum, you must be utilizing Windows Server 2003 as a server operating system and either Windows XP or Windows Vista as a client operating system. Using these four platforms, you can set up autoenrollment for your user base.

9. B. Using a stand-alone certificate authority prohibits you from using autoenrollment. To do this, you must at minimum be an enterprise authority.

10. A. In any CA implementation, the root CA should be installed first. Furthermore, in a three-tier design, this should be brought offline as soon as possible.

11. A. The Online Certificate Status Protocol is designed to alleviate the burden of having to transmit the entire list of revoked certificates. Using this, servers respond to unique claims based upon the request of individual components.

12. B. Whenever you are exposing a site to the open Internet that will use encryption (SSL), it's a good idea to install an enterprise certificate from a public company. This way, the certificate is trusted and has been validated against a third party.

13. B. To support an offline CA, you must at minimum have one additional tier for a total of two. This allows an online CA to be present to issue certificates and lets the root stay offline for security purposes.

14. C. To install an enterprise root certificate authority, you must be logged in as an enterprise administrator. Otherwise, you do not have the required authority to make such an important change to the PKI.

15. D. Restricted enrollment agents allow administrators to assign certain users and groups with the privilege of certificate enrollment. By using this, SuperCorp will be able to pass assignments down through its organization according to the requirements set forth in the problem.

16. A. `certutil.exe` is a command-line utility that allows you to create, submit, accept, and retrieve certificates, as well as run batch files or scripts. Additionally, you can use it for cross-certificate certificate requests.

17. B. The certificate policy is responsible for determining whether a certificate is assigned. Additionally, it keeps track of where keys are stored and renewed or generally how certificates are managed in the environment.

18. A. A cross-certification trust allows two organizations to trust each other's certificates and keys as if they were issued from themselves. This is a useful practice for merging companies and extended branch offices or conglomerates.

19. A. A corporate security policy is responsible for determining the acceptable use of network resources, computers, and other devices within the infrastructure. Without a corporate security policy, business lacks a validation of their standard methods and practice and compromise themselves by becoming vulnerable to a "Don't ask, don't tell" policy.

20. A. With fewer than 300 user accounts, an infrastructure this simple will require only one tier of certificate authorities. Beyond this, you expose your organization to unnecessary complication.

Chapter

8

Planning for Business Continuity and Backup

OBJECTIVES COVERED IN THIS CHAPTER:

✓ **Plan for Business Continuity**

  ▪ May include but is not limited to: service availability, directory service recovery

✓ **Design for Data Management and Data Access**

  ▪ May include but is not limited to: data security, data accessibility and redundancy, data collaboration

Ask any professional administrator who has been in the industry for a long time, and they will tell you that the job of the administrator is twofold. First, you have to make sure things work. Second, you have to make sure they *always* work.

On the enterprise level, this can be so extreme that it can include measurements up to the millisecond level of downtime. In fact, one administrator I spoke to at a major banking company told me that at their central location it was quite possible that a large majority of the staff may be losing their positions with the company because their servers were once down for an entire minute. And, in an industry where billions of dollars are swapped from hand to hand every minute, that could have meant millions of dollars in potential losses.

For the Enterprise Administrator exam, Microsoft will test you on your knowledge of service availability, business continuity, and backup by presenting questions about the full spread of technologies available with Windows Server 2008 at the professional level. This includes technologies such as RAID, backup utilities, network load balancing, and other service and backup distributing utilities.

In this chapter, I'll cover these services in detail and discuss how these services apply to the enterprise.

Introducing RAID

In the world of making backups, the first line of defense against a potential problem is a redundant array of independent (or inexpensive) disks (RAID). At this point in your career, you have probably set up or used machines that have been RAID capable, and it's even more likely that you have set up a RAID yourself. Thus, I'll cover only the basic aspects of RAID and its place within the network infrastructure.

Software RAID

The simplest form of RAID is configured in software. When this type of configuration occurs, the administrator uses multiple available drives and storage devices to combine available space into one (or multiple) logical drives for the purpose of storing large amounts of data over several volumes. Normally, a software RAID is used in situations where there is a large amount of non-mission-critical data space accessible over several drives that are not linked together in hardware.

Using Windows Server 2008, administrators can easily put a RAID together through the use of Windows disk utilities. However, each disk used in the RAID must be configured as a *dynamic* disk. Once this is complete, disk utilities can store the software RAID data in either RAID 0, RAID 1, or RAID 5, which will be discussed later in this chapter.

Hardware RAIDs

A hardware RAID is a RAID in which individual drives have been partitioned and segmented through the use of a hardware device, such as a RAID card, in such a way that the operating system or software recognizes them as one independent device, or a custom number of independent devices, as determined by the setup of the administrator. The advantage of a hardware RAID is that it is faster, is more efficient, and involves less burden on the server to set up than software RAID. However, it is also much more expensive because it requires the purchase of dedicated hardware.

RAID Configurations

Using RAID, administrators can place data across multiple volumes and create redundancy and fault tolerance in several ways. Within the enterprise, you are primarily concerned with the following types of RAID configuration:

- RAID 0
- RAID 1
- RAID 5
- RAID 10 (1+0)

RAID 0

RAID 0, or *striping*, is the process of taking several disks and combining them into one large, maximum-speed disk. In the industry, RAID 0 is often referred to as "just a bunch of disks." This phrase is often used to describe it because RAID 0 provides no fault tolerance, and thus it's used only for data that is not mission critical and can be easily recovered. However, RAID 0 does have several important key benefits. First, RAID 0 is the fastest of all RAID types. Using RAID 0 you can achieve speeds of data input and output far greater than any other RAID configuration. Second, RAID 0 is the easiest to set up.

More often than not, a lot of organizations use RAID 0 on a server that is critical to business when on a limited budget. This is because RAID 0, in combination with another technology such as tape backup, can provide an excellent means of cost-effective storage.

Obviously, RAID 0 is supported in both hardware and software configurations. However, RAID 0 cannot be booted from in software configuration. This is because the operating system as it boots has no idea where to find the drive with the existing NT loader. Thus, in order to trick the operating system into understanding RAID 0, a hardware device is required.

RAID 1

RAID 1 is a type of RAID configuration that in slang is referred to as *mirroring*. The process used with RAID 1 is a bit-for-bit copy that is exchanged from one drive to another. If a change is made to one drive, the change is matched to another drive that is a mirror image of it. This way, if one drive ever goes bad, you instantly have access to a direct copy of that drive to pick up where you last left off and recover back to your full operating potential.

The disadvantages of RAID 1 are, first, that it's slow and provides no methods for data efficiency, but more important, it also provides *less* access to space than you would normally have with two separate drives. When using RAID 0, you would have access to twice the amount of data than you would with RAID 1, because for each individual drive that is used there is a completely separate drive that remains relatively inactive because it just copies data.

RAID 5

When RAID 5 was first introduced to the world, a lot of administrators called it "black magic." And that's because they just couldn't figure out how it worked! Most administrators, including me, just looked at RAID 5 and knew it provided speed increases and redundancy.

But most people could never figure out how it really worked. The truth is, RAID 5 is actually fairly easy to explain—though I imagine it wasn't quite as easy to engineer. RAID 5 uses a *parity bit*, which, in simple language, is a 1 or 0 that is placed on a drive that is dedicated to storing parity bits.

A parity bit is responsible for answering this question: "Is this data different?"

RAID 5 uses a minimum of three drives—two that store data and one that stores the parity bits. The way the parity bit comes about is by taking data on the first drive, comparing it with data on the second drive, and saying "Is this different?" So, for example, say you have three drives, as shown in Figure 8.1.

FIGURE 8.1   Parity bits

In row A, Drive 1 has a 1 in its first bit, and Drive 2 has a 0 in its first bit. Those two numbers are different. Thus, the parity bit is set to 1. It really just says this: "True. These are different."

On row B, Drive 1 has a 1 in its second bit, and Drive 2 also has a 1. Since these are the same, the parity bit has been set to 0 and basically says this: "False. These are not different."

Let's see what this accomplishes. Say you lose one drive, such as Drive 1 in Figure 8.2.

FIGURE 8.2 Failed drive

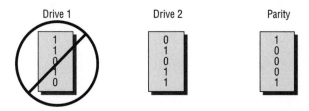

Well, my data is gone, right? Wrong. I have a parity drive! By looking at this, I can do as you see in Figure 8.3, compare this data, and say this: "Well, if the parity bit is a 0, I can assume this data is the same. If it's a 1, I can place the opposite data from what's contained in the working drive."

FIGURE 8.3 Drive rebuild

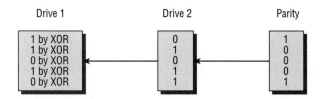

So if you lose one of the drives with your data on it, the parity bit can help you rebuild the data! But what if you lose the parity drive itself? No worries, you'll be perfectly fine. That's because this drive is used to store only parity information, not actual data like the main drives. In this case, you could replace the failed parity drive with a new drive that would rebuild its parity information by comparing the two existing drives bit by bit.

RAID 5 has a huge advantage. It's both fast and offers redundancy. But there are also some major downsides. For one thing, it's expensive and requires at least three drives. Also, just like RAID 0, RAID 5 cannot be booted from unless you have a hardware RAID card. However, for a high-budget enterprise solution, RAID 5 is priceless.

RAID 10

RAID 10, or RAID 1+0, is the first of several "mixed RAID" modes that are available as high-end storage solutions. In the enterprise, you'll often run into situations where a simple storage solution utilizing one of the main three RAID types (0, 1, 5) will not be enough, so you'll need to take advantage of another type of RAID.

The need for RAID 10 most commonly arises when an organization demands the speed and accessibility of RAID 0 but also desires the reliability that only RAID 1 can bring. In and of itself, RAID 5 can provide some of these features, in that it can both provide redundancy and improve speeds, but on its own RAID 5 cannot completely stripe together several volumes and then completely mirror them.

Using RAID 10, an entire stripe is mirrored onto a completely different stripe. What this means is that there are effectively two complete RAIDs, each of which contains mirror-like setups of their disk configuration. And within these RAIDs, they have been set up to mirror each other's data. In other words, you're mirroring an entire RAID, not just a drive.

As mentioned earlier, this is very useful for high-end, demanding environments. But it's not good for all users. First, RAID 10 is probably the single most expensive implementation of RAID because it requires multiple drives with an exact mirror of the same multiple drives. Thus, you can't really have RAID 10 without a minimum of four hard drives (two for the stripe and two for the second mirrored stripe). In the real world, you should use this configuration only when the organization can afford it and when both speed and reliability are absolutely essential.

Within Windows Server 2008, there can be a maximum of 32 logical devices assigned together in RAID 0, 1, or 5 configurations.

 Real World Scenario

RAID Decisions

OmniCorp has recently acquired a new Windows Server 2008 with more than 5TB of space spread across 10 hard drives. The server will have several purposes, functioning as a domain controller, a backup server, and a real-time video-editing machine for high-end video software. The requirements for the server are as follows:

- The operating system and required files must be redundant.

- The applications must be as fast as possible.

- The backup software must be fast and provide some redundancy.

In this case, OmniCorp would most likely take the following path:

1. Create three separate RAID volumes, two in hardware and two in software.

2. On the first hardware RAID volume, configure the operating system to be redundant using RAID 1.

3. Place the applications folder into a software RAID 0 configuration, with maximum speed.

4. Configure the remaining backup portions with RAID 5 technology, allowing for some redundancy but also allocating for speeds that are as fast as possible.

This way, the system provides all the necessary tasks with optimum efficiency.

Introducing the Distributed File System

The purpose behind the distributed file system (DFS) can be summed up into two words: simplification and consolidation. Before the days of DFS, administrators constantly ran into problems where data would be spread across the network infrastructure and its location would be difficult to describe to users. You'd hear stuff like this: "To access the videos, you can look on Server 1; the audio files, however, are on Server 2, and the stripped images for the video are on Server 3."

This became a big problem. The solution that Microsoft created for it was DFS. In effect, DFS takes multiple files and replicates them across the network based on their path. Using Windows Server 2008, Windows Server machines can consolidate files from across the network by making them appear in one central location to outside users. In fancier language, it creates a hierarchical view of network files that is easily understandable by most users.

DFS Components

A DFS infrastructure comprises five major components:

- Namespace
- Namespace server
- Namespace root
- Folders
- Folder targets

A DFS namespace is similar to a container in that the namespace contains the logical structure of the DFS system. In it are the root, folders, and other servers. The namespace is controlled by a namespace server that hosts the namespace. And logically, the namespace root is the first server in the namespace (which shows you that a DFS system can actually contain multiple servers).

And finally, at the bottom level of the DFS structure, there are folders and targets. Folders contain data that needs to be shared, and folder targets specify locations in a separate folder (similar to shortcuts) where data is stored.

 A DFS namespace can be on a stand-alone or domain-based system. However, to be supported by Active Directory Domain Services (AD DS) and support file replication, it must be on a domain-based system.

DFS Replication

The true power of DFS lies in its ability to perform a process called *replication*. With DFS, replication occurs through a series of communications with a protocol called Remote Differential Compression (RDC). Using RDC, DFS detects any changes to files that occur in the environment, such as the moving or altering of data, and ensures that the changes are made to the namespace only when the files are updated. For the certification exam, you need to make sure you understand that this process is managed through something called the *multimaster replication engine*.

DFS Features

Using DFS, administrators have many available features at their disposal that they can use to design a very robust environment. Among these features are referral ordering, target priority, failover procedures, redundant namespace servers, and namespace scalability mode.

Referral Ordering

With DFS, Windows Server 2008 is capable of making reference to several different structures called *referrals*. A referral, in a nutshell, is a type of structure that leads Windows Server 2008 toward a target or folder that contains required data specified by the administrators, such as shared files. These pieces of data appear to the client computer requesting the information as an ordered list of referral information that is prioritized by one of three methods as decided by the user:

- Lowest cost
- Random order
- Exclude targets outside the client's site

Through one of these methods, administrators can decide how they want to have referrals ordered. Thus, an administrator could do something like increase the site-link cost for an out-of-site controller and then arrange the results by lowest cost or completely ignore (exclude) results that are outside a given site.

DFS Failover

If a DFS sharing server loses its connection, *failover* lets a member server within the namespace attempt to authenticate to another server in the case of losing the original server. Then, if that server is successfully restored, the client will reconnect and *fail back* to the server if and only if the site-link cost of the recovered server is *less* than the cost of the server it has been using since the failure.

The reason behind this in simple terms is that since there has already been a failure in the first server that the DFS failover system was connected to, the DFS failover system now considers that server to be less reliable than its previous server. Thus, unless it is considerably less costly to access, the DFS failover system will not fail back unless required.

Redundant Namespace Servers

Just like there are backups in the case of DFS failover, there is a procedure that can be used for domain-based DFS namespace servers that might possibly fail. For the certification exam, all you need to be familiar with is that Windows Server 2008 supports the capability for more than one namespace server and can use a failover system for it.

Target Priority

With Windows Server 2008, you can designate certain targets to have priority over other targets. Some of the options for this include the following:

First among all targets This makes the target first, regardless of any other target priority.

Last among all targets This makes the target last, regardless of any other target priority.

First among targets of equal cost If there is a conflict involving targets of equal cost, the target with this selection will win.

Last among targets of equal cost If there is a conflict involving targets of equal cost, the target with this selection will be placed last regardless of other priorities.

Namespace Scalability Mode

Using this mode, domain controllers in domain-based DFS infrastructures are able to sense changes to the DFS namespace and respond accordingly through automated processes, rather than requiring the administrator to make manual changes.

Introducing Failover Clustering

Back in the 1990s, if you wanted to impress a few friends and gain a couple new colleagues in the industry, all you had to do was throw down the word *cluster* and watch the excitement fly. Clustering wasn't a new concept, but it wasn't really until the 1990s that clustering became a viable possibility for the average business environment.

In the network infrastructure context, the word *cluster* refers to the ability of several computers to function as one computer through the use of communications ports. Normally, clusters function by communicating via TCP/IP or by a high-bandwidth interconnect device such as Myrinet to allow the transmission of data across high-speed interconnects.

Within Windows Server 2008, the primary cluster to be concerned with is called a *failover cluster*. This refers to additional computers that are designed to carry over the tasks of a given network in case of the failure of a computer providing a primary service. Earlier in this chapter, I referenced RAID as the first line of defense in terms of redundancy and backup. A failover cluster is designed to be always ready to deploy but with any luck is never necessary.

The most common contexts in which a failover cluster might be used are with server-based applications and components such as the following:

- SQL Server
- Domain controllers
- Exchange servers
- Custom applications
- Mission-critical roles

Clustering Components

Within a cluster, you need to be familiar with two components:

- Server nodes
- Shared storage

Server Nodes

Within a server cluster, a *node* is an individual machine that performs a function in the overall picture of the cluster. Within a cluster, there are usually several nodes or individual servers. But at minimum, a cluster must contain two nodes to be considered a cluster. Without two nodes, there would be only one centralized machine.

Shared Storage

Shared storage refers to space that is allocated at a location that is accessible to multiple machines throughout the infrastructure. Within a cluster, this is usually a form of network-attached storage, iSCSI, Fibre Channel, or another space for offloaded data that is accessible by all nodes throughout the server.

Clustering with Windows Server 2008

With Windows Server 2008, Microsoft faced several challenges in creating a safe, reliable operating system that supported a highly complex system of backups and redundancy. Its customers demanded a system that not only worked but also supported multiple clustering configurations with a failover system that was second to none.

Microsoft's response was to create a 64-bit capable failover system that could take advantage of TCP/IP versions 4 and 6, support up to 16 nodes, and establish an unparalleled series of criteria for determining server availability.

Only Windows Server 2008 Enterprise and Datacenter edition support Windows failover clustering.

Introducing Quorums

One of the ways of the Windows Server 2008 clustering failover architecture improved upon the previously existing Windows Server 2003 platform was through the introduction of Windows Server 2008 quorums.

When used with reference to human beings, the word *quorum* is defined as "the number of members of a group or organization required to be present to transact business legally, usually a majority" (Source: *Random House Unabridged Dictionary*).

This definition is apt for us, because in a cluster a quorum is the number of nodes required to make an appropriate decision regarding any given subject and keep the cluster operational. Within Windows Server 2008, administrators can give several nodes within a cluster a certain amount of criteria-based decision-making authority regarding whether the cluster should continue to function in case of a failure.

Witness Disks and File Share Witness

A *witness disk* is an optional data disk within your infrastructure that contains a copy of the cluster configuration database. The purpose of this disk is to serve as another litmus test as to whether a cluster should remain functioning in addition to quorum configurations. This happens through one of four options:

- Node majority
- Node and disk majority
- Node and file share majority
- Disk only

The cluster uses the number of nodes it has access to as well as the witness disk to determine whether it should continue operating. In node majority mode, the cluster will continue to operate as long as the majority of nodes (two out of three, for example) continue to run. In node and disk majority mode, it's required that the cluster have a majority of the nodes, and the disk (or file share, in the case of node and file share majority) counts as an additional vote that can break the case of a tie in even number of node environments. Additionally, you can have the witness disk be the single factor that determines whether the cluster continues to run.

Introducing Network Load Balancing

Whenever I hear the words *network load balancing*, a little part of me still says, "Coooool!" The reason for that is that there is only one reason that you would ever need to use network load balancing: you have a huge network.

And getting to administer huge enterprises with really high-end missions is what being an enterprise administrator is all about.

The purpose of network load balancing (NLB) is to relieve the burden on one computer and place it on another. Just like in our section on Terminal Services, sometimes servers are running so many tasks or doing so many deeds that to do just one more can cause an extremely heavy and unnecessary load. Take, for example, the illustration in Figure 8.4. In Figure 8.4, the server farm is extremely unbalanced. Right now, Server 1 is so overburdened that it is constantly operating at 100 percent load, while Server 2, Server 3, and Server 4 are operating at less than 20 percent each.

FIGURE 8.4 Unbalanced server farm

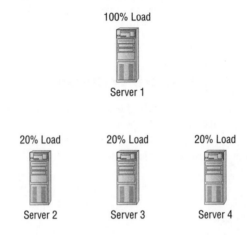

In this example, if you were using network load balancing, NLB would distribute this load to the rest of your computers.

For the certification exam, you need to know that the most common uses of NLB are for the following:

- Web farms
- VPNs
- Terminal Services
- Custom applications

You do not need to know the ins and outs of setting up an entire web farm. However, doing that is an exceedingly good way to become familiar with just about every aspect of Windows Server 2008.

With network load balancing, a single point of failure is removed, and scalability is increased to a maximum. By adding computers, you can further increase the power of your server farm and the redundancy of your infrastructure.

Using Windows Server Backup Tools

At this point I've discussed many of the fail-safes available with Windows Server, such as RAID, network load balancing, and clustering, but now let's get into the true meat and potatoes of Windows backup—the Windows Server Backup tools. Using these tools, you can back up certain portions of Windows Server 2008, including everything from important files to information regarding the exact setup of the Windows Server 2008 infrastructure.

To use Windows Server Backup, you must first add it through the Windows Server Manager by selecting Add Features ≻ Windows Server Backup.

Windows Server Backup

The Windows Server Backup feature in Windows Server 2008 is a backup recovery utility that is designed to provide simplified backup capability. Before Windows Server 2008, this backup utility was called `ntbackup.exe`. Now, it is an MMC that consists of four wizards that can back up the entire server, the system state, a selected volume, or individual files and folders. You can also use Windows Server Backup remotely.

Wbadmin

The Wbadmin command-line tool is a backup utility that runs through the Windows Server Backup feature to restore the operating system, files, folders, and even applications. However, it is accessible only after the backup features have been installed within Windows Server 2008.

Table 8.1 lists the commands that are available at the command line.

TABLE 8.1   Available Commands in Wbadmin

Command	Purpose
Enable Backup	Enables a daily backup schedule
Disable Backup	Stops an enabled daily backup
Start Backup	Executes a one-time backup
Stop Job	Stops any currently running backup
Get Versions	Lists details of previously executed backups
Get Items	Lists the items of a previous backup
Start Recovery	Runs a recovery of specified items from a backup

TABLE 8.1   Available Commands in Wbadmin *(continued)*

Command	Purpose
Get Status	Shows the status of a currently running backup or recovery
Get Disks	Lists the disks that are online and operating
Start Systemstaterecovery	Runs a system state recovery
Start Systemstatebackup	Runs a system state backup
Delete Systemstatebackup	Deletes specified system state backups
Start Sysrecovery	Runs the recovery of the entire system
Restore Catalog	Restores a catalog from a storage location if it has been corrupted
Delete Catalog	Deletes a backup catalog

Introducing the Encrypting File System

From your earlier and more basic studies of the Windows system architecture, you may remember the two overarching file systems that are used when creating an initial Windows drive partition:

- FAT32
- NTFS

Since the introduction of Windows Vista and Windows Server 2008, NTFS has become the de facto file system for use in the Windows platform. However, both Windows Server 2008 and Windows Vista still support the capability to read and interpret FAT32 and earlier volumes.

Within NTFS, Microsoft supports a technology for security and encrypting data written across NTFS volumes called Encrypting File System (EFS). This has been available since Windows 2000 and is not a new technology to Windows Server 2008. However, although it has been around for many years, it remains useful for the modern-day administrator.

Using EFS, administrators can support symmetric and asymmetric forms of encryption to protect data against being read by applications or malicious users by running the data through several standardized cryptographic algorithms. This data encryption occurs at the file level and not at the application level, making it difficult to compromise. Furthermore, EFS supports the use of keys that can be archived and exported to external media for backup.

For the certification exam's purposes, you need to know that EFS is an encrypting technology and that it is made possible through the use of certificates. Additionally, EFS can be deployed through certificate authorities, within which Group Policy can assign users as data recovery agents to retrieve data that has been encrypted and needs to be recovered.

 If data is taken from an encrypted NTFS (EFS) file system and copied to a FAT32 volume, the data will no longer be encrypted!

Introducing Windows BitLocker

In addition to the Encrypting File System (EFS), Windows Server 2008 and Windows Vista now implement Windows BitLocker. The advantage of Windows BitLocker over EFS is that BitLocker encrypts all files, including hibernation files and system files. According to Microsoft, the primary purpose of BitLocker is to secure the entire volume against the possibility of the volume being stolen or physically compromised in some manner.

Recovering Active Directory Domains Services

Within any critical Windows Server 2008 environment, one of the primary responsibilities of a prudent administrator is to make sure that, along with the critical data that is stored throughout an environment, the environment itself can be rebuilt in case of an extreme failure, such as the loss of AD DS.

According to Microsoft, two of the best practices to follow when first designing an infrastructure are, first, to make sure that your Active Directory domain controllers can be recovered, regardless of any potential loss; and, second, to make sure your operating system files are stored in another directory by themselves.

Recovering Active Directory Domain Controllers

To recover Active Directory domain controllers, you have to make sure that two critical components of the Active Directory infrastructure are stored in separate volumes:

- The SYSVOL directory
- Ntdis.dit, which is the database for Active Directory, including user accounts

By doing this, you ensure that the system volume directory and the Active Directory database are stored in places that are easily recoverable.

Storing Operating System Files Separately

As mentioned, another best practice is to make sure your operating system files are stored in another directory by themselves. This way, in the case of a single system volume, the rest will still be kept intact.

Restoring AD DS

In the case of a loss of AD DS, you can perform two types of restores: authoritative restores and nonauthoritative restores. From your earlier study of Active Directory in Windows Server 2008, you are or should already be familiar with these procedures. But in case you have forgotten, here's a review:

Nonauthoritative restores   Nonauthoritative restores are most commonly used for hardware or software failures. With nonauthoritative restores, the restoration is made from a backup, and the restored domain controller learns of the changes made since its last backup through replication of other domain controllers throughout the network.

Authoritative restores   Authoritative restores are performed where a change has been made to Active Directory that removes mission-critical information, such as the removal of a vital organizational unit that would take hundreds of hours to rebuild. The process for executing an authoritative restore is to recover from a backup and then rely on the recovered domain controller to overwrite any changes made to the network infrastructure via its own replication.

Obviously, no type of restoration is completely without risk. In fact, if you can avoid it, it's best in an environment not to do a restoration at all. Anyone who has spent a lot of time around Active Directory will tell you that although Active Directory is powerful, it can certainly have its problems, specifically when it involves the use of replication. But, with that cautionary statement out of the way, they are both very useful tools.

 If you'd like to learn how to perform an authoritative or nonauthoritative restore, consult Will Panek's *Windows Server 2008 Active Directory Configuration*, published by Sybex.

Introducing Windows Recovery Environment

The Windows Recovery Environment is a partial version of the operating system that is designed to be used to recover the Windows operating system in case of a failure. It is based on the WinRE, which includes the tools covered in the following sections.

Windows Complete PC Restore

Using Windows Complete PC Restore, Windows Server 2008 searches for the location of a full backup and uses it to restore the operating system from the ground up. At first, PC Restore will search either a DVD drive or a USB drive for the appropriate files.

Windows Memory Diagnostic Tool

Using the Windows Memory Diagnostic tool, you can search the computer's physical memory to check for any system errors. This way, if you've been experiencing consistent read, write, or access problems, you can identify them via this low-level tool.

Command Prompt

With WinRE, you have full access to the command prompt. This allows you to move files, access the Wbadmin tool, and perform functions using Windows' most basic (and arguably most powerful) mode.

Using Windows Recovery

You can access the Windows Recovery Environment via one of four methods:

Boot from the installation CD   Place the installation CD into the CD drive, reboot from the CD upon the boot selection device, and then select Repair.

Deploy from Windows Deployment Services (WDS)   You can access the Windows Recovery Environment using Windows Deployment Services.

Create a bootable WinRE disk   Using either Backup Business Deployment or the Windows Automated Installation Kit, you can create a bootable Windows recovery disk.

Create a bootable WinRE partition   You can create an entire partition dedicated to the Windows Recovery Environment.

Using Volume Shadow Copy

In earlier versions of both Windows Server and Windows Server 2008, shadow copies have always been one of the most prized resources of the busy administrator. Using Volume Shadow Copy, administrators are able to restore previous versions of files without the need for extensive backup procedures.

With Volume Shadow Copy, existing images of the current Windows Server state are taken and compared with future changes made to the Windows network environment. Then, if a version of a particular file doesn't match the original state of the image, Volume Shadow Copy stores the changes made to this file in a given area determined by the administrator. At this point, the Previous Versions tab, as shown in Figure 8.5, appears in the properties of a file.

FIGURE 8.5   Volume Shadow Copy's Previous Versions tab

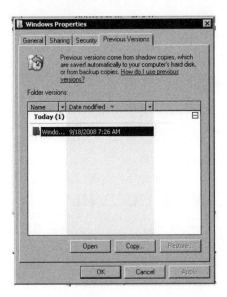

When selected, a Volume Shadow Copy will then list all the changes made to the file and the dates these changes were made. At this point, you have three choices:

Open   When you open the file, you execute the file and view it on your desktop. Then, you can decide what you want to do with the previous version, such as save it to another location.

Restore   When you use the Restore function, the current version of the existing file is replaced by the previous version selected by the administrator in Volume Shadow Copy.

Copy   When you execute the Copy command, you tell Windows Server to place the file in a new location.

In Exercise 8.1, you'll enable volume shadow copies on your machine to make future versions of your files restorable to previous states.

EXERCISE 8.1

Enabling Volume Shadow Copy

To perform this exercise, you must be running Windows Server 2008 and have access to a volume that is formatted with NTFS. FAT32 is not supported with Volume Shadow Copy. Furthermore, you must be logged in as a local administrator or someone with higher privileges.

1. Open your server's hard drives by selecting Start ➢ Computer.

2. Right-click your local drive, and select Properties.

3. Click the Shadow Copies tab, as shown here.

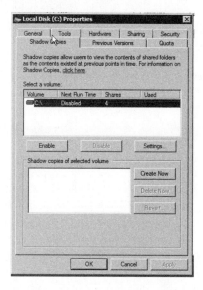

4. Select the drive you want to enable Volume Shadow Copy on, and then select Create Now. This will create a shadow copy of the selected volume to be initially used for backup.

5. Keep the drive you want to enable Volume Shadow Copy on selected, and then click Enable. A warning box will appear, as shown here. Ignore this, and select Yes.

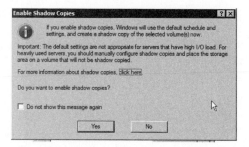

EXERCISE 8.1 *(continued)*

6. By default, Windows Server 2008 will set Volume Shadow Copy to use its default settings. To alter these, you click the Settings button. Then, you can set the maximum amount of space that can be used by Volume Shadow Copy and also can adjust the schedule of copies using the Schedule button.

To perform Exercise 8.2, you will need a large amount of space available on your server hard drive that is *not* where the local operating system is installed. The specific amount will depend on your individual server's configuration. For a basic install, 10–15GB should be sufficient to perform the full backup.

EXERCISE 8.2

Installing and Using Windows Server Backup

1. Start Server Manger by clicking the Server Manager shortcut button.

2. Select the features screen, and then click Add Feature.

3. Scroll to Windows Server Backup Features, select it, and click Next, as shown here.

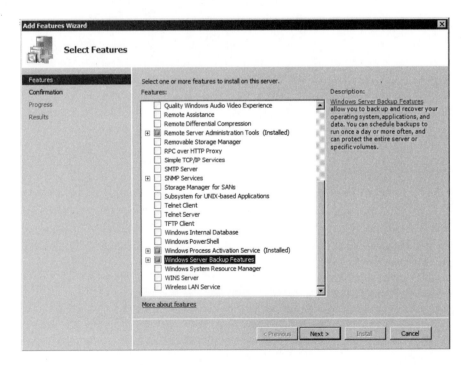

EXERCISE 8.2 *(continued)*

4. Click Install.

5. Close the install screen when complete.

6. Select Start ➢ Administrative Tools ➢ Windows Server Backup.

7. On the right portion of the screen, as shown here, click Backup Once.

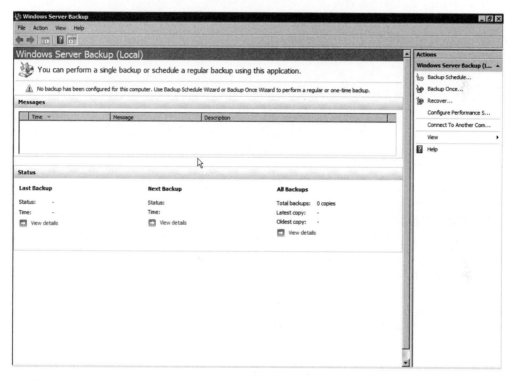

8. Since this is your first time backing up, the wizard will insist that you use different options than a previous instance because there are no previous instances. Just click Next.

9. On the next screen, click Full Server, as shown here, to back up your entire server, including your application data.

EXERCISE 8.2   *(continued)*

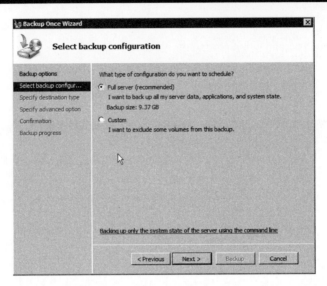

10. On the Specify Destination Type screen, you select another drive or shared folder to store the backup. For this exercise, I will assume you have access to this. However, it's impossible for me to know your exact environment, so you will have to extrapolate the exact procedures for this exercise based upon your individual environment.

11. Click either Local Drives or Remote Shared Folder (depending on your particular environment), as shown here, and then click Next. For the purposes of this exercise, I will use a remote shared folder.

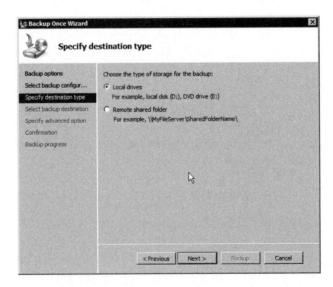

EXERCISE 8.2 *(continued)*

12. Enter either the local drive information or the proper remote information. If you want, you can permit only a specific user to access the backup. To do this, choose Do Not Inherit under Access Control. Otherwise, choose Inherit, as shown here.

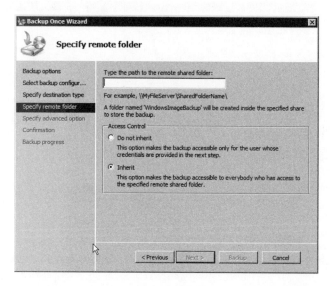

13. On the next screen, you can choose either VSS Copy Backup or VSS Full Backup. If you have another backup application, you can choose VSS Copy Backup. However, I will choose Full Backup for safety's sake in this exercise. Click VSS Full Backup and then Next, as shown here.

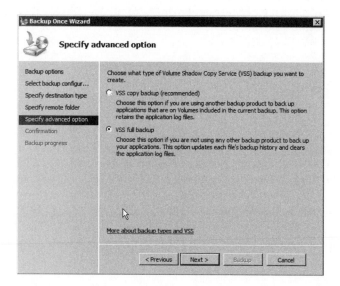

14. On the final screen, review your settings, and then click Backup. Note: This can take several hours, as the progress bar shown here indicates.

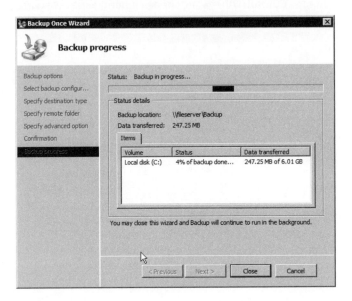

15. Once this process is complete, you will see a "Backup complete" message in the status bar area. Click Close.

At this point, you will see a message area indicating the last time a backup was completed on the server. Were you to desire to recover from that database, you could select that backup and then click the Recover option on the right.

Using Server Core

One of the most important points to make when discussing file security is that when there are fewer OS components, there is less attack surface to be compromised.

Accordingly, Microsoft security practices strongly recommend that whenever there is a great concern regarding the security of a server, Server Core should be implemented if the environment allows for this type of installation.

This is because Server Core is a light, easily managed installation that still supports security features such as BitLocker and EFS. In the real world, when you're considering an extremely secure installation, remember that Server Core may very well be the best option.

Introducing Active Directory Rights Management Services and File Protection

Active Directory Rights Management Services and File Protection (AD RMS) allows individual users to assign privileges to files. Once these permissions are assigned, they are correspondingly checked with an AD RMS server (powered through Microsoft SQL Server) to check the qualifications of users against an AD RMS client. This client is built into Windows Server 2008 and Windows Vista and is available for download with Windows XP.

With AD RMS, users can define three different components that comprise an AD RMS usage policy:

Trusted entities   These include trusted users who can access given files for an AD RMS group.

Usage rights   These include file permissions dictating how the files can be used and accessed.

Encryption   This determines whether a file is encrypted for nontrusted users.

Additionally, there are certain applications that natively support the use of AD RMS. These applications include the Microsoft Office suite (both 2003 and 2007), as well as SharePoint Portal Server 2007, Exchange 2007, and Internet Explorer 6 and newer. Thus, when you use these programs or other supported files with AD RMS, these files will be protected regardless of whether they leave the network.

Summary

With Windows Server 2008, there are a myriad of backup, recovery, and data security methods available at your administrative fingertips. In this chapter, I covered the appropriate utilities you can use at the appropriate time to create a secure and reliable backup in case of a failure.

The Windows Server Backup utility can create both full and partial backups simply and easily. It can take advantage of spare drives, file shares, and spare space in almost any location.

I also covered when to use load balancing and when to use clustering. More important, I covered the differences between each. Load balancing is primarily used to separate the processing and network demand on each server and place it upon one individual machine. Clustering is designed to provide backup of an individual service and to possibly increase the efficiency of your network.

I also covered the different types of RAID. You will possibly encounter them on your exam, but you will most certainly encounter them in the real world. Make sure you know the advantages of each type of RAID and when each should be used.

Exam Essentials

Understand RAID. By the time you take the certification exam, the different types of RAID should roll off your tongue just like your ABCs. RAID 0 is striping and the combination of disks into one large volume, RAID 1 is mirroring and creating an exact backup, and RAID 5 uses RAIDing to take advantage of a parity bit with some redundancy and some speed increases.

Understand failover, failback, and clustering. You need to understand the importance and purpose of clustering. Clustering is a very powerful and useful tool for use with failover, failback, and other forms of redundancy.

Understand network load balancing. Be familiar with the key uses of NLB, such as web farms, VPNs, and customer applications. Know that using NLB eliminates a central point of failure and is used to ensure the reliability of a complex network.

Be familiar with the Windows Backup Utility. The Windows Backup Utility can be used for very useful backups and recovery methods. It is also relatively easy to use, and backups can be stored to a file share, external drive, internal drive, or separate volume.

Understand Volume Shadow Copy. Know that Volume Shadow Copy can be used to restore previous versions of files and is one of the most powerful and commonly used tools in an administrator's repertoire. Understand that by using this tool you can both open and copy previous versions of files to anywhere in your network infrastructure with the appropriately set permissions.

Review Questions

1. In a mission-critical environment, some applications require forms of redundancy that include completely separate volumes of backup that mirror the current application's central drive. Of the following RAID types, which one most fully supports drive mirroring?

   A. RAID 0

   B. RAID 1

   C. RAID 5

   D. RAID 10

2. When initially designing an Active Directory infrastructure, one of the design elements that is strongly recommended is to make Active Directory as redundant as possible. Specifically, this recommendation strongly emphasizes placing which two components of the Windows Server 2008 infrastructure on separate volumes?

   A. The SYSVOL directory

   B. boot.ini

   C. Ntdis.dit

   D. Ntloader

   E. Repadmin.sys

3. With DFS, referrals can be organized in three ways. Of the following options, which two of the following options are available methods to administrators?

   A. By lowest cost

   B. By random order

   C. By highest cost

   D. By linear order

   E. Targets within site

   F. Targets out of site

4. Encrypted File System is a file-level system of encryption that is designed to secure data from a malicious outside source. Of the following options, which could possibly result in the EFS system being compromised and no longer encrypted?

   A. Migrating Windows Server 2003 files to a Windows Server 2008–based platform

   B. Reverse migrating from Windows Server 2008 to Windows Server 2003 or Windows 2000 Server

   C. Implementing AD RMS using DFS

   D. Transferring the Windows Server 2008 application data drive to a Windows XP FAT32 volume

5. Within OmniCorp, there has recently arisen a need to have a series of servers running to keep a custom application up and running at all times. Accordingly, OmniCorp has decided to implement a failover cluster to provide redundancy in case of a failure of a single server. If the cluster contains three nodes and it needs to remain running in case of the loss of a single node, regardless of that node's position in the cluster, what quorum configuration mode should be chosen?

   A. Node majority

   B. Node and disk majority

   C. Node and file share majority

   D. Disk only

6. Within OmniCorp, there has recently arisen a need to have a series of servers running to keep a custom application up and running at all times. Accordingly, OmniCorp has decided to implement a failover cluster to provide redundancy in the case of the failure of a single server. If the cluster contains three nodes and a file share located on a storage array set inside one of the member servers, what quorum configuration mode should be set to ensure that the server is shut down in the case of a file share loss?

   A. Node majority

   B. Node and disk majority

   C. Node and file share majority

   D. Disk only

7. To use DFS in the enterprise, a certain protocol has to be available to Windows Server in order to make this process occur. Which of the following is that protocol?

   A. RPC

   B. RDC

   C. FTP

   D. RPC over HTTP

   E. LDP

8. In a Windows Server DFS architecture, Server 1 and Server 2 are connected to Server 3. At 9 a.m., the connection between Server 1 and Server 2 suffers a failure, and Server 1 resorts to recovery via failover to Server 3. The site-link cost between Server 1 and Server 3 is 300. At noon, Server 2 is restored and the site-link cost between Server 1 and Server 2 is 200. Given this information, what should occur?

   A. Server 1 will fail over to Server 2 because the site-link cost is less.

   B. Server 1 will not fail over to Server 2 because the site-link cost is less.

   C. Server 1 will fail back to Server 2.

   D. There will be no change in the operating system environment.

9. Of the following backup types, which supports restoration of a previous version of a file?

   A. DFS

   B. Wbadmin

   C. Windows Server Backup

   D. Volume Shadow Copy

   E. NLB

10. At SuperCorp, an unfortunate disaster has occurred in that an organizational unit has been deleted within Active Directory. Since the deletion, the change has been replicated throughout the network infrastructure and additional changes have been made. Overall, the entirety of the SuperCorp infrastructure has been compromised, and the executive staff wants to restore the data from a backup using a backup domain controller stored in case of emergencies. Knowing this, how should you proceed?

   A. Perform a nonauthoritative restore to restore the OU, and replicate this change to the rest of the servers in the infrastructure.

   B. Perform an authoritative restore to have all incorrect changes made since the incident removed.

   C. Use Windows Server Backup to restore the state of the root domain controller since the last partial or full backup.

   D. Use Windows Server Backup and a nonauthoritative restore to restore the OU.

11. Of the following backup methods, which must be installed? Choose two.

   A. Volume Shadow Copy

   B. RAID

   C. DFS

   D. Windows Server Backup

   E. Active Directory Restore

12. OmniCorp, a multibillion-dollar textiles conglomerate, has recently experienced a problem with VPN authentication across its server. Apparently, clients are experiencing difficulties logging in as they receive timeouts when trying to connect. What should you do?

   A. Implement a failover cluster for the clients, and ensure that the quorum is set to node majority so the cluster will maintain availability.

   B. Implement network load balancing with at least two nodes.

   C. Install Terminal Services Gateway, and implement Terminal Services Balancing.

   D. Implement a failback procedure for a site with a lesser site-link cost. Connect to this via Terminal Services.

13. A supervisor has informed your department that it has become necessary to implement a high-performance server within your infrastructure that will be added as part of the load-balanced cluster that is responsible for serving your company's intranet web portal that serves important functions, such as providing written materials for your department. When setting up this server, what should you do?

A. Implement a member server using RAID 0, and add this server to the quorum.

B. Implement a member server using RAID 1, and do not add this server to the quorum.

C. Implement the server as a domain controller apart from the cluster, and employ network load balancing.

D. Implement the server using default status, and join this server to the cluster.

14. In exceptionally secure environments, what action can be taken to ensure that Windows Server 2008 drives cannot be accessed by individuals across the network?

A. Implement DFS.

B. Implement BitLocker.

C. Disable EFS.

D. Disable Admin Shares.

E. Implement a RAID configuration.

15. At SuperCorp, there has been a tremendous problem with previously terminated employees retaliating against the company by attempting to steal hardware. To protect against this, what should you as the administrator do to make your computers the *most* secure against this action?

A. Implement DFS.

B. Implement BitLocker.

C. Implement EFS.

D. Implement backups.

16. When attempting to view a Microsoft Word document, a consultant outside your company reports that he is unable to view the document in Word 2007. The consultant must be able to read the document, and you have to find a solution that most effectively deals with the issue. What should you do?

A. Ensure the consultant has disabled any virus software that may be interfering with file permission.

B. Instruct the user to open the document's properties, and select the Read permission.

C. Using AD RMS, instruct the consultant to add himself to the Allowed permission.

D. Add the consultant as a trusted user with AD RMS.

17. The new deployment for the MyCorp server includes a server that will be exposed to a high-risk, high-volatility environment that could include the possibility of physical vulnerability. Furthermore, in this area there will be a strong chance of electronic attack because the server will need to be connected to the open Internet. Knowing this, what should you do?

A. Implement a Read Only Domain Controller (RODC) role using BitLocker drive encryption.

B. Enable BitLocker with your drive.

C. Install Windows Server 2008 Server Core (if available), and then enable BitLocker.

D. Install Windows Server 2008 Server Core, and then promote the member server to an RODC role.

18. Within SuperCorp, executives have decided to launch a new website that will detail the SuperCorp product line. Because of the number and demand for SuperCorp's products, the website will most likely consume a great deal of bandwidth because it receives numerous hits per day. Accordingly, you've been asked to design a server structure that will support this number of computers. Of the following options, which should you choose?

A. Implement a node majority quorum–based cluster.

B. Create a network load-balanced farm that is designed to pass load to different servers.

C. Install backup servers to stand by in case of one point of failure.

D. Install a Terminal Services Gateway server to alleviate load on the web farm.

19. Using Windows recovery, Windows is capable of achieving all but which of the following tasks?

A. Promoting a domain controller

B. Moving files

C. Backing up using Wbadmin

D. Altering a directory

20. To stop sharing administrative shares with Windows Server 2008, what process must you complete in order to halt this process?

A. Remove the feature from Server Manager.

B. Remove the role from Server Manager.

C. Net stop and start the service.

D. Alter the registry.

Answers to Review Questions

1. B. RAID 1 is the form of RAID that is naturally a mirror state. RAID 5 supports redundancy through the use of a parity bit, and RAID 10 uses mirrors as well but also requires a stripe, which was not stated in the question as a requirement.

2. A, C. Best practices for maintaining a redundant Active Directory structure include placing the SYSVOL and Ntdis.dit files on a separate volume. Additionally, best practices also recommend separating these files from your core operating system files for the maximum amount of redundancy in case of a failure.

3. A, B. Using DFS referral ordering, three options are available: lowest cost, random order, and exclude targets outside of the client's site. Arranging by highest cost and linear order are not options because they wouldn't logically be useful. Also, DFS is set to "exclude" targets outside the client's site, not arrange targets within or outside of the site.

4. D. EFS requires the support of the NTFS file system. Without NTFS, EFS can no longer encrypt information, and it will therefore be stored as simple data files. When moving data between versions of Windows or different volumes, it is important to try to avoid this possibility.

5. A. If there are three member servers and node majority mode is chosen, this means that regardless of whether a single server fails, the cluster will continue to operate. To continue functioning in node majority mode, at least a majority of the clusters (more than 50 percent) must be in operation. In this case, the failure of one cluster would result in 66 percent of the clusters still being in operation.

6. C. Using node and file share majority mode, the file share counts as one node of the server. Therefore, if there are three member servers and one of these servers contains the file share, if the server containing the file share goes down, the count will be two to two, because the server containing the share receives an extra vote in the quorum. Because this is a tie, a majority is not present, and the failover cluster will shut down immediately.

7. B. The Microsoft Distributed File System takes advantage of multiple computers in a Windows infrastructure by using Remote Differential Compressions (RDC). Using this protocol, Windows is able to place multiple files across multiple nodes in a network infrastructure and have them appear to be in one contiguous location.

8. C. Failback is the process that occurs whenever a failover occurs and then the system ultimately recovers itself by repairing its original link. This occurs only if the site link between the original two servers is less than the currently established link. Otherwise, no changes will occur.

9. D. Volume Shadow Copy is a Windows technology that takes advantage of a shadow copy of a Windows volume to store previous versions of files in the Windows Server file structure. Using Volume Shadow Copy, you can click the Previous Versions tab and restore files from a certain date.

10. B. In the case of loss that has been replicated throughout the infrastructure, you should use an authoritative restore to override any changes made throughout the organization. This way, the changes made to Active Directory since the loss will be overridden by the authoritative backup.

11. C, D. Both the Windows Server Backup utility and the Distributed File System must be manually installed. Volume Shadow Copy, RAID, and Active Directory restoration all require a setup process but do not have to be installed per se.

12. B. Network load balancing is used for situations such as VPN, web farms, and other applications that may require the load to be spread amongst several servers. Using NLB, clients can be authenticated amongst several servers and alleviate the burden from one central location.

13. A. When adding a performance server to a cluster, especially one that is load balanced, it becomes imperative to use as many features available as possible, including RAID 0. Additionally, the server should be joined as quickly as possible to the quorum to act as a voting member of the cluster—this should be done be default.

14. D. By default, Windows Server 2008 allows drives to be accessed across the network through network administrative shares. These shares are identified by the $ sign and should be canceled in exceptionally secure environments.

15. B. BitLocker drive encryption provides a complete, low-level encryption of all files within the Windows Server 2008 file system. Using BitLocker, drives cannot be compromised, even if stolen.

16. D. Using AD RMS, to read files that have been encrypted, you must be a member of the trusted users group. To become a member of the trusted users group, you must be specifically added by either a user or an administrator as authorized to view the file's contents.

17. C. Using Windows Server 2008 Server Core, you ensure that as few files are exposed as possible. Furthermore, by enabling BitLocker, you ensure that the drive is protected as possible. Promoting this server to an RODC role is not required, because the problem does not state if the machine needs to be promoted to a domain controller.

18. B. Network load balancing is highly useful for applications such as web servers. Using network load balancing, data is transferred from one server to the next based on the load present on that server at particular time. This way, there is no central point of failure and more servers are available in the case of high server load, which is expected in the given problem.

19. A. Promoting a domain controller requires the Windows Start button and the Dcpromo command. In WinRE mode, this is not available.

20. D. To modify the administrative share options, you must alter the system registry by navigating to the following registry key: HKEY_LOCAL_MACHINE\SYSTEM\CurrentControlSet\ Services\LanmanServer\Parameters\AutoShareServer. Afterward, you must change the value to zero.

Chapter

9

Designing a Windows Update Strategy for the Enterprise

OBJECTIVES COVERED IN THIS CHAPTER:

✓ **Design for software updates and compliance management.**

- May include but is not limited to: patch management and patch management compliance, Microsoft Update and Windows Update, security baselines, system health models

Sometimes the majority of an administrator's day is spent looking for updates. And with the number of software programs available for use in the business sector always increasing, the need for more and more updates keeps expanding. This is further complicated by the fact that when you're going through the process of updating an entire enterprise, you have to keep track of all the following pieces of software: operating systems, applications, drivers, and firmware.

With Windows Server 2008, the process of updating has become much less complicated than it has been in the past. In this chapter, I'll discuss security practices and system health models so you can determine whether an update is needed and when it should be applied, if at all. Then I'll cover the methodology of using Windows Update, as well as best practices for using the service. By the end of this chapter, you should be familiar with all update services and Microsoft best practices.

Establishing a Security Baseline

Effectively, a security baseline is the process of formally gathering certain pieces of data and applying them throughout the enterprise in such a way that all present, past, and future server deployments use this foundation as a guideline for the rest of their lifetime. Establishing a security baseline is a multistep process that involves four major components:

- Active Directory design
- Security policies
- Server scope definition
- GPO design

I've already discussed some of these topics, such as Active Directory design, GPO design, and security policies, in detail.

For administrators creating their first deployment of Windows Server 2008, establishing a security baseline has become much easier. Previously, other versions of Windows Server required much more extensive manipulations of administrative templates and .inf files in order to create a secure environment. Now, most of this process is completely handled by Group Policy. However, server security and server scope definition are now defined as two distinct portions: enterprise client environments and specialized security environments.

Enterprise Client Environments

An *enterprise client environment* is any server environment that involves the use of multiple active users and the extensive use of Active Directory to monitor and administrate those users. Specifically, the Microsoft Windows Server security documentation further defines Windows Server 2008 deployments with heavy enterprise client environments as environments that run Windows Server 2008 or Windows Server 2003 Service Pack 2, Windows XP with Service Pack 3, and Windows Vista. They further require an enterprise client environment to exclusively use Group Policy to administer applications on all sites, domains, and organizational units.

Specialized Client Environments

A *specialized client environment*—also known as a limited-functionality environment or specialized client environment, limited functionality (SSLF)—is the portion of an infrastructure that is set aside for the specific purpose of performing a given task. Examples of limited functionality might be a file share server or a server that consistently evaluates common tasks, such as authentication.

In specialized environments, security is generally more refined than in enterprise client environments. This is because specialized environments serve fewer purposes and therefore have fewer open points of possible intrusion and less functionality. According to the Microsoft Solution Accelerator for Windows Server 2008 security (available via Microsoft TechNet), the limited functionality portion of a server dedicated to a specific task can be refined into three portions:

- Restricted service and data access

- Restricted network access

- Strong network protection

Through these three security areas, specialized servers become more secure because users are allowed to access fewer portions of the available data and fewer network resources. For your purposes as an enterprise administrator (and for the Enterprise Administrator certification exam), you'll generally need two security baselines—one for the entire enterprise and one for servers that serve specialized functions.

The exact process of defining a security baseline is rather complex and is usually evaluated by an entire staff. Thus, the topic is beyond the scope of this book. However, for your future administrative career, it's a good idea to start looking into general security management practices. You can find these in other certifications, such as the CISSP by ISC[2] and the CISM by ISACA. Either one should serve you well in your chosen field.

The Microsoft Baseline Security Analyzer Tool

The Microsoft Baseline Security Analyzer 2.1 tool is the latest in a series of incredibly powerful tools available to administrators. Using the Microsoft Baseline Security Analyzer (MBSA), you can get an idea of the overall health of your system, including needed security patches, possible security holes, recommended procedures, and a list of other important details.

The MBSA is not installed by default, so you must download it from Microsoft. Doing so requires you to validate your Windows installation as genuine, and then you can access and install it. Once it is installed, it is extremely easy to use. Through a simple menu system, you can select to evaluate Windows-based computers in a given domain or even a given range of IP addresses manually assigned by the user. Once installed, the MBSA will check the status of each provided computer and then provide a report of the status of these computers according to a list of predefined standards provided by Microsoft. The report usually looks like Figure 9.1, but it will vary based on how many computers are in your environment and how extensive the report is.

FIGURE 9.1   Microsoft Baseline Security Analyzer report

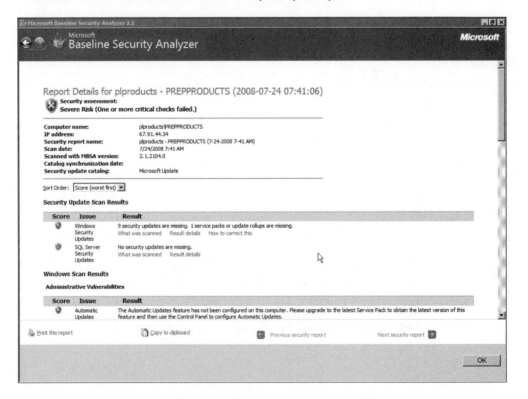

System and Environment Health Models

The term *system health model* refers to the process of ordering and tracking the overall system state of individual servers throughout the environment as time progresses. Within the enterprise, this process is particularly crucial because it gives you an indication of how much productivity is being lost because of equipment failures and a lack of application availability.

In some corporations, the loss of a single server can bring the entire company to its knees in terms of production, especially if there is no backup. However, usually in a large enterprise the loss of one machine just means that the state of the overall environment is "other than 100 percent." In other words, the environment is still functioning but not as well as it theoretically could be functioning.

Windows Server health, and server health in general, usually falls into several categories, each of which can be monitored and evaluated on an individual level. These categories include the following:

- Server availability
- Server uptime
- Server downtime
- CPU usage
- Memory usage
- Page file usage
- Disk utilization
- Network utilization
- Service availability
- Service downtime
- Application availability
- Application downtime
- Backup availability
- Backup downtime

Most of these are discussed throughout the process of becoming a Microsoft Certified Windows Server Professional. At the enterprise administrator level, you're interested primarily in the top four categories: server availability, uptime, downtime, and hardware statistics.

Server Availability

Server availability refers to the period of time in which a server is up, running, and not inaccessible. This can be achieved only when a server is operating at its full capacity. For example, a server cannot be considered "available" if the server is running but the network cable has somehow become unplugged and is now inaccessible to the rest of the network infrastructure. Thus, in order for this state to be achieved, the server has to be set up properly and functioning.

As shown in Figure 9.2, most administrators keep a chart of the times and availability of their server on a day-to-day basis, using a score of 0 percent to 100 percent. In most companies, this is usually available to all IT staff in a centralized intranet or Internet location so that it can be accessed for future study.

FIGURE 9.2   Server availability chart

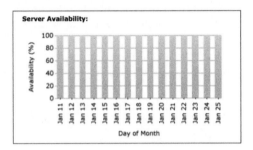

The importance of this chart and this area of study is that it determines the overall state of the enterprise. The closer it is to 100 percent, the better off the entire organization is. With anything less than 100 percent, the company is not functioning as well as it could be.

Server Uptime

Server uptime refers to the period of time that the server has been running with power in which it has not experienced a software- or hardware-based failure resulting in the loss of the critical components of an operating system. Generally, the causes of a loss of server uptime include the following:

- Power failures
- Power surges
- Operating system failures (blue screens)
- Human error (such as an accidental disconnect)

Usually, server uptime is used in conjunction with server availability to determine whether software on the operating system is causing failures. Additionally, this indicates the status of power availability and reliability throughout the infrastructure. Normally, administrators who need a justification for expensive hardware, such as battery backups, will use this statistic along with server availability to illustrate that most productivity loss comes from a lack of available power in the case of a failure.

Server Downtime

The opposite of server uptime is *server downtime*, which refers to the period of time in which the operating system is not up, running, receiving power, or functioning as it should be functioning. Ideally, the amount of server downtime is zero. Whenever this statistic is present, it means the network is not functioning as well as it could be.

Service Availability

When working with Windows Server, an important component to the overall environment health is *service availability*. When using Active Directory, a simple network service such as NetLogon can result in the entire Active Directory infrastructure becoming useless if it is an overall environment outage. With this statistic, you can pay careful attention to the availability of services overall.

If these services are automatic, you can check them against a chart that compares whether the automatic services are being enabled as they should be (based on need). If these services are manual, you can even do a human task-oriented analysis to see whether these services are enabled as they should be based on job roles and duties.

Overall, service availability plays a large role in overall server availability, because it is one of the deciding factors in determining how a computer is functioning. A server can be up, running, and operating but not have a service started and therefore not be fulfilling its given purpose, especially in a specialized client environment.

Hardware Statistics

The next general category of system health that's important is divided amongst the many different components of general server health. This includes functions such as memory usage, disk access, and the use of overall hardware. At the enterprise level, you're won't be quite as concerned with this as an operator of an individual server. You're much more concerned with the overall health of the entire infrastructure. However, it's important to note this general category.

Planning and Implementing Windows Software Update Services (WSUS)

Earlier in this chapter, I mentioned that administrators often have to deploy updates throughout the entire enterprise. This could include updates to the following:

Operating systems If you're working in a complex environment, this probably includes several different versions of Windows (possibly going back as far as Windows NT), as well as the probable presence of Linux or Unix, including Mac OS X.

Applications When I say applications, you have to consider standardized Microsoft applications, as well as third-party applications and custom applications. In total, they represent three different stages of updates that have to be conducted, because not all applications are well known enough or complex enough to support automatic updating processes.

Drivers Factoring drivers into the equation provides a conundrum for many enterprises. More often than not, the rule for drivers is "if it ain't broke, don't fix it." But the problem with that philosophy is that many vendors will say that certain driver updates are critical to the functionality of their hardware. This results in vendors and support contracts recommending or demanding updates and company policies refusing to accommodate them. Ultimately, something has to give, but which one depends on the circumstance and pure chance.

Firmware Firmware plays a major role in the enterprise. Sometimes, pieces of hardware will experience functionality problems that will have to be fixed by firmware updates. And firmware updates usually involve the certainty of one problem, downtime, and the possibility of another, critical failure. So, these present yet another problem that you have to deal with.

Accordingly, deploying updates (if done manually) can require hundreds, if not thousands, of hours of labor because each update is applied to a computer and subjected to numerous tweaks and updates. To avoid this, Windows administrators can use the Windows Software Update Services (WSUS) technology.

With WSUS, you can automate the process of deploying updates by setting up a server as a dedicated update server (the WSUS server). This server then sends updates to various computers throughout the enterprise automatically, or as determined by the user, which alleviates the need to go install each of these updates one at a time, computer by computer. Additionally, WSUS can roll back updates and install or uninstall drivers based on the administrator's decision. If you use a proper deployment, Windows software updates can become a very relaxed process.

The process can be deployed either remotely or locally —this is the administrator's decision. In either case, Windows requires the answers to two questions to deploy an update:

- Where is this update located?
- Where should this update be placed?

The first question is asked by the update server so it knows where the data it should distribute is located. Knowing this, it can make sure the right type of update is applied to computers, which factors into the second question, "Where should this update be placed?" WSUS has two separate group roles that aid in the process of answering this question:

WSUS Administrators This is a local group on the WSUS server that is responsible for preparing update policies and administering the WSUS console.

WSUS Reporters This is another local group that can run reports on updates to determine their impact on the environment.

WSUS Server Deployment

Usually whenever a WSUS deployment is created, as few servers as possible are used. There are several reasons for this, but this is mainly because WSUS is incredibly powerful and capable of supporting tens of thousands of computers at the same time, making just one server capable of supporting all but the largest of large networks. Therefore, it's not practical to have numerous update servers spread throughout the network.

This can change, however, depending on the complexity of the network. Specifically, the physical number of servers can change depending upon how many subnetworks or different sites are present throughout the enterprise. The more subnetworks, the more transitions at the packet level have to be completed through routers in order to deploy these updates. Consequently, best practices strongly recommend having a WSUS server run on your local area network. And, since it's impractical and ultimately practically impossible to have that many users on one local area network, more WSUS servers have to be implemented.

Anatomy of WSUS

The current version of WSUS as of the printing of this book is Windows Software Updates Services version 3.0 Service Pack 1. It is not available by default with Windows Server 2008, but it can be downloaded freely at Microsoft.com in either X86 or X64 version, based on the configuration of your Windows Server 2008 machine. Each version can deploy updates to any version of Windows on your network once it has been set up.

Regardless of the version, WSUS uses two different streams, called the *upstream* and the *downstream*.

Upstream

An *upstream* in WSUS is any server that functions as a central authority that is responsible for the constant broadcast and upload of Windows Update. Generally, the upstream used as the original point of authority is the actual Windows Update web server maintained by Microsoft. However, in certain deployments, WSUS servers can be configured as Windows Update upstream configuration computers in order to more thoroughly control the reception of updates throughout your enterprise.

Downstream

The next layer of server down from an upstream server is (as the name slightly implies) a downstream server. Downstream servers are servers along the WSUS path. They receive their updates from an upstream server and are then responsible for cycling and distributing the updates to the rest of the environment. Using downstream servers, WSUS adds an extra layer of complexity as these servers forward the information they are given. However, WSUS also adds a level of security if configured properly. Here's how the path works in a downstream server–based environment:

1. The originating server sends a request for an update.
2. An upstream server sends the updates.

3. A downstream server sends the update to the destination machine.

4. The destination machine applies the update.

WSUS Update Hierarchy and Administration Decisions

I have covered two WSUS components and types of servers so far: upstream servers and downstream servers. With these types of servers, you have to keep in mind a couple of considerations. The first is to identify the upstream server, in other words, the point of origin. Is it Microsoft Update? Or is it your own custom server? The answer determines how the rest of your infrastructure will be laid out. As I've said before, usually this is Microsoft Update.

The next portion is the harder part of this decision: the downstream server. Downstream servers can be deployed in two modes: replica mode and autonomous mode.

Replica Mode

With replica mode, downstream servers take the information they receive from an upstream server and replicate it through the rest of the environment. This means they receive updates and then send those updates through the entire enterprise. One of the upsides of this configuration mode is that it's simple to configure. One of the downsides is that it is very bandwidth intensive and requires a lot of dedicated time that may not be available at the moment that updates are required.

Autonomous Mode

Using autonomous mode, downstream servers function as individual entities that can be configured by lower-level update administrators. Using powers granted to them by local administrators, lower-level administrators can choose which updates are and are not applied to their network. This is highly advantageous because sometimes parts of a network are running critical pieces of software that cannot risk the volatility of an update or are running a component that is not compatible with the rest of the network.

In Exercise 9.1, you'll learn how to install and set up WSUS.

EXERCISE 9.1

Installing and Setting Up WSUS

Note that before installing WSUS, you must have IIS 7 installed and that you must have Microsoft Report Viewer installed. You can obtain each of these files through www.microsoft.com.

1. Download the WSUS install file from Microsoft at http://technet.microsoft.com/en-us/wsus/default.aspx. The file is named WSUSSetup_30SP1_x86.exe (or WSUSSetup_30SP1_x64.exe for the 64-bit version).

2. Double-click the install file.

3.   Choose Full Server Installation because a console installation will not allow for the GUI you need in this exercise. Click Next.

4.   Agree to the terms of service, and then click Next.

5.   On the Windows Server Update Services 3.0 SP1 Setup Wizard's Select Update Source screen, make sure the Store Updates Locally option is selected and that C:\WSUS is the default folder, as shown here. This makes sure that all updates are stored in this location when they are downloaded. Click Next.

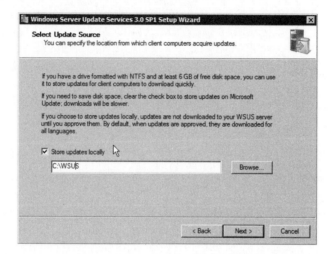

6.   On the next screen, Database Options, leave the default settings as shown here, and then click Next. Alternatively, you could use an existing database for this, but you will create a new one within the WSUS folder in this exercise. Click Next.

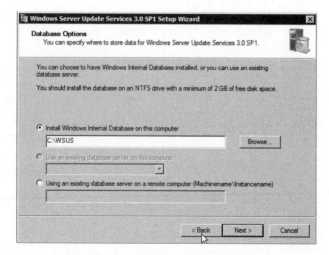

EXERCISE 9.1 *(continued)*

7. On the Web Site Selection screen, choose the Create a Windows Server Update Services 3.1 SP1 Web Site option. This creates a custom web site for you to be able to view Windows updates. Click Next.

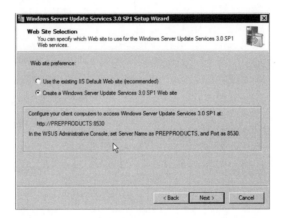

8. Click Next on the Summary screen. Afterward, WSUS will begin to install; this may take a while.

9. Click Finish.

10. Once complete, this will launch the Windows Server Update Services Configuration Wizard shown here. Upon the first step, it will ask you a couple of configuration questions about your network. Make sure these concerns are alleviated, and click Next when complete.

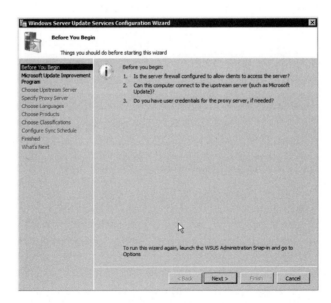

11. Click Next upon the improvement program, unless you do not want your data shared. In that case, unselect the box, and click Next.

12. On the Choose Upstream Server screen, you can choose where this server receives updates from. Since this is the only WSUS server in this exercise, choose Synchronize from Microsoft Update. Alternatively, if you have a more complex environment, you could specify the WSUS server to receive data from another WSUS server and then specify the server name and port number of that server. For now, click Next.

13. Click Next on the Specify Proxy Server screen because you do not require a proxy server.

14. On the Connect to Upstream Server screen, the Windows Server Update Services Configuration Wizard will tell you that it needs to connect to Microsoft Update to collect information. You will need to click the Start Connecting button, as shown here. This will take a few moments as the server connects to Microsoft Update. Afterward, click Next.

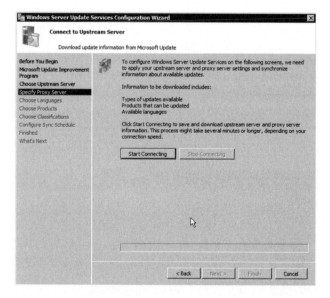

15. You can then choose any specific languages you would like to receive and even configure your updates to choose all languages available. For this exercise, choose English, and then click Next.

16. The next screen, Choose Products, is where you want to pay some careful attention. Here, you can choose any Microsoft product you want to update. As you can see, you have many choices. For this simple example, leave the default Microsoft Office and Windows selected. In a real environment, you may need to choose many more selections. For now, click Next.

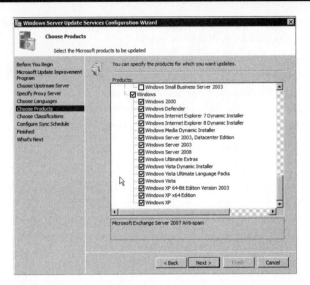

17. Next, you can choose the classification of updates. This includes special tools, updates, drivers, critical updates, and so forth. You can choose which you would like to receive, but the default selection is quite intuitive. This is because it contains the most critical information necessary to keep your environment running. Make your selection, and then click Next.

18. On the next screen, choose Synchronize Automatically, and leave it at the default time. This makes the WSUS server check Microsoft Update once per day to see whether there are any new updates. Click Next.

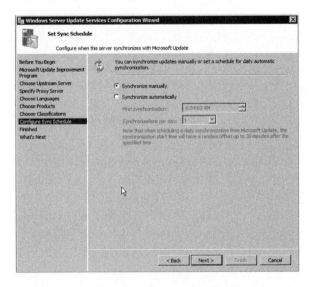

19. Click Next on the Finished screen, and then click Finish again. This launches the WSUS home screen and will signify that you have completed your installation.

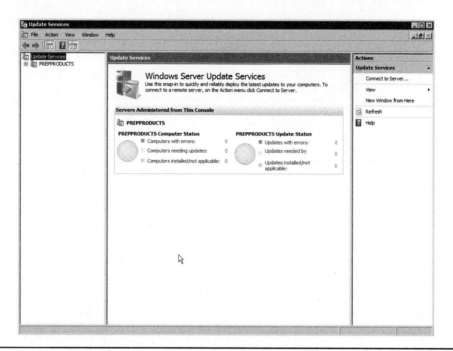

Now that you have WSUS installed, in Exercise 9.2 you'll learn how to set up WSUS.

Setting Up WSUS

To complete this exercise, you must have completed Exercise 9.1.

1. Open WSUS by selecting Administrative Tools ➤ Microsoft Windows Server Update Services 3.0 SP1. You may see a message informing you that the snap-in is being installed.

2. Based upon the number of products and classification of updates you selected, selecting your WSUS server will produce a list of several updates, as shown here.

EXERCISE 9.2 *(continued)*

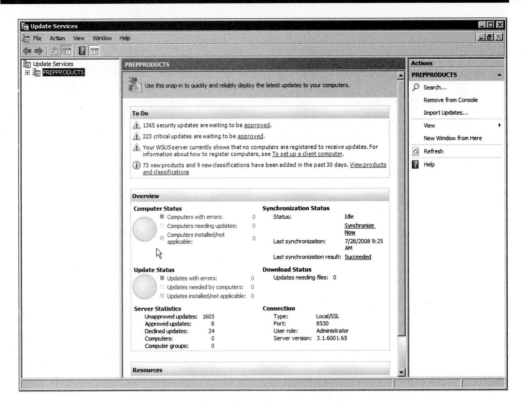

3. Now, before you can get started using Windows Software Updates Services, you have to begin by creating a GPO for your domain that lets you use WSUS. This is because WSUS is administrated through Group Policy.

4. Open the GPMC by selecting Administrative Tools ➢ Group Policy Management.

5. Expand your domain, and then select the Group Policy Objects container.

6. Right-click in the GPO area on the right side of the screen, and select New. In the dialog box, name the policy **WSUS Policy**.

7. Once the policy is created, open the Group Policy Management Editor by right-clicking the WSUS policy and selecting Edit.

8. Expand the Policies section of the Computer Configuration area, right-click Administrative Templates, and select Add/Remove Templates.

EXERCISE 9.2   *(continued)*

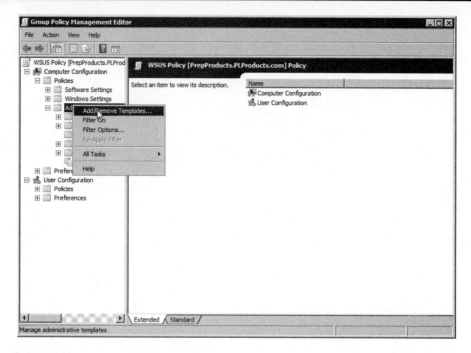

9. Select Add.

10. In the Filename box, type **wuau**, and then click Open. This opens the default administrative template that is used for administering WSUS.

11. Close the dialog box.

12. Under the Computer Configuration, select Administrative Templates ➢ Windows Components ➢ Windows Update.

13. On the right side, double-click Configure Automatic Updates.

14. Select the radio button Enabled, and then change the first drop-down list to 3-Auto Download and Notify for Install. Leave the other options default.

15. Click the Next Setting button.

16. Select the radio button Enabled, and then set the two boxes to **http://<your server name>**. Click the Next Setting button.

EXERCISE 9.2 *(continued)*

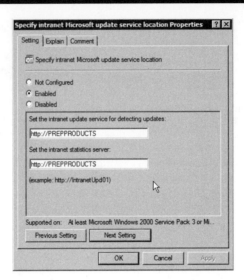

17. Select the Enabled button again, and then change the syncing period to a period of your choosing; 22 to 24 hours is appropriate.

18. Click OK.

19. Close the editor, right-click your domain in the GPMC, and select Link an Existing GPO.

20. Select WSUS Policy, and then click OK.

21. Now, return to the Windows Update Service home screen. If you click Computers on the left, at least the main computer and most likely several other computers will show up when you click the Search button in the upper-right corner. If they do not, you can issue the following command on your domain controller in the console:

    gpupdate /force

    Also, on any client computers connected to your domain controller, you can tell them to automatically look for a new update server by issuing the wuauclt.exe /detect-now **command.**

At this point, Group Policy should now be set up on WSUS, and you should be able to view computers on your WSUS home screen. If not (or if you experience trouble along the way), you can reference the Microsoft "Step-by-Step Guide" to WSUS, located on Microsoft.com.

WSUS Grouping

When the WSUS Management User Services screen is launched, by default it loads a home screen that includes several notifications and a single group on the left. This group is referred to as the Unassigned Computers group. When rolling out updates, WSUS supports the ability to group computers based on the need to update individual platforms.

As you saw earlier, WSUS supports all Microsoft business products. Thus, certain groups may require different deployments of updates, based on the type of products installed. This type of deployment is called *client-side* deployment and is used as an alternative to Group Policy–specific deployment for individual groups.

To create a new user group using WSUS grouping, you can start WSUS, select the Computers area after expanding the server name, expand the All Computers area, and click Add Computer Group on the right, as shown in Figure 9.3.

FIGURE 9.3   Adding a computer group

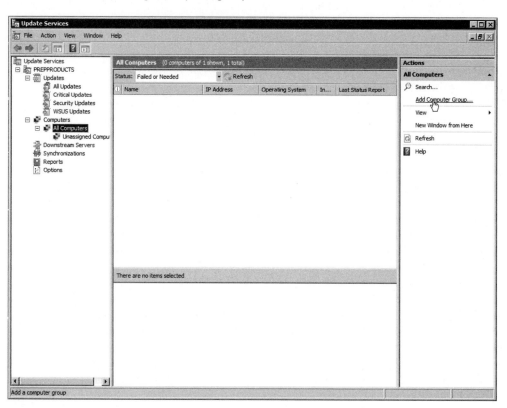

WSUS Options

Using WSUS, administrators can set a variety of options:

Update Source and Proxy Server You can redirect a WSUS server to another area of the network or to Microsoft Update.

Products and Classification You can specify new products to update or remove old products.

Update Files and Languages You can choose your languages and file locations.

Synchronize schedule You can set up your schedule for manual or automatic synchronization.

Automatic Approvals You can specify the automatic approval for updates you know will need to be deployed without user approval.

Computers You can assign computers to groups.

Server Cleanup Wizard You can clean up old updates and update files on other servers.

Reporting Rollup You can have replica downstream servers roll up updates and computer status.

Email Notifications You can set up your WSUS server to send emails and status reports.

Microsoft Update Improvement Program You can elect to join the update improvement program.

Personalization You can customize the appearance of your program.

WSUS Server Configuration Wizard You can relaunch the original configuration wizard to configure your server again.

WSUS Reports

One benefit of automating the installation of updates is that you don't have to oversee every step of the installation. However, one of the many responsibilities of a worthy administrator is to keep up with the changes in their environment. Accordingly, part of the robust nature of WSUS includes the ability to produce reports that allow you to monitor the changes made to your network infrastructure while using WSUS.

On the WSUS home screen, the Reports area is located underneath your server name, as shown in Figure 9. 4. Within this report area, there are three sections:

- Update Reports
- Computer Reports
- Synchronization Reports

FIGURE 9.4   WSUS Reports area

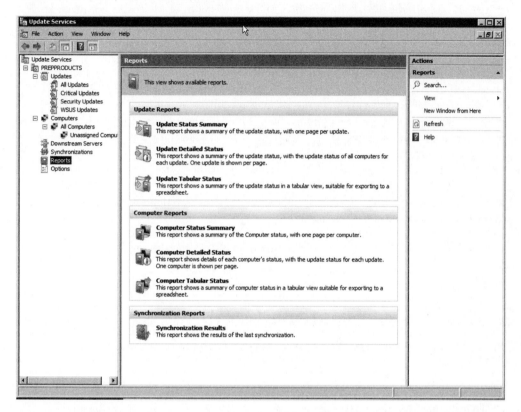

By clicking any of these report areas within the three main sections, you can open a submenu that will allow you to generate more refined reports. Additionally, using optional features of WSUS, you can set up WSUS to automatically install updates and then email you reports of the procedures it has done. This way, you can backtrack updates if they have caused a problem that requires you to remove any changes to your infrastructure.

Overview of System Center Essentials 2007

As I pointed out earlier when discussing Windows Server 2008 WSUS, WSUS is a freely available add-on from Microsoft that is designed to support the update and deployment of

Microsoft business products throughout the enterprise. The only real limitation to WSUS is that it relies on both the use of Group Policy and the existence of Microsoft products. For most businesses, this is enough functionality to prove that it is an exceptionally useful tool. However, for some higher-end enterprises, a more robust update solution is required. Enter System Center Essentials 2007 (SCE 2007).

SCE 2007 is an update solution available from Microsoft that is designed to support updates to third-party pieces of software not available from Microsoft. Unlike WSUS, SCE 2007 is not free; however, an evaluation version is available. Currently, SCE 2007 is not as popular as WSUS. This is because although SCE is a very robust piece of software, it doesn't support every application in existence. Although there's a limit to its capability, it's worth noting that this limit is extremely generous.

Another limitation is that SCE 2007 is designed for medium-sized enterprises—those that do not have more than 500 personal computers or 30 servers. For businesses larger than this, Microsoft recommends upgrading to System Center Configuration Manager 2007, covered in the next section of this chapter.

In addition SCE 2007 requires Active Directory Domain Services; it cannot be used in a workgroup. And it cannot be used in conjunction with WSUS, although they can operate side by side.

Overview of System Center Configuration Manager 2007

Enterprises with the most complex requirements for enterprise-level update needs can use the System Center Configuration Manager 2007 (SCCM 2007), designed for businesses with more than 500 PCs and 30 servers.

SCCM 2007 has been designed from the ground up with a high-end business in mind. First, the hardware requirements are high. SCCM 2007 with Service Pack 1 runs only on Windows Server 2008, and it also requires a dedicated SQL Server running at least SQL Server 2005 Service Pack 1, but SQL Server 2008 will soon be recommended for a more complete solution.

Using SCCM 2007, administrators can support updates for Microsoft-based products and third-party applications. SCCM 2007 will also support the deployment of applications through SCCM 2007 as well as entire operating systems. For the Enterprise Administrator certification exam, you need to be familiar with what SCCM 2007 is and that it is a solution available for enterprises that have high update automation needs. However, you will not need to know how to set up or utilize SCCM 2007. Thus, I will not cover SCCM 2007 in depth.

Real World Scenario

Deploying Updates to a Medium-Sized Environment

MyCorp has approximately 215 employees, all of whom are issued individual computers running Windows Vista or Windows XP, depending on hardware and software availability. MyCorp has been in business since 1999 and has been running Microsoft operating system products since then. Accordingly, it now runs Windows Server 2000, Windows Server 2003, and Windows Server 2008 in its environment.

In total, MyCorp has seven servers functioning in a single-forest architecture. However, MyCorp has been divided into four different sites, because MyCorp has offices in Brazil, Japan, the United States, and Canada. Connecting each of these sites is a WAN connection of no less than a T1, with the fastest connection being a T3 that connects the U.S. and Canadian office.

Recently, MyCorp has been forced to begin laying off employees because of the depressing economy and the possible automation that can be achieved using Windows Server 2008. To alleviate some of the burden, one of the design decisions was to incorporate Windows Software Updates Services. This way, all of the Microsoft products will stay up-to-date based on the latest updates approved by MyCorp's staff.

To support its environment, MyCorp established its main upstream server as a dedicated WSUS server in the U.S. office. This server receives manual updates attained from the administrator. In the rest of the separate sites, a single WSUS server has been added to each site as a local-area WSUS server that serves the small LAN. These WSUS servers have been set as downstream servers that receive their updates from the main WSUS server. Thus, whenever an update is issued from the upstream server, it is sent to the WSUS servers in the separate sites and then replicated throughout groups defined by the administrators.

Overview of Windows Update

Almost everyone who has used a Windows-based computer since Windows 95 is familiar with the ever-present Windows Update button. And Windows Server 2008 is no exception. But, I can summarize this topic in one sentence: enabling automatic updates is easy in its implementation but possibly dangerous in a complex environment. This is because automatic updates induce the potential to release an update that could cause a service to suddenly stop operating in a fashion that you've become familiar with. And this means that (if the service is relatively important) the entire server could stop running as a whole!

With any luck, in time, this will change. As time moves on, the days of automatic updates ruining entire infrastructures are becoming rarer and rarer. But still, to this day, sometimes updates can sneak up on us in the middle of the night and cause problems. Regardless, in Windows Server 2008 you can access the Windows Update button by clicking Start and then clicking Control Panel. Within Control Panel, you should see the Windows Update icon, as shown in Figure 9.5.

FIGURE 9.5   Control Panel

When you double-click the Windows Update button, Windows Update will default to a home screen that looks similar to Figure 9.6.

Here, you will see when the most recent check for updates was, as well as the most recent updates that were installed. You can also view the history of your updates, which can be extremely important if you need to diagnose a network issue that may have occurred around the same time as your original Windows Update. Once there, you can even double-click updates and see the specific details of a particular update, as shown in Figure 9.7.

FIGURE 9.6   Windows Update

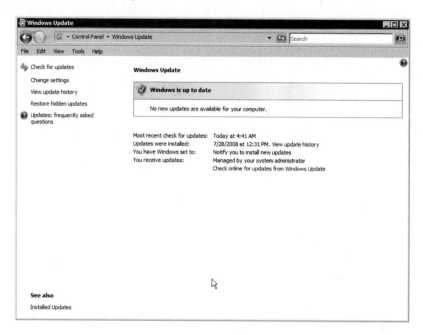

FIGURE 9.7   Windows Update history

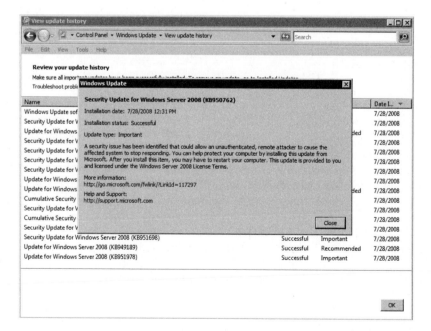

Additionally within Windows Update, you can choose to change the settings for your updates. With the Change Settings link, you can change from automatic to manual updates and choose the specific updates you want to install, or you can disable the Check for Updates option entirely. Although this isn't normally recommended, it can be useful for an offline server that is running a dedicated task or even an online server that is protected through several hardware firewalls and cannot afford even a miniscule amount of downtime.

And of course, last but not least, you can manually initiate an online check for updates by clicking the Check Online for Updates from Windows Update link on the Windows Update main page. This check even greets you with a neat-looking progress bar, as shown in Figure 9.8.

FIGURE 9.8   Windows Update progress bar

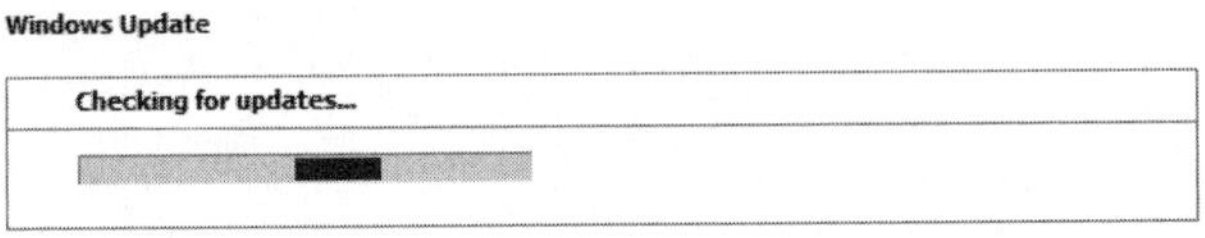

Windows Update

Checking for updates...

If there's an available update, the area where the progress bar is will be replaced either by a yellow or by a red update alert, which will display the total number of updates and the size of the download available for these updates, as shown in Figure 9.9.

FIGURE 9.9   Available updates

You can install these updates by clicking the Install Updates button. And then you will be greeted with the progress bar as the server begins to update. After that, sometimes the server may ask you to reboot, and sometimes you may have to answer a few user agreement license questions, but the process is really quite simple.

Windows Update was designed to be fairly simple in its implementation because it was originally designed with the end user in mind. In the mind of Microsoft, users shouldn't have to worry about their machines working. They should just work. And the way they fix this is by having the machine fix any problems it may have seemingly by itself, without the user being aware that anything occurred. But in an environment where we as administrators are responsible for the health and safety of all computers, it's important for us to research every update and make sure we can deploy them with little to no risk to our infrastructure. This may seem tedious, but it's ultimately the best and most safe way to operate.

Overview of Microsoft Update

Microsoft Update, which is a separate tool from Windows Update, is an update tool that serves a similar role to Windows Update, except it is used on Microsoft Windows as well as Microsoft Office and other Microsoft programs. Additionally, Microsoft Update is compatible with Windows Update. You can access Microsoft Update is first accessed through the Web by heading to http://www.update.microsoft.com.

Note that in order to access this site, you must be using Internet Explorer. Once there on a computer running Windows Server 2008, you should see a screen that looks like Figure 9.10.

FIGURE 9.10   Microsoft Update

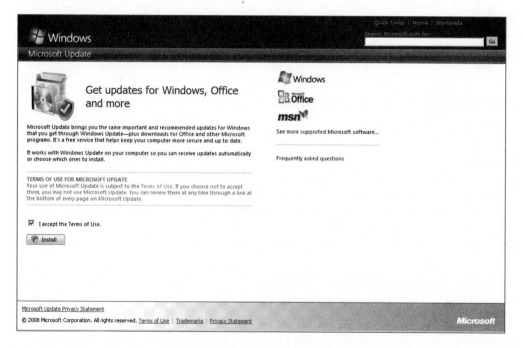

Once you install this program by clicking the Install button, it will incorporate Microsoft Update into the current Windows Update used by Windows Server 2008. Note, however, that this isn't as useful on the server side, because most servers don't run programs such as Microsoft Office.

Real-World Update Practices

Although they're not part of the certification exam, I'll offer you six procedural principles for deploying updates throughout your enterprise. By following these procedures, you'll reduce your chances of causing inadvertent failures or a lack of service availability.

Research Updates Before Downloading Them

Just about any update available from any software contains documentation. With Microsoft, every single update goes through a rigorous quality assurance process that involves verifying the functions of that update, what it changes, and what effects it may have on your enterprise. Often, you can save yourself a lot of headache by reading the update's documentation and determining whether the update is even necessary for your enterprise. After all, updates aren't worth doing just for the sake of doing. They serve a specific function. If a software update addresses services you do not use, hardware you do not possess, or functions you do not require, then avoid it. It's simply not worth your trouble.

Update Based on a Schedule

The term *patch Tuesday* is infamous because of its obvious association with Microsoft. Starting with Windows 98, every second Tuesday of each month Microsoft has released security patches in a consistent manner. This lets the industry know when to expect a fix to a problem or (humorously) when to expect a problem.

This same logic applies with the enterprise. By patching on a certain day, you create an environment that is prepared for the case of a failure. This way, users have backed up their information, administrators will have the appropriate tools on hand, and your environment will be ripe for deploying any update changes that may occur.

Inform Users of Major Updates

A major update can mean major problems. Whenever it becomes necessary for you to make a major update, you should inform users that you will be making a major change so they can prepare themselves. In the old days of IT (I mean the 1990s), this practice was discouraged because it created an environment where users weren't confident of the reliability of their IT hardware and software. But now, this is no longer the general thinking. The reason may sound funny, but it's because people now expect problems in the IT infrastructure. Just like when you used to start (or still start) your first car, you were surprised when it *did* work, not when it didn't.

Apply Updates at Low-Usage Times

One of the best ways to avoid disrupting workflow is to perform an update when there isn't much workflow to interrupt. If you have the authority to do so, try to install updates when users aren't likely to be working. This way, you won't be bogging down the network with data exchange, and the machines won't have to be shut down or restarted during peak usage periods. Chances are, it will please the executives in your company, and it will also save you a lot of headache. The dozens of hours spent answering the questions you might to answer about network slowdown far surpass the few hours it would take you to apply a patch after-hours.

Simulate Updates Before Deploying Updates

If every administrator could have their way, they would simulate all updates in a test environment routinely and eliminate any worries altogether. However, in most enterprise environments, this simply isn't feasible. This is mainly because there are so many different workstations, servers, and other factors to be changed that the enterprise environment is too difficult to replicate.

Regardless, testing an update before deploying it is almost always a good option if it is in any way possible. Even on the smallest scale, this can sometimes give you very early warnings of any serious problems.

Be Prepared for Rollback in Case of Failure

The motto of the Boy Scouts of America has always been "Be prepared." The same thing also applies to administrators. Remember Murphy 's Law—in the enterprise, it's best to assume that the worst-case situation will occur and that you will need a backup in case it does. In this case, you need to make sure you have all the available resources you need to restore your update. This includes elements such as spare computers, original update files, backup data, and anything necessary to completely recover.

Update Compliance

One of the terms you will hear a lot in the world of administration and security is *compliance*. Compliance is the process of making your network infrastructure adhere to a standard defined by a trustable third party. One commonly used set of standards is National Security Agency (NSA) standards for network security. The reason these standards are trusted is that the NSA is the federal branch of the federal government responsible for the national security of information passed across open mediums, such as the Internet and telephone lines. To add a little bit of history, the NSA was created in 1952, but the government didn't publicly recognize its existence or inform the public of its purpose until recently.

Within most companies, the process of adhering to compliance involves installing updates and implementing security policies to one standard. With a compliance standard, no update is installed unless that update is consistent with the compliance documents that have been originated by the company or from the third-party source that the company has used to draft their compliance documents.

The NSA security guide for Windows Server 2008 is not yet available. However, the NSA assisted in the development of the Windows Server 2003 guide, and it's logical to expect that the new guide, like its predecessor, will be recognized as sufficient for the most secure possible operating practices. Here is the link to these invaluable guides: www.nsa.gov/snac/index .cfm?MenuID=scg10.3.1.

Summary

In this chapter, I covered the process of accurately updating a Microsoft Windows Server 2008 environment through manual and automated processes. Specifically, I covered the Microsoft Baseline Security Analyzer tool. Using the Microsoft Baseline Security Analyzer, you can determine any deficiencies in your network concerning updates or software-level update concerns that may pose a threat to the maintained integrity of your network.

Within a Windows Server 2008 environment, many update options are available to you, each of which is suited to an individual need. Using Windows Server 2008, you have access to the following:

- Windows Update

- Microsoft Update

- SCCM 2007

- SCE 2007

- Windows Software Update Services

You also can access Windows Update by manually installing updates that you download from Microsoft.com.

I also discussed six procedural principles to safely update a Windows infrastructure in an enterprise environment:

- Research updates before downloading them.

- Download on a schedule.

- Inform users of major updates.

- Apply updates at low peak usage times.

- Simulate updates before deploying updates.

- Be prepared to roll back in case of failure.

In addition, you should make sure your updates are promulgated in conjunction with a compliance document that is either drafted in house or retrieved from a third party.

Of all the update technologies available in Windows Server 2008, the one you should concentrate most on for real-world enterprise deployment and for the certification exam is

Windows Server 2008 WSUS. Through WSUS, Group Policy can deploy various updates through a set of predefined standards outlined by the administrators through the Group Policy management console.

Finally, once Windows Server 2008 is running, you should take care to implement a standard system for monitoring the health of your environment. This includes the processes of monitoring hardware, software, network interaction, uptime, downtime, and availability. Through these measures, you can do your best to ensure a clean, healthy, and functional environment.

Exam Essentials

Understand WSUS. There is a lot to WSUS, including Group Policy, administrative roles, implementation strategies, and various options within WSUS. To succeed on the certification exam, you need to be familiar with all of them and need to have completed the exercises in this book, as well as used WSUS extensively in either your home lab or in the real world. WSUS can get quite expansive, and the certification exam will assume you've dealt with WSUS in addition to lots of other technologies.

Be familiar with the advantages of different types of updates. It goes without saying that you need to know the different types of updates available from Microsoft and the different software methods available to deploy each. But, you also need to know when it is appropriate to use one type of software and when it's appropriate to use another. Know *when* to use something as well as when *not* to use something.

Understand compliance. This doesn't just mean understanding what it takes to adhere to a standard. By understanding compliance, you understand a business's need to implement a complex strategy of deploying updates throughout several hundred or thousand workstations and servers.

Know your health models. To pass the certification exam, you don't necessarily need to know health "models" as much as you need to understand what it takes to maintain a healthy IT environment. This includes procedures such as best practices as well as routine maintenance and plans for maintaining system availability.

Know the difference between SCCM/SEC 2007. It might seem like a surface-level distinction, but the certification exam will throw a lot of different technology names at you. Don't get confused if SCCM and SEC 2007 both appear as an option. Know which one is used for larger demographics and which one is used for smaller implementations.

Remember update strategies. Remembering update strategies means knowing how updates can be deployed to a system environment, from the largest-scale implementation to the simplest. In the enterprise, you deal with several nested layers of updates that can be used with multiple pieces of Microsoft software. Know how they all work together, and know how each of these can benefit you.

Review Questions

1. If your organization requires an update strategy that can accommodate more than 200 users that is deployed through Group Policy and supports automation for the least amount of long-term administration, what update strategy should you deploy?

   A. Automatic updates

   B. Microsoft Update

   C. Windows Update

   D. WSUS

2. As the lead administrator, you want a way for your lower-level administrators to deploy updates with WSUS according to their desires. What should you do?

   A. Implement a group policy that grants rights to the lower-level administrators to create WSUS accounts, and link the policy to their user group.

   B. Implement a group policy that links WSUS computers to the administrators user group.

   C. Create a WSUS Reporters group on the domain controller, and link that group in Group Policy to the Windows Server 2008 domain controllers.

   D. On the server level, implement a local WSUS Administrators local group.

3. Your current server architecture consists of three member servers that are attached to a domain controller that functions as the primary server for the rest of your enterprise. Accordingly, this server is the root of your domain architecture, and the member servers are used for additional tasks, such as file sharing and email. If you wanted these member servers to take advantage of WSUS, what should you do?

   A. Implement WSUS using an upstream server from the domain controller, and feed the flow up to your remaining member servers.

   B. Implement WSUS using a downstream server from the domain controller, and feed the flow down to your remaining member servers.

   C. Link a GPO using the WSUS policy to the domain controller, and send the link to the member servers.

   D. Create a GPO that fixes your member servers as a downstream distractor, set your domain controller as an upstream, and then link the policy.

4. Which of the following components cannot be updated through the use of standard Windows enterprise update tools available through Windows Server 2008?

   A. Drivers

   B. Third-party applications

   C. Software components

   D. OS updates

   E. Firmware

5. MegaCorp, an international conglomerate with more than 2,000 users, has recently become aware of major security concerns within its enterprise and has decided to tighten security measures. Part of this process is the decision to create a new security baseline. Knowing what you know of this process, which of the following five processes will not be necessary?

   A. Securing Active Directory design

   B. Securing Group Policy design

   C. Securing security scope definition

   D. Securing user passwords

   E. Securing social engineering

6. When selecting to use the Microsoft Baseline Security Analyzer (MBSA) tool, there are two ways your network can be analyzed. Of the following options, which two are available?

   A. Domain-wide analysis

   B. IP address range analysis

   C. GPO analysis

   D. Active Directory analysis

7. Within OmniCorp, it's of paramount importance that all servers be active and running as much as possible. This is so important that OmniCorp has just announced that a single second of downtime will result in written penalties for all employees within the IT department. Ironically, they've also asked the IT department to prepare a system health model that reflects this. Knowing what you know of system health models, what factors is Omni-Corp asking you to monitor?

   A. Server uptime

   B. Server availability

   C. Backup availability

   C. Backup downtime

   D. Application availability

   E. Application downtime

8. Your organization, OmniCorp, requires that a certain third-party program be accessible at all times. Accordingly, OmniCorp has asked you to create a system health model to record the times that this does not occur. What should you do?

   A. Monitor server uptime

   B. Monitor server availability

   C. Monitor backup availability

   C. Monitor backup downtime

   D. Monitor application availability

   E. Monitor application downtime

9. Of the following options, which system health category can be hardware related only? (Choose all that apply.)

   A. Server uptime

   B. Server downtime

   C. CPU usage

   D. Memory usage

   E. Page File usage

   F. Network utilization

   G. Service availability

   H. Backup downtime

10. MyCorp is a medium-sized business that runs a fully operating and functional WSUS deployment. Recently, lower-level administrators have requested a method to determine the impact that individual updates have on their environment. What should you do?

   A. Promote the junior-level administrators to the Enterprise Admins group.

   B. Implement WSUS monitoring.

   C. Run MBSA.

   D. Create a system health model before updating.

   E. Use the WSUS Reporters group.

11. You are the senior enterprise administrator for OmniCorp. You need to devise a way for individual administrators beneath you to authorize updates that are passed down through WSUS. What should you do?

   A. Implement a GPO for WSUS, and link it to the Administrators group.

   B. Implement a GPO for WSUS, and link it to the WSUS updates computers.

   C. Implement WSUS in replica mode.

   D. Implement WSUS in autonomous mode.

12. You are the senior enterprise administrators for OmniCorp. You need to devise a way to automate WSUS in such a fashion so that updates you create are applied to all servers in the same method as your root server, regardless of their setup. What should you do?

   A. Implement a GPO for WSUS, and link it to the computers in your organization.

   B. Implement a GPO for WSUS, and link it to the WSUS All Computers group.

   C. Implement WSUS in replica mode.

   D. Implement WSUS in autonomous mode.

13. If you are going to deploy an update and you need this update to be given to all your users, regardless of their desires, what should you do?

   A. Use Windows Update, and set it to automatically install updates.

   B. Use Microsoft Update, and set it to automatically install updates.

   C. Use WSUS with automatic approval.

   D. Use WSUS with GPO links to the computers using access lists.

14. You work for MyCorp, a medium-sized business that creates toys for children ages 9 to 13. At your office, you use less than 500 computers and a total of 12 servers. In addition to using Windows Server and Microsoft Office, you also use third-party applications. Knowing this, which of the following technologies would suit your enterprise best?

    A. WSUS

    B. SCE 2007

    C. SCCM 2007

    D. Windows Update

    E. Microsoft Update

15. You work for MegaCorp, a large-sized business that manufacturers cars. At your office, you use more than 500 computers and a total of 120 servers. In addition to using Windows Server and Microsoft Office, you also use third-party applications. Knowing this, which of the following technologies would suit your enterprise best?

    A. WSUS

    B. SCE 2007

    C. SCCM 2007

    D. Windows Update

    E. Microsoft Update

16. You are the administrator for the OmniCorp corporation. Within OmniCorp, WSUS and automatic updates are disabled for security reasons, and users will instead update through manual updates sent through instructional emails. Today, your organization has to do a system-wide update of Windows Server 2008 servers and Microsoft Office 2007. What should you instruct your users to do?

    A. Manually download the updates through Microsoft.com.

    B. Use Windows Update.

    C. Use Microsoft Update.

    D. Use WSUS because it poses no potential risk.

17. As you are working for an online service provider, a fellow co-worker comes to you and informs you of a critical security update that has just been recommended by Microsoft. Without this update, your organization will be vulnerable to exploitive attacks that could compromise the system and application integrity. What should you do?

    A. Act immediately. Turn off the system, apply the update, and then reboot.

    B. Inform the users of the update, then take the system offline, and apply the update.

    C. Wait until the end of business or a low peak operating time, and then apply the update.

    D. Do not apply the update unless specifically directed to by your superior.

18. In a mission-critical environment, security patch #34 has come out in accordance with Knowledge Base article KB293421. This patch addresses minor concerns regarding performance and possible reliability during heavy server use periods. Knowing this, what should you do? Choose the best answer.

   A. Apply the patch during nonpeak periods.

   B. Test the patch in a lab environment.

   C. Do not apply the patch.

   D. Inform the users of the patch, and then apply it immediately.

19. When using WSUS, you've decided you would like only updates to be sent throughout the rest of your environment. Disregarding Microsoft Update or Windows Update, what should you do?

   A. Establish your root domain controller as an upstream server, and set the rest of your servers up in autonomous mode.

   B. Establish your root domain controller as a downstream server, and set the rest of your servers up in replica mode.

   C. Establish your root domain controller as an upstream server, and set the rest of your servers up in replica mode.

   D. Establish your root domain controller as a downstream server, and set the rest of your servers up in autonomous mode.

20. Which of the following documents is *not* considered an acceptable workplace security baseline document standard or tool?

   A. MBSA

   B. NSA standards

   C. Microsoft standards

   D. Third-party standards

   E. In-house standards

   F. IT department standards

Answers to Review Questions

1. D. In order to use group policy, the best solution available is WSUS. WSUS is designed to be deployed through a completely automated solution that frees administrators to concentrate on other aspects of the network infrastructure.

2. D. The WSUS Administrators local group is used to allow individual users at a lower level to pick their own updates.

3. B. WSUS servers can be either upstream or downstream servers. An upstream server is designed to upload and serve as the primary and trusted source of the updates. Usually, Microsoft Update serves as an upstream server. A downstream server is used to filter the received authoritative updates to other member servers.

4. E. Firmware needs to be manually updated. This is because most firmware requires a reboot, power-off, or specialized reload procedure in order to proceed. Accordingly, Windows Update methods do not support this.

5. E. Social engineering is a security risk but not part of the establishment of a security baseline. A security baseline is the process of hardening the software and hardware-level components of an architecture.

6. A, B. Using the MBSA, you can select either a domain or a list of IP addresses in order to process. The MBSA doesn't concentrate on GPOs or Active Directory.

7. B. Server availability refers to the time that a server is up, running, not down, and accessible. In other words, to monitor server availability, you are monitoring every moment that the server is functioning properly.

8. E. Application downtime refers to the period in which an application is not available, for whatever reason. This could be a hardware, software, or even human error. But regardless, every moment it doesn't work is recorded here.

9. C, D, E. Server uptime, downtime, network utilization, service availability, and backup downtime are all possible through various causes, including software issues and operating system crashes. Only the CPU, memory, and page file categories uses are hardware-related statistics. However, note that software is required to utilize these hardware devices.

10. E. WSUS Reporters is a local group on servers that allows junior-level administrators to run reports to determine the impact of WUS updates on their environment. Using this, they can determine what will happen after WSUS updates occur.

11. D. Autonomous mode allows administrators to individual choose which updates are applied to their network. Autonomous mode is useful with networks that need to be closely monitored in case of a change.

12. C. Replica mode is used to simply replicate the updates that are sent from one server to another. This is used as a method to increase the deployment of updates and create a fallback method in case of a failure.

13. C. WSUS has the ability to deploy updates without the need for approval for users. WSUS offers this option as well as email notifications and several other important features.

14. B. System Center Essentials 2007 is an add-on available for Windows Server that supports updates of both Microsoft software and third-party software. It is available for purchase from Microsoft.

15. C. System Center Configuration Manager 2007 (SCCM 2007) is a purchasable tool from Microsoft designed to support update configurations for large-scale businesses. It is designed for high-end use only and is quite expensive.

16. C. Microsoft Update provides updates for Windows as well as updates for Microsoft software. WSUS, while convenient, can have potential for security risks.

17. C. When applying updates, it's wise to apply updates only during nonpeak usage times. Otherwise, you can disrupt business for the sake of only possible security risks.

18. B. Whenever a patch has to be applied to a live, mission-critical environment, it is best to test it extensively. Without this vital step, there is an extreme potential for disaster.

19. C. By placing the root domain controller as an upstream server, you make it the centralized point for all updates. Placing the rest of the servers in replica mode helps distribute the updates without having to bother with the process of allowing junior-level administrators to choose updates while in autonomous mode.

20. F. Several sources exist to create an effective security baseline. But any baseline that is created through the use of documents that do not have complete company approval is not advisable. They should be verified with the executive branch or a third party.

Chapter

10

Using Virtualization to Increase Productivity and Facilitate Consolidation

✓ **Design the operating system virtualization strategy**

- May include but is not limited to: server consolidation, application compatibility, virtualization management, placement of servers

It's sometimes hard to remember that information technology is still a relatively young industry. And just like any other new industry, IT has gone through dramatic changes, so much so that there have been entire books written on the subject of change in IT. It's particularly easy for most people to relate to IT, because they were alive and thriving at some point during its origin, less than 100 years ago with the birth of the first computer.

And although I'm not here to provide a history lesson, it's important to discuss that the very subject of this chapter originates from the centralized problem that IT is still a young industry and there are so many changes associated with it that they're sometimes hard to keep track of. Just think about a normal user who decides to buy a computer, new or used (remember, not everyone buys a computer fresh out of the box). A new user might be running one of more than 100 operating systems. Beyond the familiar versions of Windows, there are many different generations of Mac OS and untold flavors of Linux. All of these vary in some form or another, support different devices, and have different interfaces.

On the server side, this variety persists. In fact, some of the case studies in this book deal with environments running different versions of Windows. Sometimes the servers are old boxes that won't be upgraded, and at other times they're new boxes that still need to support old technologies. Basically, almost all environments contain various computers. And more computers, ultimately, means more money—more money for hardware, more money for software, and more money for operating costs such as electricity. And although we computer gurus may love the idea of more hardware, the folks in the executive suite probably don't share this opinion. Instead, they'd rather have a single point of focus. In other words, they'd rather have a single point of origin where they can focus all their IT needs or simply consolidate the need for several different server options. Can they do that? Well, yes, they can, through the power of something called *virtualization*.

Introducing Virtualization

You'll find a lot of long-winded, technical descriptions for virtualization. But the best way I can explain it at the introductory level is by providing you with a scenario. So, for the moment, let's say you work at a company called UniCom. Within UniCom, a lot of different versions of software are being used. And, because any good example should be a fun example, let's say UniCom is a movie studio that specializes in 3D computer graphics.

Within 3D, there is certainly more than one way to skin a cat—or render a scene, for that manner. UniCom uses tons of different 3D software clients, such as Alias Maya, 3DS Studio Max, Lightwave, and even some of the free and available apps like Blender. At the end of the day, they all can produce the same result. But the problem is, at the high end, 3D studios often use CPU-intensive rendering servers in the background to support tasks that may take a very long time. And not all these computers run the same rendering software. So here's our ultimate dilemma: not all the software supports the same version of server software.

In fact, more often than not, rendering software supports only one specific version of software for one specific version of the rendering client. And just to throw a last log on the fire, licensing schemes for these very expensive pieces of software usually do not allow for upgrades. Why buy one when you can buy two at twice the price? (If you don't get that joke, go watch the movie *Contact*.)

Anyway, this long-winded explanation is my way of pointing out that many environments have a lot of technical limitations. 3D graphic artists don't grow on trees, and anyone who has worked with a good artist will tell you they don't exactly like the idea of limitations. So, what do you do? Install multiple servers? Well, let's take a look at what that would be like if you installed multiple servers. Check out Figure 10.1. Say, in that figure, you have twelve different graphic artists, four of which use 3DS Max, four of which use Alias Maya, and four of which use Blender. And, for the sake of argument, say that one piece of software requires Windows 2000 Server, one requires Windows Server 2003, and one requires Windows Server 2008. We're already up to three servers for twelve users. That's not exactly efficient.

FIGURE 10.1   Servers without virtualization

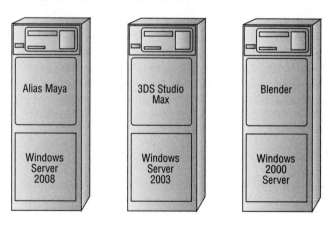

And so we think, "Well, what a waste. If only there were another way, we could run all the clients on the same server." Well, there is. And that process is called *consolidation,* which I will talk about in a moment after I talk a little bit more about the different types of virtualization and what they really are.

The Different Types of Virtualization

Windows Server 2008 presents a ton of different possibilities for virtualization, and with all the different types of virtualization that are available with Windows Server 2008, it's pretty easy to feel a little lost. It's sometimes difficult to keep track of what each of the different types of virtualization actually does. Accordingly, I'll give a brief summary of some of the principal types of virtualization in the following sections.

Presentation Virtualization

Whenever you hear the words *presentation virtualization* and *Windows Server 2008* in the same breath, you should instantly think of one concept: Terminal Services. The idea of presentation virtualization is that programs should appear to be running on a client's desktop computer but actually be operating behind the scenes on a computer separate from the main server that is doing the real work. The advantage of this is that it creates a central focus point for all users to operate and allows that point to be heavily monitored.

Application Virtualization

Just like presentation virtualization should make you think of Terminal Services, application virtualization should instantly make you think of SoftGrid. The idea behind SoftGrid, and behind application virtualization, is that users should be able to log on to a server and have that server provide for them a semblance of a desktop where they can use programs and applications in a safe, predetermined environment. It's designed as a method of control and application delivery to facilitate a steady business flow.

Desktop Virtualization

Finally, we get into true operating system virtualization. Using desktop virtualization, an administrator can run a child operating system at the same time that they are running a parent operating system. And this isn't purely limited to Windows. As an example, Figure 10.2 shows a Mac OS X installation running Windows XP through a virtualized desktop.

FIGURE 10.2   Mac virtualization

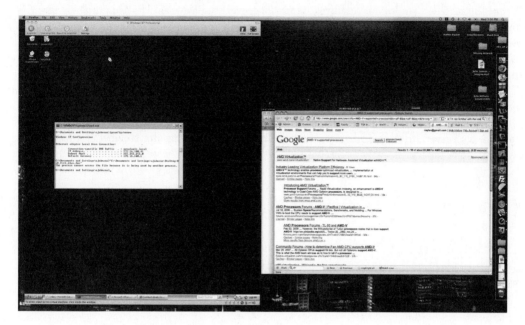

Server Virtualization

Server virtualization is high-end virtualization, and it's the type you'll focus on in this chapter. There are two main programs used for this with Windows Server 2008: the Hyper-V server role and Virtual Server 2005 Release 2. With these two programs, you can run extra server operating systems alongside your main Windows Server 2008 operating system and save a dramatic amount of time and money.

   Server virtualization is also possible through programs such as VMware.

Virtualization vs. Multitasking

A common misconception about virtualization is that a virtualized environment is simply another program, running within the operating system, that uses an application to emulate an operating system. Although that's easy to understand and makes a lot of sense, it isn't necessarily true.

When virtualizing an entire operating system, the way this is accomplished is slightly different. First, when you're multitasking, your computer's CPU (or CPUs) are going through the process of allocating the piece of software across your computer's memory and then accessing the software across that memory in a very linear fashion. Technically, the computer is reading the memory from spot 0 to spot X, where along the way it's executing commands that programs are issuing.

With virtualization, a virtualized computer will "virtually split" the CPU into multiple portions. In such a manner, CPU1 will become VirtualCPU1 and VirtualCPU2. And each of these VirtualCPUs will then allocate themselves completely to the isolated operating system. It's pretty amazing and very effective. It allows for a computer to view its processes as completely separated, rather than embedded with application after application.

Introducing Server Consolidation

The *Random House Unabridged Dictionary* defines *consolidate* as "to bring together (separate parts) into a single or unified whole; unit; [to] combine." So, it's almost self-explanatory that *server consolidation* is the process of unifying different servers into one. In the example from Figure 10.1, there are three different servers. Consolidating them into one server would look a lot like what what's shown in Figure 10.3.

FIGURE 10.3   Server consolidation

As you can see there, even though the figure shows only one computer, three different operating systems are running. And furthermore, different applications are running within each of those operating systems. Back in the 1980s and 1990s, this concept was presented at a lot of technical conferences. Most people, even famous scientists, said they didn't think it would be possible for the next 20 years. Well, lo and behold, 20 years later—it's possible. Using virtualization, you can consolidate the work of what was three operating systems in one centralized location by running one of the operating systems natively and then *virtualizing* the other two operating systems within the first operating system. In other words, the OS architecture is still in place, but multiple operating systems and multiple applications are layered on top of it.

Normally, you implement virtualization by initializing the native install of the most prevalent (or newest) operating system. In our case (and in the case of the Windows Server 2008 certification exam), this will almost always be Windows Server 2008. That's mostly because Windows Server 2008 uses a new tool called Hyper-V.

Hyper-V

Hyper-V is a new tool, available with Windows Server 2008 Standard, Enterprise, and Datacenter x64-bit builds, that is designed to support individualized virtualization of different platforms on a single Windows Server 2008 server workstation. The name *Hyper-V* comes from a technology called a *hypervisor*, which is a piece of monitoring software that is designed to track the status of multiple operating systems that run on a single machine at the same time and allow them to access system resources without interfering with one another. Rather than functioning like most normal applications, which sit on top, Hyper-V runs operating systems natively as a core part of the OS.

 Hyper-V requires Windows Server 2008 x64, but it can run 32-bit operating systems within it.

One of the best practices for using Hyper-V on a server is to install a virtualized operating system onto a RAID-enabled system. Preferably, this RAID-enabled system includes redundancy, such as RAID 0 or RAID 5. But in any case, a virtualized imagine should be placed on a separate volume from the host system. This is because placing the two operating systems in the same location can create a lot of complications as the individual platforms try to read and write data at excessive speeds and frequency.

Hyper-V Hardware Requirements

One of the unfortunate side effects of such impressive software is that it has equally impressive hardware requirements. To effectively use Hyper-V—or rather, use Hyper-V at all—you must have an x64-compatible computer with a process that contains one of two technologies:

Intel VT or AMD-V. One of these two features is built into certain product lines of AMD and Intel processors that support a form of hardware-accelerated virtualization.

According to Intel's website, Intel VT lets you optimize flexibility and maximize system utilization by consolidating multiple environments into a single server, allowing you to perform the same tasks using fewer systems. Therefore, it does the following:

- Simplifies resource management

- Increases IT efficiency

- Decreases disaster recovery time

- Improves systems reliability and availability

- Reduces corporate risk and real-time losses from downtime

- Lowers hardware acquisition costs because you can make increased use of existing machines

You can find a complete explanation of Intel VT and AMD-V technology on their respective websites, currently available at the following locations:

    www.intel.com/technology/virtualization/

    www.amd.com/us-en/Processors/ProductInformation/0,,30_118_8796_14287,00.html

Each of these websites provides a great deal of documentation regarding the hardware-specific portions of onboard virtualization in hardware devices. But what's important to remember is that in both of these technologies, virtualization is disabled by default. This is for good reason. Enabling onboard virtualization greatly magnifies your potential to receive a possibly crippling virus. If you've ever heard of a rootkit, you can just imagine the granddaddy of all rootkit viruses—the hardware virtualization-based rootkit. If present, it can metaphorically rock your world, and not in a way you might enjoy.

Lastly, Hyper-V requires that data execution prevention be available and enabled. This means you need to enable the Intel XD bit or the AMD NX bit.

 Although it might be cool in a very "hardcore geek" sort of way, it is impossible to run Hyper-V inside another virtualized environment, such as VMware. This is because Hyper-V requires direct access to the hardware virtualization technology, which isn't available when running in a virtualized environment.

Hyper-V Limits

When you are planning your deployment of Hyper-V, you should keep in mind that Hyper-V has some practical limitations that should suffice for all but the most demanding user, as shown in Table 10.1.

TABLE 10.1   Hyper-V Limits

Component	Limitation
Processor	16 or fewer logical processors
Memory	64GB per virtual machine, 1TB maximum
Network	12 network adapters
Hard disks	Virtual drives up to 2040GB (2TB)
Virtual optical drives	Up to 3 DVD drives
Virtual COM ports	2 virtual COM ports
Virtual floppy drive	1 virtual floppy drive

Supported Guest Operating Systems with Windows Server 2008 Hyper-V

You can run these editions of Windows Server 2008 with 32- and 64-bit Windows Server 2008 virtual machines:

- Windows Server 2008 Standard and Windows Server 2008 Standard without Hyper-V
- Windows Server 2008 Enterprise and Windows Server 2008 Enterprise without Hyper-V
- Windows Server 2008 Datacenter and Windows Server 2008 Datacenter without Hyper-V
- Windows Web Server 2008
- Windows Server 2008 HPC edition

You can run the following editions of Windows Server 2003 with up to two virtual processors:

- Windows Server 2003 R2 Standard edition with Service Pack 2
- Windows Server 2003 R2 Enterprise edition with Service Pack 2
- Windows Server 2003 R2 Datacenter edition with Service Pack 2
- Windows Server 2003 Standard edition with Service Pack 2
- Windows Server 2003 Enterprise edition with Service Pack 2
- Windows Server 2003 Datacenter edition with Service Pack 2
- Windows Server 2003 Web edition with Service Pack 2
- Windows Server 2003 R2 Standard x64 edition with Service Pack 2

- Windows Server 2003 R2 Enterprise x64 edition with Service Pack 2
- Windows Server 2003 R2 Datacenter x64 edition with Service Pack 2
- Windows Server 2003 Standard x64 edition with Service Pack 2
- Windows Server 2003 Enterprise x64 edition with Service Pack 2
- Windows Server 2003 Datacenter x64 edition with Service Pack 2

You can run the following versions of Windows 2000 on a virtual machine configured with one virtual processor:

- Windows 2000 Server with Service Pack 4
- Windows 2000 Advanced Server with Service Pack 4

You can run the following Linux distributions on a virtual machine configured with one virtual processor:

- SUSE Linux Enterprise Server 10 with Service Pack 2 (x86 edition)
- SUSE Linux Enterprise Server 10 with Service Pack 2 (x64 edition)
- SUSE Linux Enterprise Server 10 with Service Pack 1 (x86 edition)
- SUSE Linux Enterprise Server 10 with Service Pack 1 (x64 edition)

You can run the following 32-bit and 64-bit versions of Windows Vista on a virtual machine configured with up to two virtual processors:

- Windows Vista Business with Service Pack 1
- Windows Vista Enterprise with Service Pack 1
- Windows Vista Ultimate with Service Pack 1

You can run the following versions of Windows XP on a virtual machine:

- Windows XP Professional with Service Pack 3 (configured with one or two virtual processors)
- Windows XP Professional with Service Pack 2 (configured with one virtual processor)
- Windows XP Professional x64 Edition with Service Pack 2 (configured with one or two virtual processors)

Understanding Virtualized Machine Components

Whenever a new virtual machine is created, some necessary hardware components are allocated through the use of software emulation. Think about it. Whenever you use an individualized operating system, it has to access its own hard drive, network card, and system memory. Some of these components are vital for operation. Say, for instance, you're running an instance of SUSE Linux, and you're going to be using this instance of Linux to run a website that takes advantage of PHP Hypertext Preprocessor (PHP). To do this, you'd need to have an individual installation that had its own network settings, memory, and disk. Imagine for a moment that this is a medium-traffic web server. The I/O operations alone would be difficult for a single server to hold, but since this is a consolidated and "hypervised" (monitored by Hyper-V) system, it's even harder to maintain.

A lot of the reason behind this is that although there may be two operating systems running two of every single operating component, on most low-end, low-cost servers there is only one memory bus, or one memory card, and maybe even one RAID configuration. And that isn't likely to change. Thus, the hypervisor has the task of determining where the resources are allocated. At times, this can be very complicated.

Thankfully, most of what the hypervisor does has been automated to a point that it doesn't require much administrative work on the part of the lowly administrator who has been tasked with designing a consolidated server role. Really, using Hyper-V is as simple as opening up the virtualization management console (VMC).

Using the Virtualization Management Console

The VMC in Windows Server 2008 is called the Hyper-V Manager. Using the Hyper-V Manager, you're allowed access to the central brains of the hypervised machines. Here, you can create new virtualized machines, take snapshots, manage the licensing, and alter the hardware settings discussed earlier. You can access the VMC by selecting Start ➤ Administrative Tools ➤ Hyper-V Manager.

Snapshots

If you've used Windows XP or Windows Vista, a *snapshot* is pretty easy to understand. In a way, it's similar to a system restore. A VM snapshot gives you the ability to take a "photo" at a certain time of the condition of that virtualized operating system. The mother operating system (Windows Server 2008 when using Hyper-V) has the virtual machine record a data list of all its settings that will allow you to roll back to the previously established settings within Hyper-V at any point. So, if for some reason your virtual machine stops working, you can revert to a snapshot and continue working unimpeded as if nothing ever happened. Of course, any changes made after the snapshot will be lost. But part of the real advantage of snapshots is that you can decide where you want to place them on the system. This is useful if you want to deposit a snapshot on an external resource, such as a networked drive or external hard drive, for recovery purposes.

Snapshots are not exclusive to Windows Server. Snapshots are used in all sorts of virtualized machine software, such as VMware and Parallels for the Mac. In case you're interested in being certified on another platform, this is good information to remember.

Failover and Recovery with Hyper-V

One of the primary objectives of Hyper-V is, surprisingly, disaster recovery. When you first think about it, this may not make a lot of sense. At first glance, Hyper-V is just virtualization software that allows the really nifty deployment of other platforms. However, there's more to it than that. Using Hyper-V and snapshots, administrators are able to take entire installations and store them at a given point and time.

Logically, this means that these snapshots are available for recovery. Thus, failover recovery is quite easy. And furthermore, in the case of an upgrade or move, the process of migration is greatly simplified because downtime is almost entirely removed. But the final advantage of Hyper-V is that it also supports Volume Shadow Copy. This functionality, which we discussed in Chapter 8, "Planning for Business Continuity and Backup," creates a specific recovery point for easy recovery.

Network Setups with All Types of Virtual Machines

When a virtual machine is initially created, you can set it up in several ways. But of particular concern to most any administrator is the method that allows you to possibly use a single network card for multiple computers. In sharing the Ethernet port, you have three available options: using the host's NAT, using a bridged connection, and allowing only a network with the host.

Host NAT

Using host NAT, the host actually creates a virtualized DHCP pool and assigns an IP address to the virtual machine running in it. This is ideal for a machine that won't have to be communicated with but will communicate with machines outside the network. The reason behind this is that NAT, by its very nature (as discussed in Chapter 2, "Naming Conventions, Networking, and Access Principles"), serves as an internal firewall. It's kind of funny, but by installing a virtual machine and using host NAT, you are effectively setting up a machine within a software firewall.

This said, the machine can still reach out and access the Internet, send email, and do the tasks it needs to perform in order to function (most of the time). Problems start to arise only when you want to use this server for, say, a web server or for a platform such as Microsoft Exchange. This is relatively difficult, if not impossible, because NAT doesn't play well with others.

Bridged Connection

A bridged connection is by far the best method if it's available. Using a bridged connection, the VM creates its own unique IP address and authenticates to the network as if it is something completely separate. It can be a pretty surreal feeling to look at two distinct machines on one computer, each with their own network card. It still makes many of us say, "Huh… well, that's something." Not only does the virtual machine function on the same network, but outside resources from your network can individually access the logical address of that virtual machine and have no idea that it isn't really a whole other entity. To them, it just looks like another host.

Host Only

The least desirable method of connection is to allow connection only with the host. This creates an environment where VMs cannot communicate with the outside world and can run only in the virtual environment. Sometimes, this can be useful if you'd like to test a software program in a secure environment, because the two OS installations can still communicate. But it has little other practical use and is thus less common.

Virtual Networks

Now that you understand how network cards can be physically shared through software implementation (try getting your head around that for a minute!), let's talk a little bit about virtual networks and the role they play within Windows Server 2008 Hyper-V installations.

When you first set up a Hyper-V installation, you have the option of creating special types of *virtual networks*. In total, there are three types: internal virtual networks, external virtual networks, and private virtual networks.

Using a virtual network, Windows Server 2008 Hyper-V can isolate communication types with child machines. In the following sections, I'll discuss in detail each type of network you can create.

Internal Virtual Networks

The primary use of an *internal virtual network* is testing. Using an internal network, an administrator can create a network that will communicate between the child virtual server and the parent host server. This is convenient if you need to test applications because it isolates the communication that will be done within the virtual network. This enables the following types of communication:

- Virtual machine to virtual machine within the same physical server
- Virtual machine to parent host server

External Virtual Networks

The word *external* in *external virtual network* implies that the network is not necessarily a network outside the virtual server but nevertheless can be accessed externally. This means that users outside of the area you define within your network can access the virtual server through its own unique IP address. This enables the following types of communication:

- Virtual child machine to virtual child machine
- Virtual child machine to parent
- Virtual child machine to outside world

Private Virtual Networks

A *private virtual network* is created when you want two virtual machines to communicate but it's imperative that they be able to communicate only with one another. Usually, this is done for testing. For example, imagine you have an application that needs two servers to run. Instead of getting two separate computers and then installing operating systems on them both, you can create two virtual machines and give them a private network to communicate to each other. This enables the following type of communication: virtual machine to virtual machine.

Multiple Network Interface Cards with Virtual Networks

The already-common practice technique of using multiple network interface cards (NICs) for different missions will be used even more in the future of Hyper-V. Generally, the Microsoft documentation strongly encourages the use of several Ethernet adapters because there are three distinct needs in a virtualized operating environment:

- The host OS (Windows Server 2008) requires a port.
- The virtualized environment should have a dedicated port.
- The iSCSI array (which is recommended) should have a dedicated port.

As you can see, the need for a large amount of network connectivity grows extremely quickly. Fortunately, Microsoft Windows Server 2008 supports a large number of NICs already, including NICs that have onboard packet management and other useful tools.

Installing Hyper-V

In the following exercises, you will apply what you have learned in the preceding sections by installing Hyper-V. To complete Exercise 10.1, you must have a computer that supports at least Windows Server 2008 Standard edition and either AMD-V or Intel VT. You will not be able to get past the first step of Exercise 10.1 if you do not have that hardware. In addition, please note that these exercises build on one another, so you will need to do them in the sequence presented here.

EXERCISE 10.1

Preparing to Install Hyper-V

1. Download the Server 2008 Hyper-V update. As of the time of the publication of this book, you have to manually download it from Microsoft at the following URL:

   `www.microsoft.com/downloads/details.aspx?FamilyId=F3AB3D4B-63C8-4424-A738-BADED34D24ED&displaylang=en`

2. Once you have downloaded this update, double-click the `.msu` file, and install the update. The computer will ask you to reboot. Then, you can proceed with the install.

3. Enable hardware virtualization in the BIOS. The details of this step will vary depending on who produced your BIOS. As an example, on a Dell computer, you can achieve this by pressing F2 upon the computer startup, navigating to the Performance portion of the BIOS, and enabling Intel VT or AMD-V.

In the next exercise, you will proceed with the installation of Hyper-V. You must have completed Exercise 10.1 in order to do Exercise 10.2.

EXERCISE 10.2

Installing Hyper-V

1. The install process for Hyper-V begins like most any server role install with Windows Server 2008. First click the Server Manager button, and then select Add Roles ➤ Hyper-V.

2. At this point, if you do not meet the hardware requirements, you will be greeted with the warning shown here.

EXERCISE 10.2   (continued)

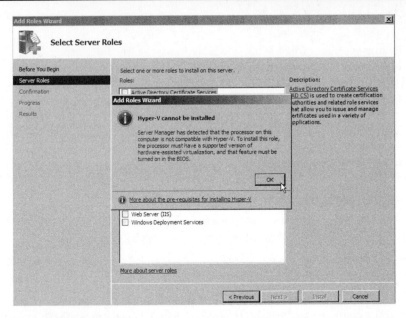

Otherwise, you will be able to select the Hyper-V check box, as shown here.

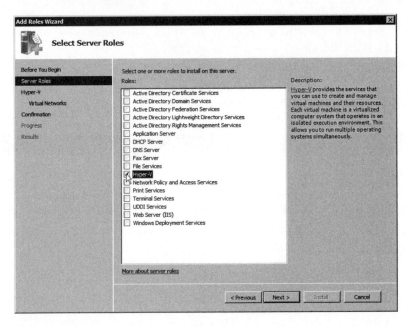

3. Click Next.

4. On the next screen, you can select a network card for use in your virtual network. In the example shown here, only one network card is available, so you will choose that one. However, if you have multiple network cards and don't select one, they would not be set up as virtual networks.

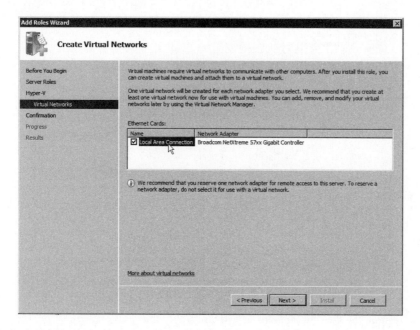

5. The install will continue, as shown here, after you click Next.

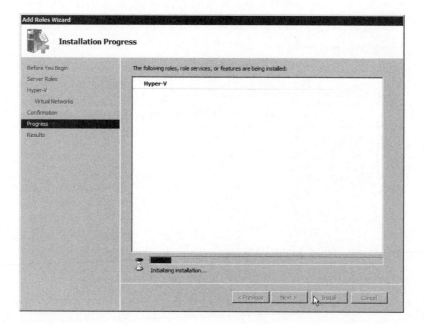

EXERCISE 10.2 *(continued)*

6. Once you've completed the install process, you will be prompted to close the installer and reboot, as shown here.

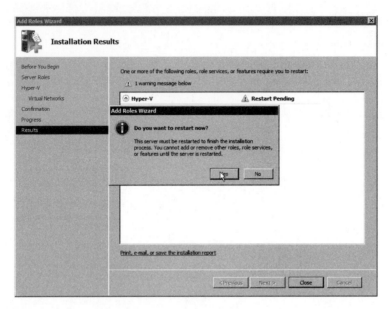

7. Upon reboot, the resume installer will begin.

8. When complete, you'll be presented with a summary screen. Click Close.

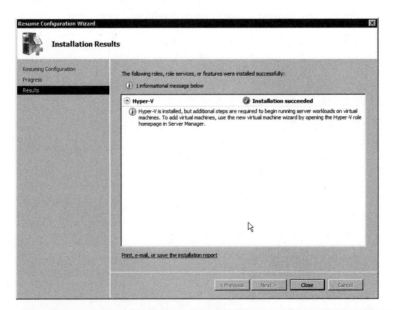

In Exercise 10.3, you will set up Hyper-V. To complete this exercise, you must have completed Exercises 10.1 and 10.2.

EXERCISE 10.3

Setting Up Hyper-V

1. To begin setting up Hyper-V, select Start ➢ Administrative Tools ➢ Hyper-V Manager. This opens the Hyper-V Manager home screen shown here.

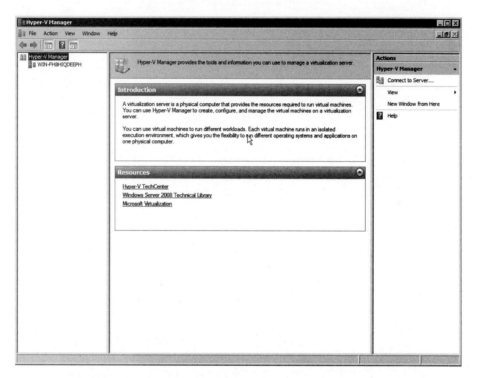

2. In the Hyper-V Manager, select the name of your computer, and in the upper-right portion of the screen, select New ➢ Virtual Machine, as shown here.

3. On the initial configuration screen, if it's shown, click Next.

4. On the Specify Name and Location screen, name the virtual machine something appropriate, such as SUSE Linux. Click Next.

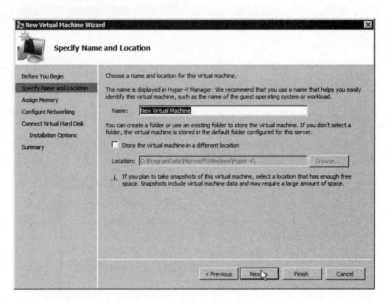

5. On the Assign Memory screen, you can pick the amount of memory to be assigned to this virtual machine. Keep in mind that this is limited by the amount of memory you possess. For our purposes, 512MB should suffice. Place this (if available) in your box, and click Next.

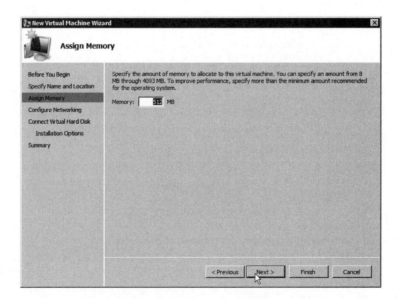

6. When the Configure Networking screen appears, you can select from the drop-down menu any virtual networks that have been created in this or any previous installs. Otherwise, there will be no virtual networks. Click Next when complete.

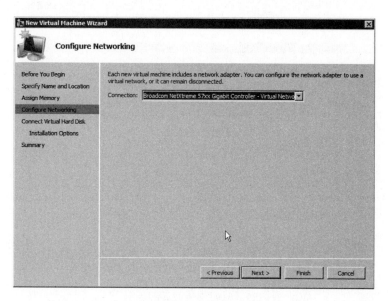

7. On the next screen, Connect Virtual Hard Disk, you can choose to either create a new hard disk or work from a preexisting virtual disk. In this exercise, you will create a new disk and assign 15GB. Click Next when complete.

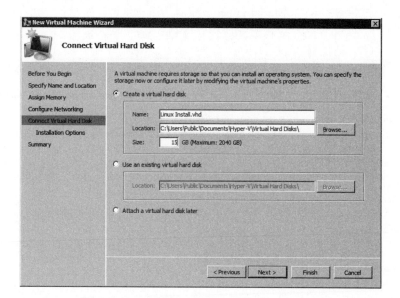

EXERCISE 10.3   *(continued)*

8. You will install an operating system later, so select Install Operating System Later, and click Next.

9. When the screen shown here appears and the Finish button is available, make sure you select the check box to start the virtual machine upon exiting the wizard.

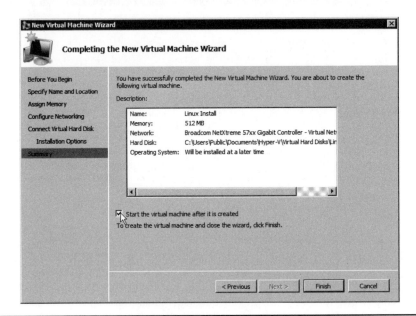

In Exercise 10.4, you will install an operating system on a preexisting virtual machine. You must have completed Exercises 10.1 to 10.3 to do this exercise.

EXERCISE 10.4

Installing an Operating System on a Previously Created Virtual Machine

1. Upon exiting the previous exercise, the virtual machine for your install Linux Install should have begun and appeared on your screen, as shown here.

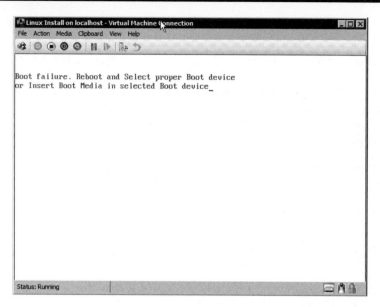

2   To load a disk, it's recommended you download a version of SUSE Linux Enterprise edition for free from Novell.com. Depending upon your choice, you can either
burn it to DVD or leave it in ISO format. For this exercise, you will leave it in ISO format.

3. Once it's downloaded, select Media ➢ DVD Drive ➢ Insert Disk, as shown here.

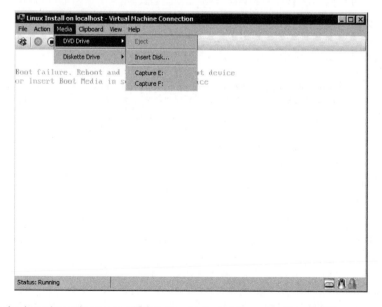

4. Select the location where your ISO is located, and then double-click it.

EXERCISE 10.4 *(continued)*

5. Choose Action and then Reset. This will bring you to the default loading screen for SUSE Linux.

6. Enter linux at the command prompt to begin the installation, as shown here.

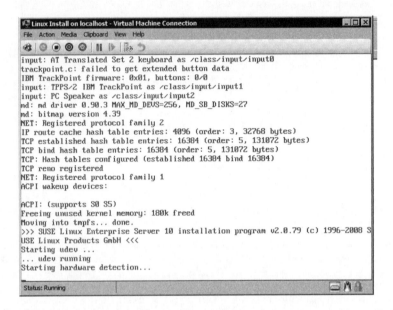

7. Follow the installation instructions on the SUSE screen, and the machine will then start upon VM reboot.

 If you try to use Hyper-V through Remote Desktop, the mouse will not be enabled unless you turn on Integration Services, which is available through the Microsoft Download Center (www.microsoft.com/downloads/).

Introducing iSCSI

One of the most popular methods for storing both data and virtual operating systems is iSCSI. A relative new kid on the block, Internet Small Computer Systems Interface (iSCSI) is very popular for virtualization solutions because iSCSI devices can be installed via TCP/IP protocols and receive standard SCSI commands.

In the enterprise, most iSCSI configurations are stored in arrays of disks that are managed through external software in proprietary enclosures, such as those made by EMC[2] and other companies that produce disk arrays. Using iSCSI, administrators can easily create RAIDs of various disks and then assign further details to these RAIDs using logical unit numbers (LUNs).

Logical Unit Numbers

To understand logical unit numbers, it's best to first understand SCSI. In case you're not too much of a hardware guru, SCSI is a type of I/O method that takes advantage of a dedicated card that interconnects directly with the PCI bus.

In the old days, or at least the "older" days, of computing, SCSI was used because it could interface with higher-frequency buses and transfer more information faster than the standard PCI bus using IDE technology. SCSI supported a maximum of 16 devices per bus, each of which had its own individual and unique identifier, or number. You could, for example, have four hard drives that exist on logical numbers 0, 1, 2, and 3. You could then specify which drive you wanted to communicate with via some relatively simple I/O operations.

LUNs come into play when you have a large device that's attached to one particular SCSI port. Say, for instance, you have a four-drive disk array that takes only one SCSI port. If you wanted to break that array into, say, four individual volumes, you'd have to use both the SCSI port and a logical number for each drive—the logical unit number.

Using LUNs, the drives can be identified as individual volumes and be accessed individually. This is particularly important if you want to use these drives for virtualization, because for each virtual operating system you have, you have to have one dedicated volume. With an iSCSI system, you can take a single array, break this array down into multiple volumes, and assign them each logical unit numbers. Then, you can take each volume and assign it individually to a virtualized system.

Windows Vista x64 Hyper-V Management

Because of the inherent flexibility of both the Vista operating system and Server 2008's robust architecture, Microsoft has made the process of administering Hyper-V relatively easy. Using Windows Vista 64-bit edition with Service Pack 1, administrators can log on to a client host operating system and use the Remote Server Administration Toolkit in conjunction with the Hyper-V Manager to administer a Hyper-V server from a remote location.

This is useful for a variety of reasons, but primarily it is useful because it means an administrator doesn't have to go through the bother of using Remote Desktop to access a machine or manually logging in. Instead, the administrator can just sit at their remote location and gain easy access to the Hyper-V server.

NOTE   You have to enable WMI for this installation.

Server Core and Virtualization

Just to prove to you exactly how powerful Windows Server 2008 Server Core really is, Server Core does indeed support Hyper-V! In this book, I won't go into the procedures for this, because it isn't practical for our use. However, in your own environment, it may be a good idea to implement Hyper-V on Server Core. According to both Microsoft and common sense, a Server Core installation of Hyper-V reduces your attack surface by using fewer bells and whistles.

In addition to reducing your attack surface, you free up valuable memory, which is a rare commodity with any type of server. Additionally, SUSE Linux and other installations of Linux-based platforms in the future are often installed in command-line-only forms. Thus, it doesn't make a lot of sense to have a full GUI-enabled machine if a command-line-based server will do.

The main difference between Server Core and full installation Hyper-V setups, beyond the lack of graphics, is that Windows Server 2008 Server Core has to have its Hyper-V installation managed remotely via Windows Vista Service Pack 1 or another installation of Windows Server 2008. But, although it's a downside, it isn't the end of the world. Furthermore, if you have time on your hands, you can even set up an unattended installation of Server Core that prevents you from having to set up Server Core again after you've done it once.

Using System Center
Virtual Machine Manager 2007

Just like the old saying goes, "There's the individual way to do it, and then there's the enterprise way to do it." Well, maybe that's not really an old saying, or even a saying at all, but it certainly applies here. System Center Virtual Machine Manager 2007 (SCVMM 2007) is an application available from Microsoft that deals directly with the process of managing multiple virtual machines in an enterprise or data-center environment. With consolidation, it can be pretty easy to get carried away. First you start with one machine, and before you know it, your entire enterprise starts to take advantage of the available features of a completely consolidated environment.

With SCVMM 2007, an individual administrator or team of administrators can support up to 8,000 virtual machines. That's a heck of a lot of operating systems in one environment. But there are a couple of gotchas. First, "only" 400 Hyper-V installations are supported. I put *only* in quotation marks, because that is a tremendous number of 64-bit platforms running Windows Server 2008.

Among other features, SCVMM 2007 allows you to do the following:

- Easily create virtual machines.
- Swap VM from one Hyper-V to another.
- Move virtual machines.
- Delegate permissions.

Using SCVMM 2007, the sometimes painstakingly long process of creating virtual machines can be dramatically abbreviated. In a clustered array, you can use SCVMM 2007 to simply move one virtual machine's data files from one location to another. Furthermore, you can delegate certain permissions with little administrative overhead, as opposed to the long process of manually moving files from one place to another. The SCVMM 2007 architecture has two main components: the SCVMM server and the SCVMM agent. I will also discuss two other components—the database and the library server.

SCVMM Server

The SCVMM server is the component that serves the centralized process of the entire virtual machine environment. Usually, there is only one SCVMM server, and the rest of the machines communicate with it through the use of SCVMM hosts, discussed in the next section.

Here are a couple of tidbits you should remember for the Enterprise Administrator exam:

- SCVMM requires a connection to a database SQL server of some sort.
- SCVMM requires an active and functioning DNS environment—preferably one with Active Directory completely functioning.

SCVMM Agent

This component of the SCVMM 2007 is automatically installed with Hyper-V. The SCVMM agent is a process that is designed to communicate with the SCVMM server and allow certain tasks to be completed automatically. Note that SCVMM agents need to be in the same forest in order to properly communicate with the SCVMM server.

SCVMM Database

The SCVMM database is the location of the SQL server used to support the SCVMM server. Best practices recommend that this server be running at least SQL Server 2005, but with the release of SQL Server 2008, this will soon become the recommended best practice.

SCVMM Library Server

All virtual servers require a certain amount of data in order to be created. This includes stuff like the image files required to install the operating systems, as well as a couple scripts and profiles. The SCVMM library server serves as central depository for these components by allowing SCVMM access to these files in one location. This way, you can create or alter images from a central location and not have to worry about changing CDs or swapping files. It's quite convenient.

 Real World Scenario

Windows and Linux

OmniCorp, an extremely large corporation, currently hosts two websites, both of which serve an extremely vital function to OmniCorp. One of these websites is hosted on SQL Server 2008 and IIS7. However, the other website uses PHP and Apache. Normally, Omni-Corp would be forced to utilize two servers, one running a version of Linux such as SUSE and the other running Windows Server 2008.

However, using Hyper-V, OmniCorp could instead run both web server applications on a single platform. First, OmniCorp could install Windows Server 2008. Next, it could install Hyper-V. Finally, OmniCorp could create a child virtual machine for the SUSE Linux install, which would allow the company to install whatever resources it required. By bridging these connections in this fashion, OmniCorp could have two separate network resources that could each host an individual website.

Using Virtual Server 2005 R2

Although quickly becoming replaced by Windows Server Hyper-V, Microsoft Virtual Server 2005 R2 is still a completely viable solution for virtual machine implementations. In some ways, it is more robust in Hyper-V, because it does not have the extreme hardware require-ments of Microsoft Hyper-V. It is also available free of charge from Microsoft. Addition-ally, Microsoft has issued a management pack that allows Virtual Server 2005 to be man-aged from a remote distance and administer it, as well as its virtual machines.

Summary

In this chapter, I covered Hyper-V, which is the latest development in the long history of virtualization throughout the enterprise. Available only with Windows Server 2008, Hyper-V is an extremely powerful and useful tool for enterprise administrators and server administrators alike. Using Hyper-V, administrators can consolidate multiple server roles by installing multiple operating systems in one centralized location.

I also covered virtualization. When virtualizing, network cards, CPU, and memory are shared on virtualized buses that access data at different times and locations through "virtual" networks, CPUs, and memory DIMMs. In particular, Hyper-V takes advantage of three different types of network pools: internal, external, and private. Internal is designed to communicate only within the host and virtual machines, private is only between virtual machines, and external virtual networks can communicate to the outside world.

Most virtual machines, according to best practices, should be placed on iSCSI devices or locations that can be easily migrated to external areas. Keep in mind that the capabilities of Hyper-V have some limitations involving the number of CPUs, amount of memory, and disk space it can address. But ultimately, using Hyper-V can prove extremely cost effective for most enterprises.

Exam Essentials

Know the limits of Hyper-V. Hyper-V has a certain number of CPUs, memory, and hard disk space that it can address; it's best to be familiar with it.

Be familiar with the Hyper-V compatible operating systems. Hyper-V can't virtualize every operating system on the planet; it does have its limitations, and you should know what they are for the certification exam.

Understand SCVMM 2007. The exact procedures for using this tool will probably not appear on the Enterprise Administrator exam, but you should know the purpose of the tool and its components.

Understand virtual networks. Know the types of virtual networks and what they're used for.

Know about storage purposes. You should know your different RAID types, LUNs, SCSI, and iSCSI purposes. And you should know how they can assist in the development of a complex and robust infrastructure.

Understand that Windows Vista can play a role in Hyper-V. Remote administration plays a major role in almost all forms of enterprise administration. Know how Windows Vista 64-bit edition can play a role in the remote administration of Hyper-V.

Review Questions

1. To function as a depository location for a Hyper-V install of a virtualized machine of SUSE Linux on Windows Server 2008, which of the following is required for an iSCSI storage device attached through a network installation?

   A. A SCSI port

   B. At least 20GB of hard disk space

   C. A logical unit number

   D. At least 512MB of memory

2. Windows Server 2008 Hyper-V has a few very stringent and demanding hardware requirements. Of the following hardware features, which are necessary in order for Hyper-V to function properly? (Choose all that apply.)

   A. Intel VT

   B. Intel V

   C. AMD-V

   D. AMD-VT

   E. Intel XD

   F. Intel DX

   G. AMD ND

   H. AMD NX

3. You are the administrator for OmniCorp, an experimental software company. OmniCorp has a centralized domain controller with six different branch offices, all of which run Windows Server 2008. At one of the branch offices in Seattle, the administrators need to run three different virtual machines of SUSE Linux to test an experimental piece of software. However, they do not want the virtual machines to communicate with any other machines than each other. What should you do?

   A. When creating the virtual machines, set up a virtual network. Ensure that this virtual network is internal, and connect the virtual machines through the piece of software.

   B. When creating the virtual machines, set up a virtual network. Ensure that this virtual network is external, and connect the virtual machines through the piece of software.

   C. When creating the virtual machines, set up a virtual network. Ensure that this virtual network is private, and connect the virtual machines through the piece of software.

   D. When creating the virtual machines, set up a virtual network. Ensure that this virtual network is experimental, and connect the virtual machines through the piece of software.

4. MyCorp, a medium-sized textile company, has a central office in New York City where it produces sweaters and vests. MyCorp uses a great deal of manufacturing equipment that runs off Windows servers. For security purposes, these servers will be relocated to Atlanta,

Georgia, and must run a version of Windows Server for the manufacturing equipment as well as a version of Linux for MyCorp's file server needs. As the lead administrator, what should you do?

A. Create a Server 2008 install, virtualize the Windows Server install, and set up the network as an external network to access the virtual machine over the Internet.

B. Create a Server 2008 install, virtualize the Linux Server install, and set up the network as an external network to access the virtual machine over the Internet.

C. Create a Server 2008 install, virtualize the Windows Server install, and set up the network as an internal network to access the virtual machine over the Internet.

D. Create a Server 2008 install, virtualize the Linux Server install, and set up the network as an internal network to access the virtual machine over the Internet.

5. You work in an environment that would like to take advantage of System Center Virtual Machine Manager 2007 to support a planned install of approximately 100 virtual machines. What should you do?

A. Install one SCVMM 2007 server and some agents on a few centralized networked machines.

B. Install one SCVMM instance per 10 virtual machines, and link them through SCVMM hosts.

C. Install one SCVMM server, and set the rest of the VMs up as hosts.

D. Install SCVMM on one server and the rest of the machines as SCOM agents.

6. Which of the following is *not* a benefit of Hyper-V?

A. Server consolidation

B. Failover clustering

C. Ease of migration

D. Network efficiency

E. 32-bit native compliance

7. You are the administrator of AnimalCorp, a large business responsible for the placement of endangered species and the preservation of the environment. AnimalCorp currently runs SQL and a MySQL database that runs off a centralized server that is under consistent security risks. AnimalCorp would like to install Linux on this server as well as Windows Server 2008. Security and reliability are of extreme concern. What should you do?

A. Perform a full install of Windows Server 2008 behind a firewall, and run Hyper-V on the local hard drive.

B. Perform a Server Core install of Windows Server 2008, and install Hyper-V on the local hard drive.

C. Perform a Server Core install of Windows Server 2008 behind a firewall. Install Hyper-V, and store the install on a secure network-attached location.

D. Do not install Hyper-V.

8. Which of the following are *not* benefits of SCVMM 2007?

   A. Easily create virtual machines.

   B. Swap VM from one Hyper-V to another.

   C. Move virtual machines.

   D. Delegate permissions.

   E. None of the above.

9. What is the maximum number of processors that can be used by Hyper-V?

   A. 2

   B. 4

   C. 8

   D. 16

   E. 32

10. What is the maximum amount of memory supported by Hyper-V?

   A. .5TB

   B. 1TB

   C. 2TB

   D. 4TB

11. Which of the following supports remote management and administration of the Hyper-V Manager through the addition of an administration download that is available from Microsoft?

   A. Windows XP Home edition

   B. Windows XP Pro

   C. Windows Vista

   D. Windows Vista x64

   E. Windows Server 2008

12. In an installation where the reliability of four virtual machines is critical and the implementation of an iSCSI device is recommended through the use of a SAN, what setup would you use?

   A. One RAID 0 implementation on the SAN with four unique LUNs

   B. Four RAID 0 implementations with four LUNs

   C. One RAID 1 implementation with four LUNs

   D. RAID 5 implementation with one LUN

13. You are the administrator for OmniCorp, and OmniCorp has just recently installed a centralized server that contains six virtualized machines that are backed up through RAID 1 redundancy on an iSCSI device. Because of security reasons, executives have asked you to create a system of recovery to support the possible loss of data in the case of system failure. What should you do?

    A. Create a failover cluster, and direct the failover cluster to take over the virtual machines in the case of a failure.

    B. Implement a separate RAID 1 configuration in the case of failure.

    C. Take snapshots of the OmniCorp virtual machines, and store them in an easily recoverable location.

    D. Use the Windows Server 2008 Backup and Recovery tool.

14. Which of the following SVMM components are required in order to create a centralized place to store operating system components, including install files and certain scripts?

    A. SCVMM agent

    B. SCVMM server

    C. SCVMM library server

    D. SCVMM administrator

15. What type of virtualization involves the process of making applications appear to be located on the desktop but in fact is present on a server in a dedicated location?

    A. Application virtualization

    B. Server virtualization

    C. Presentation virtualization

    D. Desktop virtualization

16. What type of virtualization involves the emulation of entire operating systems within a server while virtualizing CPUs and memory in such a fashion that it can operate entirely independently from the host operating system?

    A. Application virtualization

    B. Server virtualization

    C. Presentation virtualization

    D. Desktop virtualization

17. You are the administrator for the SuperCorp network and need to make a recommendation for an upgrade to Windows Server 2008 for the central office. This installation must support Hyper-V. What do you recommend?

    A. A dual-processor machine with Windows Server 2008 Web edition

    B. A single-processor machine with Windows Server 2008 Enterprise edition

    C. A single-processor machine with Windows Server 2008 Datacenter edition

    D. A dual-processor machine with Windows Server 2008 Standard edition

18. What is the main difference between Hyper-V and Microsoft Virtual Server 2005 SP2?

    A. Hyper-V supports Windows Server 2003 installations.

    B. Virtual Server 2005 supports Linux, and Hyper-V does not.

    C. Hyper-V supports Linux installations, and Virtual Server 2005 does not.

    D. Virtual Server 2005 does not support x64 host installations.

    E. Virtual Server 2005 does not support x64 virtual machines, while Hyper-V does.

19. To support Hyper-V, what must be done on the BIOS in order to support virtual machines?

    A. Enable data execution.

    B. Create a dedicated partition.

    C. Enable hardware virtualization.

    D. Enable Virtual Memory Manager.

20. Using multiple forms of virtualization, you can set up a network address in many ways. If you are working in an environment where it's required for you to be able to uniquely address a machine in order to retrieve services from NAT, what type of shared network connection must be established in order to facilitate this?

    A. Host-NAT connection

    B. Host-only connection

    C. Bridged connection

    D. Dedicated connection

Answers to Review Questions

1. C. To function as an iSCSI network-attached storage device, the device needs to have a logical unit number so that network resources can access it. iSCSI is currently the most popular method of installing network-attached storage locations.

2. A, C, E, H. The two marketed hardware virtualization features available on hardware chips are Intel VT and AMD-V. Additionally, these chips must support either Intel XD or AMD NX data execution technology.

3. C. Private virtual networks are designed only for communication between virtual machines. Using a private network, the piece of software being testing will not affect the branch office computers or any computers connected through the rest of the network.

4. B. By virtualizing the Linux install and running it on an external network, you will create an environment where it can be accessed over the Internet and be allowed its own individual network access for the file server needs.

5. C. To utilize SCVMM, you need to have only one SCVMM server and the rest of your computers set up as SCVMM agents The SCVMM server manages the environment of the host machines.

6. E. Although Windows Server 2008 Hyper-V can support 32 bit installations, it is not natively supported on 32-bit installations. Instead, it requires 64-bit x64 installations.

7. C. Server Core installs, firewalls, and networked-attached storage solutions all aid in the development of extra security. By installing all three, you're making your virtualized environment as secure as possible.

8. E. SCVMM 207 can create virtual machines, swap VM, move virtual machines, and delegate permissions. It is an extremely robust and powerful large-scale administration tool.

9. D. Hyper-V can support up to 16 logical processors. And with Hyper-V, you can specify the way you want processors to be virtualized.

10. B. Hyper-V can support up to 1TB of memory. Currently, this is beyond the needs of almost any practical application.

11. D, E. Both Windows Vista x64 and Windows Server 2008 support remote management tools for Microsoft Hyper-V. Through these tools, administrators can manage Hyper-V virtualized machines through the use of remote tools that allow easy administration.

12. C. To provide redundancy, you need to implement RAID 1 to have an exact mirror of the installation in the case of failure. Furthermore, for each volume, setting up an individual LUN for the virtual machine will ensure that the VMs have all they require in order to function properly.

13. C. Snapshots are designed to create recoverable points in time can be used to restore virtual machines in the case of failure. RAID 1 and failover clusters are designed to be points of redundancy, not points of recovery.

14. C. An SCVMM library server is designed to serve as a central repository for various files used in the administration of virtualized machines. Using this library server, you can store install files and other important information.

15. C. Presentation virtualization in Windows Server 2008 is also referred to as Terminal Services. Terminal Services gives users multiple ways to access programs that are executed on servers but appear to be on users' desktops.

16. D. Desktop virtualization is used to create an environment where two separate operating systems can be used through a graphical user interface at the same time. Technologies that make this possible include Hyper-V and VMware.

17. D. Windows Server 2008 Standard, Enterprise, and Datacenter editions support Hyper-V, but Web edition does not. Additionally, best practices recommend the installation of a dual processor so one processor can be dedicated to the host and one toward the virtual machine.

18. E. Hyper-V supports Windows and Linux installations, as well as 64-bit installations. Virtual Server 2005, however, supports 32-bit guest installations.

19. C. Before Hyper-V can be installed, the computer must be able to support hardware virtualization. This is done by enabling either AMD-V or Intel VT.

20. C. Bridged network connections share a single network interface card between the host operating system and virtualized machines. Using a bridged connection, the VM will receive its own unique IP address that is accessible externally and set apart from the host.

Glossary

Numbers

6to4   The process of translating IPv6 packets over IPv4 packets, allowing hosts to communicate via both techniques.

A

AD DS   Active Directory Domain Services.

administrative autonomy   The process of ensuring that an individual location in the network has the freedom and capability to do whatever is necessary to conduct business and not interrupt the rest of the organization.

application virtualization   The process of making applications available through virtual servers that appear as if they are readily accessible on the user's own computer.

AP-TLS   A certificate-based authentication that always authenticates on the server end and can be configured to require both client and server authentication.

audit compliance   Compliance with a set of predefined audits and whether these audits comply to standards.

audit policies   Specific settings for audits, including what will be audited and how it will be audited.

B

back-to-back firewall   Two firewalls placed back to back.

bastion host   An individual computer designed to serve a single purpose and be inherently secure because of its limited functionality.

BitLocker   A bit-level file encryption system available with Windows Server 2008 and Windows Vista that ensures the physical security of data disks.

built-in/local groups   Groups that are built into Windows Server 2008 by default for specific purposes assigned to Windows Server 2008.

C

centralized   When resources are placed in a central location, either computer based or personnel based.

certificate authority (CA)   A part of Public Key Infrastructure that is responsible for validating certificates, issuing certificates, and revoking certificates.

certification policy   Determines whether a certificate will be assigned and under what circumstances.

certification practice statement   Outlines how a certificate authority manages its security and certificates.

Challenge Handshake Authentication Protocol (CHAP)   An outdated authentication method used by Point-to-Point Protocol that uses a three-way handshake.

consolidation   The process of reducing the number of servers by consolidating services or objects to fewer servers.

Cryptography Next Generation   A new suite of encryption algorithms that allow for custom-created security for digital signatures, key exchange, hashing, and other features for all encryption-requiring applications in the enterprise.

D

DACL   A list of zero or more access control entries (ACEs) that specify who has which access to the object.

decentralized   When resources are placed away from the main office.

delegation   The process of assigning control permissions to another entity in the Windows infrastructure.

desktop virtualization   The complete virtualization of an entire desktop within another operating system.

Distributed File System   A file system that creates a hierarchical view of network files that is easily understandable by most users.

DMZ/perimeter network   A network that exists outside of a firewall.

domain local groups   Groups that are created from accounts that can come from any domain but access resources only on the local domain.

Domain Name Server (DNS) round-robin   The process of responding with a list of available DNS servers in an attempt to load balance server requests.

domain trusts   Trusts that exist between two domains.

downstream autonomous mode   A mode in which downstream servers function as individual entities that can be configured by lower-level update administrators.

downstream servers   Servers that first receive their updates from another server and then replicate these updates to the rest of the environment through WSUS.

dual IP layer   When both the IPv4 and the IPv6 protocol access the same information in the same TCP/IP stack.

dual stack   Creates a complete separate stack through which each protocol travels.

dynamic libraries   Compiled code that can be accessed at different instances of a program. Dynamic libraries exist in .dll format and are sometimes required for installing Terminal Services programs.

E

Easy Print   A Terminal Services method that is designed to create an easy system of printing when logged in via Terminal Services.

Encrypting File System   An encryption system available with NTFS that encrypts files on a Windows Server drive partition.

enrollment agents   A user configured with the ability to issue smart card certificates on behalf of users.

enterprise CA   A CA that takes advantage of Active Directory to control the enrollment process.

enterprise client environments   Any server environment that involves the use of multiple active users and the extensive use of Active Directory to monitor and administrate those users.

external trusts   A trust that exists between an active directory supporting domain and a Windows NT domain.

F

failover clustering   A cluster made of additional computers that are designed to carry over the tasks of a given network in the case of the failure of a cluster providing a primary service.

firmware   The core software used by a particular component to function at its core level. Without firmware, a device requiring software I/O cannot function.

forest   The highest administrative level in Microsoft Windows, which contains domains.

forest trusts   Trusts that exist between two forests.

forestwide authentication   A trust that permeates the entire forest.

G

global groups   Groups that can access resources on any domain but can contain accounts only from its unique domain.

GlobalNames Zone   A zone used to support NetBIOS legacy name resolution clients.

Group Policy filtering   The process of ensuring that certain policies are applied at certain locations because of user settings.

Group Policy scope   The administrative level a GPO is applied. This can be local, site, domain, or OU.

H

health model   A business-like model of overall system health that informs administrators of the state of the infrastructure.

host-to-host   Communication that occurs between two individuals hosts.

host-to-router/router-to-host   Communication that occurs between a router and a host or a host to a router.

hybrid   When resources are placed both at the main office location and at a remote location.

Hyper-V   The Microsoft virtualization system available with Windows Server 2008 that is designed to virtualize both Microsoft Windows and Linux.

I

inheritance   The process of child objects inheriting attributes from parent objects.

INI files   System files that are used to provide configuration information.

Internet Small Computer Systems Interface (iSCSI)   A connection that takes advantage of the TCP/IP protocol to store data over network locations.

IPsec   A very secure, network-layer authentication protocol that can support certificates.

ISATAP   An IPv6 transition mechanism between dual-stacked nodes within an IPv4 network.

L

licensing mode   The mode of licensing that a Terminal Services server is placed in. Examples of this include per user and per device.

licensing scope   The range of the network infrastructure that is covered by Terminal Services Licensing, including forest, domain, and workgroup.

line-of-business application   An application that is required to both do business and keep the business functioning.

load balancing   The process of distributing server load throughout multiple different servers in an attempt to keep servers balanced.

logical unit numbers   The number assigned to a logical unit that dedicates it for I/O operations.

loopback merge mode   A user's policies and a machine's policies combined.

loopback processing   Used on Terminal Services machines to make sure that users, regardless of their location, are given specific policies according to that individual Terminal Services machine.

loopback replace mode   All policies that were once granted to a user are now instead defined by the machine on which the user is logged on.

M

MBSA   The Microsoft Baseline Security Analyzer, which will diagnose an environment and determine its security baseline.

Microsoft SoftGrid   An application virtualization program designed to virtually deploy applications to end users.

Microsoft SoftGrid client: SystemGuard   What Microsoft describes as a "sandbox" that allows applications to run in a framework on an individual client computer using Microsoft SoftGrid.

Microsoft SoftGrid management web service   A snap-in tool that integrates within the Microsoft Management Console. It is capable of interacting with Active Directory and database-driven applications for line-of-business or general virtualization purposes.

Microsoft SoftGrid sequencer   The portion of Microsoft SoftGrid that determines which .ini, .dll, and other such files are required in the interaction between the operating system and the application.

Microsoft System Center Configuration Manager   A high-end utility designed to administrate an extremely large-scale enterprise.

Microsoft System Virtual Application Server   A component of Microsoft SoftGrid that is responsible for streaming application data to users who have requested that data throughout the enterprise.

Microsoft Update   The update service available from Microsoft that is used to support Windows and other Microsoft products.

Microsoft Virtual PC   An earlier version of desktop emulation used by Microsoft for multiple operating systems in one desktop.

migration   The process of transferring Active Directory objects from one forest or domain to another.

MS-CHAP   The Microsoft version of CHAP that exists in two versions, version 1 and version 2. Windows Vista no longer supports version 1.

N

nesting   The process of embedding OUs within OUs.

network device enrollment   The process of enrolling network devices with certificates for increased security.

network load balancing   Balancing load across multiple servers to conserve network bandwidth.

Network Policy Server (NPS)   A technology designed by Microsoft to replace RADIUS and serve as a replacement for the Windows Server 2003 Internet Authentication Service (2003). In addition to performing RADIUS functions, it also supports VPNs and network access protection.

O

object-based delegation   Delegating control permission based on specific objects.

one-way trusts   A trust that exists in only one direction, with only one forest or domain trusting the other.

online responders   Any machine that is currently running the Online Responder service.

P

PAP   A simple, unencrypted form of authentication that sends plain-text ASCII passwords as an authentication method.

PEAP   A certificate using server-side techniques that takes advantage of SSL and TLS tunnels to authenticate users.

presentation virtualization   Using Terminal Services to make applications appear as if they are running on a desktop but instead are running through a terminal server.

primary zone   The main zone that contains the main DNS database that can be either integrated or not integrated with Active Directory.

Public Key Infrastructure (PKI)   The inherent design for administering and receiving certificates for job-specific and enterprise-specific tasks.

Q

quorum   The number of nodes required to make an appropriate decision regarding any given subject and keep the cluster operational.

R

RAID 0   The process of taking several disks and combing them into one large, maximum-speed disk.

RAID 1   A bit-for-bit copy that is exchanged from one drive to another.

RAID 5   Drives that use a parity bit to ensure data redundancy and spread data across as many drives as possible, creating points of failure but also expanding overall drive capacity.

read-only domain controllers (RODC)   Domain controllers that are designed to be placed in secure locations and require writable domain controllers to be placed with them.

realm trust   Trusts that exist between a Windows infrastructure and a Unix domain.

Remote Authentication Dial-in User Service (RADIUS)   A protocol designed to support and administer remotely connected users to a server. RADIUS can determine rights, as well as authorization and accounting.

replica mode   A mode in which downstream servers simply take the information they have received from an upstream server and replicate it through the rest of the environment.

restricted enrollment agents   Users or security groups with the ability to enroll other security groups or users.

root CA authority   The first installed and most important CA in the entire infrastructure.

router-to-router   Communication that occurs between two routers.

S

SACL   A list of access controls used for auditing.

secondary zone   Read-only, host copies of known DNS information, designed to reduce traffic in an enterprise.

security baseline   An initial analysis that acquires data concerning the security of Active Directory, security policies, server scope, and GPO design.

security policy   A set of predefined standards to determine the security rules and regulations for an enterprise. Usually this is a document or set of easily accessible standards.

selective authentication   A trust that exists only in certain distinct locations throughout the infrastructure.

server availability   The time period in which a server is up, running, and not inaccessible.

server downtime   The period of time in which the operating system is not up, running, receiving power, and functioning as it should be functioning.

server uptime   The period of time that the server has been running with power in which it has not experienced a software- or hardware-based failure that results in the loss of the critical components of an operating system.

server virtualization   Virtualizing servers through the use of programs like Hyper-V to create dedicated, consolidated servers for the use of various purposes.

shortcut trust   A direct trust from one point in the forest architecture to another.

SoftGrid administrator   Users granted access to the SoftGrid Management Console, as well as the SoftGrid Management Web Services. Administrators can also add/delete/and remove accounts within SoftGrid, as well as manage application-based software.

SoftGrid browser   A read-only account type that is designed to allow users to browse SoftGrid applications to see what is available.

SoftGrid user   Accounts used to access available SoftGrid applications throughout the infrastructure.

stand-alone CA   A CA that does not take advantage of Active Directory and cannot be merged by Group Policy.

starter GPOs GPOs that can be created based on administrative templates settings that can be defined in the GPMC and then applied to a newly created GPO with that starter as a base.

static libraries Complied libraries of code that can be accessed from only one point in an application.

stub zone Zones that delegate information to another namespace.

System Center Configuration Manager 2007 (SCCM 2007) An update solution similar to SCE 2007 that is designed for higher-end environments with more than 500 users.

System Center Essentials 2007 (SCE 2007) An update solution available from Microsoft that is designed to support updates to third-party pieces of software not available from Microsoft. SCE 2007 supports up to 500 users.

T

task-based delegation Delegating control permissions based upon task analysis.

Teredo One of the IPv4 to IPv6 translational techniques that is designed to support IPv6-unaware NAT devices.

terminal server A server set aside to allow access to remote applications and remote services through Terminal Services.

Terminal Services Gateway Allows users to connect to internal servers running remote applications via an Internet device that can run Remote Desktop connections.

Terminal Services Licensing A license manager that maintains client access licenses for users of devices.

Terminal Services RAP Allows you to allocate a specific resource to which users have access in your given infrastructure.

Terminal Services Server Drain A feature that allows administrator to shut down any new sessions being established with a server.

Terminal Services Session Broker A load balancing service for Terminal Services in an enterprise.

Terminal Services Web Access Required to use RemoteApp programs and Remote Desktop connections through the Internet.

three-home firewall A firewall connected to a DMZ, an intranet, and the Internet.

tunneling The process of embedding data from a certain medium inside another medium.

two-way trust A trust that exists both ways, with both forests trusting one another.

U

universal groups   Groups that can contain membership from any domain and can access resources in any domain.

upstream   In Windows Software Update Services (WSUS), any server that functions as a central authority that is responsible for the constant broadcast and upload of Windows updates.

V

version 1, 2, and 3 certificates   The three different types of X.509 certificates available with Windows Server 2008.

Virtual Management Console   The management console used with Hyper-V to manage virtual machines.

virtual private network (VPN)   A virtual connection to a network that is connected through either L2TP or PPTP encryption. Once connected to a VPN, a host will function as if it is physically connected to that network.

visibility   The determination of whether an OU is visible to the infrastructure. OUs can be designed using this as a basis for determining where the OU can be placed.

Volume Shadow Copy   A service available through Windows Server that is designed to create partial backups as files go through different iterations on a server through user-based or computer-based changes.

W

Windows Server Backup   A freely available tool that can be installed to Windows Server 2008 to support full backups.

Windows Software Update Services (WSUS)   An automated update solution available through Windows Server for ease of update installation in enterprise environments.

Windows Update   An update solution available from Microsoft that is designed to support updates only to Microsoft Windows.

WMI filters   Filtering Group Policy based on machine settings.

Appendix A

About the Companion CD

IN THIS APPENDIX:

- What you'll find on the CD
- System requirements
- Using the CD
- Troubleshooting

What You'll Find on the CD

The following sections are arranged by category and summarize the software and other goodies you'll find on the CD. If you need help with installing the items provided on the CD, refer to the installation instructions in the "Using the CD" section of this appendix.

Some programs on the CD might fall into one of these categories:

- *Shareware programs* are fully functional, free, trial versions of copyrighted programs. If you like particular programs, register with their authors for a nominal fee and receive licenses, enhanced versions, and technical support.

- *Freeware programs* are free, copyrighted games, applications, and utilities. You can copy them to as many computers as you like—for free—but they offer no technical support.

- *GNU software* is governed by its own license, which is included inside the folder of the GNU software. There are no restrictions on distribution of GNU software. See the GNU license at the root of the CD for more details.

- *Trial, demo,* or *evaluation* versions of software are usually limited either by time or by functionality (such as not letting you save a project after you create it).

Sybex Test Engine

For Windows

The CD contains the Sybex test engine, which includes all of the assessment test and chapter review questions in electronic format, as well as two bonus exams located only on the CD.

PDF of the Book

For Windows

The CD includes an electronic version of the text in .pdf format. You can view the electronic version of the book with Adobe Reader.

Adobe Reader

For Windows

The CD also includes a copy of Adobe Reader so you can view PDF files that accompany the book's content. For more information on Adobe Reader or to check for a newer version, visit Adobe's website at www.adobe.com/products/reader/.

Electronic Flashcards

For PC, Pocket PC, and Palm

These handy electronic flashcards are just what they sound like. One side contains a question or fill-in-the-blank question, and the other side shows the answer.

System Requirements

Make sure your computer meets the minimum system requirements shown in the following list. If your computer doesn't match up to most of these requirements, you may have problems using the software and files on the companion CD. For the latest and greatest information, please refer to the ReadMe file located at the root of the CD-ROM.

- A PC running Microsoft Windows 98, Windows 2000, Windows NT 4 (with SP4 or later), Windows Me, Windows XP, or Windows Vista
- An Internet connection
- A CD-ROM drive

Using the CD

To install the items from the CD to your hard drive, follow these steps:

1. Insert the CD into your computer's CD-ROM drive. The license agreement appears.

 Windows users: The interface won't launch if you have autorun disabled. In that case, click Start ➢ Run (for Windows Vista, Start ➢ All Programs ➢ Accessories ➢ Run). In the dialog box that appears, type **D:\Start.exe**. (Replace *D* with the proper letter if your CD drive uses a different letter. If you don't know the letter, see how your CD drive is listed under My Computer.) Click OK.

2. Read the license agreement, and then click the Accept button if you want to use the CD.

The CD interface appears. The interface allows you to access the content with just one or two clicks.

Troubleshooting

Wiley has attempted to provide programs that work on most computers with the minimum system requirements. Alas, your computer may differ, and some programs may not work properly for some reason.

The two likeliest problems are that you don't have enough memory (RAM) for the programs you want to use or you have other programs running that are affecting installation or running of a program. If you get an error message such as "Not enough memory" or "Setup cannot continue," try one or more of the following suggestions and then try using the software again:

Turn off any antivirus software running on your computer. Installation programs sometimes mimic virus activity and may make your computer incorrectly believe that it's being infected by a virus.

Close all running programs. The more programs you have running, the less memory is available to other programs. Installation programs typically update files and programs; so if you keep other programs running, installation may not work properly.

Have your local computer store add more RAM to your computer. This is, admittedly, a drastic and somewhat expensive step. However, adding more memory can really help the speed of your computer and allow more programs to run at the same time.

Customer Care

If you have trouble with the book's companion CD-ROM, please call the Wiley Product Technical Support phone number at (800) 762-2974. Outside the United States, call +1 (317) 572-3994. You can also contact Wiley Product Technical Support at http://sybex.custhelp.com. John Wiley & Sons will provide technical support only for installation and other general quality-control items. For technical support on the applications themselves, consult the program's vendor or author.

To place additional orders or to request information about other Wiley products, please call (877) 762-2974.

Index

Note to the reader: Throughout this index **boldfaced** page numbers indicate primary discussions of a topic. *Italicized* page numbers indicate illustrations.

The Absolute Best MCITP: Windows Server 2008 Enterprise Administrator Book/CD Package on the Market!

Get ready for your Windows Server 2008 Enterprise Administrator certification with the most comprehensive and challenging sample tests anywhere!

The Sybex Test Engine features the following:

- All the review questions, as found in each chapter of the book
- Challenging questions representative of those you'll find on the real exam
- Two full-length bonus exams available only on the CD
- An assessment test to narrow your focus to certain objective groups

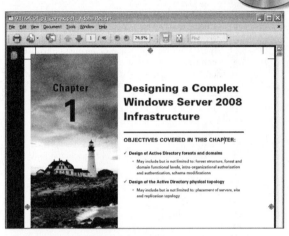

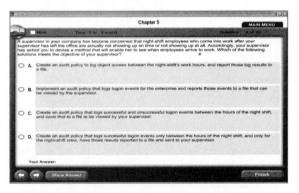

Search through the complete book in PDF!

- Access the entire *MCITP: Microsoft Windows Server 2008 Enterprise Administrator Study Guide*, complete with figures and tables, in electronic format.
- Search the *MCITP: Microsoft Windows Server 2008 Enterprise Administrator Study Guide* chapters to find information on any topic in seconds.

Use the electronic flashcards for PCs or Palm devices to jog your memory and prep on the go for the exam:

- Reinforce your understanding of key concepts with these hardcore flashcard-style questions.
- Download the flashcards to your Palm device and go on the road. Now you can study for the MCITP: Windows Server 2008 Enterprise Administrator (70-647) exam anytime, anywhere.

Your Group Policy Companions

For Windows Server® 2008 and Windows Vista®

When you're doing something tough or learning something new, it's always nice to have help—a companion or two to make things easier for you. And if you're enhancing your skills in Active Directory Group Policy, you'll want to have Group Policy MVP Jeremy Moskowitz and his two fully-updated companion books on Group Policy at your side.

Stay Informed

Get additional resources, download eChapters, and get follow-up tips and tricks at Jeremy's website www.GPanswers.com/books.

About the Books

Group Policy Fundamentals, Security and Troubleshooting builds on previous editions to cover the latest in Group Policy essentials. Get updates and new coverage for Windows Vista, Windows Server 2008, the Advanced Group Policy Management tool, Group Policy with PowerShell, and the all-new Group Policy Preference Extensions.

Creating the Secure Managed Desktop: Using Group Policy, SoftGrid®, Microsoft® Deployment Toolkit, and Other Management Tools picks up where the first book leaves off. Here, you'll learn the secrets of crafting the smoothest possible desktop experience. Save money and implement faster using the tools Microsoft already provides, and ensure the best experience possible for your users.

Jeremy Moskowitz, Group Policy MVP, is the Chief Propeller-Head for Moskowitz, inc., and GPanswers.com. He is a nationally recognized authority on Windows Server, Active Directory, Group Policy, and other Windows management topics. He is one of less than a dozen Microsoft MVPs in Group Policy. He runs GPanswers.com, ranked by *Computerworld* as a "Top 20 Resource for Microsoft IT Professionals." Jeremy frequently contributes to *Microsoft TechNet Magazine, Windows IT Pro* magazine and *Redmond* magazine. Jeremy is a sought-after speaker at many industry conferences and, in his training workshops, helps thousand of administrators every year do more with Group Policy. Contact Jeremy by visiting GPanswers.com.

Go to www.sybex.com/go/moskowitz for more information

SYBEX

An Imprint of ⓦWILEY
Now you know.